Critical Perspectives

on Bilingual Education Research

ɞp

Bilingual Press/Editorial Bilingüe

General Editor
Gary D. Keller

Managing Editor
Karen S. Van Hooft

Associate Editor
Ann M. Waggoner

Editorial Consultants
Jennifer Hartfield Prochnow
Linda St. George Thurston
Janet Woolum

Address:
Bilingual Review/Press
Hispanic Research Center
Arizona State University
Tempe, Arizona 85287
(602) 965-3867

Critical Perspectives

on Bilingual Education Research

Edited by

Raymond V. Padilla
Alfredo H. Benavides

Bilingual Press/Editorial Bilingüe

TEMPE, ARIZONA

ISBN 0-927534-20-7

Library of Congress Cataloging-in-Publication Data

Critical perspectives on bilingual education research / edited by
    Raymond V. Padilla and Alfredo H. Benavides.
        p.   cm.
    Papers from a series of symposia held April 23–25, 1990,
concurrently with the National Association for Bilingual Education
annual meeting in Tucson, Arizona.
    Includes bibliographical references.
    ISBN 0-927534-20-7
    1. Education, Bilingual—United States—Congresses. 2. Second
language acquisition—Congresses. 3. Education and state—United
States—Congresses. I. Padilla, Raymond V. II. Benavides,
Alfredo.
    LC 3731.C735   1991
    371.97'00973—dc20   91-21873
                                        CIP

PRINTED IN THE UNITED STATES OF AMERICA

Cover design by Thomas Detrie

Acknowledgments

The editors wish to thank the following organizations for permission to reprint material appearing in this volume:

Modern Language Association and the University of Wisconsin Press, for the table appearing in J. F. Lee and D. Musumeci, "On Hierarchies of Reading Skills and Text Types," *Modern Language Journal*, 72, 2 (September 1988), 174.

HarperCollinsAcademic, for the table appearing in J. Richards, *Classroom Language: What Sort?* (London: George Allen & Unwin, 1978), 90.

Arte Público Press, for the poem "asimilao," appearing in T. Laviera, *AmeRícan* (Houston: Arte Público Press, 1985), 54.

The table on page 266 first appeared in J. Liskin-Gasparro, "Teaching and Testing for Oral Proficiency: Some Applications for the Classroom," *Teaching Our Students a Second Language in a Proficiency Based Classroom*, ed. A. Papalia (Schenectady, NY: New York State Association of Foreign Language Teachers, 1986), 93.

Contents

Introduction
Raymond V. Padilla and Alfredo H. Benavides   1

Part One
DEVELOPING NEW FRAMEWORKS

A Theoretical and Pedagogical Framework for Bilingual
Education Based on Principles from Cognitive Psychology
Amado M. Padilla and Hyekyung Sung   11

Bilinguality, Intelligence, and Cognitive Information Processing
José E. Náñez, Sr., Raymond V. Padilla, and Becky López Máez   42

The Sociolinguistic Basis for Code Switching in Bilingual
Discourse and in Bilingual Instruction
Adalberto Aguirre, Jr.   70

Alternate Paradigms in Bilingual Education Research
Lourdes Díaz Soto   93

Critical Pedagogy in Bilingual Education: Language Proficiency
and Bilingualism
Antonio Simões   110

Linking Critical Pedagogy to Bilingual Education: An Ethno-
historical Study Contextualizing School Policies in an Urban
Community
Martha Montero-Sieburth and Mark LaCelle-Peterson   125

Ethnoterritorial Politics and the Institutionalization of Bilingual
Education at the Grass-Roots Level
Armando L. Trujillo   162

Part Two
IMPROVING PRACTICE IN BILINGUAL EDUCATION

Two-Way Bilingual/Immersion Education: Theory, Conceptual
Issues, and Pedagogical Implications
Kathryn J. Lindholm   195

A Metacognitive Approach to Teaching Bilingual Students
María Cardelle-Elawar and José E. Náñez, Sr.   221

Mathematics Instruction in Bilingual Education
Sheryl L. Santos   242

Language Proficiency and Bilingualism
Arnulfo G. Ramírez   257

Toward a Definition of Exemplary Teachers in Bilingual
Multicultural School Settings
Christian J. Faltis and Barbara J. Merino   277

Part Three
BILINGUAL EDUCATION AND THE PUBLIC INTEREST

Bilingual Education, Public Policy, and the Trickle-Down Reform
Agenda
John J. Halcón and María de la Luz Reyes   303

Shifts in Bilingual Education Policy and the Knowledge Base
Ursula Casanova   324

History and Status of Bilingual Special Education for Hispanic
Handicapped Students
*Nadeen T. Ruiz, Richard A. Figueroa, Robert S. Rueda,
and Carol Beaumont*   349

Assessment of Bilingual Preschool Children
Maryann Santos de Barona and Andrés Barona   381

Mexican American Student Segregation and Desegregation in
California
M. Beatriz Arias   401

Contributors   423

Approximately ten years ago the coeditors of this volume participated in a project at Eastern Michigan University called Ethnoperspectives in Bilingual Education Research. This project was designed to stimulate critical thinking and empirical research on bilingualism and bilingual education. Up to that time, mainstream researchers in the United States had largely ignored the apparent research needs of a field that only a few years before had been introduced by practitioners as a great experiment to improve the educational achievement of language minority students. To the extent that mainstream researchers did take an interest in bilingual education research, they often played an adversarial role, relentlessly demanding proof that "bilingual education works." Consequently, a great deal of the research on bilingual education during the 1970s was oriented either to demonstrating that bilingual education was working or that it was not.

As the decade of the seventies came to a close, it became evident to some of us involved in bilingual education that the national research agenda for bilingual education was heading in the wrong direction. Little attention was being given to developing the theoretical, technological, and policy foundations of the field, and far too much effort was being expended on polemical arguments about the effectiveness of bilingual education. It was time for a change. We argued then that bilingual education should be grounded in a knowledge base, and that the first order of business was to define, expand, and continuously refine the content and structure of that knowledge base. Our view has not changed during the intervening decade. In fact, it has been reaffirmed.

The 1980s ushered in the Reagan era with its shrill and devastating attacks on bilingual education. Seldom has a federal program received such virulent attacks and scurrilous treatment. Bilingual education advocates hunkered down and tried to weather the storm. Under such harrowing circumstances, only token efforts were made to conduct serious research on bilingual education. The research agenda continued to focus on effectiveness, as if bilingual education either worked flawlessly or did not work at all. There could be no middle ground, no qualification, no contextualization, no specification of circumstances and conditions. But even that peculiarly distorted research became increasingly obscured. It appears that during the Reagan era government agencies tried to conceal findings that were favorable toward bilingual education and eagerly paraded studies aimed at discrediting bilingual pedagogy. Although those efforts largely have failed, those were not good days for advocates of bilingual education.

Yet, by a curious twist of fate, the changing demographics of the United States was becoming increasingly apparent while this strange debate was going on. Minority leaders began to point out that sometime during the 21st century minorities would be in the majority, that social security would be jeopardized if minority youth were not adequately educated, that the responsibility for educating all of the nation's young people must be owned collectively, and that the nation's economic survival would be at stake in an increasingly competitive world economy. Some political leaders and educators were awakened by these sobering prospects and the reform movement in education began to take shape and to gain momentum. Many task forces, commissions, groups, and blue ribbon panels were activated and asked to recommend solutions to the educational crisis facing the nation. Unfortunately, these special bodies did little to address the pressing needs in the field of bilingual education. Those with fresh ideas, with the desire to innovate, with the commitment to improve the educational system for the benefit of neglected youth were left outside the official discussions. As a result, much commotion, but very little educational change of value, occurred during the 1980s, and the education crisis persisted into the 1990s to challenge both practitioners and politicians.

When we became aware that the 1990 annual meeting of the National Association for Bilingual Education (NABE) would be held in Tucson, Arizona, we decided that it was time once again to stimulate serious research on bilingual-ism and bilingual education. To that end, we organized a series of symposia that were held concurrently with the NABE annual meeting. In designing the symposia, we were looking for critical, emic perspectives on bilingual education. Arid polemics about its effectiveness are not the central issue. How to develop a quality knowledge base, a well-defined set of professional practices, and a proven technology are central to our concern. We are not out to prove anything to anyone: we are out to improve what we do for ourselves and the nation.

We got an enthusiastic response from our colleagues across the country. Many submissions were received. From these we selected those papers that we think reflect a critical understanding of important issues in bilingualism and bilingual education. The resulting symposia were held on April 23-25, 1990. Although the symposia were well attended and well received, only a small number of the people potentially interested in the topics covered by the symposia were able to attend. In order to reach a wider audience and to further stimulate research in this important educational field, we decided to publish the papers presented at the symposia.

The first part of this book focuses on developing new frameworks or expanding current areas of research interest. Amado M. Padilla and Hyekyung Sung seriously consider the potential application of principles from cognitive psychology to bilingual education theory and practice. Similar assessment of existing theories and findings from a variety of disciplines must be done by bilingual educators. Padilla and Sung provide a model for doing this kind of work. José E. Náñez, Sr., Raymond V. Padilla, and Becky Máez review the psychometric and chronometric literature on bilinguality to argue for a new research initiative aimed at isolating the effects of bilinguality on cognitive information processing. How bilinguality affects cognitive processes needs to be assessed very carefully so that we may draw out implications for bilingual pedagogy.

Adalberto Aguirre, Jr. takes a sociolinguistic perspective and reminds us that for bilingual teachers to be truly effective they must be truly bilingual. The intricacies of alternating languages, or code switching, and their implications for bilingual pedagogy require much more attention than researchers have given to this technical subject in the past. Lourdes Díaz-Soto challenges us to discard the apologist perspective on bilingual education research and to look at bilingual education as something that has to be made to work given its promising start over the past two decades. Along the same line, Antonio Simões introduces a critical theory perspective in bilingual education research that has been sorely lacking. Given the recent expansion of critical theory research in education, it is timely to introduce such a perspective in the field of bilingual education research.

In fact, Martha Montero-Sieburth and Mark LaCelle-Peterson adopt such a critical theory perspective in their ethno-historical study of school policies. Their work shows that various immigrant groups throughout history have reshaped the educational establishment and that bilingual education must be seen in such a social and historical context. Shifting the focus from the east coast to Texas, Armando L. Trujillo provides a detailed analysis of bilingual education politics at the grass roots level. This study clearly shows the larger political context within which bilingual education has had to struggle and develop. Collectively, the papers in the first part of the book show examples of how bilingual education researchers must reexamine old paradigms and introduce new ones.

The second part of the book focuses on pedagogical issues. At some point, someone has to do bilingual education rather than just talk about it. Bilingual educators can be expected to do a good job only if researchers provide them with proven bilingual education technology. To that end, Kathryn J. Lindholm begins to clarify the concepts and issues related to two-way bilingual immersion education. In the wake of great polemical debates about various bilingual education ideologies, Lindholm's work shows that the issues should be approached more pragmatically and dispassionately.

Following such pragmatism, María Cardelle-Elawar and José E. Náñez, Sr. point out that metacognitive skills can be used to advantage by bilingual students to increase their overall school achievement. When bilingual students have difficulty with math problems, is it because they do not know the relevant mathematical concepts or because they do not understand the language being used to describe the problem? These authors suggest that the latter is often the real problem. Here again we come face to face with Aguirre's warning about the need for truly bilingual teachers. Meanwhile, Sheryl L. Santos argues that mathematics must be taught in an appropriate social context, and that bilingual educators should redouble their efforts to increase the attainment of bilingual students in mathematics. To that end she offers a sampling of resources that are available to interested teachers.

This connection between language proficiency and bilingualism is treated from a technical point of view by Arnulfo G. Ramírez who summarizes the various frameworks that have been used to assess language proficiency. This highly technical area deserves much more attention from psychometricians and language specialists. Certainly the field of bilingual education could use many more diagnostic instruments to determine with precision the bilingual skills of students with dual language abilities.

The second part of the book closes with a much needed discussion of exemplary bilingual teachers by Christian J. Faltis and Barbara J. Merino. One of the most astounding lapses in the field of bilingual education is its lack of professional standards that define a competent bilingual teacher. Perhaps this chapter will stimulate further work in the important area of professional practice. Here again there is a great need to develop adequate and versatile assessment instruments and procedures along with reasonable standards.

The last part of the book is devoted to bilingualism and the public interest. As amply demonstrated by those who have chronicled the demographic revolution, bilingual education is no longer simply a minority or ethnic concern. The issues that are being addressed by this field affect everyone and the problems that it is trying to resolve belong to everyone. All levels of government must become involved in developing effective bilingual pedagogy if the national in-

terest is to be served. In this context, John J. Halcón and
María de la Luz Reyes critique the Reagan era trickle down
reform philosophy and its devastating effects on bilingual
education during the eighties. In the same voice, Ursula
Casanova asks why federal policy shifts and changes in the
bilingual education knowledge base are moving in the opposite direction: even though bilingual education increasingly has proven to be an effective approach, federal policy
has moved steadily toward English only instruction.

At the school building and classroom level, educational
policy has profound impacts on which students will receive
what kind of educational services. In the intricate field of
bilingual special education, the policy questions and issues
are still evolving. Nadeen T. Ruiz, Richard A. Figueroa,
Robert S. Rueda, and Carol Beaumont make a special contribution by tracing the history and status of bilingual special
education. In this speciality, one can see clearly the conver-
gence of multiple risk factors and how educational policies
can affect the lifetime chances of students. In this situation,
errors can occur in two directions, either through unnecessary stigmatization or through failure to provide services
that are truly needed. At the preschool level, there is still
much discussion as to how assessment of bilingual students
should be performed and how educational policies have
affected these issues. Maryann Santos de Barona and
Andrés Barona provide a thorough discussion of issues in
this speciality. They demonstrate the intersection between
educational policies and the highly technical business of determining and assessing language skills in bilingual populations.

The book closes with a case study that highlights the
dilemmas and contradictions that must be confronted by
educational systems having to respond simultaneously to
multiple demands from diverse populations. For example,
an interface between the needs of desegregation programs
and bilingual education is not easy to construct. Beatriz
Arias shows how such an interface was designed and how it
functioned in a northern California school district faced
with competing pressures from special populations and at

the same time experiencing changes in its urban environment.

Collectively, the contributors to this volume challenge the entire field of bilingual education to redouble its efforts in bilingual research. It is time to develop new frameworks for old issues; to devise new theories based on empirical research, careful reflection, and discussion; and to improve practice based on well-designed studies. There does exist a knowledge base that supports the practice of bilingual education. It is up to the researchers to develop further and maintain this knowledge base. It is up to the teacher educators to use it to create the best possible corps of bilingual teachers. And it is up to the policy-makers to insist that both researchers and educators fulfill their critical roles. If we can encourage further development in this direction, the main goal of this book will be achieved.

Raymond V. Padilla
Alfredo H. Benavides
Arizona State University

Part One

Developing New Frameworks

A THEORETICAL AND PEDAGOGICAL FRAMEWORK FOR BILINGUAL EDUCATION BASED ON PRINCIPLES FROM COGNITIVE PSYCHOLOGY

Amado M. Padilla and Hyekyung Sung
Stanford University

ABSTRACT

In this article, a theoretical framework based on cognitive ~ *theory* psychology are proposed for the pedagogy of bilingual education. First, a general model of information processing in human memory is presented. Then several models explaining how two languages are acquired and used by the bilingual are introduced. From this the cognitive mechanisms involved in second language learning are discussed. Language educators need teaching and learning strategies that facilitate second language acquisition and function among students. This chapter discusses the strategies for facilitating memory storage and retrieval of two languages including cognitive, metacognitive, and metalinguistic strategies. Finally, guiding principles based on the framework of cognitive psychology that can be used in the classroom context are identified.

For the past two decades there has been considerable debate in the educational literature surrounding the efficacy of bilingual education. This debate often has been more sociopolitical than pedagogical (Padilla, 1990). Bilingual educators frequently have been on the defensive in terms of asserting the educational merits of their programs to critics. Thus, less time and resources have been devoted to the development of sound theoretical and pedagogical frameworks. This is unfortunate because while this unproductive debate has gone on in the area of bilingual education, there have been considerable advances in the language sciences, including applied linguistics, which have served to inform educators in foreign language education and English as a Second Language (ESL) instruction. Today there are a large number of theoretical and pedagogical frameworks underpinning foreign language education and ESL instruction, compared with those of bilingual education (e.g., Oxford, 1990).

In this chapter, we propose that a theoretical framework based on cognitive psychology be instituted in the pedagogy of bilingual education. We do this because of our conviction that such an approach offers advantages to bilingual educators. These advantages include an approach that is both theoretically and methodically relevant to second language acquisition and use and to issues of concern to bilingual researchers. We will offer an explanation of second language learning from an information processing perspective. In addition, we will extend our discussion of cognitive principles of second language learning to the implications of how language educators can use these principles in their classrooms.

We will begin by presenting a general model of information processing in the first language that is widely accepted and used today (e.g., Anderson, 1985). This model is useful for describing how information enters and is stored in human memory, and how it is retrieved from memory. This general model will be expanded to show how two languages are processed by the bilingual and how memory operates in the bilingual individual, and will lead to a discussion of acquisition and use of a second language in bilinguals. In addition, several models explaining the bilingual's memory processing have been proposed, and we will examine and discuss them in detail in a later section of this chapter. Then we will explain the relevance of these models to second language learning and instruction.

As language educators, we are interested in finding strategies that facilitate second language learning and function among students. The most discussed strategies involve ways of facilitating memory storage and retrieval in the first and second language of the bilingual. Here we are addressing both cognitive and metacognitive strategies used knowingly or unknowingly by students to become more efficient second language learners. In addition, we have to consider the knowledge that the learner has about language and how this knowledge can be put into service in learning a new language. A person's conscious knowledge of language as an object of the analysis is termed metalinguistic knowledge and the use of such knowledge in language-related tasks is termed a metalinguistic strategy. We will argue that the use of metalinguistic knowledge facilitates second language learning. Our goal is to develop a set of guiding principles, based on information processing within the framework of cognitive psychology, that can be used by language instructors in teaching students a second language.

This chapter consists of four sections: (1) a presentation of the basic components of a general information processing model; (2) the function of these components in bilinguals and their involvement in second language learning; (3) knowledge-based strategies for second language learning as major instructional implications that emerge from the examination of bilingual information processing; and (4) guiding principles for second language and bilingual instructors according to each memory system in the model.

A General Information Processing Model

Although a number of information processing models are available today, they all share a set of basic assumptions. Among these is the view that a person operates as an information-processing system, selectively filtering and storing relevant information. According to these models, cognition involves the active processing of information beginning with encoding, moving to memory storage, and ending with retrieval of stored information. A representation of information processing is shown in Figure 1.

In this model, information moves through three memory systems. All stimulus information from the environment first enters into sensory memory, based on its saliency it may then be transferred to short-term memory (STM), and then to long-term memory (LTM). Once information is in LTM, it is assumed to be learned and available for use in any situation or context.

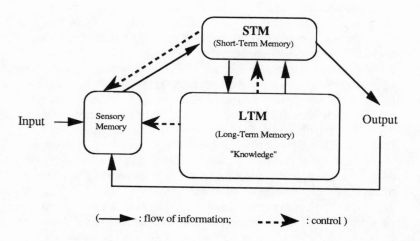

(⟶ : flow of information;   ▬ ▬ ▶ : control)

Figure 1

Representation of information flow showing the different levels of
processing in memory.

Sensory Memory

When we experience events or notice objects in our environment such as engaging in a conversation with someone or reading a poster on a bulletin board, the stimulus
information first enters into sensory memory. Perception is
the cognitive process that involves the assignment of meaning to these incoming stimuli (Glover, Ronning, & Bruning,
1990). Stimulus information must be perceived by the individual for it to be registered in sensory memory. Otherwise,
it will be lost. Sensory memory includes an echoic memory
for auditory information and an iconic memory for visual
information. In sensory memory we can store a great deal of
information, but only for a brief period of time. Therefore,
in order to operate on information that is registered in sen-

sory memory, the information must be transferred to short-term memory (STM). If the information in sensory memory is not transferred to STM, it will be lost very quickly.

Attention, which is interwoven with perception in human cognition, is also very critical in sensory memory. Attention allows the person to allocate cognitive resources to the tasks at hand. However, an individual has a very limited attention span and cannot attend to more than one or two events simultaneously. Therefore, some information that enters sensory memory will not necessarily be perceived and transferred to STM. Thus, attention plays an important role in selecting sensory information for further processing into STM.

Since attention is a very limited mental resource that can be allocated to a limited number of cognitive processes at a time, the more frequently the processes have been practiced, the less attention they require; and eventually they can be performed without interfering with other cognitive processes (Anderson, 1985). Processes that are highly practiced and require little or no attention are referred to as automatic, while processes that require attention are called controlled processes. Automatic processes complete themselves without deliberate effort by the subject. Registering the stimuli in sensory memory is generally an automatic process. Many aspects of our everyday behavior such as driving a car and comprehending language appear to be automatic.

Controlled processes require deliberate attention. We become aware of this control when we deliberately set about to listen to a lecture on a difficult topic and decide to take elaborate notes on the lecture. Many higher order cognitive processes, such as performing mental arithmetic, also demonstrate controlled processing (Anderson, 1985; McLaughlin, et al., 1983).

To get a good idea of how this sensory memory system works, imagine listening to someone speaking a language you do not know. You hear the sounds that the speaker is making, but you cannot understand even when listening attentively because you cannot process these sounds as meaningful. You cannot process and transfer the information received in sensory memory to STM because of the lack of prerequisite knowledge of the language. At a minimum, we need knowledge of the sound system in a language that leads to the development of feature detectors necessary for processing linguistic information. These feature detectors enable us to make sense of the multitude of auditory signals that we are exposed to and also permit us to understand these sounds as meaningful words.

What we have to notice here is the relationship between sensory memory and long-term memory (LTM). Feature detectors function in sensory memory, but information about these feature detectors is stored in LTM. As shown in Figure 1, the dotted arrow from LTM to sensory memory indicates that information in sensory memory is controlled by LTM. An example would be students learning English as a second language. Initially, the students have great difficulty in understanding the teacher because of their lack of knowledge of the language. As they begin to learn the sounds of the language they also begin to recognize more and more words in spoken English (i.e., they are developing feature detectors in English). Eventually, they possess good listening skills in English, however, these skills may be confined largely to the teacher and to a small number of other English speakers. When they encounter a speaker of English who has a dialect other than the teacher's, they may have difficulty in understanding this new speaker because their feature detectors for English do not yet extend into the range needed to process this new speaker's dialect of English.

Short-Term Memory (STM)

If we attend to the information in sensory memory, the information then can be transferred to short-term memory (STM). Short-term memory refers to the capacity for keeping a limited amount of information in a special active state during a very limited time. Information can be used only when it is in this active state. For example, when we hear a new phone number, we can memorize it just long enough to dial it and then we may forget it. Since we attended to the phone number that we had heard through sensory memory, the phone number was transferred to STM and kept only long enough to use it. Information that is transferred to

STM is lost within about one minute unless it is rehearsed, repeated, or meaningfully encoded and transferred to long-term memory (LTM).

When information is in STM, we are generally conscious of it because the information is in an active state. However, when information has been transferred to LTM, we are no longer conscious of it unless we need it for something we are doing at the moment. Because of this STM is also called a transient working memory.

Another major property of STM is limited storage capacity. There is just so much information that we can hold in STM at any given moment. Studies of STM show that if in a rote memory lesson on vocabulary the teacher reads words to students at a rate of about one every second, students are only able to hold between five to nine of them in STM. This is sometimes referred to as the "7 plus or minus 2" rule of STM. If the teacher continues reading words beyond 7 plus/minus 2, each new word will bump out one of the words previously read.

Encoding of information is a crucial part of STM. To transfer information into LTM the information must be actively practiced until it is learned and moved on to LTM. There are various encoding strategies that can be employed to learn information. Such strategies include rehearsal, mediation, imagery, and use of mnemonics (Glover, Ronning, & Bruning, 1990). Once information gets to LTM it does not have to be practiced again to be maintained because it is now permanently stored.

Long-Term Memory (LTM)

The best way to think of long-term memory is as a library where knowledge is stored permanently when not in use. Unlike STM, the capacity of LTM is relatively unlimited, and we can continue to add new information to our library throughout our lifetime. Information in LTM is normally in an inactive state and we are usually unaware of it. To use information from LTM it is necessary to activate that knowledge. Once the information is activated, it is moved back to STM and is ready for use (see Figure 1). For example, suppose you are in your office working and one of your colleagues stops by for consultation about a paper that she/he is writing. She/he asks if you would please read the paper for both content and form. As you begin reading the paper you realize that the writing could be improved and that important references need to be incorporated into the paper. Without being conscious of it, you are retrieving grammatical rules and content knowledge stored in LTM, moving them to STM, and preparing them to be used to assist your colleague in understanding how parts of the paper need to be revised for greater clarity or accuracy. This shows the power of LTM in controlling the event that transpires between you and your colleague.

An important feature of LTM is how knowledge is organized and stored in LTM. Some of the most interesting research on LTM has to do with how semantic information is stored. This research has led to a number of semantic-network models for describing how information is represented in LTM. In one way or another these models all assume that the best way to think about semantic knowledge is in terms of multiple, interconnected associations, relationships, or pathways. Accordingly, information is assumed to be embedded in an organized, structured network composed of semantic units and their functional relationships to one another.

In the semantic-network model called the spreading-activation model (Collins & Loftus, 1975), the relationship between words is assumed to be very complex. For example, the word *red* might activate *fire engine, roses,* and *apples.* In turn, *fire engine* activates *truck, ambulance,* and *house,* while *roses* activates *violets* and *flowers.* Similarly, *apples* might call forth *cherries* and *pie.* In some of these connections, the relationship to the word *red* might be stronger or more meaningful than in other cases. In addition, the spreading-activation model stipulates that an activated word can be more easily processed than an inactivated one (Anderson, 1983). For example, you are given the word *bird* and then shown one of three target words, *canary, box,* or *pielf* (a nonsense word) for a very brief period of time. You are instructed to decide as quickly as possible if the new word belongs to the same category as *bird* or whether it is a word at all. If you are like other persons given this task, you will show the fastest reaction time to the word *canary*, followed by *box*, and finally *pielf*. This occurs because the starter word (*bird*) activates material in the network. The closer this word is to the target, the more activated, and thus the more easily processed that target is.

It is difficult to separate in an easy fashion how knowledge is actually stored in LTM and how such knowledge is retrieved. Retrieval includes at least two processes: recall and recognition. In a recall task, the person is required to actively reproduce stored information, while a recognition task requires the person to verify if certain information is correct or not. For example, a student asked to write an essay on the meaning and intent of the U.S. Declaration of Independence would use a recall process. However, a student asked to identify individuals who participated in the writing of the Declaration of Independence would use recognition memory. Obviously, the retrieval processes involved in these two types of tasks are quite distinct.

Our discussion to this point has been confined to a general model of information processing. We will now turn our attention to the role of information processing in bilinguals. The models to be presented have been developed to describe the language use of proficient bilinguals. In these models, what is most apparent is the importance of LTM in the processing of information across linguistic systems. Although these models are confined to proficient bilinguals, we will show how information processing models of the type described can be used to explain the learning of a second language. Further, from examination of these models we will offer recommendations to language teachers on how they can more effectively structure second language learning environments. The focus of our discussion in the following section will include only situations where learners already have a moderately well-developed first language and are now learning a second language. This includes children beginning at about five years of age, and excludes children simultaneously exposed to two languages.

Bilingual Information Processing

LTM Models in Bilinguals

Common storage vs. separate storage model. In the area of
bilingual information processing a debate has long ensued
over whether there is a separate or a shared LTM store.
Kolers (1968) placed the issue of the independence versus
interdependence of the bilingual's two languages in the context of information-processing approaches to human cognition. Based on Kolers's initial ideas about the bilingual's
memory system, two competing hypotheses were advanced:
the common storage model and the separate storage model.
According to Hamers and Blanc (1989), the interdependence
or common-store hypothesis states that bilingual memory is
a single system in which information is stored as a complex
set of attributes or tags that enables the bilingual to store
nonsemantic information such as modality, frequency, spatial and temporal aspects, and type of language (e.g., English,
Korean). Language is then one of these tags through which
the common store taps into two lexical systems via a
"switching mechanism." Conversely, the independence or
separate-memory hypothesis holds that there are two independent language-specific memory stores in contact with
each other via a "translation mechanism."

Both models postulate the existence of a "mechanism"
that permits the bilingual to switch from one linguistic system to the other; they differ from each other in where they
locate this mechanism during processing. In the common-
store model, this switch is situated before semantic memory.
The switching mechanism is set to whichever language is
being processed and then information is sent to a common
memory store. In the separate-store model information in
each language is stored separately unless it is required in the
opposite language and is then translated via the translation
mechanism.

If the independence hypothesis is correct, a balanced
bilingual should react as a monolingual in both the languages, independently from what is learned in the other
language. The evidence for the separate-storage model
stems from studies in which bilinguals either respond dif-

ferently in their two languages or fail to transfer from one language to the other. On the other hand, if the interdependence hypothesis reflects a common memory store, then we should be able to test the model using a variety of memory tasks such as association tasks, language-recognition tasks, and free recall in the two languages. Generally speaking, the common-storage model is supported by evidence indicating that intralingual behavior does not differ from interlingual behavior in bilinguals.

Based on their reviews of the literature, McCormack (1977), McLaughlin (1978), and Dornic (1980) all conclude that the evidence supports the common store hypothesis. However, Kolers (1978) advocates for the separate-storage model on the grounds that empirical evidence using a variety of tasks such as word association, free recall, and recognition tasks cannot be explained by the common-storage model. In a current review of the literature on information processing in bilinguals, Hamers and Blanc (1989) conclude that the controversy between the two opposing points of view is still very much an open question and that existing data can be marshalled to support either position. Similarly, Grosjean (1982) states that perhaps the question of independence versus interdependence was fated for mixed findings from the beginning.

Although we have been only discussing semantic memory, which permits the storage of words and their meanings, there are other types of memory such as episodic memory (autobiographical experiences such as childhood experiences, details of conversations with friends, etc.) that are important. However, they will not be discussed within the framework of bilingual information processing in this chapter.

Dual-coding model. In order to resolve the controversy between the common storage and the separate storage models, Paivio and Desrochers (1980) and Paivio and Lambert (1981) applied the dual-coding theory that Paivio (1971) had proposed earlier for monolinguals. Dual-coding theory is based on the assumption that memory and cognition are served by two separate symbolic systems, one specialized for dealing with verbal representation (*logogens*) and the other with nonverbal representation (*imagens*). The two systems of representations are presumed to be interconnected, but capable of functioning independently. Paivio and Desrochers (1980) suggest that the bilingual has two verbal representations, one for each language, in addition to a representation in the imagery system. These three systems are independent and autonomous from each other but are interconnected at the referential level. Actually, the two verbal representational systems function independently from each other, but there is one memory in imagery which is in constant interaction with the two verbal systems. Interconnectedness means that representations in one system can activate those in the other, so that, for example, pictures can be named and images can occur for words. Independence implies, among other things, that nonverbal and verbal memory codes, aroused directly by pictures and words or indirectly by imagery and verbal encoding tasks, should have additive effects on recall.

Hamers and Blanc (1989) state that the dual-coding model is a promising alternative to the unresolved issue of the common-store or the separate-store models. In this model, a surface level exists on which two separate representations store specific characteristics, including tagging and perceptual aspects associated with language. In addition, a deeper cognitive level, that of semantic storage, draws on both languages. This higher-order, non-language-specific organization, together with the imagery process, is then further organized into concepts and propositional representations. This approach is consistent with recent trends in psycholinguistics and information processing. However, it must be noted that the dual-coding model concerns access to representation rather than the organization of memory. Furthermore, the dual-coding model, although it has attempted to resolve the controversy between the separate and shared models, does not explain the process engaged in by the bilingual in processing information in one or both languages. Rather, it is limited only to the representation in LTM and does not explain the full processing of information from stimulus presentation to eventual LTM storage and retrieval. Therefore, we will now discuss bilingual information processing beginning with sensory memory and proceeding to bilingual STM and LTM storage to show how LTM is related to all aspects of information processing. It is in fact impossible to process information without LTM involvement.

Sensory Memory in Bilinguals

As we discussed earlier, feature detectors are critical in understanding the language spoken around us. Similarly, the only way the learner of a second language can actually learn the new language is by developing the necessary feature detectors for the new language. If we have a certain prerequisite level of knowledge of the language in LTM, then we know that language well enough to process it from sensory memory to STM and possibly to LTM. For example, if we hear the language we know, it can be filtered by feature detectors in sensory memory and transferred into STM. An example would be an English speaker entertaining a Japanese guest who speaks little English. The English speaker asks, "Do you want to go to the *sushi* restaurant?" The Japanese guest easily catches the word sushi, even though little of anything else is understood. In the large flow of communicative discourse, the guest might filter the conversation something like, " . . . sushi . . . " because of the familiarity with the Japanese word sushi, which is part of his/her prerequisite knowledge in LTM. Here, we conclude that for the guest the word "sushi" is easily filtered in sensory memory because of fully developed Japanese feature detectors, while the surrounding English discourse may be partly or completely lost because of insufficiently developed English feature detectors (Padilla & Sung, 1990).

In second language learning, we often make interesting and sometimes comical errors in filtering a new language through our sensory memory because we may not yet have sufficiently developed feature detectors to process our second language. If the feature detectors are not quite developed in the second language, we often process the auditory signals using our first language feature detectors. For example, the native Spanish speaker in an adult ESL class

hears the instructor say, "Please watch the card," and interprets it as "Please wash the car," and then is confused about
what is being asked since the request is not appropriate to
the context.   In Spanish the /ch/ sound is pronounced
nearly like the English /sh/ (e.g., like the /ch/ in *machine*).
Thus the native speaker filters the word *watch* as *wash*.
Similarly, the final /d/ sounds in Spanish are infrequent
and when they do occur they are like the English /th/ sound
and not likely to be filtered, resulting in the perception of *car*
rather than *card*.

Another problem that often occurs in second language
learning is the difficulty in producing certain sounds in a
new language because of an insensitivity to those sounds.
Take the native Chinese-speaking restaurant owner who
recommends to his English-speaking customers a special
dish that comes with fried rice, which he/she pronounces as
"flied lice!" In this case, the English sounds /r/ and /l/ are
not differentiated and therefore the Chinese speaker uses /l/
where /r/ is required when he is speaking English.

These examples demonstrate that it is essential for second
language instructors to be knowledgeable of the linguistic
contrasts between the first language and the language being
acquired to understand the types of problems that second
language learners encounter.   Such information also enables
instructors to plan better language instruction programs for
limited English proficient students.

Since sensory memory also includes iconic memory for
visual information as well as echoic memory for auditory
information, using the imagery system in LTM enhances
processing in sensory memory. For example, to learn a certain word in a new language, if the learner either has a
paired picture-word representation or uses imagery, better
learning will occur. According to the dual-coding memory
model, this occurs because the imagery system produces an
additive effect in learning.

Short-Term Memory in Bilinguals

In our discussion of the general information processing
model, we described the function of STM as the location
where relevant information is rehearsed prior to storage in

LTM. We showed that STM has limited storage capacity and that it is of short duration. The same constraints operate in the STM of bilinguals. The only difference may be in the STM processing of material in the less dominant language. It is true that when we are called upon to learn material in our less proficient language we spend more time in simply trying to understand the message, rather than engaging in the rehearsal that is necessary to encode the information for transfer to LTM. For example, a student in a class who has some proficiency in English, but who is still limited in English may require more time simply to decode the meaning of a teacher's lecture on the application of some mathematical principle. As a consequence, the student misses parts of the lecture because of the time needed to comprehend the message, which lags behind the rate at which the message is being received. Therefore, it is likely that only parts of the message are being processed. It is as if every few words or phrases were being deleted from a text. The meaning of the message may still be understandable, but critical aspects of the message may be lost causing the loss of valuable time in having to do additional work to fill in the information that was not processed.

A review of literature on the information processing in bilinguals shows that very little research has been conducted on the STM system in bilinguals (Hamers & Blanc, 1989). For whatever reason, the study of memory in bilinguals has been largely confined to LTM. This may be due to the fact that most researchers see STM as an intermediate stage to LTM with the most important and intriguing issues occurring in LTM.

Knowledge-Based Second Language Learning Strategies

Cognitive and Metacognitive Strategies

One aspect of an information processing approach to second language learning that has not received much attention is the role of cognitive and metacognitive strategies in second language instruction. Cognitive strategies refer to the direct action taken by a learner to assimilate, transform, and manipulate the material to be learned. Oxford (1986, 1990) states that these strategies operate directly on the language and are linked to the specific task demands of the learning situation. Metacognitive strategies, on the other hand, refer to the learner's ability to monitor, regulate, and assess his/her progress and to create conditions that are conducive to effective learning based on understanding of his/her own strengths and weaknesses. According to Oxford (1986), metacognitive strategies can be envisioned as support strategies since their role is to enhance or support language learning in a more general domain, by establishing learning goals and progress assessment techniques as well as by creating good attitudes and reducing frustration and anxiety.

This is a very useful distinction because it defines two separate and important aspects of the second language learning situation: the student's direct approach to the many information processing tasks inside and outside the classroom (cognitive strategies and behaviors) as well as the student's awareness of the nature of the learning process that should lead to the ability of constructive progress assessment (metacognitive strategies and behaviors).

Chamot and O'Malley (1986) and O'Malley and Chamot (1989) view metacognitive strategies as involving thinking about the learning process, planning for learning, monitoring of comprehension and production while it is taking place, and self-evaluation of learning after the language activity is completed. On the other hand, cognitive strategies concern the direct relationship between the individual learning task and the immediate manipulation of the present material. According to these authors, students need to recognize that learning how to handle second language material (cognitive strategy) is as important as learning how to learn a second language (metacognitive strategy). O'Malley and Chamot (1989) maintain that students who approach language learning without metacognitive strategies are essentially learners without direction or opportunity to review their progress, achievement, or future learning directions.

Oxford (1990) has developed an extensive taxonomy of skills for both cognitive and metacognitive strategies.

According to this taxonomy, the following are all classified as cognitive strategies: getting organized, getting the meaning, showing you understand, communicating, practicing, learning the rules, learning outside of class, and memory building. The metacognitive strategies include: setting the stage, dealing with attitudes and motivation, planning and goal setting, self-management, social cooperation, creating practice opportunities, and cultural orientation.

Although useful, Oxford's taxonomy is of limited value because the strategies are not organized according to any theoretical framework which would show how they are maximally beneficial. Our approach is to present some important cognitive and metacognitive strategies that teachers can incorporate into their bilingual program irrespective of the age of the learners. In the next section, we will identify these strategies according to whether they influence sensory memory, STM, or LTM. Our position is that second language learning is facilitated by the proper employment of cognitive and metacognitive strategies because these strategies enhance the processing of information in the new language and thereby learning.

Metalinguistic Strategies

It is true that a person does not develop proficiency in a second language through the mere attainment of a few words and grammatical rules. Also a person does not learn to comprehend a second language through indiscriminate language exposure to the second language. Rather, a person learns a second language through reflecting upon and making explicit one's knowledge of how language works. This conscious and explicit knowledge of how language works is referred to as metalinguistic awareness.

Learning a second language presents an interesting challenge to the learner since he/she already has the basic abilities to use and comprehend language, but through the added ability of treating language as an object of analysis is able to use first language knowledge to facilitate second language learning. Odlin (1989) refers to this as cross-linguistic transfer in language learning. The knowledge that we have about language exists on many different levels—knowledge about its sound system, words, sentence structure, semantics, and discourse structure. The good second language learner understands the skills used in going about the business of learning the new language. At the most basic level and operating through our sensory memory is phonemic awareness, which is the ability to "hear" sound units and the knowledge that spoken units can be analyzed and compared across linguistic systems. Take, for example, the distinction between the sounds /ch/ and /sh/ in English which are easily detectable as different sounds by the native English speaker, but which are not perceived as distinct by the native Spanish speaker learning English as a second language. Accordingly, the good second language learner knows that it is essential to pay attention to every sound in the early stages of second language acquisition in order to recognize the basic sound distinctions between the first and second languages. Similarly, through syntactic awareness of the native language, the second language learner is able to recognize sentence patterns and to transfer this knowledge to the second language in order to construct the syntactic rules necessary in the new language (Odlin, 1989). Obviously, the learner also possesses semantic awareness, which is transferable to the development of semantic networks in second language acquisition. Depending upon the similarity between languages such knowledge and its use in the learning of a new language can either facilitate or impede the rate of second language learning.

Implications then for the language instructor are: (a) to identify or create language exercises and other curriculum devices that capitalize on the positive transfer of linguistic skills across languages, and (b) to design curriculum that sensitizes students to their inherent linguistic knowledge in their first language so that they can apply such knowledge to the development of linguistic skills in the second language. In this way, the learner becomes an active participant in the acquisition of the new language and does not rely solely on the instructor to demonstrate similarities and differences between the native language and the new language being learned. It is through the active cognitive construction of language during the acquisition process that the learner demonstrates the characteristics of a good second language learner.

Guiding Principles for Second Language Instructors

The learning strategies that can be used in second language or bilingual education classrooms include both cognitive and metacognitive strategies and metalinguistic strategies based on knowledge of information processing. We will discuss strategies according to each of the components described in the processing (learning and retrieval) of information, providing guidelines for efficient second language learning and instruction, and showing how such guidelines are related to our general model of information processing. Our assumption in presenting these guidelines is that understanding the cognitive processes involved in first and second language processing will make possible the development of curriculum materials and techniques for teaching that are theoretically driven and that result in improved second language pedagogy and learning. While suggesting some strategies that may facilitate second language learning, we expect that second language instructors will expand upon these strategies in their instructional practices.

Sensory Memory

As discussed previously, sensory memory has three identifiable components that are important in second language learning. We will discuss how they can be involved in pedagogical strategies.

Feature detectors. The input linguistic signals in a new language cannot be correctly filtered unless the feature detectors in the language are sufficiently developed. Incoming information can only be perceived once a minimal level of feature detectors has been developed in the new language. This means that at a minimum the learner needs to have the basic sound system of the language to be able to assign meaning to spoken words. Although it is important to recognize that feature detectors also include written forms of the language, we will confine ourselves to examples from spoken forms to simplify this discussion.

To be proficient in a second language, especially for oral proficiency, the learner has to develop the feature detectors necessary for understanding speech. Initially, this means learning the phonology of the new language and the ways in which sounds are combined to produce words, and words combined to form sentences. Because this learning involves an active cognitive process, it is possible to identify strategies to facilitate this component of second language acquisition.

Both cognitive and metacognitive strategies can be called upon to facilitate the development of second language feature detectors. One useful cognitive strategy is the mental or actual repetition of the sound(s) in order to create an auditory representation of the sound(s). This strategy improves echoic memory. We can think of this as the playing back of a sound, word, or phrase, in our mind in order to assist comprehension and recall of the material. To make sure of the new sound used in a certain word, or a new expression (phrase) used in a certain context, the learner should ask a teacher or other native speaker for repetition, explanation, and/or examples. Such questioning for clarification is a good example of the use of another cognitive strategy that helps in the development of echoic memory.

Self-monitoring is an important metacognitive strategy that also helps in the development of feature detectors in the second language (L2). By deliberately checking comprehension during listening or reading, or by checking the accuracy and appropriateness of oral or written production while it is taking place, the learner can efficiently improve proficiency in L2. The value of this metacognitive strategy is frequently underestimated by language instructors. Students who are taught self-monitoring skills demonstrate improved learning on complex tasks (Perkins, 1987).

In addition, language instructors can use direct strategies to facilitate the learner's development of feature detectors in the second language. Although these strategies are certainly not novel to bilingual teachers, their recognition in this section indicates how they operate to enhance learning of the new language. The strategies include the instructor's clear articulation in L2 along with a rate of speech that is commensurate with the learner's fluency in the second language. These strategies show the instructor's sensitivity to the student's insufficiently developed language detectors. By means of clear articulation and pacing of language input, the instructor enables the learner to begin to develop "an ear" for the new language. As the learner develops proficiency in the new language, the instructor can begin to increase the rate of speech to approximate the normal speech rate of the community. Coupled with instruction in the critical differences that exist between the home language and the target language, this assists the learner in recognizing the differences between the two languages.

Attentional processes. Information enters into sensory memory only when the learner attends to it. Paying attention is a sufficient condition for activating sensory memory. By focusing attention to what he/she is hearing, the learner facilitates the development of the sensory memory system in L2. There are two metacognitive strategies that enhance attentional processing. One is directed attention, in which the learner decides in advance to attend in general to a learning task and to ignore irrelevant distractions. The other is selective attention, in which the learner decides in advance to attend to specific aspects of language input or situational details that will help in the perception and acquisition of the language input. Another important second language learning skill involves a metalinguistic strategy of attending to the ends of words because it is the word endings in most languages that convey meaning about gender, number, verb tense, and so on. Recognizing and attending to the importance of word endings facilitates both second language acquisition and comprehension.

The language educator can play an important role in attentional processing by arranging a classroom environment that is as distraction free as possible. By reducing the distractions the student is better able to employ directed and selective attention. For example, we know from work on information processing that noise can disrupt learning of unfamiliar information, including things to be learned in a

nondominant language (Dornic, 1980). The disruption takes
two forms. In the first, the learner finds it difficult to use
inner speech (thinking) when there are many environmental noises and the situation demands processing in the
nondominant language. In the second, distractions, including noise, seem to elicit second language processing
through the dominant language. This means that the
language learner relies more heavily on translating from
the weaker to the stronger language. This creates a situation
where the student is slow to respond to classroom activities
because it takes longer for the student to comprehend the
auditory information that he/she is receiving in L2.
Further, the long latency in responding and the incomplete
comprehension that sometimes occurs because of lost information often leads the teacher to the mistaken conclusion that the student was not attending to the material or
has not mastered it. However, this happens when the problem is more a situation of an environmental stressor (e.g.,
distracting noise in the classroom) causing the learner to
revert to older learned habits and thereby processing the L2
through his/her native language.

In this discussion, it is important to clarify that the noise
that we are targeting for reduction is extraneous noise from
the environment, for example, traffic on a busy thorough-
fare or talking in the class that is not task relevant. We are
not excluding talking and/or recitation by the students in
the classroom that occurs when learners are engaged in the
active practice of the new language. Noise created by students who are actively practicing their new language skills is
important.

Automaticity. The essential difference between a native
speaker of English and one who is just beginning to learn
English is the naturalness and automaticity that the native
speaker has in comparison to the beginner. Fluency thus
means the processing of information in an efficient and
seemingly effortless manner. Similarly, as one gains proficiency in the second language the learner reports greater automaticity in the use of the new language. It is important

then in second language instruction to set as a goal the automatic processing of information in the second language. Teachers need to strive to have students begin to think in the new language as soon as possible. One technique to achieve automaticity involves teaching students self-monitoring metacognitive skills. At the beginning stage of second language learning, this implies teaching students to think about language and to try to engage in thinking in a new language. The purpose for striving for automaticity is that less time is spent in evaluating incoming information when the learner is prepared to receive information in the second language.

The natural tendency for the second language learner is to rely heavily on the dominant language in making sense of the new language. For many second language learners this entails translation, however, the sooner learners can be taught not to translate between the two languages the more rapidly learning will proceed because thinking in the new language will not be encumbered by the dominant language.

It is important for language instructors to continuously monitor a student's level of proficiency. Students' level of proficiency even within a class may vary widely depending on education, age, motivation, and strategies employed for learning a second language. For example, adult second language learners with good academic preparation in their native language can more efficiently use their highly developed cognitive, metacognitive, and metalinguistic strategies than their counterparts with less formal education. Accordingly, instructors can maximize the efficacy of their pedagogy by knowing a priori the L2 learning capability of their students and tailoring specific L2 learning strategies for them. To do this effectively the instructor must be aware of both the characteristics of sensory memory and the cognitive and metacognitive strategies that can be used to enhance the processing of information through sensory memory. An important part of this is the teaching of critical "thinking" skills including the use of cognitive, metacognitive, and metalinguistic strategies to facilitate overall cognitive processing.

Short-Term Memory (STM)

Consciousness. STM is an activated stage and learners are very conscious of their efforts to store information in STM. To enhance the processes in STM, directed attention is recommended as a metacognitive strategy. This means that the learner ideally should be directing his/her attention to the task of learning the material being presented by the teacher.

Rehearsal. To help in the rehearsal process, instructors should employ methods of repetition of material at a speed of presentation that allows adequate rehearsal to take place. In addition, students can be taught to engage in active rehearsal strategies in the second language that improve the ability to process L2 input from sensory memory to STM and then to LTM. Imagery is an important cognitive strategy that requires some consideration. This refers to relating new information to visual concepts in memory via familiar, easily retrievable visualizations, phrases, or locations. Language instructors frequently rely on pictures for linking words to objects. This use of pictures becomes even more useful when the students are encouraged to engage in active imagery. Use of iconic memory for visual information as well as use of echoic memory for auditory information are also known to facilitate learning in monolinguals. Further, the importance of imagery is noted in the dual-coding memory model discussed earlier.

Another very effective strategy in the learning of a L2 is recombination. This refers to instructional exercises that require the student to construct, for example, meaningful sentences or larger language sequences by combining new linguistic elements in new ways. Recombination tasks require that the student engage in active metacognitive and metalinguistic planning in order to arrive at new combinations of elements not practiced before.

With practice and continued encouragement to self-monitor their rehearsal, students will show a decrease in processing time as they gain proficiency in L2. Note-taking is another cognitive strategy that can be used to facilitate rehearsal in STM. By writing down main ideas and important points, and by outlining or summarizing information presented orally or in writing, the learner can increase processing capability in STM. Taking enough time in processing a second language is a cognitive strategy that is often not well understood by both instructors and learners. Learning new and difficult material often requires repeated presentations and rehearsal before learning occurs in meaningful enough "chunks" for it to be stored in LTM. Accordingly, considerable time must be devoted to repetition and practice before the benefits to learning are apparent.

Self-questioning can be both a metacognitive and metalinguistic strategy that the learner can use to facilitate second language learning. By consciously engaging in self-questioning about the content or linguistic structure of the language being learned, the student can better comprehend what is being studied because self-questioning increases the amount of rehearsal that is necessary to achieve STM.

Unfortunately, L2 processing is not automatic and is much more deliberate and controlled. As a consequence, L2 learning is likely to be very fatiguing especially when the learner is very motivated and is employing the strategies discussed here. Because of the fatigue factor, the student may necessarily require frequent time-outs. These time-outs allow the student to recover from the fatigue and to consolidate the learning that is taking place in L2.

Long-Term Memory (LTM)

A large number of strategies have been shown to be useful for memory enhancement. Most of the knowledge that we have about these strategies comes from experimental laboratory work with monolinguals or adult bilinguals (mostly college students), however, there is no reason for believing that these strategies do not also have ecological validity for L2 learners. Further, it may appear from what has been said about the relationship between STM and LTM that information passes into LTM in some indiscriminate fashion. However, this impression is far from accurate. In fact, there are numerous strategies, that if used, can assist in the organization of knowledge in LTM. We will now turn our attention to a discussion of what we consider to be some useful strategies in L2 that can be used by learners of any age.

Organization of information. Second language instruction
and learning should be carried out in a way that maximizes
the separation of L1 and L2 in LTM. Therefore, the four
metacognitive strategies that we will discuss first should be
viewed from this perspective. Two of the metacognitive
strategies involve preparation for memory organization are
advance organization and organizational planning. The
other two, self-evaluation and self-management, refer to
learner oriented regulation of L2 performance. In advance
organization, we refer to previewing the main ideas and
concepts of the material in L2 to be learned, often by skim-
ming the text for the organizing principles. In organizational planning, the central notion is to plan the parts,
sequences, and main ideas to be expressed orally or in writing in L2. Self-evaluation involves the students' monitoring of how well they have performed on a second
language acquisition task. In this type of monitoring,
students evaluate their performances as either meeting
some standard or falling below the standard. If performances fall below the standard, they should practice the task
until performance attains the standard. If attainment of the
standard is too difficult then the learners may need to re-
assess his/her or the teacher's standard and set the goal a
little lower until the desired performance level is attained.
As a part of this, the student can engage in self-management
of the learning environment, which entails finding opportunities for improving L2 proficiency. This may include
seeking out native speakers of L2, using L2 learning aids,
and not avoiding challenges that demand the use of the
second language.

In addition to these metacognitive strategies, a number of
cognitive strategies also can be employed in planning instruction in a second language. Students must be instructed
in the use of these strategies by their language teachers,
meaning that not only must the teacher plan the lesson to
include language content, but must plan time devoted to
learning and practicing those cognitive strategies that have
been shown to be very helpful in facilitating LTM.

The first of these cognitive strategies is summarizing. In
summarizing the student is shown the power of making

written summaries of the information gained through listening and reading. With practice, older students will be able to engage in mental summation. The important consideration here is the active engagement in the learning process that occurs when summarizing is going on. During appropriate opportunities the teacher must allow time for students to engage in note-taking and in reviewing the notes so that the material can be rehearsed again. Another useful strategy is elaboration, which refers specifically to the learner relating new information to what is already known. The idea here is to look for ways new information is related to old knowledge already in LTM. To maximize the use of this strategy teachers must be constantly on the alert to draw bridges or connections between information that is being taught and material that has already been learned. Once the learner realizes that much of what is being taught about a language can be related to what was learned earlier, or what is known in the native language, then the learner understands the interconnections between what possibly had earlier seemed to be many disconnected bits of information. Through summarizing and elaboration, second language learning becomes less a series of rules to be acquired through rote memorization and more the generation of production based on self-generated rules and connections between parts of language.

A cognitive strategy that is not used enough in language education is deduction. When children begin to learn their home languages they generate their own linguistic rules for how they believe the language is used. We see evidence of this, for example, when we listen to children overgeneralize the rules of regular grammatical forms to otherwise non-regular forms (e.g., foots for feet, goed for went, etc.). In learning a second language the learner needs to have ample opportunity to explore the rules of the new language and to apply these rules in the production of the language. Rule generation and deduction of rules in speech production is bound to be more illuminating than rote memorization of grammatical rules in a new language without the chance to put these rules to the test in language production. Obviously, there is a large metalinguistic component inherent in the process of deducing how the new language works and how to go about acquiring it. Language acquisition is in some respects similar to other problems to be solved and we know from the literature that deduction is an effective strategy in problem solving.

Another important strategy is inferencing which calls for the learner to use information in a text to guess the meaning of new items, to predict outcomes, or to complete missing parts. Again this strategy is not unique or in any way surprising. In fact, the merits of inferencing may appear as commonsense to many. However, for a learner to exercise the skill of inferencing there needs to be an atmosphere of exploration in the classroom that permits the student to practice inferencing skills (i.e., a classroom where second language instruction takes place in a nonrestrictive atmosphere and learners can play with language without sanctions or penalty). This is the type of naturalistic environment that usually exists for children learning their first language. Unfortunately, most second language learning occurs in formal classroom settings that require structure and order rather than language exploration.

Another strategy that is easily identifiable is transfer where what is already known facilitates the learning or incorporation of new information. In transfer, we are specifically referring to the positive transfer of knowledge that is available to us in LTM and which we can bring to bear in the learning of new knowledge. When prior knowledge can be used to facilitate acquisition of new knowledge, then we describe this as positive transfer. If prior knowledge detracts from new learning, this is referred to as negative transfer. Positive transfer may include the categorizing of new words in L2 based on already established L1 organizational structures in memory, or it may involve the extrapolation of L1 concepts to new L2 information. Whatever the particulars, the essential point is that prior knowledge, including linguistic knowledge, is used to shape the organization and retention of new knowledge in LTM.

In second language learning, one important strategy is the cross-linguistic transfer of L1 knowledge and skills to L2 acquisition. Essentially, in L2 learning, it is not necessary to

relearn all the language skills that have already been acquired in L1, but which now must be used in L2. For example, if a child has already learned to read in his/her native
language and is now learning English as his/her new language, it is obvious that he/she does not have to start from
zero, but can easily transfer the skills of reading in the native language to reading in the new language. There are
numerous ways in which L1 linguistic knowledge can be
applied to the acquisition of L2. However, both teacher and
student must seek ways to enhance positive transfer during
the course of L2 learning.

Finally, a much explored cognitive strategy that has been
shown to facilitate memory involves imagery. Here the
learner is encouraged and, if needed, instructed in ways to
use mental imagery of information that requires storage in
long-term memory. We know from research on the relationship between the use of imagery and LTM that some
types of information (e.g., concrete words) are more readily
accessible to imagery techniques than other types of material
(e.g., abstract concepts). It is also known that mnemonic
techniques that rely on imagery strategies are very useful in
assisting in the learning process of large masses of information. Such techniques may be very useful in learning vocabulary in L2 and in other types of L2 knowledge.

Conclusion

In this section we have discussed some of the more
salient cognitive, metacognitive, and metalinguistic strategies that can be employed by both the language educator and
student in bilingual education, ESL, or any other second
language instructional methodology. Further, we have organized our discussion of these strategies according to the
location in our information processing model where their
contribution to second language learning can be maximized.
Accordingly, ours is not a shopping list of hints, suggestions,
or strategies for learning a second language as seen in other
works (e.g., Oxford, 1990; Rubin and Thompson, 1982).
Rather, we have described a cognitive processing model de-

veloped with monolinguals that can be extended to account for bilingual information processing. This model can also be used to describe the acquisition and the use of a second language. The principles that emerge from this model regarding the learning of L2 have implications for both language educators and learners. Finally, we firmly believe that a cognitive information processing model of the type described in this paper has great potential for bilingual education as well as heuristic value because of the research questions that it lends itself to when considering second language learning.

References

Anderson, J. R. (1983). A spreading-activation model of memory. *Journal of Verbal Learning and Verbal Behavior, 22*, 261-295.

____. (1985). *Cognitive psychology and its implications* (2nd edition). New York: Freeman.

Chamot, A. U., & O'Malley, J. M. (1986). *A cognitive academic language learning approach: An ESL content-based curriculum.* Washington, D.C.: National Clearinghouse for Bilingual Education.

Collins, A. M., & Loftus, E. F. (1975). A spreading-activation theory of semantic processing. *Psychological Review, 82*, 407-428.

Dornic, S. (1980). Information processing and language dominance. *International Review of Applied Psychology, 29*, 119-140.

Glover, J. A., Ronning, R. R., & Bruning, R. H. (1990). *Cognitive psychology for teachers.* New York: Macmillan Publishing Company.

Grosjean, F. (1982). *Life with two languages: An introduction to bilingualism.* Cambridge, MA: Harvard University Press.

Hamers, J. F. and Blanc, M. H. (1989). *Bilinguality & bilingualism.* Cambridge: Cambridge University Press.

Kolers, P. A. (1968). Bilingualism and information processing. *Scientific American*, March, pp. 78-86.

____. (1978). On the representation of experience. In D. Gerver & H. W. Sinaiko (Eds.), *Language, interpretation and communication* (pp. 245-258). New York: Plenum Press.

McCormack, P. D. (1977). Bilingual linguistic memory: the independence-interdependence issue revisited. In P. A. Hornby (Ed.), *Bilingualism:*

Psychological, social and educational implications (pp. 57-66). New York: Academic Press.

McLaughlin, B. (1978). *Second-language acquisition in children.* Hillsdale, NJ: Lawrence Erlbaum Associates.

___, Rossman, T., & McLeod, B. (1983). Second language learning: an information-processing perspective. *Language Learning, 33*(2), 135-158.

Odlin, T. (1989). *Language transfer: Cross-linguistic influence in language learning.* Cambridge, MA: Cambridge University Press.

O'Malley, J. M., & Chamot, A. U. (1989). *Learning strategies in second language acquisition.* Cambridge; MA: Cambridge University Press.

Oxford, R. L. (1986). *Second language learning strategies: Current research and implications* (Technical Report #3). Los Angeles, CA: UCLA Center for Language Education and Research.

___. (1990). *Language learning strategies: What every teacher should know.* New York: Newbury House Publishers.

Padilla, A. M. (1990). Bilingual education: Issues and strategies. In A. M. Padilla, H. Fairchild, & C. Valadez, (Eds.), (pp. 15-26) *Bilingual education: Issues and strategies.* Newbury Park, CA: Sage Publications.

___, & Sung, H. (1990). Information processing and foreign language learning. In A. M. Padilla, H. Fairchild, & C. Valadez, (Eds.), *Foreign language education: Issues and strategies* (pp. 41-55). Newbury Park, CA: Sage Publications.

Paivio, A. (1971). *Imagery and verbal process.* New York: Holt, Rinehart & Winston.

___, & Desrochers, A. (1980). A dual-coding approach to bilingual memory. *Canadian Journal of Psychology, 34,* 388-399.

___, & Lambert, W. E. (1981). Dual coding and bilingual memory. *Journal of Verbal Learning and Verbal Behavior, 20,* 532-539.

Perkins, D. N. (1987). Thinking frames: an integrative perspective on teaching cognitive skills. In J. B. Baron & R. J. Sternberg (Eds.), *Teaching thinking skills: Theory and practice* (pp. 41-61). New York: W. H. Freeman and Company.

Rubin, J., & Thompson, I. (1982). *How to be a more successful language learner.* Boston, MA: Heinle & Heinle Publishers, Inc.

BILINGUALITY, INTELLIGENCE, AND COGNITIVE INFORMATION PROCESSING*

José E. Náñez, Sr.
Arizona State University West

Raymond V. Padilla
Becky López Máez
Arizona State University

ABSTRACT

This chapter provides a brief historical overview of chronometric and psychometric research concerning the interaction between bilinguality and cognitive processes. Three chronometric paradigms, Hick (1952), Sternberg (1966)/Posner (1969), and Jensen, et al. (1988), are suggested for initiating a research program based on information processing theory, which should progress from the study of the relationship between bilinguality and cognition on elementary cognitive tasks to their relationship on complex cognitive tasks. Ultimately, the research should identify possible applications contributing to theory, practice, and policy regarding bilingual education.

> At present, much bilingualism research on cognition is unsophisticated, and it seldom draws on information processing paradigms for research.
> — *Richard Durán and Mary Enright, 1983*

How does bilinguality, the ability of an individual to communicate in two languages, affect mental functioning?

---

*Primary support for this chapter was provided by a research support grant from the Hispanic Research Center, Arizona State University. Support for a graduate research assistant was provided by the Graduate College, Arizona State University. The authors thank Richard Durán, Jenifer J. Partch, and Miguel A. Moreno for their helpful comments on earlier versions of this chapter.

Researchers have studied and debated this question for almost a century. Yet, no clear answer has been forthcoming. The debate over bilingual education in the United States and elsewhere over the past 30 years, emphasizes the importance of this question. Bilingualism at the societal level will continue to be a prevalent feature in a world where different languages are in contact almost everywhere, thus it is important to intensify our efforts to determine the interaction between bilinguality and cognition.

The basic goal of this chapter is to suggest strategies and techniques for studying the interaction between bilinguality and cognitive processing. In this context, we discuss two important research paradigms, psychometry and mental chronometry, that historically have been used to examine cognitive functions. Although there is some overlap in the research conducted within these two paradigms, the distinction is useful for organizing what is known about the interaction between bilinguality and cognition, and to highlight the different methods and approaches that investigators have used to study this issue. We conclude the chapter by proposing that information processing theory may be a good platform for launching a new research agenda that should advance our knowledge of how bilinguality and cognition interact. More specifically, we suggest several chronometric paradigms that can provide a sound methodological base.

The Psychometric Paradigm

Psychometry attempts to quantify the elusive concept of mental ability. It focuses on how much of a particular kind of information the brain can process within a relatively long time frame. The many problems encountered when trying to measure intelligence through psychometric techniques have fueled historical controversies that are well-documented elsewhere so they need not be discussed in detail here. However, Hunt (1976) captured well some of the biases of psychometry in his statement:

. . . intelligence, as the term is commonly used, is a concept that was introduced to cope with problems that could only exist within a world view stemming from democracy. . . . and Darwinism . . . Some way had to be found to relieve the state of the burden of opening doors to people who could not pass through them. The way chosen was to produce an objective ordering of the citizenry. In abstract theory each citizen was to be described relative to the other citizens, and the description would be used to determine how the state should support the individual's personal development. (p. 237)

The literature on bilinguality and psychometrics is extensive and will be reviewed here selectively. However, there are a number of excellent literature reviews, some of which are listed in Table 1.

TABLE 1

Chronological Listing of Selected Reviews of the Psychometric Literature Related to Bilinguality

Author	Date of Publication
Arsenian, S.	1937
Darcy, N. T.	1953
Jensen, J. V.	1962
Peal, E., & Lambert, W. E.	1962
Darcy, N. T.	1963
Macnamara, J.	1966
Cummins, J.	1979
Dornic, S.	1980
Hamers, J. F., & Blanc, M. H.	1989

Four key issues can be used to categorize bilinguality studies conducted within the psychometric paradigm. The first issue concerns whether bilinguality has a positive or negative effect on cognitive abilities. The second issue attempts to specify the conditions under which bilinguality produces positive versus negative effects on cognition. Assuming that bilinguality produces positive effects in the form of increased cognitive abilities and flexibility, the third issue concerns whether some theoretical proficiency threshold is required before the positive effects can occur. The final issue is whether a causal relationship exists between bilinguality and increased cognitive abilities, and if so, what is the direction of the relationship. Tables 2-5 summarize selected studies that investigate the interaction(s) between bilinguality and cognitive processes using a psychometric paradigm. Some of these studies are further discussed below because they shed light on these four issues.

Regarding the first issue, psychometrically driven research conducted in the United States prior to 1962 tended to find that bilinguality had negative effects on the individual's cognitive processes. These findings were rooted in late-19th and early-20th century paranoia focused on excluding non-English-speaking immigrants from the United States. If it could be shown that non-English speakers scored lower on standardized IQ tests, this could be taken as evidence of their "genetically inferior" intellect when compared to earlier immigrants from Western and Northern Europe. On the basis of such findings, a case could be made to curtail widespread immigration by such individuals (Hakuta, 1986).

This political agenda influenced psychometric researchers of that period to produce a steady flow of studies indicating that bilinguality hinders cognitive processes. For example, a prominent early developmental psychologist suggested that the language of origin persisted among some groups of immigrants because their genetic intellectual inferiority prevented them from learning the new language (Goodenough, 1926). In hindsight, such research confounded the effects of bilinguality on intelligence, with language proficiency and balance, culture, social class, and the

TABLE 2

Selected Studies Addressing the Effects of Bilinguality on Cognitive Processes

Issue One: Does Bilinguality Have a Positive
or Negative Effect on Cognitive Abilities?

Author	Date of Publication	Result
Jordan, R. H.	1921	Negative
Mann, C.	1921	Negative
Berry, C. S.	1922	Negative
Pintner, R., & Keller, R.	1922	Negative
Giardini, G., & Root, W. T.	1923	Neutral
Feingold, G. A.	1924	Negative
Madsen, I. N.	1924	Neutral
Garretson, O. K.	1928	Neutral
Koch, H. L., & Simmons, R.	1928	Negative
Rigg, M.	1928	Negative
Haught, B. F.	1931	Neutral
Goodenough, F. L.	1926	Negative
Peal E., & Lambert, W. E.	1962	Positive
Liedtke W. W., & Nelson, L. D.	1968	Positive
Balkan, L.	1970	Positive
Ben-Zeev, S.	1972	Positive
Ianco-Worrall, A. D.	1972	Positive
Bain, B.	1974	Positive
Cummins, J.	1976b	Positive
Gorrell, J. J., Bregman, N. J., McAllistair, H. A., & Lipscombe, T. J.	1982	Positive
Powers, S., & Lopez, R. L.	1985	Positive
Kessler, C., & Quinn, M. E.	1987	Positive

TABLE 3

Selected Studies Addressing the Effects of Bilinguality on Cognitive Processes

Issue Two: Under What Conditions Does Bilinguality Produce Positive Versus Negative Effects on Cognition?

Author	Date of Publication	Type of Acquisition	Result
Lambert, W. E.	1973	Additive Subtractive	Positive Negative
Long, K. K. & Padilla, A. M.	1970	Additive	Positive
Bhatnagar, J.	1980	Additive	Positive

TABLE 4

Selected Studies Addressing the Effects of Bilinguality on Cognitive Processes

Issue Three: Do the Positive Effects of Bilinguality on Cognitive Processes Occur Before or After Some Theoretical Proficiency Level?

Author	Date of Publication	Result
Landry, R. G.	1974	After
Cummins, J.	1977, 1979, 1981	After
Duncan, S. E. & De Avila, E. A.	1979	After
Díaz, R. M.	1985	Before
Hakuta K., & Díaz, R. M.	1984	Before

TABLE 5

Selected Studies Addressing the Effects
of Bilinguality on Cognitive Processes

Issue Four: What Is the Likely Causal/Directional
Relationship between Bilinguality and Cognition?

Author	Date of Publication	Result
Peal, E., & Lambert, W. E.	1962	Bilinguality to cognition
Macnamara, J.	1964	Cognition to bilinguality
Díaz, R. M.	1985	Bilinguality to cognition
Hakuta, K., & Díaz, R. M	1984	Bilinguality to cognition

mental abilities measured by standardized psychometric intelligence tests.

Decades later, researchers in Canada (e.g., Peal & Lambert, 1962) concluded that there are no negative consequences to being bilingual. In fact, bilinguality was credited with the enhancement of intelligence and cognitive flexibility. Peal and Lambert's (1962) landmark study found that balanced bilinguals outperformed monolinguals on both verbal and nonverbal measures of intelligence when variables such as SES, language proficiency, sex, and age were controlled. Their findings were supported by numerous subsequent studies (see Lambert & Anisfeld, 1969).

Macnamara (1964) criticized Peal and Lambert's (1962) findings because, in his opinion, they confounded bilinguality and intelligence. Given that a positive relationship exists between verbal abilities and psychometric intelligence, Macnamara argued that the more intelligent individuals also were more likely to become bilingual, while the less intelligent remained monolingual. But Lambert and Anisfeld (1969) were disinclined to accept Macnamara's (1964) conclusion:

> . . . [Macnamara] suggests that it is more reasonable to argue that the more intelligent children become bilin-

gual than it is to argue that becoming bilingual influences intellectual development. He supports his preference for the former interpretation by reference to the previous studies in the field which found that bilingual children scored lower on tests of intelligence. This seems to be a dubious argument. It is difficult to understand how studies purportedly showing that bilingual children are inferior can be used to support the interpretation that the more intelligent become bilingual rather than vice versa. Is it reasonable to argue that children become bilingual because they are inferior intellectually? . . . In fact, our experiences with bilingual communities, bilingual homes, and bilingual youngsters suggest to us that anyone would become bilingual if the motivation of those teaching and learning the two languages were appropriate . . . and if a favourable time period were chosen to introduce the two languages. (Lambert & Anisfeld, 1969, p. 126)

According to Peal and Lambert, the positive effects of bilinguality on cognition are attributable to the balanced, proficient bilingual's access to two symbolic language-based systems with which to address cognitive tasks (see Hamers & Blanc [1989] for a detailed discussion and listing of research supporting Peal & Lambert's hypothesis).

The second issue presented above is a result of Lambert's (1973) suggestion that bilinguality affects cognition positively when the bilingual acquires a second language (L2) in an "additive" versus a "subtractive" mode. The additive model applies to the language learner whose first language (L1) is the prominent and prestigious language of the culture. In this type of acquisition, L1 remains strong during the learning process because it is a common and prominent feature of the individual's daily environment; L2 is merely being added to the individual's language repertoire. The additive effects of acquiring L2 under these conditions are increased cognitive abilities and flexibility. Alternatively, when L2 is both the dominant and prestigious language, L1 atrophies because its use and prestige are significantly decreased in the learner's daily social and education environment. The devaluation and dismantling of L1 coupled with a lack of command of L2 is seen as having subtractive (negative) effects on the individual's cognitive abilities.

Cummins (1977) summarized the additive/subtractive perspective as follows:

> It seems reasonable to posit qualitative differences in the linguistic competence attained by bilingual subjects in earlier and more recent studies on the basis of the fact that recent studies have included only balanced bilinguals and have been carried out in "additive" environments whereas the majority of earlier studies were carried out in "subtractive" environments with no controls for the bilingual subjects' level of competence in L1 and L2. (p. 5)

The third issue concerns whether there is a proficiency threshold beyond which bilinguality affects cognition positively (Cummins, 1976a, 1977, 1979, 1981). Cummins supported Lambert's (1975) additive/subtractive model; however, Cummins also wanted to know at what point in the L2 additive acquisition process the positive effects of L2 become evident. In his view, the positive effects of bilinguality on cognitive flexibility and divergent thinking do not take effect unless there is a high "threshold" level of language proficiency in L1 during the initial stages of L2 acquisition and the learner also passes an L2 threshold.

> . . . the twofold threshold hypothesis explains the apparently contradictory results from the different studies. The first threshold must be reached in order to avoid an intellectual handicap as a consequence of childhood bilingual experience; if this lower threshold is not attained, a below-normal level of competence in both languages might result. Above the first threshold and below the second a handicap will be avoided. But it is only when the second threshold is passed that bilingual experience can have a positive effect on cognitive processing and that competence in both languages tends towards balance (Hamers & Blanc, 1989, pp. 53-54).

According to Cummins, the thresholds are not absolute or fixed levels of bilingual balance or proficiency, and may differ for individuals at different ages and stages of cognitive development, and also for individuals with different conditions or in different programs in which the L2 is acquired.

Cummins (1979) proposed that the threshold may differ for individuals in which instruction time is divided equally between the learner's two languages as opposed to those learning through immersion programs:

> The threshold for a child in a full immersion program is likely to be higher (in absolute terms) than for a child in a bilingual program in which 50% of the time is spent in L1. Because a greater proportion of his cognitive operations in the school setting must be expressed through the medium of his second language, the immersion child is more likely than the child in the bilingual program to suffer cognitively (and academically) if he fails to develop adequate skills in that language. However, by the same token, the immersion experience seems more likely to promote full functional bilingualism than bilingual programs in which a sizeable proportion of the time is spent through L1. Thus, the child in an immersion program may more rapidly gain the threshold level of L2 competence required to reap the cognitive benefits of his bilingual learning experience. This raises the possibility that there may be not one but two thresholds. The attainment of the first threshold would be sufficient to avoid cognitive retardation but the attainment of a second, higher level of bilingual competence might be necessary to lead to accelerated cognitive growth (Cummins, 1979, p. 25).

Landry's (1974) research supported Cummins's hypotheses: Landry found that there were no significant differences between first-grade and fourth-grade students enrolled in a Foreign Languages in the Elementary Schools (FLES) program and non-FLES controls; but by sixth grade, the FLES students exhibited significantly greater scores on verbal ability and divergent thinking tasks than monolinguals.

An alternative to Cummins' (1979) threshold model has been proposed by Hakuta and Díaz (1984) and Díaz (1985). Supporters of this model contend that the significant positive effects of bilinguality on cognition occur *prior* to some theoretical proficiency level:

> . . . degree of bilingualism will predict significant portions of cognitive variance only *before* a certain

> level of second language proficiency has been achieved
> (Díaz, 1985, p. 1386).

Thus, Hakuta and Díaz are proposing that the positive effects of bilinguality on cognition occur earlier than supposed by Cummins. It remains an empirical question whether Cummins' threshold model or Hakuta and Díaz' early effects explanation best accounts for the positive effects of bilinguality on cognition.

The fourth substantive issue concerns whether a causal relationship exists between bilinguality and cognition. To determine the directionality of the causal effects, level of bilingual proficiency must be utilized as an independent variable, while controlling for the effects of other important confounding variables such as ethnicity, SES, intelligence, and L1 proficiency (Duncan & De Avila, 1979). However, it will be difficult to settle this issue unequivocally, if bilinguality studies continue to be limited to correlational research methods.

The Chronometric Paradigm

The chronometric approach (mental chronometry) focuses on time as a dependent variable, more specifically, on the time required by an individual to react to a stimulus or elementary cognitive task. When carefully measured, this reaction time (RT) can be used to make inferences about cognitive processes. A typical early experiment on reaction time was described by Woodworth (1938) as follows:

> [The subject] is seated at a table on which is a telegraph key. At the fore-signal "Ready" he closes the key with his finger and is prepared to raise the finger instantly on receiving a certain stimulus. Apparatus is present for recording the time between the application of the stimulus and the opening of the telegraph key by [the subject's] reaction. This time usually lies between 100 and 200 [milliseconds]. . . . The task here is about the simplest possible. It can be complicated in various ways. (p. 298)

The telegraph key has long been replaced by modern electronic equipment, but the general design of the experiment as described by Woodworth is still in use. A contemporary description of the chronometric paradigm is provided in Meyer, Osman, Irwin, and Yantis (1988):

> . . . chronometry involves experimental procedures in which a subject experiences a series of test trials. Each trial starts with a warning signal . . . followed by a brief foreperiod. The foreperiod serves to maximize the subject's alertness and attention. After the foreperiod, a test stimulus . . . is presented. Given this stimulus, the subject must make an appropriate overt response . . . quickly and accurately. The subject's reaction time (RT) is measured from the onset of the test stimulus until the response occurs. In a *simple reaction-time procedure*, for example, there would be only one possible stimulus and one possible response. In a *choice reaction-time procedure*, there would be multiple stimuli and multiple responses with different responses assigned to different stimuli. (p. 5)

To someone unfamiliar with the chronometric literature, it would appear that the measurement of RT is standardized. However, researchers have measured and defined RT in nearly as many ways as there are RT studies. Kolers (1968) labeled the time required to complete a mental operation "call time . . . the amount of time the mind needs to organize a set of procedures for handling a piece of information" (p. 80). Patchella (1974) defined reaction time ". . . as the interval between the presentation of a stimulus to a subject and the subject's response" (p. 45). Johnson (1953) defined RT as the ratio between the number of words produced in Spanish versus the number produced in English during a five-minute interval. Lambert (1955) used the amount of time required for a subject to move his/her finger from a home button to a target button in response to simple instructions such as "press the blue key." Dornic (cited in Magiste, 1979) required subjects to ". . . check off a series of items defined by position, value, shape, or color" (p. 80). Durán and Enright (1983) also used a response key technique and a microcomputer to measure RT in the dominant versus the weaker language of bilingual Hispanics. Magiste

(1980) used differences in naming latencies between naming common objects in the dominant versus the weaker of two languages.

As an index of intelligence, mental chronometry has a lengthy and controversial history that in some respects reflects the development of psychology as a discipline (Jensen, 1980, 1982; Meyer et al., 1988; Woodworth, 1938; Woodworth & Schlosberg, 1954). It is rooted in 19th-century psychophysiological research that was stimulated by a practical problem in astronomy concerned with measuring the precise moment that a stellar body was perceived to cross the hairline on a telescope (Bessei, 1823). By the end of the 19th century, reaction time studies involving various sense modalities had been conducted in a variety of laboratories in Europe and the United States (Cattell, 1886; Exner, 1873; Gilbert, 1894; Helmholtz, 1850/1853; Jastrow, 1890; Lange, 1888; Merkle, 1885; Wissler, 1901; Woodworth, 1899; Wundt, 1880). Psychologists of the period had expanded the reaction time paradigm considerably beyond the original intent of astronomers and were trying to apply reaction time measures to the assessment of mental abilities. These efforts were eclipsed in the late-19th and early-20th centuries by the work of psychometrists, who concluded that there was little or no relationship between reaction time and mental abilities (e.g., Binet, 1900; Wissler, 1901; Whipple, 1904). In addition, Donders's logic, the subtractive method, which involved estimating processing time for various mental stages by subtracting the reaction time to a simple task from the reaction time to a more complex task (Donders, 1868/1969; Meyer et al., 1988), had reached a methodological dead end by the turn of the 19th century (Kulpe, 1893/1909). With Binet's development of psychometric techniques, research on the use of mental chronometry as a measure of intelligence ceased for about half a century (Meyer et al., 1988).

More recently there has been renewed interest in mental chronometry resulting primarily from technological advances, the development of sophisticated electronic equipment, the refinement of statistical methods of analysis, and the serious criticisms that have been leveled against the psychometric approach (Meyer et al., 1988.) These advances are returning the focus of investigation to "hardware" (i.e., how the brain processes information), instead of merely continuing to categorize people on some abstract scale. This fits well with a major interest of information processing researchers, namely to understand mental processing well enough to produce computer models of the working brain (e.g., Hunt, 1976).

Advances in mental chronometry have led to renewed interest and controversy regarding the relationship between reaction time measures and intelligence (Longstreth 1984, 1986; Jensen & Vernon, 1986; Vernon, 1986; Larsen & Saccuzzo, 1986). However, our interest in reaction time research does not have this focus. Our initial research goal is to study how bilinguality affects cognitive information processing. That is, we wish to find out whether or not bilinguality independently affects the time needed to carry out mental processes, and whether the effects first occur at some basic sensory/perceptual level, at the level of short-term memory, at a cognitive level between short-term and long-term memory, or at some higher level involving long-term memory and complex problem solving. If there are significant differences in reaction time which can be traced to bilinguality, they might be important to consider in structuring teaching situations for bilinguals. Such differences also would have to be accounted for in terms of cognitive processes, thus potentially improving our understanding of how the bilingual brain receives, processes, stores, and retrieves information.

There have been only a few chronometric studies conducted with bilingual subjects. Some of these studies are listed in Table 6 and will be discussed briefly. In one study, Durán and Enright (1983) found that bilingual Hispanics achieved the same proportion of correct answers in their weaker language as monolinguals, although they also noted that the bilinguals completed fewer items than monolinguals. Because Durán and Enright did not counterbalance the order of English-Spanish presentation between some of their problem-solving tasks, it is not possible to distinguish whether their results were attributable to differences in language balance or to practice effects.

TABLE 6

Selected Bilinguality Studies Conducted with the Chronometric Paradigm

Author	Date of Publication
Johnson, G. B.	1953
Lambert, W. E.	1955, 1956
Lambert, W. E., Havelka, J., & Crosby, C.	1958
Lambert, W. E., Havelka, J., & Gardner, R. C.	1959
Ervin, S. M.	1961
Macnamara, J.	1967
Kolers, P. A.	1968
Dornic, S.	1969, 1977, 1978, 1980
Preston, M. S., & Lambert, W. E.	1969
Hamers, J. F., & Lambert, W. E.	1972
Gutierrez-Marsh, L., & Hipple-Maki, R.	1976
Magiste, E.	1979, 1980, 1982, 1986
Kirsner, K., Brown, H. L., Abrul, S., Chadha, N. K., & Sharma, N. K.	1980
Durán, R., & Enright, M.	1983

Magiste (1979, 1980) found that bilinguals were slower at both decoding and encoding word and number tasks in their chosen language than monolinguals. Magiste did not match her subjects on intelligence. However, given that the tasks required very basic cognitive abilities, this is probably not a problem with her work. There is also no evidence that Magiste counterbalanced the presentation of test items between Swedish and German. Moreover, Magiste failed to match the subjects on reading ability, which may represent a major confound in the text-reading portion of her study:

The group differences found in this test may be due to
the time limits. Since one minute was sufficient for all
monolingual subjects—some of them reported that they
had read the text more than twice—for the bilingual
group the time was short, generally allowing only one
reading. Some subjects did not have time to get through
the text (Magiste, 1980, p. 66).

Given the obvious reading superiority of the monolinguals, the poor performance of the bilinguals in this study is
likely attributable to their decreased reading ability rather
than to their bilinguality. Further, since some monolinguals read the text up to three times more often than the
bilinguals, their superior performance also may be attributable to practice effects. Kolers (1968), for example,
noted that the ability to recall a given item is directly proportional to the number of times one is exposed to it within a
unilingual list. Kolers found that for words presented three
times more often than other words in a list, the probability
is three to one in favor of their recall relative to words presented only once. Interestingly, Kolers (1968) also found that
this phenomenon holds across languages:

> . . . the percentage of recall increased linearly with the
> frequency of occurrence of meaning. Presenting *fold* and
> *pli* twice produces the same effect on the recall of
> either one as presenting either one four times. (p. 83)

Studies such as those described above are examples of
how the chronometric approach has been used to study the
interaction between bilinguality and cognition. In spite of
some methodological weaknesses these studies are helpful
to researchers interested in formulating a new chronometric
research agenda to identify the independent effects of bilinguality on cognition.

A Framework Based on Information Processing Theory

Newell and Simon (1972) describe a research framework
based on information processing theory. For them, "the
theory posits a set of processes or mechanisms that produce

the behavior of the thinking human" (p. 9). The focus is on the mind as a symbol processor that can accept input from the external world, process the input, and direct observable behaviors that reflect intelligence. In essence, they are more interested in accounting for the thinking processes involved in the calculation of a chess move than the neural-motor commands directing the hand to move a pawn a particular distance in a given direction.

Durán and Enright (1983) used an information processing perspective like the one described by Newell and Simon (1972) to conduct research aimed at determining the effects of a bilingual's weaker language on performance of the cognitive tasks. They presented the subjects with various problem-solving tasks which incorporated the idea that there are three interactive sets of activities involved in formal problem solving: "problem input, problem representation and conceptual solution, and physical execution of the solution steps" (pp. 2-4). Durán and Enright's work is a significant example of the application of the information processing approach to the study of the interaction between bilinguality and cognition. Their work focused almost exclusively on the intermediate to higher ranges of the information processing continuum (Figure 1).

In our opinion, information processing research should be expanded both downward and upward along the continuum to incorporate more basic cognitive processes, such as those involved in sensory/perceptual tasks, as well as highly sophisticated cognitive processes such as those involved in complex problem solving. Further, we suggest that in order to identify where in the information processing continuum the initial interaction between bilinguality and cognition occurs, future research should initially concentrate on basic sensory/perceptual and elementary cognitive tasks at the lower levels of the continuum and progress systematically to tasks at the higher levels. This approach should not only reveal the type of interaction existing between bilinguality and cognition, it should also help to identify the major factors contributing to the interaction.

Figure 1 presents schematically what may be called the "information processing continuum," depicting the brain as

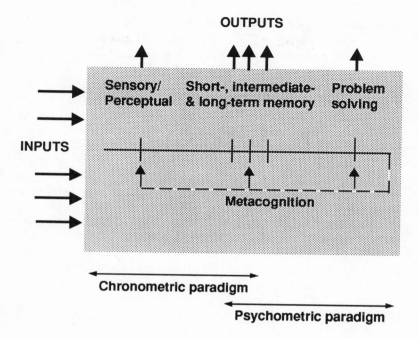

Figure 1

The chronometric and psychometric paradigms in the context
of the information-processing continuum.

capable of receiving input from the external environment
and as an efficient processor of that input. The outcome of
the mental processing phase is an observable or measurable
output. The idea of the continuum presented in Figure 1 is
that the brain is capable of processing input that ranges from
very basic sensory/perceptual to highly complex input requiring feedback, reflection, mental representation, and
other metacognitive skills. The chronometric and psychometric paradigms can be overlaid against this schema. As
Figure 1 shows, research conducted within these paradigms
concentrates on different ends of the information processing
continuum, although there is some overlap in the middle
ranges. The psychometric and chronometric paradigms also
differ in that they utilize quite different approaches to the

measurement and assessment of mental abilities. In the chronometric paradigm, the fundamental question is how quickly can an individual perform a particular reaction-time task. This approach derives from the idea that in cognitive processing, "quicker is also better."

In the psychometric paradigm, the intent is to classify an individual's performance level by administering a series of problem-solving tasks. The tasks are standardized across representative samples of the relevant population so that an individual's performance can be ranked and compared with the performance of other individuals in the population. This approach, therefore, inherently results in a hierarchical classification of individuals according to their performance on the selected problem-solving tasks. Historically, certain sets of cognitive tasks have been defined as measuring "intelligence" so that the ranking established through these procedures is said to reflect the intellectual level of the individual(s) so categorized.

Developing a New Research Agenda

Bilinguality has been studied from a variety of methodological perspectives. Research to date has failed to provide a clear answer to the fundamental question: Does bilinguality independently affect the time required to carry out mental processes given that correlated variables such as language proficiency, L1 and L2 balance, IQ, SES, reading level, etc., are adequately controlled? This question needs to be addressed on at least two levels:

1. Does bilinguality affect the time required to process simple reaction time (SRT) or choice reaction time (CRT) tasks?

2. Does bilinguality affect the time required to process other more demanding cognitive tasks?

If bilinguality affects processing time on cognitive tasks, then a third question arises:

3. How and under what conditions does bilinguality affect information processing time?

These questions are important for two reasons. First, if level of bilinguality were found to correlate significantly with increased RT or PST, this would stimulate research aimed at identifying the cognitive processes that account for these differences, and what these differences might mean in practical learning situations such as those found in the class-room.

Second, it is also important to determine how bilingual-ity affects problem solving. This issue can be addressed on several levels of cognition as well as problem complexity. As already stated, it may not be a good strategy to focus ini-tially on the study of complex problems that require higher-order cognitive processes. A better strategy may be to start with simple tasks that can be studied with time as a very precisely measured dependent variable. This strategy re-quires a research program designed to investigate bilinguals' differences in processing time on sensory/perceptual tasks, decoding, encoding, inferring, and other cognitive tasks that require increasingly greater cognitive demands. Such a re-search program should utilize methods that are commonly used in traditional chronometric research but which have not been used extensively in bilinguality research.

Three of these general methods are of special interest to the research program that we propose (Hick, 1952; Sternberg, 1966, and Posner, 1969; Jensen et al., 1988). These three reac-tion time approaches are similar because they require the subject to respond to visual stimuli (e.g., to a light on a panel or text on a computer monitor) by moving his or her finger from a depressed home button to the appropriate but-ton on a panel as soon as possible after the stimulus is de-tected and understood. Movement of the finger off the home button is labeled reaction time (RT), while the time from lifting the finger off the home button to pressing the response button is labeled movement time (MT). The two can be analyzed separately or together as indices of the cogni-tive information processing interval. Correct and incorrect responses also can be recorded. Hick's approach has resulted in "Hick's Law," which holds that reaction time increases linearly as a function of the number of bits being processed in simple or choice reaction time tasks. Does bilinguality affect Hick's Law? This question has not been answered, but it is very unlikely that bilinguality meaningfully affects information processing at this level.

The Sternberg/Posner method focuses on short-term memory. Typically, a small set of digits is presented to the subject along with a probe digit. The subject is asked to indicate whether or not the probe is contained within the stimulus set by depressing the "yes" or "no" button on a panel. In general, it has been found that reaction time increases linearly as a function of the number of digits in the stimulus set. The linear relationship in this case is with the number of digits in the set. We are interested in finding out whether bilinguality affects the linear relationship typically found in the Sternberg/Posner paradigm. Differences in RT on this task would indicate that bilinguality initially affects cognitive information processing at the level of short-term memory.

The Jensen et al. (1988) version of the sentence verification technique (SVT) is designed to measure a subject's reaction time to stimuli, which are evaluated on the basis of physical appearance or logical/semantic relationships. For example, a statement such as: "A before C" is presented briefly on the monitor screen and is followed by a probe such as "BAC." The subject presses the "yes" or "no" button in response to these stimuli. Presumably, the subject's response requires access to long-term memory to compare the test stimuli with previously stored information. Does bilinguality affect reaction time on this task? To our knowledge, this question has not yet been carefully addressed.

These three research paradigms are by no means the only methods available for conducting reaction time research with bilinguals. However, since the tasks require relatively simple, albeit progressively more difficult, cognitive processes, they are a good starting point for assessing the possible effects of bilinguality on cognitive information processing. If significant effects are found for different levels of bilingual proficiency and balance, then a new area of research will develop to investigate the sources of the differences. If no significant differences are found on the cognitive tasks encompassed by these paradigms, then researchers should apply information processing methodology to study tasks that require higher cognitive processes. Eventually, the results of this research should advance our theoretical understanding of bilinguality and cognitive information processing and lead to practical applications in the field of bilingual education.

References

Arsenian, S. (1937). *Bilingual and mental development.* New York: Teachers College Contribution to Education, Columbia University.

Bain, B. (1974). Bilingualism and cognition: Toward a general theory. In S. T. Carey (Ed.), *Bilingualism, biculturalism, and education: Proceedings from the conference at College Universitaire Saint Jean* (pp. 119-128). Edmonton: University of Alberta.

Balkan, L. (1970). *Les effets du bilinguisme francais-anglais sur les aptitudes intellectuelles.* Brussels: AIMAV.

Ben-Zeev, S. (1972). The influence of bilingualism on cognitive development and cognitive strategy. Unpublished dissertation. Chicago: University of Chicago.

Berry, C. S. (1922). Classification by tests of intelligence of 10,000 first grade children. *Journal of Educational Research, 6,* 185-203.

Bessel, F. W. (1823). *Astronomische Beobachtungen in Konigsberg, 8,* iii-viii.

Bhatnagar, J. (1980). Linguistic behaviour and adjustment of immigrant children in French and English schools in Montreal. *International Journal of Applied Psychology, 29,* 141-158.

Binet, A. (1900). Attention et adoption. *L'année Psychol., 6,* 248-404.

Cattell, J. McK. (1886). The time taken by cerebral operations. *Mind, 11,* 20-242.

Cummins, J. (1976a). The influence of bilingualism on cognitive growth: A synthesis of research findings and explanatory hypotheses. *Working Papers on Bilingualism, 9,* 1-43.

_____. (1976b). *Bilingualism and the development of metalinguistic abilities.* Unpublished manuscript, University of Alberta.

_____. (1977). Cognitive factors associated with the attainment of intermediate levels of bilingual skill. *Modern Language Journal, 61*, 3-12.

_____. (1979). Linguistic interdependence and the educational development of bilingual children. *Review of Educational Research, 49*, 222-251.

_____. (1981). The role of primary language development in promoting educational success for language minority students. In *California State Department of Education, schooling and language minority students: A theoretical framework*. Los Angeles: Evaluation, Assessment and Dissemination Center.

Darcy, N. T. (1953). A review of the literature on the effects of bilingualism upon the measurement of intelligence. *Journal of Genetic Psychology, 82*, 21-57.

_____. (1963). Bilingualism and the measurement of intelligence: Review of a decade of research. *Journal of Genetic Psychology, 103*, 259-282.

Díaz, R. M. (1985). Bilingual cognitive development: Addressing three gaps in current research. *Child Development, 56*, 1376-1388.

Donders, F. C. (1868/1969). On the speed of mental processes. [W. G. Koster Trans.] in W. G. Koster (Ed.), *Attention and performance II* (pp. 412-431). Amsterdam: North-Holland Publishing Co. Original work published in *Onderzoekingen gedaan in het Physiologisch Laboratorium der Utrechtsche Hoogeschool, Tweede reeks, 1868-1869, II*, 92-120.

Dornic, S. (1969). Verbal factor in number perception. *Acta Psychologica, 29*, 393-399.

_____. (1977). *Human information processing and bilingualism*. Reports from the Institute of Applied Psychology, University of Stockholm, No. 67.

_____. (1978). The bilingual's performance: Language dominance, stress, and individual differences. In D. Gerber & V. Sinaiko (Eds.), *Proceedings from the interdisciplinary symposium on language, interpretation, and communication* (pp. 259-271). New York: Plenum Press.

_____. (1980). Language dominance, spare capacity and perceived effort in bilinguals. *Ergonomics, 23*(4), 369-377.

Duncan, S. E., & De Avila, E. A. (1979). Bilingualism and cognition: Some recent findings. *NABE Journal, 4*, 15-50.

Durán R., & Enright, M. (1983). *Reading comprehension proficiency, cognitive processing mechanisms, and deductive reasoning in bilinguals*. Final Report (Grant No. NIE-G-80-0157). Princeton, NJ: Educational Testing Services.

Ervin, S. M. (1961). Semantic shift in bilingualism. *American Journal of Psychology, 74*, 233-241.

Exner, S. (1873). Experimentelle Untersuchung der einfachsten psychischen Processe. *Pflugers Archiv fur gesamte Physiologie, 7,* 601-660.

Feingold, G. A. (1924). Intelligence of the first generation of immigrant groups. *Journal of Educational Psychology, 15,* 65-82.

Garretson, O. K. (1928). A study of the causes of retardation among Mexican children. *Journal of Educational Psychology, 19,* 31-40. Giardini, G., & Root, W. T. (1923). A comparison of the Detroit First Grade Tests given in Italian and English. *Psychological Clinic, 15,* 101-108.

Gilbert, J. A. (1894). Research on the mental and physical development of school children. *Stud Yale Psychol Lab, 2,*40-100.

Goodenough, F. L. (1926). Racial differences in the intelligence of school children. *Journal of Experimental Psychology, 9,* 388-397.

Gorrel, J. J., Bregman, N. J., McAllistair, H. A., & Lipscombe, T. J. (1982). A comparison of spatial role-taking in monolingual and bilingual children. *Journal of Genetic Psychology, 140,* 3-10.

Gutiérrez-Marsh, L., & Hipple-Maki, R. (1976). Efficiency of arithmetic operations in bilinguals as a function of language. *Memory & Cognition, 4*(4), 459-464.

Hakuta, K. (1986). *Mirror of language; The debate on bilingualism.* New York: Basic Books.

____, & Díaz, R. M. (1984). The relationship between bilingualism and cognitive ability: A critical discussion and some new longitudinal data. In K. E. Nelson (Ed.), *Children's language* (pp. 319-344). Hillsdale, NJ: Erlbaum.

Hamers, J. F., & Blanc, M. H. (1989). *Bilinguality and bilingualism.* Cambridge: Cambridge University Press.

____, & Lambert, W. E. (1972). Bilingual interdependencies in auditory perception. *Journal of Verbal Learning and Verbal Behavior, 11,* 303-310.

Haught, B. F. (1931). The language difficulty of Spanish-American children. *Journal of Applied Psychology, 15,* 92-95.

Helmholtz, H. L. F. von (1850). Uber die Methoden, kleinste Zeittheile zu messen, und ihre Anwendung fur physiologische Zwecke. Original work translated in *Philosophical Magazine,* 1853, *6*(4), 313-325.

Hick, W. E. (1952). On the rate of gain of information. *Quarterly Journal of Experimental Psychology, 4,* 11-26.

Hunt, E. (1976). Varieties of cognitive power. In I. B. Resnick (Ed.), *The nature of intelligence* (pp. 237-259). Hillsdale, NJ: Erlbaum.

Ianco-Worrall, A. D. (1972). Bilingualism and cognitive development. *Child Development, 43,* 1390-1400.

Jastrow, J. (1890). *The time relations of mental phenomena*. New York: Hodges.

Jensen, A. R. (1980). Chronometric analysis of intelligence. *Journal of Social and Biological Structure, 3*, 103-122.

____. (1982). Reaction time and psychometric *g*. In H. J. Eysenck (Ed.), *A model for intelligence* (pp. 93-132). New York: Springer-Verlag.

____, & Vernon, P. A. (1986). Jensen's reaction-time studies: A reply to Longstreth. *Intelligence, 10*(2), 153-179.

____, Larsen, J. & Paul, S. M. (1988). A chronometric semantic verification test and psychometric intelligence. *Personality and Individual Differences, 9*, 243-255.

Jensen, J. V. (1962). Effects of childhood bilingualism, I. *Elementary English, 39*, 132-143.

Johnson, G. B. (1953). Bilingualism as measured by a reaction-time technique and the relationship between a language and non-language intelligence quotient. *Journal of Genetic Psychology, 82*, 3-9.

Jordan, R. H. (1921). *Nationality and School Progress*. Bloomington, IL: Public School Publishing Co.

Kessler, C., & Quinn, M. E. (1987). Language minority children's linguistic and cognitive creativity. *Journal of Multilingual and Multicultural Development, 8*, 173-186.

Kirsner, K., Brown, H. L., Abrul, S., Chadha, N. K., & Sharma, N. K. (1980). Bilingualism and lexical representation. *Quarterly Journal of Experimental Psychology, 32*, 585-594.

Koch, H. L., & Simmons, R. (1928). A study of the test performance of American, Mexican and Negro children. *Psychological Monographs, 35*, 1-116.

Kolers, P. A. (1968). Bilingualism and information processing. *Scientific American, 218*, 78-86.

Kulpe, O. (1909). *Outlines of psychology: Based upon the results of experimental investigation* (3rd ed.). New York: Macmillan. Translation of original work published in 1893.

Lambert, W. E. (1955). Measurement of the linguistic dominance in bilinguals. *Journal of Abnormal and Social Psychology, 50*, 197-200.

____. (1956). Developmental aspects of second-language acquisition I: Associational fluency, stimulus provocativeness, and word-order influence. *Journal of Social Psychology, 43*, 83-89.

____. (1973). Culture and language as factors in learning and education. Paper presented at the Fifth Annual Learning Symposium on "Cultural Factors in Learning," Bellingham, WA: November 1973.

____, & Anisfeld, E. (1969). A note on the relation of bilingualism and intelligence. *Canadian Journal of Behavioral Science, 1,* 123-128.

____, Havelka, J., & Crosby, C. (1958). The influence of language acquisition contexts on bilingualism. *Journal of Abnormal and Social Psychology, 56,* 239-244.

____, Havelka, J., & Gardner, R. C. (1959). Linguistic manifestations of bilingualism. *American Journal of Psychology, 72,* 77-82.

Landry, R. G. (1974). A comparison of second language learners and monolinguals on divergent thinking tasks at the elementary school level. *Modern Language Journal, 58,* 10-15.

Lange, L. (1888). Neue Experimente uber den Vorgang der einfachen Reaction aud Sinneseindrucke. *Philosophische Studien, 4,* 479-510.

Larsen, G. E., & Saccuzzo, D. P. (1986). Jensen's reaction-time experiments: Another look. *Intelligence, 10*(3), 231-238.

Liedtke, W. W., & Nelson, L. D. (1968). Concept formation and bilingualism. *Alberta Journal of Educational Research, 14,* 225-232.

Long, K. K., & Padilla, A. M. (1970). Evidence for bilingual antecedents of academic success in a group of Spanish-American college students. Unpublished research report. Bellingham: Western Washington State College.

Longstreth, L. E. (1984). Jensen's reaction-time investigations of intelligence: A critique. *Intelligence, 8*(2), 139-160.

____. (1986). The real and the unreal: A reply to Jensen and Vernon. *Intelligence, 10*(2), 181-191.

Macnamara, J. (1964). The commission on Irish: Psychological aspects. *Studies,* Summer, 164-173.

____. (1966). *Bilingualism and primary education.* Edinburgh: Edinburgh University Press.

____. (1967). The effects of instruction in a weaker language. *Journal of Social Issues, 23,* 121-135.

Madsen, I. N. (1924). Some results with the Stanford Revision of the Binet-Simon tests. *School and Society, 19,* 559-562.

Magiste, E. (1979). The competing language systems of the multilingual: A developmental study of decoding and encoding process. *Journal of Verbal Learning and Verbal Behavior, 18,* 79-89.

____. (1980). Memory for numbers in monolinguals and bilinguals. *Acta Psychologica, 46,* 63-68.

____. (1982). Automaticity and interference in bilinguals. *Psychological Research, 44,* 29-43.

____. (1986). Selected issues in second and third language learning. In J. Vaid (Ed.), *Language processing in bilinguals: Psycholinguistics and neuropsychological perspective.* (pp. 97-122). Hillsdale, NJ: Lawrence Erlbaum Associates.

Mann, C. (1921). Failures due to language deficiency. *Psychological Clinic, 13,* 230-237.

Merkle, J. (1885). Die zeitlichen Verhaltnisse der Willenstatigkeit. *Philosophische Studien, 2,* 73-127.

Meyer, D. E., Osman, A. M., Irwin, D. E., & Yantis, S. (1988). Modern mental chronometry. *Biological Psychology, 26,* 3-67.

Newell, A., & Simon, H. A. (1972). *Human problem solving.* New Jersey: Prentice-Hall.

Pachella, R. G. (1974). The interpretation of reaction time in information-processing research. In B. H. Kantowitz (Ed.)*Human information processing: Tutorials in performance and cognition* (pp. 41-82). Hillsdale, NJ: Erlbaum.

Peal, E., & Lambert, W. E. (1962). The relation of bilingualism to intelligence. *Psychological Monographs: General and Applied, 76* (27, Whole No. 546), 1-23.

Pintner, R., & Keller, R. (1922). Intelligence tests of foreign children. *Journal of Educational Psychology, 13,* 214-222.

Posner, M. I. (1969). Abstraction and the process of recognition. In G. H. Bower & J. T. Spence (Eds.), *The psychology of learning and motivation, 3* (pp. 43-100). New York: Academic Press.

Powers, S., & López, R. L. (1985). Perceptual, motor, and verbal skills of monolingual and bilingual Hispanic children: A discriminant analysis. *Perceptual and Motor Skills, 60,* 999-1002.

Preston, M. S., & Lambert, W. E. (1969). Interlingual interference in a bilingual version of the Stroop color-word task. *Journal of Verbal Learning and Verbal Behavior, 8,* 295-301.

Rigg, M. (1928). Some further data on the language handicap. *Journal of Educational Psychology, 19,* 252-256.

Sternberg, S. (1966). High speed scanning in human memory. *Science, 153,* 652-654.

Vernon, P. A. (1986). He who doesn't believe in speed should beware of hasty judgments: A reply to Sternberg. *Intelligence, 10*(2), 93-100.

Whipple, G. M. (1904). Reaction times as a test of mental ability. *American Journal of Psychology, 15,* 489-498.

Wissler, C. (1901). The correlation of mental and physical tests. *Psychology Review, Monograph Supplements, 3*, 2-62. Woodworth, R. S. (1899). The accuracy of voluntary movement. *Psychological Review, 3*, (2, Whole No. 13).

Woodworth, R. S. (1938). *Experimental psychology.* New York: Holt.

____, & Schlosberg, H. (1954). *Experimental psychology.* New York: Holt, Rinehart and Winston.

Wundt, W. (1880). *Grundzuge der physiologischen Psychologie* (2nd ed.). Leipzig: W. Engelmann.

THE SOCIOLINGUISTIC BASIS FOR CODE SWITCHING IN BILINGUAL DISCOURSE AND IN BILINGUAL INSTRUCTION[*]

Adalberto Aguirre, Jr.
University of California, Riverside

ABSTRACT

The alternation or switching of languages is an observed phenomenon in bilingual speech. Researchers refer to this phenomenon as code switching. This paper is a review of studies that attempt to define and describe the general features of code switching. On the basis of that review, the discussion focuses on the utility of code switching to bilingual instruction. The paper concludes by outlining a set of observational statements regarding the uses of code switching in bilingual instruction.

A bilingual speaker may be described, in general terms, as either a member of two speech communities or as a member of a stable bilingual community who alternates use of his or her two languages by social situation and/or who mixes his or her two languages in everyday conversation. For example, Herman (1968) has noted that language choice among bilingual speakers reflects situational adjustment; Rayfield (1970) has observed that language choice serves as a rhetorical device for bilingual speakers in everyday conversation; and Limon (1982) has noted that bilingual speakers use language choice as an interactional vehicle for symbolizing political and cultural values. (For other con-

---

[*]The ideas presented in this paper owe their development to my numerous conversations with Eduardo Hernández-Chávez. Over the years, numerous graduate and undergraduate students have assisted me in the collection of bibliographic references regarding code switching—at last count, there were well over 500 references. Finally, the comments I received from the participants at the Tucson symposium were extremely useful in revising this paper. Any shortcomings or omissions in this paper are my own.

trastive examples, see: Hasselmo, 1970; McConvell, 1985; Scotton, 1986).

Another description of a bilingual speaker is Weinreich's (1953) view of a speaker who makes regular use of his or her two languages. Similarly, Haugen (1956) views bilingual persons as speakers with the ability to produce some complete and meaningful utterances in a second language. In contrast, Bloomfield (1933) describes a bilingual speaker as a person with native-like control of a second language. In general, one may note that a bilingual speaker is a person who uses his or her two languages for communicative facility to ". . . conduct ordinary daily activities in the world as it is" (Hertzler, 1965, p. 415).

Because one of the purposes of language use in everyday life is to communicate negotiated participation within social contexts, the choice of language expressed by a bilingual speaker is a tool with which he or she communicates shifts in either participatory contexts or shifts in social identity within those contexts. Regarding the nature of participatory contexts in bilingual social interaction, Haugen (1953) observed that ". . . speakers will often be quite unaware that they are switching back and forth; they are accustomed to having bilingual speakers before them and know that whichever language they use they will be understood" (p. 65). Regarding the situational use of language by bilingual speakers, Weinreich (1953) noted that ". . . the ideal bilingual switches from one language to the other according to the appropriate changes in the speech situation (interlocutor, topics, etc.) . . ." (p.73). As a result, in the everyday conversation of the bilingual speaker, language choice is congruent with social context and with shifts within social context that are often reflected in language alternation within the same utterance. Thus, for bilingual speakers, language choice in everyday life is a primary dimension in the fabrication of social meaning.

This chapter will discuss one facet of bilingual speech: *code switching* (the switching or alternation of languages by bilingual speakers). By focusing on code switching as an aspect of bilingual speech performance, I will develop a set of metatheoretical observations that can be used to construct a conceptual framework for using code switching in bilingual instruction. A caveat, however, is necessary regarding the use of the term "bilingual speaker." To avoid confusion regarding references to bilingual speakers, I assume that a bilingual speaker is a person with a relative, but complementary, degree of proficiency in two languages that permits him or her to switch or alternate languages by social situations and within utterances in everyday conversation. My notion of a bilingual speaker is also limited to those persons who have the highest probability of performing as bilingual speakers in everyday life.

Regarding the association between social identity and communicative interaction, Mead (1934) noted:

> Of these abstract social classes or subgroups of human individuals the one which is most inclusive and extensive is, of course, the one defined by the logical universe of discourse (or system of universally significant symbols) determined by the participation and communicative interaction of individuals. . . . It is the one which claims the largest number of individual members and which enables the largest conceivable number of human individuals to enter into some sort of social relation . . . a relation arising from the universal functioning of gestures as significant symbols in the general human social process of communication. (p. 222)

Communicative interaction then serves to create a social relation among persons that provides them with a social identity and membership. Regarding bilingual speakers, code switching serves to define the social relation of bilingual speakers to everyday life.

Code Switching and Interference

Early language contact studies, such as those of Weinreich (1953) and Haugen (1956), have documented that when bilingual speakers are faced with a choice of two languages, one language may be dropped or elements of one language may be incorporated into the other language, or the two languages may appear to merge into a "style of speaking." What has often been referred to as a style of speaking among bilingual persons by language contact researchers also has been regarded as "free variation." That is, because the nature of this style of speaking is difficult to analyze and define, and because it is affected by both situational and personal dimensions, it has been treated as a dimension of bilingual speech that inexplicably happens in the speech of bilingual persons. By contrast, the psychoanalytic literature recognizes that language switching in bilingual speech is not really free variation, but rather that language switching serves as an internal reflection of psychological adaptation in a bilingual person (Greenson, 1950; Krapf, 1955; Marcos, 1980; Marcos et al., 1977, 1973).

It is not unexpected then to find that code switching in bilingual speech has been regarded in language contact studies as either a form of linguistic borrowing and/or linguistic interference. Weinreich (1953) thus came to define interference as: ". . . instances of deviation from the norms of either language which occur in the speech of bilinguals as a result of their familiarity with more than one language" (p. 1). Weinreich even suggested that interference in bilingual speech was due to an excessive amount of intrautterance switching that was a result of a youngster being indiscriminately addressed in both languages by the same speaker. Similarly, Haugen (1956) defined interference as ". . . linguistic overlapping when certain items must be assigned to more than one language at a time" (p. 40). In addition, as a student of interference in bilingual speech, Mackey (1965) regards interference as ". . . the use of elements from one language while speaking or writing another" (p. 240). One result of classifying code switching as a form of interference has been confusion regarding the occurrence of code switching in bilingual speech and the function of code switching in bilingual communication.

As a form of linguistic interference, code switching has been described as either ". . . a transitional stage in the shift from the regular use of one language to the regular use of the other" (Weinreich, 1953, pp. 68-69) or as a first stage in linguistic diffusion (Haugen, 1956). On the other hand, in those few instances when code switching has been noted by researchers, it has either been dismissed as language mixture (Whitney, 1881), incorrectly implying that a new language is made up of two existing ones, or as a hybrid language, presupposing that the other languages are pure (Vildomec, 1963).

For example, in his studies of New Mexican Spanish, Espinosa (1909) identified code switching as the principal cause of speech mixture in New Mexican Spanish—the random intermingling of Spanish and English words and phrases. As a result, code switching as interference implies that bilingual speech is indicative of an unstable structure of social and linguistic meaning rather than a pattern of sociolinguistic behavior that is characteristic of stable bilingual communities. Second, code switching as interference implies that code switching is random speech mixture that can occur at any time, thus making bilingual speech unpredictable. Code switching as interference eliminates consideration of code switching as the product of a complex interplay of social and linguistic behavior in stable bilingual communities.

Regarding the appropriateness of the label interference for code switching, Clyne (1967) argues that the term interference is not appropriate for code switching because it merely looks at a partial cause of the phenomenon (e.g., language contact) rather than providing a description of the phenomenon (bilingual communication) (also see: Valdes-Fallis, 1980). Perhaps one of the most ardent critics of applying the label interference to code switching has been John Gumperz. Gumperz (1967) suggested that labeling code switching as interference assumes that bilingual speakers are switching or mixing languages in order to arrive at some standard language or standard form of speaking. As such, code switching becomes a transitional process that reflects the bilingual speaker's attempt to imitate a standard language. Consequently, Gumperz argues that treating code switching as interference ignores the importance of code switching as a communicative resource for bilingual speakers and the utility of code switching for the production of norms for communication in bilingual settings.

The labeling of code switching as interference also ignores the function of code switching as a verbal strategy in stable bilingual communities. Rather, by labeling code switching as interference, code switching is conceptualized as a breakdown in a bilingual speaker's ability to maintain his or her two languages separately, which stems from a breakdown in the bilingual community's communication patterns. In particular, the labeling of code switching as interference implies that a bilingual speaker is confused in his or her speech production. As Lance (1969) noted: "The switching occurs not because the speaker does not know the right word but because the word that comes out is more readily available at the time of production" (p. 93).

In addition, the labeling of code switching as interference implies that a bilingual speaker mixes his/her languages rather than ordering them into meaningful linguistic production. As Ure (1972) noted regarding the treatment of code switching as simple language mixture: ". . . grammatical and lexical cohesion obtains *between* the two languages in question: the difference of language does not make any difference in situation—all the bits belong together situationally and linguistically as part of one whole" (p. 225). Code switching then appears in bilingual speech not because of a breakdown in a bilingual speaker's ability to produce meaningful speech, but because code switching is an expression of a bilingual speaker's social and linguistic identity.

Bilingual Speech and Code Switching

Kolers (1968) proposed that the skilled use of two languages by bilingual speakers presumes a readiness to switch between them, and to switch completely without elements of one language intruding in the other. Gumperz (1976) defines code switching as ". . . the juxtaposition of passages of speech belonging to two different grammatical systems or subsystems within the same exchange" (p. 1). Similarly, Gingras (1974) refers to code switching as ". . . the alternation of grammatical rules, drawn from two different languages, which occurs within sentence boundaries" (p. 167). Implicit in these two definitions of code switching are the observations that: (a) code switching in bilingual speech reflects the co-existence of two separate grammars or two general language systems; and (b) code switching is an intrasentential process. Both of these observations are crucial in the identification of code switching as a feature in the bilingual speaker's communicative competence (Di Prieto, 1978; Oksaar, 1972). As Dua (1984) noted:

> Code-switching as a process of language use implies that the individual speaker has the competence of two codes at his disposal and that he can use them alternately, consciously or unconsciously, in accordance with linguistic and extra-linguistic constraints to achieve certain communication goals and convey sociosemantic connotations. This further implies that the two codes are kept distinct whether the competence in them is balanced or non-balanced and that the speaker can identify the elements of the respective codes. (p. 136)

Though they are not mutually exclusive, the observations outlined serve to characterize the principal areas of sociolinguistic research in code switching. On the one hand, the observation that code switching reflects the co-existence of two separate grammars or two general language systems has focused attention on the rules of speaking or communicative competence for bilingual speakers. The rules of speaking are examined by observing the participation of bilingual speakers in social contexts that require linguistic exchange. By outlining the association between rules of speaking and on-going social interaction, the attempt is made to observe the process by which speakers select the appropriate code (language), and how code selection contributes to the maintenance of the social context.

For example, in his study of the Norwegian language in America, Haugen (1953) observed that his bilingual informants switched completely from one language to the other in their conversation with him. In particular, Haugen noted that one of his informants switched from Norwegian to English four times in 15 minutes—to show that he could speak English, to describe his pastor's illness, in reference to his own health, and to quote an English speaker. Similarly, Denison (1968) in his study of Sauris observed that his informants switched languages completely in order to achieve greater or less formality, or a different style of social interaction. In their study of code switching in a community in northern Norway, Blom and Gumperz (1972) also observed among their informants that switching languages completely served as a marker for topic, setting, and role shifts within the same social context.

Following the notion of "communicative competence" developed by Hymes (1974) that speakers have the ability to use their speech varieties for specific functions, social or linguistic, the observation that code switching reflects the co-existence of two separate grammars or two general language systems has resulted in an area of sociolinguistic interest that examines the association between code switching and the interpretation of social contexts. In this area of interest, code switching is regarded as a tool with which the researcher can create a general interpretative framework for the rules of speaking in bilingual discourse by isolating code switching to features of the social environment in everyday life (Lipski, 1980; St. Clair & Valdes, 1980). This analysis of code switching, as a result, focuses on the extent of its rule-governed behavior by demonstrating that regularity in code switching is related to features that comprise individual speech events. As a result, a general interpretative framework of rules that outline the selection of one code (language) over another is derived from the observation of how bilingual speakers negotiate meaning in everyday life.

On the other hand, the observation that code switching is an intrasentential process has focused sociolinguistic interest in those linguistic environments in which code switching occurs. This area of sociolinguistic interest attempts to demonstrate that bilingual speakers possess a subset of grammatical knowledge that permits an ordered switching of languages. For example, Gumperz and Hernández-Chávez (1975), in their study of code switching among English/Spanish bilingual Mexican American speakers in California, noted that adverbial constructions may be switched, "Vamos next week," but not as interrogatives, "When vamos?"; a code switch may occur at a noun phrase only after a determiner, "Se lo di a mi grandfather," but not as "Se lo di a my grandfather"; an adverb may be switched before an adjective, "Es very friendly," but not, "Es very amistoso."

Similarly, using the term code mixing to refer to intra-sentential code switching, Singh (1985) noted that grammatical constraints operate on Hindi-English code switching. Schmid (1986) also documented the presence of linguistic constraints in Swedish-English code switching, Pandharipande (1983) has noted the operation of linguistic constraints in Hindi-Marathi code switching, and Joshi (1985) has examined the nature of linguistic constraints in English-Marathi code switching. While it is difficult to make general comparative observations about linguistic constraints in code switching, Pfaff (1979) and Hasselmo (1972) observed that linguistic constraints do operate in the production of code switching by bilingual speakers.

The presence of linguistic or grammatical constraints in code switching implies that bilingual speakers who code switch are fully proficient in both languages, rather than in just one of the two languages. On the one hand, not to be fully proficient in both languages suggests that code switching is a result of language interference. On the other hand, as a feature in the bilingual speech of fully proficient bilinguals, code switching reflects the communicative competence of bilingual speakers in stable bilingual communities. As Doron (1983) noted: "Producing and understanding utterances with intrasentential alternating of two languages—code switching—appears to be part of the linguistic competence of members of communities where the languages are in contact" (p. 35).

While there appears to be general consensus in the sociolinguistic research literature regarding the operation of linguistic constraints in code switching, a small amount of sociolinguistic research suggests that bilingual speakers can evaluate the acceptability of code switching samples in bilingual speech. For example, Timm (1975) examined the syntactic limits on code switching by eliciting from three bilingual speakers their responses to a number of test

sentences extracted from a short story.   Each of the test
sentences occurred in a variety of switched formats, such as:

> Yo fui a la store.
> Yo fui to the store.
> I went a la tienda.
> Yo went to the store.

According to Timm (1975), the level of acceptability for each
of the switched sentences determines ". . . at exactly what
points switching becomes unacceptable to those familiar
with the art" (p. 477).

Aguirre (1985b, 1981b, 1978, 1977) has demonstrated that
bilingual speakers can rank-order the level of acceptability
for code-switched sentences.   By constructing a series of
sentences that have code switches at different points, he has
shown that (1) some types of code switches are more acceptable to bilingual speakers than other switches, and (2) the
ability to rate the acceptability of code-switched sentences is
directly associated with a speaker's bilingual proficiency.
Regarding the latter finding, Aguirre has shown that a bilingual speaker's ability to evaluate the acceptability of code-
switched sentences is directly associated with the speaker's
approximation of full proficiency in both languages.   Similarly, Valdes-Fallis (1976a) has shown that the ability to code
switch by bilingual speakers is associated with their linguistic dominance, and that ". . . bilinguals of the same type employed strikingly similar code-switching patterns" (p. 98).

In addition, research that has examined the lexical
processing abilities of bilingual speakers shows that bilingual speakers utilize a combination of grammatical knowledge from their two languages in the processing of bilingual
speech (Altenberg & Cairns, 1983), and that bilingual speakers can evaluate the use of code switching by bilingual
speakers on the basis of situational norms, interpersonal accommodation, and in-group favoritism (Genesse, 1984).   In
general, then, this area of sociolinguistic research shows that
bilingual speakers are able to utilize some notion of communicative competence to evaluate levels of acceptability
for certain forms of code switching (also see: Sridhar &
Sridhar, 1980; Valdes-Fallis, 1976b).

Regarding the association of communicative competence to code switching, Gumperz and Hernández-Chávez (1975) stated that "social structure, like syntax, aids in the interpretation of sentences. It is part of what a speaker has to know in order to judge the full import of what is said. Two speakers will make similar interpretations of a sentence only if they interpret it in terms of the same social assumptions" (p. 162). Code switching, thus, is a sociolinguistic feature in bilingual speech and bilingual social interaction. Second, the production of code switching is associated with fully proficient bilinguals who possess the necessary social knowledge for utilizing code switching to fabricate and interpret meaning in everyday life. Third, the social knowledge required for the meaningful production of code switching is derived from participation in bilingual speech situations and membership in a stable bilingual speech community. As a result, one can make the following metatheoretical observations regarding the association of code switching to bilingual discourse. First, code switching is a sociolinguistic feature in bilingual speech that demonstrates a bilingual speaker's social knowledge for language use and language choice in stable patterns of social interaction in bilingual contexts. Second, code switching in the everyday discourse of bilingual speakers demonstrates a bilingual speaker's ability to utilize the linguistic knowledge he or she possesses for two languages to produce language (code) switches in bilingual discourse that have sociolinguistic meaning. Finally, code switching in bilingual discourse demonstrates a bilingual speaker's social and linguistic accommodation to the communicative norms in his or her bilingual speech community.

Code Switching and Bilingual Instruction

If code switching is a sociolinguistic feature in bilingual speech then how can the bilingual teacher in a bilingual classroom utilize code switching as an instructional vehicle in bilingual instruction? Before we proceed any further we must make obvious the assumptions implicit in bilingual instruction:

1. teachers in bilingual classrooms are bilingual

2. bilingual teachers are proficient in the languages of their bilingual students in the classroom

3. bilingual teachers possess social knowledge of the communicative norms in their students' speech communities

The preceding assumptions are important because they recognize the importance social knowledge about communication and interaction in bilingual contexts plays in utilizing code switching as a feature of assessment and learning in bilingual instruction (Aguirre, 1985a, 1981a).

If a teacher in a bilingual classroom is not bilingual then the classroom context is meaningless. Secondly, if a teacher in a bilingual classroom is not proficient in the languages of his or her students then he or she reduces the communicative value of the classroom to bilingual instruction. Third, a nonfamiliarity with the norms that guide social and linguistic behavior in a bilingual student's speech community places the teacher in a position of not understanding a bilingual student's sociolinguistic behavior (Haugen, 1977). Thus, bilingual teachers in bilingual classrooms must reflect the sociolinguistic make-up of their students and share a sociolinguistic understanding for bilingual behavior. If both bilingual teachers and bilingual students share the same pool of sociolinguistic knowledge then both teacher and student will operate in the bilingual classroom with a base of social knowledge that reduces the degree of ambiguity in the interpretation of classroom behavior.

Jacobson (1981, 1979) has proposed that intersentential code switching can be used in bilingual instruction to develop and enhance the bilingual student's sociolinguistic competence in each language (also see Faltis, 1989). In particular, Jacobson identifies the following guides for employing code switching in bilingual instruction:

1. the extent to which the native language must
   be developed in order to succeed in learning a
   second language

2. the extent to which the home language
   should be used in school to develop a positive
   attitude toward it

3. the extent to which first language maintenance in the primary grades would not interfere with the transition to English in post-
   primary education

4. the extent to which the use of both languages
   would lead to an understanding of the
   bilingual functioning of some sectors of our
   society

5. the extent to which school subjects could be
   learned through two language media

González (1972), however, has suggested that code
switching is not appropriate in bilingual instruction because:

1. children can learn a second language while
   maintaining their first language, but allowing
   code switching deprives the child of the
   opportunity to practice using the two languages as separate modes of communication;

2. code switching in the bilingual classroom
   encourages the student to use the stronger
   language (usually English) rather than attempting new linguistic expressions in the
   weaker language;

3. the use of code switching prevents the teacher
   from identifying language areas in need of
   remediation

In a later revision of this viewpoint, González and Máez
(1980) proposed that: "Code-switching of the intersentential
type can and should be used in teaching, while intrasentential code switching should be accepted (as should

any variety of language the child brings with him) but should not be used by the teacher. In addition, the teacher should assure that when the child does engage in intrasentential code switching, the word switched to English is in his repertoire" (p. 133).

In general then, code switching is considered as a valuable tool in bilingual instruction when it occurs in separate and independent linguistic environments—such as intersentential code switching. In addition, code switching that is intrasentential, while regarded as a sociolinguistic feature in bilingual speech, is regarded as an obstacle to the development of independent bilingual language use. The concern then appears to be not so much with the presence and occurrence of code switching in bilingual instruction, as much as it is with what "form" it assumes. In a sense, the concern with form (intersentential versus intrasentential) reflects the general concern with code switching in the sociolinguistic literature: Is code switching a form of linguistic interference or is code switching an ordered sociolinguistic process?

One thing is clear though, the bilingual teacher in the bilingual classroom will encounter code switching in the student's speech at both the intersentential and intrasentential levels. Regardless of its form, code switching is an unavoidable sociolinguistic feature in the bilingual classroom. Bilingual teachers in bilingual classrooms should regard code switching as a meaningful and purposeful communicative strategy. By doing so, the teacher in the bilingual classroom may be able to use his or her own intuitive knowledge about bilingual behavior to develop a sociolinguistic profile of the bilingual student. Code switching, as a result, is a valuable resource for bilingual instruction because it assists the bilingual teacher in "making sense" of the bilingual student's sociolinguistic complexity in the classroom. For example, Schutz (1962) observed that: ". . . all interpretation of this world (of daily life) is based upon a stock of previous experiences of it . . . which in the form of 'knowledge at hand' function as a scheme of reference" (p.208). Similarly, Kjolseth (1972) stated that while ". . . there are many differences between individual stocks of 'everyday knowledge' a good deal is shared with others and this [is] called 'commonsense' knowledge" (p. 59). Thus, code switching as a shared feature (e.g., commonsense knowledge) among bilingual speakers in everyday knowledge can be utilized by a bilingual teacher as an interpretative tool in bilingual instruction in order to make sense of what he or she observes in the classroom.

I have proposed that code switching, as part of a teacher's base of intuitive knowledge, allows him or her to infuse order into the meaning of everyday life in the bilingual classroom (Aguirre, 1988b). My notion of intuitive knowledge focuses on only one feature—understanding. Where an epistemologist may focus on intuitive knowledge as a mode of evidence, I am more concerned with the use of intuitive knowledge in developing levels of social understanding. A bilingual person's base of intuitive knowledge for bilingual behavior and bilingual communication expands in correspondence with his or her ability to approach a state of balance in the use of his or her two languages. The term *balance* follows Macnamara's (1969) observations: ". . . the term 'balanced' is commonly used to describe persons who are equally skilled in two languages in all aspects and all styles of the language skills he possesses . . . a person is balanced in understanding or in speaking two languages, or at least in some particular facet of linguistic competence" (p. 80). A prerequisite, however, for approaching a state of bilingual balance is active participation in bilingual contexts. As a result, simply speaking two languages is not sufficient to permit the development of a base of intuitive knowledge for bilingual behavior. Since code switching is a sociolinguistic feature in bilingual communication, as a person's base of intuitive knowledge for bilingual behavior expands, he or she will increase proficiency in code switching as part of his or her own bilingual communicative competence.

In discussing the use of code switching as a sociolinguistic resource for bilingual instruction, I need to stress an initial assumption in this paper—that bilingual teachers are proficient in the languages of their students. This assumption is vital to establishing sociolinguistic congruence between teachers and students in the bilingual classroom.

Based on this assumption, some observations can be outlined that are reflective, rather than inclusive, regarding the use of code switching as a sociolinguistic resource in bilingual instruction (Aguirre, 1988a, 1986-1987).

Code switching can be used by the bilingual teacher to promote the functional separation and specialization of language use. The teacher can listen to students' code switching in order to identify what is being switched and how it is being switched—such as word repetition across languages. If the bilingual teacher's base of intuitive knowledge allows him or her to identify the child as possessing a similar linguistic ability in each language, then the teacher may choose to alternate languages with the student in order to build on sentence complexity and word power.

Second, the bilingual teacher's base of intuitive knowledge for bilingual behavior may tell him or her that a bilingual student's code switching is language mixture that communicates confusion. That is, the bilingual teacher may observe that the language alternation is incongruent with what is socially and linguistically probable within the social context. The bilingual teacher is then able to separate simple language confusion from cognitive difficulties associated with a student's language learning abilities. The bilingual teacher can then use code switching to instruct the student in the transfer of concepts and their linguistic symbols from one language to another. The goal is to use code switching to develop within the student's linguistic knowledge two separate symbol systems with their appropriate meaning.

Finally, the bilingual teacher can use his or her base of intuitive knowledge for bilingual behavior to develop criteria for separating meaningful from meaningless language alternation. That is, the bilingual teacher can identify those speakers whose code switching is reflective of participation in bilingual contexts from those speakers who have learned how to code switch as part of some social activity. The former will usually be proficient bilinguals, while the latter will be limited in their use of both languages. The bilingual teacher can then develop sets of classroom lessons that are bilingual in goals and that depend on some reinforcement outside of the classroom.

The preceding observations are only those associated with the use of intuitive knowledge for code switching by bilingual teachers with bilingual students. The limited classroom time available for bilingual teachers to observe and assess the sociolinguistic competence of their bilingual students enhances the use of code switching as a tool for facilitating the bilingual teacher's identification of sociolinguistic behavior in the bilingual classroom. By focusing on code switching, the bilingual teacher can employ his or her intuitive knowledge for identifying global, rather than particularistic, features in a student's bilingual behavior. Since the general educational process is oriented toward students' global rather than particularistic features, the use of code switching by bilingual teachers to understand their bilingual students is compatible with what is both possible and probable in the school classroom. Thus, as a feature of bilingual behavior, code switching can be employed by the bilingual teacher to observe the sociolinguistic skills bilingual students bring to the bilingual classroom and to enhance their language skills in two languages.

Conclusion

Code switching is an integral aspect of bilingual discourse. Code switching is not merely the product of co-occurring social and linguistic variables, but it is an abstract entity with its own sociolinguistic grammar. We can speak of a sociolinguistic grammar for code switching because its production is governed by social rules for communication (social competence) and linguistic rules for meaningful speech (linguistic competence). For the fully proficient bilingual speaker, code switching is a reflexive process that symbolizes his or her social identity in bilingual discourse. Thus, code switching amounts to a form of sociolinguistic behavior in that it typifies the everyday life experiences of bilingual persons.

I have derived a set of metatheoretical observations regarding the operation of code switching in bilingual discourse in order to discuss its usefulness in bilingual instruction. Code switching can be utilized by the bilingual teacher to unravel the complexity in a bilingual student's sociolinguistic behavior. However, the usefulness of code switching in bilingual instruction requires that the teacher and student share a social identity and social reality. In sum, the bilingual teacher and bilingual student must share social features, and not just language features, in order to maximize the use of code switching in bilingual instruction.

Finally, one of the difficulties in thinking about social phenomena is that one must cross various conceptual levels in an attempt to make sense of one's observations. Regarding code switching, one must begin at the micro level in order to examine the interpersonal interpretative features of code switching, then shift to the macro level in order to outline the utility of code switching to a generalized social process. Consequently, just as people tend to get lost in a crowd, the meaning of code switching at the interpersonal level tends to get lost when placed within an institutional process, such as classroom instruction, that generalizes everyday experiences. Thus, code switching may have maximum utility to bilingual instruction only if a bilingual teacher is capable of particularizing everyday experiences within a shared context of sociolinguistic knowledge with his or her students.

References

Aguirre, A., Jr. (1977). *Acceptability judgements of code-switching phrases by Chicanos.* Arlington, VA: Center for Applied Linguistics, ERIC Clearinghouse for Language and Linguistics.

_____. (1978). *An experimental sociolinguistic study of Chicano bilingualism.* San Francisco: R & E Research Associates.

_____. (1981a). In search of a paradigm for bilingual education. In R. Padilla (Ed.), *Ethnoperspectives in bilingual education, volume III: Bilingual education technology* (pp. 3-13). Ypsilanti, MI: Eastern Michigan University.

_____. (1981b). Toward an index of acceptability for code alternation: An experimental analysis. *Aztlán: International Journal of Chicano Studies Research, 11,* 297-322.

_____. (1985a). Opinions of parents, teachers, and principals on select features of bilingual education. In E. García & R. Padilla (Eds.),

Advances in Bilingual Education Research (pp. 212-225). Tucson: University of Arizona Press.

___. (1985b). A sociolinguistic approach to the experimental study of language alternation in bilingual speech. *Revue Roumaine de Linguistique, 30*, 293-302.

___. (1986-1987). A commentary on bilingual students and bilingual teachers. *Educational Research Quarterly, 11*, 5-9.

___. (1988a). Code switching and intuitive knowledge in the bilingual classroom. In D. Bixler-Márquez & J. Ornstein-Galicia (Eds.), *Chicano speech in the bilingual classroom* (pp. 83-89). New York: Peter Lang.

___. (1988b). Code-switching, intuitive knowledge and the bilingual classroom. In H. García & R. Chávez (Eds.), *Ethnolinguistic issues in education* (pp. 28-38). Lubbock, TX: Texas Tech University College of Education.

Altenberg, E., & Cairns, H. (1983). The effects of phonotactic constraints on lexical processing in bilingual and monolingual subjects. *Journal of Verbal Learning and Verbal Behavior, 22*, 174-188.

Blom, J., & Gumperz, J. (1972). Social meaning in linguistic structure: Code-switching in Norway. In J. Gumperz & D. Hymes (Eds.), *Directions in sociolinguistics* (p. 407-434). New York: Holt, Rinehart & Winston.

Bloomfield, L. (1933). *Language*. New York: Holt, Rinehart & Winston.

Clyne, M. (1967). *Transference and triggering: Observations on the language assimilation of postwar German-speaking migrants in Australia*. The Hague: Martinus Nijhoff.

Denison, N. (1968). Sauris: A trilingual community in diatypic perspective. *Man, 3*, 578-592.

Di Prieto, R. (1978). Code-switching as a verbal strategy among bilinguals. In M. Paradis (Ed.), *Aspects of bilingualism* (pp. 275-282). Columbia, SC: Hornbeam Press.

Doron, E. (1983). On a formal model of code-switching. *Texas Linguistic Forum, 22*, 35-59.

Dua, H. (1984). Perspectives on code-switching research. *International Journal of Dravidian Linguistics, 13*, 136-155.

Espinosa, A. (1909). *Studies in New Mexican Spanish, part I: Phonology*. Chicago: University of Chicago Press.

Faltis, C. (1989). Code-switching and bilingual schooling: An examination of Jacobson's new concurrent approach. *Journal of Multilingual and Multicultural Development, 10*, 117-127.

Genesee, F. (1984). The social-psychological significance of bilingual code-switching for children. *Applied Psycholinguistics, 5*, 3-20.

Gingras, R. (1974). Problems in the description of Spanish-English intrasentential code-switching. In G. Bills (Ed.), *Southwest areal linguistics* (pp. 167-174). San Diego: San Diego State University Institute for Cultural Pluralism.

González, G. (1972). Analysis of Chicano Spanish and the problem of usage. *Aztlán: International Journal of Chicano Studies Research, 3*, 223-231.

____, & Máez, L. (1980). To switch or not to switch: The role of code-switching in the elementary bilingual classroom. In R. Padilla (Ed.), *Ethnoperspectives in bilingual education research, volume II: Theory in bilingual education* (pp. 125-135). Ypsilanti, MI: Eastern Michigan University.

Greenson, R. (1950). The mother tongue and the mother. *International Journal of Psychoanalysis, 31*, 18-23.

Gumperz, J. (1967). The linguistic markers of bilingualism. *Journal of Social Issues, 23*, 48-57.

____. (1976). *The sociolinguistic significance of conversational code-switching*. Berkeley, CA: University of California at Berkeley Papers on Language and Context.

____, & Hernández-Chávez, E. (1975). Cognitive aspects of bilingual communication. In E. Hernández-Chávez, A. Cohen, & A. Beltramo (Eds.), *El lenguaje de los chicanos: Regional and social characteristics of language used by Mexican Americans* (pp. 154-163). Arlington, VA: Center for Applied Linguistics.

Hasselmo, N. (1970). Code-switching and modes of speaking. In G. Gilbert (Ed.), *Texas studies in bilingualism* (pp. 179-210). Berlin: Walter de Gruyter.

____. (1972). Code-switching as ordered selection. In E. Kirchow (Ed.), *Studies for Einar Haugen* (pp. 261-280). The Hague: Mouton.

Haugen, E. (1953). *The Norwegian language in America*. Philadelphia: University of Pennsylvania Press.

____. (1956). *Bilingualism in the Americas: A bibliography and research guide*. Publication of the American Dialect Society, Philadelphia, No.26.

____. (1977). Norm and deviation in bilingual communities. In P. Hornby (Ed.), *Bilingualism: Psychological, social and educational implications* (pp. 91-102). New York: Academic Press.

Herman, S. (1968). Explorations in the social psychology of language choice. In J. Fishman (Ed.), *Readings in the sociology of language* (pp. 492-511). The Hague: Mouton.

Hertzler, J. (1965). *A sociology of language.* New York: Random House.

Hymes, D. (1974). *Foundations in sociolinguistics: An ethnographic approach.* Philadelphia: University of Pennsylvania Press.

Jacobson, R. (1979). Can bilingual teaching techniques reflect bilingual community behaviors?—A study in ethnoculture and its relationship to some amendments contained in the new bilingual education act. In R. Padilla (Ed.), *Ethnoperspectives in bilingual education research, volume I: Bilingual education and public policy in the United States* (pp. 483-497). Ypsilanti, MI: Eastern Michigan University.

____. (1981). The implementation of a bilingual instruction model: The NEW concurrent approach. In R. Padilla (Ed.), *Ethnoperspectives in bilingual education research, volume III: Bilingual education technology* (pp. 14-29). Ypsilanti, MI: Eastern Michigan University.

Joshi, A. (1985). Processing of sentences with intrasentential code switching. In D. Dowty, L. Karttunen, & A. Zwicky (Eds.), *Natural language parsing: Psychological, computational, and theoretical perspectives* (pp. 190-205). New York: Cambridge University Press.

Kjolseth, R. (1972). Making sense: Natural language and shared knowledge in understanding. In J. Fishman (Ed.), *Advances in the sociology of language, volume II* (pp. 50-76). The Hague: Mouton.

Kolers, P. (1968). Bilingualism and information processing. *Scientific American, 218,* 78-86.

Krapf, E. (1955). The choice of language in polyglot psychoanalysis. *Psychoanalytic Quarterly, 24,* 343-357.

Lance, D. (1969). *A brief study of Spanish-English bilingualism: Final report (Research Project ORR-Liberal Arts-15504).* College Station, TX: Texas A&M University.

Limon, J. (1982). El meeting: History, folk Spanish, and ethnic nationalism in a Chicano student community. In J. Amastae & L. Elías-Olivares (Eds.), *Spanish in the United States: Sociolinguistic aspects* (pp. 301-332). New York: Cambridge University Press.

Lipski, J. (1980). Bilingual code-switching and internal competence: The evidence from Spanish and English. *Le langage et l'homme, 42,* 30-39.

Mackey, W. (1965). Bilingual interference: Its analysis and measurement. *Journal of Communication, 15,* 239-249.

Macnamara, J. (1969). How can one measure the extent of a person's bilingual proficiency? In L. Kelly (Ed.), *Description and measurement of bilingualism* (pp. 80-97). Toronto: University of Toronto Press.

Marcos, L. (1980). Bilinguals in psychotherapy. In M. Simpson (Ed.), *Psycholinguistics in clinical practice* (pp. 91-109). New York: Irwington Publishers.

____, Eisma, J., & Guimon, J. (1977). Bilingualism and sense of self. *The American Journal of Psychoanalysis, 37,* 285-290.

____, Urcuyo, L., Kesselman, M., & Alpert, M. (1973). The Language barrier in evaluating Spanish American patients. *Archives of General Psychiatry, 29,* 655-659.

McConvell, P. (1985). Domains and code-switching among bilingual Aborigines. In M. Clyne (Ed.), *Australia: Meeting place of languages* (pp. 95-125). Pacific Linguistics, Series C - No. 92.

Mead, G. H. (1934). *Mind, self, and society.* Chicago: University of Chicago Press.

Oksaar, E. (1972). Bilingualism. In T. Sebeok (Ed.), *Current trends in linguistics, volume 9* (pp. 476-511). The Hague: Mouton.

Pandharipande, R. (1983). Mixing and creativity in multilingual India. *Studies in the Linguistic Sciences, 13,* 99-113.

Pfaff, C. (1979). Constraints on language mixing: Intrasentential code-switching and borrowing in Spanish/English. *Language, 55,* 291-318.

Rayfield, J. (1970). *The languages of a bilingual community.* The Hague: Mouton.

St. Clair, R., & Valdes, G. (1980). The sociology of code-switching. *Language Sciences, 2,* 205-221.

Schmid, B. (1986). Constraints on code-switching: Evidence from Swedish and English. *Nordic Journal of Linguistics, 9,* 55-82.

Schutz, A. (1962). *Collected papers, volume I: The problem of social reality.* The Hague: Mouton.

Scotton, C. (1986). Diglossia and code-switching. In J. Fishman, M. Clyne, Bh. Krishnamurti, & M. Abdulaziz (Eds.), *The Fergusonian impact, volume 2: Sociolinguistics and the sociology of language* (pp. 403-415). Berlin: Mouton de Gruyter.

Singh, R. (1985). Grammatical constraints on code-mixing: Evidence from Hindi-English. *Canadian Journal of Linguistics, 30,* 33-45.

Sridhar, S., & Sridhar, K. (1980). The syntax and psycholinguistics of bilingual code mixing. *Canadian Journal of Psychology, 34,* 407-416.

Timm, L. (1975). Spanish-English code-switching: El porque y how-not-to. *Romance Philology, 28,* 473-482.

Ure, J. (1972). Code-switching and "mixed speech," in the register systems of developing languages. In A. Verdoodt (Ed.) *Applied Linguistics, 2,*

Papers from the Third International Congress of Applied Linguistics (pp. 222-239). Heidelberg: J.S. Verlag.

Valdes-Fallis, G. (1976a). Code-switching and language dominance: Some initial findings. *General Linguistics, 18*, 90-104.

___. (1976b). Social interaction and code-switching patterns: A case study of Spanish/English alternation. In G. Keller, R. Teschner, & S. Viera (Eds.), *Bilingualism in the bicentennial and beyond* (pp. 53-85). New York: Bilingual Press.

___. (1980). Is code-switching interference, integration, or neither? In E. Blansitt & R. Teschner (Eds.), *Festchrift for Jacob Ornstein* (pp. 314-325). Rowley, MA: Newbury House.

Vildomec, V. (1963). *Multilingualism.* Leyden: A. W. Sythoff.

Weinreich, U. (1953). *Languages in contact.* The Hague: Mouton.

Whitney, W. (1881). *On mixture in language.* Philadelphia: Transactions of the American Philological Association.

ALTERNATE PARADIGMS IN
BILINGUAL EDUCATION RESEARCH[*]

Lourdes Díaz Soto
Pennsylvania State University

ABSTRACT

The majority of the quantitative research investigating linguistically and culturally diverse learners has utilized a
deficit philosophy, and this has permeated psychological
literature. The purpose of this paper is to question and
discuss this research; to examine new possibilities; and to
gain awareness of such alternate research models as the
possibilities-oriented paradigm.

Much of the quantitative research investigating linguistically and culturally diverse learners has tended to originate
from a perspective employing a deficit philosophy. A biased
philosophy pointing to inherent deficiencies and patholo-
gies has permeated the psychological literature to such an
extent that the successful aspects of growing up as enriched
individuals capable of speaking a variety of languages and
negotiating diverse learning environments has been largely
overlooked. Deficiencies, problems, difficulties, and mental
health issues have overshadowed the contributions, talents,
and success stories. A large body of research relating attributes of second language learners and members of underrepresented groups reflects the fact that we live in a society
where some groups of people are viewed as more desirable,
while others as less so.

The purpose of this article is threefold: (1) to raise questions and introduce discussion about research emanating
from deficit philosophies; (2) to examine pioneering research endeavors that explore new possibilities; and (3) to
gain awareness of alternate research paradigms.

---

[*]Gratitude is expressed to Dr. Ursula Casanova for editorial suggestions helpful in enhancing this manuscript.

Bilingual Handicaps

Historically, research viewing bilingual/bicultural learners in the United States has employed a deficit point of view. Bilinguals have been referred to as handicapped, mentally confused, and less intelligent than mainstream learners. The initial research viewing bilingualism is largely responsible for creating what Cummins (1984) refers to as the "myth of the bilingual handicap." The stereotypical findings so prevalent in the research of the 1920s through the early 1960s continue to impact the lives of many of our learners. The attitude from earlier work has been translated by practitioners into the notion that bilinguals are not only inherently lacking, but deficient, and retarded. Since bilingualism has been seen as a harmful attribute, teachers continue to employ subtractive (Lambert, 1975) strategies, replacing one language for another. Examples of linguistic repression directed toward Native Americans and Mexican American learners in the classroom are cited by Crawford (1989).

Major reviews of the era clearly document the flawed research paradigms and the accompanying negative, biased results. Jensen (1962) reviewed more than 200 studies relating the disadvantages of childhood bilingualism and listed the "handicaps" that the literature of the day attributed to bilingualism: handicaps in speech development and in emotional and intellectual progress, mental fatigue, impaired originality of thought, handicapped on intelligence tests, handicapped in reading and studying, inadequate adjustment to school and education in general, loss in self-confidence, schizophrenia, shyness or aggressiveness, direct feelings of arrogance, and indications of contempt and hatred toward parents (pp. 132-136). Common sense dictates that such negative attributes are absurd, yet this was the state of the art and the initial base guiding mainstream practitioners in the field of bilingual education for nearly 40 years.

Other major reviews (Darcy, 1953; Weinreich, 1953) also report the negative consequences of bilingualism from the 1920s to the 1960s. Frequently cited in these major reviews is the work of Saer (1923), who failed to match bilingual and monolingual learners on demographic variables; Pintner and Arsenian (1937), who relied on the child's surname as the indication of bilingualism; and Smith (1939), who counted "errors" of second language learners and then attributed preschool speech retardation to the use of two languages. Hakuta (1986) notes that it is important to view the early literature in light of historical debates in our nation over the quality of immigrant groups. The companion debate continued regarding whether bilingualism presented a handicap, with the advent of the psychometric saga, and the measurement of intelligence. Goodenough (1921), for example, stated: "Those nationality groups whose average intellectual ability is inferior do not readily learn the new language" (p. 393).

There were but a few notable exceptions in the literature at this time, consisting of case studies such as Leopold's (1939) investigation. In general, researchers during this era, viewed bilingualism as an independent variable contributing to both intellectual and emotional ill effects. Cummins (1976) and Peal and Lambert (1962) have related the severe methodological flaws with the initial negative findings including careless sampling procedures, classifying bilinguals by surname, comparisons of students labeled either as monolingual or bilingual, and reliance on intelligence testing, to name but a few.

It was not until the 1962 publication of Peal and Lambert's study of bilingual learners in Montreal that a brighter and positive view of bilingualism began to emerge:

> A youngster whose wider experiences in two cultures have given him advantages which a monolingual does not enjoy. Intellectually his experiences with two language systems seems to have left him with a mental flexibility, a superiority in concept formation, a more diverse field set of mental abilities . . . (p. 20)

Peal and Lambert responded to previous research that did not take into account language proficiency by attempting to distinguish between "pseudo" bilinguals and "balanced" bilinguals. Peal and Lambert's research paradigm is considered a methodological pioneering effort in the field. The new paradigm included the control of demographic variables, and the possibility of documenting findings from previous case studies (e.g., Leopold, 1939).

The 1970s ushered an era for the initiation and replication of controlled experimental conditions by researchers in the United States and other countries as a result of the dramatic findings from the St. Lambert Project (Lambert & Tucker, 1972). (The St. Lambert Project was the field study largely responsible for confirming Peal and Lambert's work.) Examples of these research endeavors include:

1. Ianco-Worrall's (1972) study indicating that children raised bilingually were more attentive to semantic relationships than monolinguals

2. Ben-Zeev's (1977) work documenting bilingual childrens' superiority to monolinguals in awareness of linguistic rules and structures

3. Cummins' (1978) investigation, which found bilingual children out-performing monolinguals on a variety of measures of metalinguistic awareness

In addition to the latter work, the positive effects of bilingualism on a variety of cognitive performance measures have been well documented. For example:

1. with regard to divergent thinking and creativity (Torrance, Gowan, Wu, & Alliotti, 1970)

2. concept formation (Cummins & Gulutsan, 1974; Bain, 1974; Liedtke & Nelson, 1968)

3. Piagetian conservation and field independence (De Avila, 1979)

4. the ability to monitor cognitive performance (Bain & Yu, 1980)

5. significant contributions of second language
   proficiency to a variety of cognitive measures
   including the Raven Progressive Matrices
   (Hakuta & Díaz, 1985)

These studies point to the enhancing and positive effects
of bilingualism on cognitive development, yet the negative
deficit philosophy continues to be disseminated across the
educational and political systems of the United States. As
Cummins and Gulutsan (1974) point out, the early negative
findings research continue to have a contemporary ring.
To cite one example:

> Much of this language retardation reflects a loss of a
> vocabulary in the first language that is not fully com-
> pensated for by a corresponding gain in the second lan-
> guage . . . it does have an adverse effect on the growth
> of functional intelligence as measured by verbal tests
> (Ausubel, Sullivan, & Ives, 1980, p. 372).

Negative stereotypical notions continue to misinform
teachers, parents, and policy makers, in spite of the clear research evidence pointing to positive effects. The public's
ambivalent attitude toward language continues to impact
the daily lives of increasingly culturally and linguistically
diverse classrooms. The fact that clear research evidence has
not informed practitioners and the general citizenry needs
to be addressed. The need to disseminate research and literature *counter to current societal perspectives* is vital in
order to enhance classroom practices and the world of the
bilingual learner.

Each generation of researchers bases its investigations on
currently existing knowledge, theoretical frameworks, and
methodologies. Building on previous efforts is essential for
continued enhancement in the field of bilingual education
research. The pioneering efforts of exemplary work include:
Cazden (1988), Cummins (1984), Heath (1983), Hakuta (1986),
Leopold (1939), Krashen, et al. (1982), Peal and Lambert
(1962), Kessler and Quinn (1982), Duncan and De Avila
(1979), Trueba (1987), Wong Fillmore (1976), to name but a
few. These researchers have helped to guide additional

work as well as the examination of theoretical and research concerns.

The intent of this portion of the paper is to highlight selected research endeavors that exemplify broader conceptual frameworks allowing for the discovery of possibilities and away from deficit perspectives. These particular studies are examined more carefully in order to view particular contexts, constructs, and methodologies guiding the research.

Selected research endeavors that exemplify broader conceptual frameworks include:

1. Hawaiian KEEP Project (Au & Jordan, 1981) which found that changing classroom interactions was compatible with existing home participant structures

2. Cazden's (1988) descriptions of classroom discourse

3. Heath's (1983) comparison of two culturally different communities

4. Macías's (1987) descriptions of Papago teacher's intervention strategies

5. Moll's (1989) study viewing classroom literate environments and outstanding teachers

6. Ogbu's (1987) ethnographic descriptions of minority learners responses to schooling

7. Phillips's (1983) view of implicit rules governing interaction patterns at home and at school among students in the Warm Springs Indian Reservation

8. Soto's (1990) descriptions of the home process variables contributing to differential school achievement

9. Wong Fillmore's (1976) descriptions of the individual differences among young second language learners at play

Au and Jordan's (1981) study employed qualitative strategies as well as additional collaborative and interdisciplinary expertise. Researchers in this study observed Hawaiian learners at home and at school and designed school practices that were congruent with the home culture. The learners in the Hawaiian KEEP program experienced success in reading because of an emphasis on mutual turn taking resembling the Hawaiian "talk story" concept, and the encouragement of the comprehension process instead of narrowly focused phonetic approaches. In this particular program the classroom interactions and practices were adapted to meet the needs of the learners and their accompanying home culture. This study underscores the importance of viewing learners' capabilities in a variety of contexts (home and school) and the critical contributions of a culturally compatible classroom to learning. The collaborative interdisciplinary contributions by anthropologists and others to educational research is highlighted since the investigation led to practical classroom applications on behalf of culturally and linguistically diverse learners.

Cazden's (1988) work vividly relates interactions, dialogues, and descriptions of sharing time, teacher and child conversations, lesson implementations, instructional communicative strategies, peer interactions and recent research findings. This particular investigation is chosen as an example because critical analysis of classroom language can enhance children's learning in all settings, including the bilingual classroom. Dr. Cazden's publication is valuable to both practitioners and researchers.

Heath's (1983) description of two communities in the Piedmont Carolinas allows for comparisons among the socialization of language learning within one geographic area. The ethnographic observation of Roadville, a white working-class community with four generations of laborers in the textile mills, and Trackton, a black working-class community whose ancestors farmed the land and became mill workers, illustrates how the language learning experiences of working-class families differs from middle- and upper-middle-class families. The differences in the language learning environments led to very different language learning strategies. In Roadville, the children are "taught" to talk via numerous adult-child interactions and props while the Trackton children live in a world of human verbal and nonverbal communication devoid of props; where children learn to talk without adult interpretations. Heath's study included observations from teachers as researchers, and in a variety of contexts (e.g., community, textile mill). The descriptions and comparisons allowed for careful interpretations of home and community contributions to the language learning environment.

Macías's (1987) ethnographic case study viewed the transition of Papago preschoolers entering their very first school encounter. Descriptions of the discontinuities experienced by the learners and the accompanying teacher reactions revealed the implementation of a "hidden curriculum" by teachers. The hidden curriculum was an attempt on the part of the teachers to ease the discontinuities experienced by the children based upon the teachers' prior experiences. Examples of classroom discontinuities included expectations for speaking up, rule-governed communication, and self-differentiation. The discontinuity lies in the fact that Papago learners are encouraged to rely on nonverbal communication, autonomy, and group norms at home.

Moll's (1989) participant observations viewed literate environments provided by outstanding teachers on behalf of second language learners. The initial theoretical framework proposed by the researcher includes a social perspective, proposed by Vygotsky, and a qualitative methodological approach. The idea of observing expert teachers and describing common themes and salient features enhancing learning is important in helping practitioners to implement successful strategies and successful learning environments. Moll and Díaz (1985) also have described how teacher assumptions about student's proficiency in English affect the quality of instruction. The authors implemented "ethnographic experiments" indicating that the practice of using English oral language proficiency assessment for placement of students in a reading curriculum has created misunderstandings.

Ogbu's (1987) ethnographic investigation and theoretical formulations are important because they explicate the recurrent differential themes affecting culturally and linguistically diverse learners. Ogbu distinguishes immigrant and nonimmigrant status and the accompanying societal responsibility. The schools and the society are given the onus for persistent school failure of the "castelike" minorities in the United States. Both national and international examples are cited by Ogbu in determining a classification system that includes: (1) autonomous groups such as Amish and Mormons; (2) immigrant groups such as Cuban Americans and Japanese Americans; and (3) castelike minorities exemplified by African Americans, Native Americans, and Mexican Americans. "Schools are implicated because they tend more or less to treat minorities so as to prepare them for subordinate positions in the prevailing stratification system" (p. 274).

Phillips's (1983) observation at the Warm Springs Indian Reservation is an example of the need for careful analysis and sensitive interpretations on behalf of culturally and linguistically diverse learners. The interaction patterns taking place in the classroom, when compared with the home cultural expectations, helps to paint a vivid picture of why Native American children have been regarded as "quiet." Differing styles of classroom participation were noted by Phillips's since non-Indian children are expected to impart individualized self-differentiated behaviors by adults; while Indian children are socialized to participate in controlled patterns of language use. The interaction patterns expected at home and the interaction patterns experienced in the classroom differed significantly. This study provides for insight to practitioners interested in gaining a deeper understanding about home and school continuities and discontinuities.

Soto (1991a) compiled a daily diary of observations as a secondary focus to a largely quantitative research design. The qualitative information obtained revealed the important contribution of a bilingual home environment to Puerto Rican (mainlanders) school achievement. The learners considered to be successful by the school district, "higher achievers," came from homes where "language rich environments" were evident. One language was not emphasized to the detriment of another, but instead both the native language and the second language were valued. This information is important for practitioners who make recommendations to parents and for parents raising bilingual learners. Soto (1988) also indicates that parents are told to emphasize English only at home by school teachers; yet the pioneering bilingual researchers (Lambert, 1975; Cummins, 1984) have indicated the importance of native language facility in order to benefit and enhance academic, social, and second language learning. Parents are made to feel that they lack the ability to help their young learners with school work and yet concept learning in the native language is known to transfer to the second language.

Wong Fillmore's (1976) ethnographic study describes the individual differences of five young learners in a variety of environmental contexts (cafeteria, playground, classroom), tasks, strategies, interactions, and accompanying personalities. Among the critical factors suggested by Wong Fillmore as enhancers of second language learning are: personality variables such as social needs, language habits, problem-solving approaches, and motivation. Both the social and cognitive strategies observed by Wong Fillmore indicate that personality factors interacting with the nature of the task and the required strategies determine the rate of second language learning to a great extent. This investigation led researchers to note the pervasiveness of formulas in normal speech and the interplay between formulas and creative speech in second language learning. The qualitative, observational research methods employed by Wong Fillmore allowed for thicker descriptions and the careful analysis of recurrent themes.

The investigations described have originated from a qualitative perspective with either participant observations or ethnographic methodologies. Each of the studies has shed light on the positive attributes of culturally and linguistically diverse learners. In most cases, group observation has avoided yardstick comparisons pointing to one group as having to ultimately measure up to other groups. Most of the investigators have attempted to relate the insider's perspective and have actively observed interactions and the grass-roots, everyday lives of learners and their accompanying learning environment.

These research endeavors have allowed for possibilities and positive perspectives within the initial design, without predetermined or stereotypical philosophies. This type of research will reach a goal of ultimately allowing the present society as a whole an opportunity to view learners in a different light by interpreting a realistic view of strategies, programs, and interactions that are optimal for enhancing learning. The fact that we have learners who are naturally occurring resources for the nation's economic and global advantage shows the need to value the educational research depicting these learners as well as the programs, methodologies, and interactions impacting their educational future.

Researchers, practitioners, and others have a tremendous responsibility to share, if we are truly interested in changing deficit philosophies and perspectives. The positive, successful, and redeeming aspects of growing up with unique capabilities and possibilities must begin to overshadow the deficiencies in order to impact a society that has for too long labeled learners and their accompanying learning environments as limited, deficient, and at risk.

Alternate Paradigms

Bilingual education research stands to benefit from both quantitative and qualitative research designs. Trueba (1987) notes that there are two major theoretical approaches exploring the sociocultural factors of learning and the language minority students: (1) the cultural-ecological approach viewing broad sociological factors; and (2) the context-specific approach relating the organization of teaching and learning activities. Trueba relates the complementary role that these approaches represent and calls for additional theories capable of providing insights regarding "how children can increase their knowledge" (p. 11).

The world of the bilingual learner consists of complex interactions, developmental milestones, learning processes, and personal perceptions; it is embedded in a sociopolitical system, and must negotiate among and between a variety of other systems. Young bilingual learners are introduced to significant others, and later to larger systems and contexts as they travel, interact, and affect their environment. Bilingual learners should not be thought of as deficient vessels nor as helpless victims but rather as lifelong learners, capable of enhancing the surrounding environment. In order to view the enhancing and enriching contributions by learners' alternate paradigms and experimental approaches need to be pursued, encouraged, and mentored. Qualitative research, in particular, allows for the world of the learner to be viewed within a broader theoretical framework, and ultimately helps to uncover important and critical contributions within an ecological context.

For the purpose of this paper, a "possibilities-oriented" paradigm is proposed. Figure 1 shows a possible research model allowing for possibilities within a broad ecologically oriented paradigm.

The idea is to provide more information and thicker descriptions of processes, behaviors, and interactions without being overly concerned with outcome variables or predetermined stereotypical comparisons and notions. For example, a researcher interested in viewing the second language acquisition of young newly arrived immigrants can begin to observe both the intrinsic and extrinsic contributions to the language acquisition process within a variety of contexts. Issues of race, class, gender, and ethnicity are a necessary component of the model due to the sociopolitical implications and contributions to learning from these variables.

Careful qualitative descriptions can begin to explicate the learning process. This type of research underscores the need for sensitive interpretations as has been the case in past research using qualitative and ethnographic approaches. Participant observation, ethnographic methodology, specific, well-grounded evidence, and face-to-face interview formats lend themselves to viewing existing practices and processes without predetermined comparisons. Descriptions of the grass-roots, everyday world of the learner, with the accompanying ecological features, may begin to explicate issues

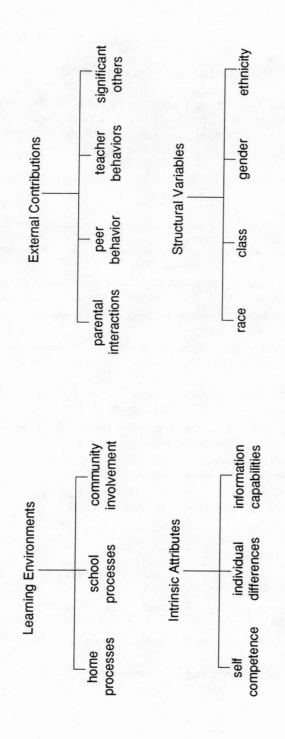

Figure 1

Possibilities-Oriented Paradigm

emanating from the learners' as well as the outsiders' point of view.

As we continue to define a research agenda for the next decade, it is vital to include possibilities-oriented paradigms on behalf of bilingual/bicultural learners in order to ultimately eliminate pervasive deficit philosophies.

References

Au, K., & Jordan, C. (1981). Teaching reading to Hawaiian children: Finding a culturally appropriate solution. In H. T. Trueba & G. P. Guthrie (Eds.), *Culture and the bilingual classroom: Studies in classroom ethnograpy* (pp. 139-152). Rowley, MA: Newbury House.

Ausubel, D., Sullivan, E., & Ives, S. (1980). *Theory and problems of child development* (3rd ed.). New York: Grune and Stratton.

Bain, B. (1975). Toward an integration of Piaget and Vygotsky: Bilingual considerations. *Linguistics, 160,* 7-9.

___, & Yu, A. (1980). Cognitive consequences of raising children bilingually: One parent, one language. *Canadian Journal of Psychology, 34,* 304-313.

Ben-Zeev, S. (1977). The influence of bilingualism on cognitive strategy and cognitive development. *Child Development, 48,* 1009-1018.

Bronfenbrenner, U. (1977). Toward an experimental ecology of human development. *American Psychologist, 32*(7), 513-531.

Cazden, C. (1988). *Classroom discourse. The language of teaching and learning.* Portsmouth, NH: Heinemann.

Crawford, J. (1989). *Bilingual Education: History, politics, theory and practice.* New Jersey: Crane Publishing Company, Inc.

Cummins, J. (1976). The influence of bilingualism on cognitive growth: A synthesis of research findings and explanatory hypotheses. *Working Papers on Bilingualism, 9,* 1-43.

___. (1978). Bilingualism and the development of metalinguistic awareness. *Journal of Cross-cultural Psychology, 9* (2), 131-149.

___. (1979). Linguistic interdependence and the educational development of bilingual children. *Review of Educational Research, 49,* 221-251.

___. (1984). *Bilingualism and special education.* Avon, England: Multilingual Matters.

___, & Gulutsan, M. (1974). Bilingual education and cognition. *The Alberta Journal of Educational Research, 22*(3), 259-269.

Darcy, N. T. (1953). A review of the literature on the effects of bilingualism on the measurement of intelligence. *Journal of Genetic Psychology*, *82*, 21-57.

De Avila, E. (1987). Bilingualism, cognitive function, and language minority group membership. In P. Homel, M. Palij, & D. Aaronson (Eds.), *Childhood bilingualism: Aspects of linguistic, cognitive, and social development*. (pp. 149-166) New Jersey: Lawrence Erlbaum Associates, Publishers.

Díaz, S. (1985). The intellectual power of bilingualism. *The Quarterly Newsletter of the Laboratory of Comparative Human Cognition, 7*, 16-22.

Duncan, S., & De Avila, E. (1979). Bilingualism and cognition. Some recent findings. *NABE Journal, 4*, 15-50.

Hakuta, K. (1986). *Mirror of language*. New York: Basic Books.

____, Ferdman, B. M., & Díaz, R. (1986). *Bilingualism and cognitive development: Three perspectives and methodological implications*. Los Angeles: University of California, Center for Language Education and Research.

Heath, S. (1983). *Ways with words*. Cambridge: Cambridge University Press.

Homel, P., Palij, M., & Aaronson, D. (Eds.). (1987). *Childhood bilingualism: Aspects of linguistic, cognitive, and social development*. New Jersey: Lawrence Erlbaum Associates, Publishers.

Ianco-Worral, A. (1972). Bilingualism and cognitive development. *Child Development, 43*, 1390-1400.

Jensen, V. (1962). Effects of childhood bilingualism, I. *Elementary English, 39*, 132-43.

Kessler, C., & Quinn, M. (1982). Cognitive development in bilingual environments. In B. Hartford, A. Valdman, & C. Foster (Eds.), *Issues in international bilingual education* (pp. 53-79). New York: Plenum.

Krashen, S., Scarcella, R., & Long, M. (Eds.). (1982). *Child-adult differences in second language acquisition*. Massachusetts: Newberry House Publishers, Inc.

Lambert, W. (1975). Culture and language as factors in learning and education. In A. Wolfgang (Ed.), *Education of immigrant students*. (pp. 55-83). Toronto: Ontario Institute for Studies in Education.

Lambert, W. E., & Tucker, G. R. (1972). *Bilingual education of children: The St. Lambert experiment*. Rowley, MA: Newbury House.

Leopold, W. (1939). *Speech development of a bilingual child: A linguist's record. Vol. 1 Vocabulary growth in the first two years.* Evanston, IL: Northwestern University Press.

Liedtke, W., & Nelson, L. (1968). Concept formation in bilingualism. *Alberta Journal of Educational Research, 14*, 225-232.

Macías, J. (1987). The hidden curriculum of Papago teachers. In G. & L. Spindler (Eds.), *Interpretive ethnography of education* (pp. 363-384) New Jersey: Lawrence Erlbaum Associates, Publishers.

McLaughlin, B. (1985). *Second-language acquisition in childhood: Volume 1. Preschool children.* New Jersey: Lawrence Erlbaum Associates, Publishers.

Moll, L. (1987). Teaching second language students: A Vygotskian perspective. In D. Johnson & D. Roen (Eds.), *Richness in Writing.* (pp. 55-67). New York: Longman.

_____, & Díaz, S. (1985). Ethnographic pedagogy: Promoting effective bilingual instruction. In E. García & R. Padilla (Eds.), *Advances in bilingual education research* (pp. 127-149). Tucson: The University of Arizona Press.

Ogbu, J. (1987). Variability in minority responses to schooling. In G. & L. Spindler (Eds.), *Interpretive ethnography of education* (pp. 255-280). New Jersey: Lawrence Erlbaum Associates, Publishers.

Pallas, A., Natriello, G., & McDill, E. (1989). The changing nature of the disadvantaged population: Current dimensions and future trends. *Educational Researcher, 18*(5), 16-22.

Peal, E., & Lambert, W. E. (1962). The relation of bilingualism to intelligence. *Psychological Monographs: General and Applied, 76* (27, Whole No. 546), 1-23.

Phillips, S. (1983). *The invisible culture: Communication in classroom and community on the Warm Springs Reservation.* New York: Longman.

Pintner, R., & Arsenian, S. (1937). The relation of bilingualism to verbal intelligence and school adjustment. *Journal of Educational Research, 31*, 255-263.

Saer, D. J. (1923). The effects of bilingualism on intelligence. *British Journal of Psychology, 14*, 25-38.

Slavin, R. (1989). Disadvantaged vs. at-risk: Does the difference matter in practice? Paper presented at the American Research Association, San Francisco.

Smith, M. E. (1939). Some light on the problem of bilingualism as found from a study of the progress in mastery of English among preschool children of non American ancestry in Hawaii. *Genetic Psychology Monographs, 21*, 119-284.

Soto, L. D. (1988, Spring). A collaborative bilingual parent education program. *Journal of Educational Issues of Language Minority Students, 2*, 27-29.

____. (1990). The relationship between home environment and the motivational orientation of higher and lower achieving Puerto Rican children. *Educational Research Quarterly, 13*(1), 22-36.

____. (1991a). Families as learning environments: Reflections on critical factors affecting differential achievement. The Pennsylvania State University, University Park, PA. (under review)

____. (1991b). Success stories. In C. Grant (Ed.), *Research directions for multicultural education*. New York: Falmer Press.

Spradley, J. (1980). *Participant observation*. Fort Worth: Holt, Rinehart and Winston, Inc.

Torrance, E., Gowan, J., Wu, J., & Alliotti, N. (1970). Creating functioning of monolingual and bilingual children in Singapore. *Journal of Educational Psychology, 61*, 72-75.

Trueba, H. T. (Ed.). (1984). *Success or failure? Learning and the language minority student*. New York: Newbury House Publishers.

Weinreich, U. (1953). *Languages in contact: Findings and problems*. New York: Linguistic Circle of New York. Reprinted by Mouton, The Hague, 1974.

Wong Fillmore. (1976). *The second time around: Cognitive and social strategies in second language acquisition*. Unpublished doctoral dissertation, Stanford University, Stanford, CA.

CRITICAL PEDAGOGY IN BILINGUAL EDUCATION: LANGUAGE PROFICIENCY AND BILINGUALISM

Antonio Simões
Fairfield University

ABSTRACT

This work examines first and second language acquisition by using sociology of knowledge as a major theoretical framework. It is suggested that language development is grounded in the distribution of knowledge and that second language development is not a neutral social act. It is inferred that the relationship between first and second language acquisition is not only a political act but that there is also a linguistic correspondence between the first and second language. This chapter also examines the role of positivism as it relates to language proficiency, testing, and language assessment.

This chapter provides an analysis of language production, language use, language proficiency, and bilingualism from the perspective that first and second language acquisition are based on the social construction of reality. From this point of view, several general themes will be addressed throughout this chapter. They are:

1. Language production, language use, language proficiency, and bilingualism are not neutral social acts. Since language development and language acquisition are a social construction of reality, first and second language acquisition must be analyzed from different paradigms in the social sciences.

2. The relationship between the first and a second language in language production, use, and proficiency may be more powerful than we realize. A political, social, and linguistic

correspondence may take place while one is learning a new or second language.

3. Language production, use, and proficiency are not acts that are outside of what society values. The use of language at home, in a social gathering, or in school reflects what society values and what society rewards within the political and educational realm.

4. Language production, use, and proficiency as these phenomena relate to first and second language acquisition, will be used synonymously. Although language production may be viewed as a domain where language can be measured or tested, and although language use may be a domain for a social context, and although language proficiency has its own literature in first and second language acquisition and bilingualism, for the purposes of this chapter all of these categories will be known as language development. For us, language development is a result of the distribution of knowledge, and consequently, language development is a socially constructed reality.

The Distribution of Knowledge in Society as it Relates to First and Second Language Acquisition

Language development is by no means a simple issue. There are many layers of inquiry that permeate several fields in the social sciences. Each level of analysis has its own logic. Language development in first and second language acquisition is governed by the distribution of knowledge and the distribution of language. Language development in the first and second language is socially constructed and is interdependent, and possibly a singular additive process (Botha, 1989; Chomsky, 1965, 1980, 1982; Ellis, 1986; Ervin-Tripp, 1978). It is an attempt to construct a theoretical framework that infers that second language acquisition is not only interdependent with one's first language, but may be an integral extension of its own social construction or first language universe.

The timeworn but still very useful Kuhnian (1962) idea that each paradigm reflects *one* finite view of reality is particularly important because of the focus on knowledge distribution and how this process affects linguistic development and second language acquisition. For us, the major question is the following If it is assumed that knowledge and language development in the first and second language possess the same characteristics in language learning, then, are "both" of these domains socially constructed into one language universe?

Language proficiency is not just a neutral and quantifiable entity but also a sociopolitical process based on the social construction of the child's reality. Many empirical researchers tend to reject the approach that language development in the first and second language are products of a distribution of knowledge and distribution of language. For them to accept this premise is to accept that language can not be studied in an "objectified" way. Giroux (1981) speaks to this issue when he claims that the process of schooling is controlled by the positivistic school or by empirical researchers. What is more important is his claim that empiricism is an ideology where knowledge is analyzed from a positivistic paradigm. This is also true, in part, in the field of bilingual education where theory building, decision making, and evaluating children's first and second language is derived from a positivistic model. An example is the popular use of the Language Assessment Battery Test, where children are tested and then placed or tracked into specific educational programs. I am not suggesting that the use of empiricism is not a valuable tool to better understand our society. However, by only using an empirical paradigm to evaluate a child's language without understanding the sociological nature of first and second language acquisition, the ideology of empiricism shuts out other ways to explore the meaning of language development.

The fundamental premise considered here is that language development in the first and second language has roots in the distribution of knowledge and the distribution of language. If one accepts this assumption, some of the literature in bilingual education may be reconsidered from the perspective that language development is a political act. From this point of view, language development has an important role dealing with complex sociopedagogical issues.

By using the sociology of knowledge or the sociology of language as a social distribution of what reality is and how it is "objectified," one can infer that first- and second-language acquisition may be a single process where the semantic system becomes additive as one learns a "new" language. This premise does not deny the existence of two language systems. It implies that the process of acquiring a new language is much more complex if one adds social construction as a variable to the study of language development. One question of many is the following What is the on-going relationship in language development between L1 and L2? Our problem goes further because we are accepting the fact that there is a relationship between the first and second language. The idea of an on-going-relationship brings on different questions (Burt, Dulay & Hernández, 1973; Cummins, 1980, 1982; Simões, 1983; Weinreich, 1974). Understanding first- and second-language interaction as an "on-going relationship" becomes problematic in that L1 must be examined as it *forms, influences, shapes, and creates* L2.

Language Development and Bilingualism as They Relate to Knowledge and Language Distribution

It is generally accepted in the field of sociology that knowledge use and function produces different ways of knowing, depending on the sociopsychological background of the individual (Berger & Luckmann, 1967; Fishman, 1989; Krashen, 1980). It is also assumed that knowledge is valued differently The possession of specific knowledge in one society may have a totally different contextual value in another (Simões, 1979). Even in monolingual settings, the distribution of knowledge and language is contextualized in terms of value in both *qualitative* and *quantitative* terms. The use of language both in quantitative terms (how much I know) and qualitative terms (what is valued by what I know) is important when one understands how language is used in relation to cultural capital (Apple, 1979). For example, when someone asks me what I do for a living, the first response is I am a college professor. This reply usually brings a positive reaction. When asked what do I teach, I have a variety of responses. I can say that I teach curriculum theory, sociolinguistics, language acquisition, or bilingual education. The former three usually bring further discussions about the field, and I rarely have to defend what I teach. In many instances, however, when I say that I teach bilingual education, the reactions are usually hostile and negative. Hence, I have the same quantitative knowledge but, how society *values* knowledge brings on different emotions.

The possession of knowledge in different contexts brings on different ways that language is used and produced both in the first and second language. From a qualitative point of view, the use of the distribution of knowledge and language leads us to many complex issues about social class, the use of a "dialect," and language-in-contact. This is because we use language through concrete, immediate forms of objectivity to convey a meaning. As Berger and Luckmann (1967) state:

> Language originates in and has its primary reference to everyday life; it refers above all to reality I experience in wide awake consciousness, which is dominated by the pragmatic matrix (that is, the cluster of meaning directly pertaining to the present or future actions) and which I share with others in a taken-for-granted manner. Although language can also be employed to other realities.it even then retains its rootage in the common sense reality of everyday life. As a sign system, language has the quality of objectivity. (p. 35)

It is important that we accept that language development has the "quality" of objectivity in what-I-know is true-and-real-to-me. As stated previously, the school of empiricism treats knowledge as something to "know" in a quantitative form and has a "neutral" quality (Apple, 1979; Giroux, 1981). Knowledge and language development are usually measured by normed tests. What is critical is that normed tests and even individualized tests, do not explain the sociological process of language distribution between the first and second language. Quantifiable tests center around knowledge and language distribution where the results relate to a fixed discriminatory entity that places children in prescribed categories. More dangerously, "objective" tests are seen as neutral, valid, reliable, and bias free. However, I contend that knowledge is expressed through language, and language development is not a fixed domain. Language used by the members of a society has a sociohistorical context in which knowledge and language development are valued in specific sociopedagogical contexts (Simões, 1982, 1984). When knowledge is viewed as a socially distributed function, both knowledge and language become qualitative in nature. The distribution of knowledge and language always represents value on what society considers important. If this paradigm is accepted, other questions arise in the field of second language acquisition and "bilingualism."

Now what about language development in particular? Is first- and second-language acquisition a representation of knowledge and reality? How is language learned from a value point of view? Let us investigate these notions in detail.

Language and knowledge create a sociolinguistic reality in which the production of language reflects "objectivity" or what is known-to-me. Language can be used to express "what is" and can be used in many forms. The use of knowledge is constructed through language that represents a social construction with a value-latent orientation. Due to the assumption that language development has a neutral value, society tends to "standardize" language as something spoken by the majority. If one deviates from the "norm," sometimes it is suggested that one is "below a standard." However, language is used by different people in different social classes to convey similar and different meanings. Haugen (1976) expressed this view several years ago when he wrote:

> The concept of "norm" in reference to language is highly ambiguous and slippery. It may refer to a standardized language like French, codified in grammars and sanctified by an Academy, taught in schools, and

> written by authors, but spoken by no one, except under
> duress. Any deviation from such a norm is deemed to
> reveal one's lack of a proper education, and is regarded
> as barbarism if it is unintentional. But it may be ac-
> ceptable if it is an intentional stylistic variation,
> either as a mockery of the lower classes or as a relax-
> ation of standards, a kind of "old shoe." (p. 91)

If language development is a political act that is socially constructed where language distributes knowledge, does the literature in second-language acquisition and bilingualism suggest sociopolitical and pedagogical relationships between the first and second language? Let us now review some of the literature in the field.

Language Development from a Sociopolitical Perspective in the Literature on First and Second Language Acquisition

Before I begin this discussion, I do realize that the litera- ture in the field on first and second language acquisition and bilingualism is extensive. I have selected some of the popu- lar researchers in bilingual education not to refute their assumptions but to create a way to analyze language development through the use of the sociology of knowledge and the sociology of language. It is only *one* way to look at and understand first-and second-language acquisition.

The field of bilingual education has changed much of its emphasis from socioeconomic and cultural factors related to the success of schooling to positivistic paradigms, especially in the areas of first- and second-language acquisition (Fantini, 1985; Krashen, 1980; Rivera, 1984 a & b; Lantolf & Dipietro, 1984) and language proficiency and assessment (Cummins, 1980; Simões, 1983).

This is not to say that social factors such as language loy- alty, (Fishman, 1966; Gardner & Lambert, 1972) language sta- tus, (Simões, 1984), and social class (Simões & Correia, 1974) are not discussed in curriculum design. To void socioeco- nomic factors and cultural variations in linguistic theory, especially in first and second language acquisition, would be to negate an essential analysis in understanding what language development entails in relation to language production in society. That is, the *process* of language acquisition may implicitly carry other domains other than the analysis of the distribution of knowledge that profoundly affect the acquisition of a second language. In the context of knowledge distribution, one basic question must be asked "Does the acquisition of the first language affect the acquisition of the other languages? Although the research in this area is contradictory, there are strong indications that there is a relationship between first-language acquisition and the acquisition of other languages (Cummins, 1979, 1982). Cummins discusses the interdependent hypothesis and how the first language affects and interacts with the second language. Since his first writings, the field has evolved. Now, the paradigm of interlanguage has replaced interdependence (Ellis, 1986). The concept of interlanguage creates new questions in both language transfer and social class. Although Cummins' recent writings do not use the terms BICS (Basic Interpersonal Communicative Skills) and CALP (Cognitive Academic Language Proficiency), his early writings introduced the paradigm of language interdependence in relation to BICS and CALP. BICS describes a stage of language where the child is able to communicate in the second language. CALP describes a stage where a child is able to communicate on a social level and compete on an academic level. Although these assumptions are valuable for educators to understand schooling and the bilingual child, they do not *directly* address the issue of the distribution of knowledge and the distribution of language. Cummins's theory becomes politically neutral and does not directly address the *social* relationship between the first and the second language. Edelsky, Hudelson, Flores, Barkin, Altwerger, and Jilbert (1983) took on this issue and questioned some of Cummins and Swain's conclusions about the relationship between BICS and CALP. Edelsky et al. (1983) went further to label Cummins and Swain's assumptions on second language learning as a "deficit theory" Cummins and Swain (1983) responded to this issue, but never directly dealt with language development as it relates to the distribution of knowledge. It is true that some of their arguments revolved around "conceptual-linguistic knowledge," but the concepts of BICS and CALP give us a way to look at knowledge and language development. If one accepts that language is concrete and real and that language is distributed in society, the concepts of BICS and CALP become confusing. BICS in one language or in a specific context may be CALP in a different language. If language is concrete and if language is contextualized through knowledge, BICS and CALP may be interchanged depending on the knowledge of the individual. For example, I am not knowledgeable about farming nor do I posses the language of farming, therefore a farmer's language may be BICS for him or her where this language becomes a CALP situation for me. I also do not possess knowledge in medicine or in accounting. If I were to understand these fields, would I have to enter a new CALP stage? In other words, one's knowledge may have a direct relationship to second language acquisition. If one does not accept that knowledge is socially constructed and distributed through language development, and if one does not accept that first and second language acquisition is an interdependent process that may have a socially constructed universe, then language development becomes "neutralized" as only something to be measured.

Accepting that knowledge is socially constructed and that first and second language acquisition may be in the same socially constructed universe, many issues come into focus. For example, if a student is not proficient in the first language in the areas of mathematics, grammar, reading, writing, and social studies, what will be the knowledge transfer from one language to another? If *knowledge is language,* are the concepts of BICS and CALP somewhat artificial constructs when it comes to the distribution of knowledge, the distribution of language, and social class? A CALP concept in one language may be a BICS concept in another. Complicating the thesis further, if a student is proficient in the first language, second language communicative competence in a school environment does not guarantee that a child is capable of performing *academic* tasks in the second or third language.

Although more research is needed, several inferences can be made. Language is not only a linguistic function, it is a function of knowledge use. Knowledge is distributed in society and consequently, when linguistic relationships between first and second language are used, knowledge transfer must be recognized. The research seems to indicate that success in schooling is related to language proficiency, usually in the native language of the child. However, language proficiency can no longer be defined as *only* knowledge in a specific domain. It is not known if CALP can be reached in the second language without passing through CALP in the first language. Again, the more the variables introduced in the area of language development, the more complicated the research.

Another avenue to explore is what Krashen (1980) termed the "silent period." He claimed that children need to listen to language for a long period of time before uttering the speech, the word, or the concept. However, using our point of departure that language development may be based on the distribution of knowledge, the "silent period" may not be silent at all. Krashen (1977) also discussed the monitor model in which children "filter" language from one language to another. However, there seems to be no indication that both processes are evolving at different time frames. Besides Krashen's filter theory, one has to consider the Input Hypothesis. According to Krashen (1980), one acquires the second language by understanding the linguistic input equal to, or a little beyond, the level of the first language. Krashen's theoretical frameworks seem to be correct, but he does not answer the *sociological* question on what is "input" or "monitored."

Research indicates that age may make a difference in language acquisition both in quality and quantity (McLaughlin, 1985). On the other hand, there are some researchers who claim that age is *not* the crucial factor in language acquisition, but that certain features of language acquisition occur at different ages (Chun, 1980). As Chamot (1981) stated "Ervin-Tripp (1978) studied the acquisition of French by thirty-one English speaking children in Geneva, ranging in age from four to nine, and found that the older children learned phonology, morphology, and syntax faster than the younger children. She attributed this to the fact that older children know more about language through their first language proficiency and they have developed more sophisticated cognitive strategies for learning in general" (p. 2). Here is where the sociopolitical framework, knowledge, and language distribution come into play. That is, there seems to be a relationship of the first and second language *depending* on the research focus. The question is what point does the sociology of language come into play when learning a second language?

Some researchers argue that there may be no extension between the first and second language and that language development could be a single process with only semantic changes (Chomsky, 1965, 1980, 1982; Ellis, 1986; Ervin-Tripp, 1978). This paradigm suggests that language development is a *single additive process.* I do realize that using the phrase a "single additive process," can create several conflicting paradigms. Be that as it may, what is important is being aware of various schools of thought when using the term additive to language development.

Again, accepting that the distribution of knowledge relates to the distribution of language and language development, second language acquisition cannot be analyzed as a neutral process. Critical pedagogy comes into play here because to consider language acquisition from an apolitical point of view is to accept theoretical frameworks that skirt the issue of social class and knowledge distribution. Unfortunately, it is now popular in the educational literature in bilingual education to be "objective," bias free. Using this so-called objective position, it becomes an ideological framework, a sort of hegemony in the literature. In bilingual education, the phenomenon of objectivity has gained more support than it deserves. Although it may serve to soothe the opposition when the field is attacked on its failures, it muffles a true dialogue among our colleagues.

There are many more fundamental questions that deal with the complex issue of language acquisition, social class, and the distribution of knowledge. Several assumptions can be formulated within the context of this chapter. Based on the latest research findings, one general inference can be formulated. There is a strong relationship between first language acquisition and the learning of other languages. This seems to indicate that the child should remain in the native language *until* he or she is able to succeed academically in the second or third language. Based on these generalizations, the following statements can be made:

1. Second language development/acquisition seems to be similar to first language learning.

2. Language development/learning/second language acquisition may be a political act.

3. Language development/learning/acquisition may be socially constructed.

4. Second language should be contextualized to relate to the native language.

5. Testing children for language proficiency does not deal with social issues nor with many types of language use.

6. The literature in the field of bilingual education generally does not incorporate the sociology of knowledge in language development and in first and second language acquisition.

Finally, I feel that I would be guilty by omission if I did not deal with some of the political issues that revolve around the thesis that knowledge and language development are socially constructed. To accept that language use and language development are a political acts is to be politically and culturally sensitive to children and parents who are not presently empowered to make educational decisions. The misplacement of many bilingual children, especially in special education classes, is unacceptable. An ideological system that historically has refused to look at and value children who are not English proficient cannot lead to a sound educational system. The field of bilingual education must go beyond testing language proficiency. We must be careful with the ideology of empiricism. Quality education goes beyond testing. Quality education deals with a true multicultural curriculum where children have access to knowledge in a warm, supportive, and familiar educational environment.

I will end with a quotation that in some ways summarizes this chapter "In this dynamic rivalry between house and universe, we are far removed from any reference to simple geometrical forms. A house that has been experienced is not an inert box. Inhabited space transcends geometrical space." (Bachelard, 1958, p. 47). Could it be that our "inhabited space" is our experienced knowledge that we carry from one language to another?

References

Apple, M. W. (1979). *Ideology and curriculum.* London: Routledge and Kegan Paul.

Bachelard, G. (1958). *The poetics of space.* NY: The Orion Press.

Berger, P., & Luckmann, T. (1967). *The social construction of reality.* New York: Anchor.

Botha, R. (1989). *Challenging Chomsky:The generative garden game.* New York : Basil Blackwell Ltd.

Burt, M., Dulay, H., & Hernández, E. (1973). *Bilingual syntax measure.* New York: Harcourt Brace Jovanovich.

Chamot, A. U. (1981). Applications of second language acquisition research to the bilingual classroom. *Focus, 10,* 1-8. Rosslyn, VA: National Clearinghouse for Bilingual Education.

Chomsky, N. (1965). *Topics in the theory of generative grammar.* Cambridge, MA: M.I.T. Press.

____. (1980). Rules and representations. *The Behavioral and Brain Sciences, 3,* 1-15, 42-61.

____. (1982). *The generative enterprise A discussion with R. Hubregys and H. van Riemsdiljk.* Dordrecht Foris Publications.

Chun, J. (1980, Fall). A survey of research in second language acquisition. *Modern Language Journal,* 287-96.

Cummins, J. (1979). Linguistic interdependence and the educational development of bilingual children. *Review of Educational Research, 49,* 222-51.

____. (1980). The cross-lingual dimensions of language proficiency Implications for bilingual education and the optimal age issue. *TESOL, 14*, 175-188.

____. (1982). *Interdependence and bicultural ambivalence regarding the pedagogical rationale for bilingual education.* Rosslyn, VA: National Clearinghouse for Bilingual Education.

____, & Swain, M. (1983). Analysis-by-rhetoric Reading the text or the readers' own projections? Reply to Edelsky et al. *Applied Linguistics,* 4 (1), 23-41.

Edelsky, C., Hudelson, S., Flores, B., Barkin, F., Altwerger, B., & Jilbert, K. (1983). Semilingualism and language deficit. *Applied Linguistics,* 4(1), 1-21.

Ellis, R. (1986). *Understanding second language acquisition.* Oxford: Oxford University Press.

Ervin-Tripp, S. (1978). Is second language learning like the First? In E. Hatch, (Ed.), *Second language acquisition* (pp. 190-206). Rowley, MA: Newbury House Publishers.

Fantini, A. E. (1985). *Language acquisition of the bilingual child A sociolinguistic perspective.* San Diego, CA: College Hill Press.

Fishman, J. (1966). *Language loyalty in the United States.* The Hague, Netherlands: Mouton & Co.

____. (1989). *Language & ethnicity in minority sociolinguistic perspective,* Philadelphia, PA : Multilingual Matters.

Gardner, R. C., & Lambert, W. E. (1972). *Attitudes and motivation in second language learning.* Rowley, MA : Newbury House.

Giroux, H. A. (1981). *Ideology culture & the process schooling.* Philadelphia, PA : Temple University Press.

Haugen, E. (1976). Norm and deviation in bilingual communities. In P. A. Hornby (Ed.), *Bilingualism Psychological, social, and educational implications* (pp. 91-102). New York Academic Press.

Krashen, S. (1977). Some issues relating to the monitor model. In H. D. Brown, Yorio, C., & Crymes, R. (Eds.), *On TESOL 75, TESOL,* 144-158.

____. (1980). The input hypothesis. In E. Alatis (Ed.), *Current issues in bilingual education* (pp.168-180). Washington, D.C.: Georgetown University Press.

Kuhn, T. S. (1962). *The structure of scientific revolutions.* Chicago: University of Chicago Press.

Lantolf, J., & Dipietro, R. (1984). *Second language acquisition in the classroom setting.* Norwood, NJ : Ablex Publishing Co.

McLaughlin, B. (1985). *Second language acquisition in childhood.* Hillsdale, NJ : Lawrence Erlbaum Associates.

Rivera, C. (1984a). *Communicative competence approaches to language proficiency assessment Research and application.* Clecedon, England: Multilingual Matters Ltd.

____. (1984b). *Language proficiency and academic achievement.* Clecedon, England: Multilingual Matters Ltd.

Simões, A. (1979). Systems context approach in bilingual education. In M. Montero (Ed.), *Bilingual education teacher handbook strategies for the design of multicultural curriculum* (pp. 7-25). Cambridge, MA: National Assessment and Dissemination Center, Lesley College.

____. (1982). Data banks revisited The use of informational systems in a multilingual-multicultural environment. In R. V. Padilla (Ed.), *Ethnoperspectives in bilingual education research, volume 3* (pp. 144-159). Ypsilanti: Eastern Michigan University.

____. (1983). Image production in two languages Its implications in testing the bilingual child. In S. Seidner (Ed.), *Issues of language assessment Language assessment and curriculum planning, volume 2* (pp. 39-34). Chicago: Illinois State Board of Education.

____. (1984). Technology and literacy Who gets the economic benefits? New York University, *University, 3*(4), 12.

____, & Correia, V. (1974, May 25). O sistema escolar americano e o imigrante. *The Portuguese Times,* New Bedford, MA.

Weinreich, U. (1974). *Languages in contact.* The Hague: Mouton Publishers.

LINKING CRITICAL PEDAGOGY TO BILINGUAL EDUCATION: AN ETHNOHISTORICAL STUDY CONTEXTUALIZING SCHOOL POLICIES IN AN URBAN COMMUNITY[1]

Martha Montero-Sieburth
Mark LaCelle-Peterson
Harvard Graduate School of Education

ABSTRACT

In the current debate on bilingual education, misrepresentations of the past and misconceptions of the present and the future are invoked by critics. We describe the past and present realities of an immigrant community in the northeast as a case study. Guided by Paulo Freire's critical pedagogy, we present an analysis of past and present interactions between immigrants and the community's schools. Though today's bilingual education program was not intended to foster politicization of the immigrant community, we suggest that it has created institutional space for greater politicization and for greater human agency on the part of present-day immigrants than was available to their predecessors in earlier waves of newcomers.

Each successive generation of immigrants to the United States is met by institutions embodying expectations that have developed in the experiences of previous immigrants and immigrant groups. Education policies embody these expectations, and represent the results of negotiation between earlier generations of immigrants and the established members of the community. During the four decades between 1924 and 1965, however, restrictive immigration laws practically halted immigration, and the memories of immigrant adjustment and education became more distant. Temporal distance has led to a somewhat idealized version of the experiences of earlier immigrant groups (Perlmann, 1990). Today's "established community members" commonly believe that immigrants of the 19th and early 20th centuries were able to learn English, assimilate into American society, and succeed economically because of the influence of schooling. This belief, embodied in local school policies and practices, today shapes the controversial institutional environment of bilingual education programs.

This chapter presents an analysis of the ethnohistorical context of one urban community as embodied in the development of school policies from 1890 to 1920 and from 1970 to 1990 in order to: (1) describe a community that has experienced ongoing cultural diversity and transitions, (2) consider the economic and political significance of schooling for immigrant groups in these two periods, (3) challenge the misconceptions of uniform and unilinear acculturation and assimilation of the earlier groups, and (4) examine the role of bilingual education as the site of contestation over the meaning of schooling for today's immigrants.

We will consider the political interests that operate in establishing and maintaining bilingual education as the current method of induction for immigrants. Guided by Freire's conception of critical pedagogy, we will look at the historical experience of this concrete local context, consider the implications of cultural analysis, and discuss the contradictions inherent in educational differentiation that purports to maintain equality of educational opportunity. Before turning to a description of the context and analysis, we will describe our research method and data sources.

Research Questions and Method

We considered a range of questions about immigration and school policies:

1. What policies developed between 1890 and 1920 and between 1970 and 1990 for integrating immigrants into this urban community's schools?

2. Whose interests were represented in the differentiation within the common school?

3. What political and economic commitments were at play in the policy implementation at the local level?

4. Have these interests and commitments been perpetuated in present policies?

Though not conclusively answered, these questions have guided our examination and analysis of historical and current sources. Because personal accounts of students' and teachers' daily experiences in the classrooms of the late 19th and early 20th centuries were not available, we have used policy statements from the earlier period to examine the schooling processes. The issues of interests, commitments, and political roles will be examined through: (1) historical documentation, (2) bilingual education program sources, and (3) field notes and transcripts from teacher meetings.

Personal computers facilitated the data management and analysis. An extensive corpus of notes summarizing pertinent information and quoting particularly salient passages from the narrative portions of historical and contemporary policy documents was compiled. We developed a software application using HyperCard™2 to manage the data from the historical documents; each note or excerpted passage was entered into a facsimile of a note card on the computer and assigned one or more code words, which were also entered on the card. Each card included an additional "field" for initial interpretive or analytic comments by the researcher. Both printed compilations of the data that had been assigned a certain code, and on-line searches of the data were used in analysis. The Ethnograph software package was used for the analysis of interview and teacher meeting transcripts and field notes from classroom observations. Triangulation of the data sources resulted in a matrix of categories from which propositional statements were developed.

The Community: A History of Cultural Diversity and Transition

This Northeastern urban community, situated on 1.86 square miles of land two miles north of the region's urban center, has been an immigrant community since its incorporation in 1739. Our analysis focuses on the periods of 1890 to 1920 and 1970 to 1990. Both of these periods saw the arrival of significant numbers of non-English speaking immigrants. In the first period, different waves of Irish, Italian, Polish, and Jewish immigrants came to the community. Beginning in the 1960s and continuing through the present, large numbers of Southeast Asians, Caribbeans, Central and South Americans have moved there. The latest arrivals have made up the student body of the bilingual program. The local schools have responded to these recent demographic changes following patterns of expectations carried over from the experience of previous groups.

The community grew rapidly in the "old immigration" period; in 1830 its inhabitants numbered under 1,000, and by 1865 its total population exceeded 14,000. Immigrants accounted for 28 percent of the population in 1855, and for 20 percent in 1865. Irish immigrants were the most numerous, accounting for 17 percent of the population in 1855 and for 12 percent in 1865 (Handlin, 1979). After the Civil War, the proportion of immigrants in the community grew slightly, and the population continued to grow steadily. In the 1890s, changes in the immigrant population that would set the tone for the ethnic make-up of the city for the first half of the 20th century began. The composition of the community's population in the period of the "new immigration" is summarized in Tables 1 and 2. Immigrants from the Russian, rather than the British, empire became the largest group of newcomers; Russian Jews made up the majority of these new arrivals.

Fire ravaged the community in April of 1908. Losses in life and property were large, and the city was placed under

TABLE 1

Nativity of Residents, 1875 to 1915

Year	All Immi- grants	(%)	British Empire	(%)	Russian Empire	(%)	Total Pop- ulation
1875	4,511	21	4,207	20	3	—	21,200
1890	7,934	29	6,899	25	82	—	27,800
1900	11,203	33	7,815	23	2,194	7	34,000
1905	13,883	37	6,713	18	4,487	12	37,300
1910	13,829	43	4,770	15	6,922	21	32,500
1915	19,297	44	5,362	12	11,225	26	43,400

Source: Kopf (1974, p. 44). Figures derived from federal and state censuses.

TABLE 2

Nativity of Residents, 1900 to 1915

Year	U.S. Born of U.S. Parents	(%)	U.S. Born of Immigrant Parents	(%)	Foreign Born	(%)
1900	10,728	33	11,534	34	11,029	32
1905	11,686	31	11,720	31	13,883	37
1910	6,969	22	11,460	35	13,748	43
1915	7,168	16	16,694	38	19,188	46

Source: Kopf (1974, p. 43) Figures derived from state and federal censuses.

the governance of a Board of Control by the state government for the period of recovery. The dip in population from 37,300 in 1905 to 32,500 in 1910 reflects the loss of housing in the conflagration (see Table 1). Likewise, the school census in the spring of 1908 found only 4,630 school-aged children, a sharp drop from 7,440 the year before. The decline in population and enrollment was temporary, however; by 1916 population, enrollment, and the proportion of immigrants in the population had all reached new highs.

Many of the old settler families left the city beginning in the 1880s (Pratt, 1930), and those that remained generally lived in the hill sections of town in single-family houses. Table 2 shows that people whose parents were born in the United States decreased in proportion to the total population from 1900, and in absolute terms from 1905. By 1915, 84 percent of the population was made up of first- and second-generation immigrants. The occupation of the work force in this era was split between manufacturing (which employed half the workers), trade (which employed one fifth), and transportation, clerical, and domestic service (which each occupied an equal part of another quarter of the work force) (Kopf, 1974, p. 35).

The Community Present: 1950-1990

Unskilled and skilled immigration to the community reached its peak in 1925 when the population was 47,505, of whom over 40 percent were foreign-born. The great depression of the 1930s resulted in a steady decline in industries and businesses. Beginning in the 1940s and continuing through the mid-1950s, construction of a major bridge and expressway through central residential neighborhoods forced many residents to move. The building of the bridge had significant consequences:

1. Since the bridge went *over* the city, a transportation "vacuum" was created, making the adjacent city inaccessible to many in the community.

2. Health risks and complications, resulting
   from lead paint peeling off the bridge, from
   the heavy traffic fumes, and noise pollution,
   have contaminated nearby homes and schools
   (Beltran, Rodríguez, Straussman, & Zweig,
   1976).

Densely settled, the community has the highest concentration of multiple family dwellings in the state (Beltran et
al., 1976:9). It is also the third poorest community in the
state; total annual family income averages around $11,500,
and it is estimated that one fourth of the total population of
over 25,000 receive welfare funds. Conflagrations and urban
development have changed the character of this community
from an "intimate" city of small neighborhoods at arms-
length from its urban neighbor to an impoverished, isolated
urban center.

In the face of physical and economic changes, many pros-
pering families left the city for the suburbs, creating "white
flight" and an overall decline in the city's population. "The
out-migration of middle- to high-income families, propor-
tionate growth in numbers of aged and youth remaining or
coming into the city," plus the fact that "approximately *50
percent of [the city's] limited land is non-taxable, which re-
stricts the flow of capital within the city*," (Beltran et al.,
1976, p. 10, emphasis added) contributed to the limited
economic growth and development. The city has been characterized recently as suffering from "institutionalized neglect"—not much is done to deal with drop-out rates, poor
achievement scores, retention of students, absenteeism,
teenage pregnancy, and underpaid teachers (Botsford, 1989).
New school facilities have not been built for over 50 years.

Against this background of declining population, limited
economic base, and capital flow, the influx of Latinos[3] began
in the 1950s when the first three families from Puerto Rico
arrived (Rosa, 1985). Other groups followed from the 1960s
to the present: Dominicans, Cubans, Costa Ricans, Mexicans, Columbians, and Argentinians. By the 1970 census,
Puerto Ricans accounted for 15 percent of the total population. More recently, in the 1980s, immigrants from El Sal-

vador, Nicaragua, Honduras, and other Central American countries have added to their numbers. Peoples' reasons for immigrating vary; many come seeking attainment of a better economic life, others to reunite with family, to pursue educational opportunities, and to find refuge from war-torn homelands or from political repression (Rosa, 1985).

Individual Latinos' access to positions in the city's political structure, (e.g., in the police and fire departments, in the city hall offices, and in the schools), and most recently on the school committee and in the superintendency contrasts with the lack of organizational unification of Latinos (Rosa, 1985). While their rise in the *political* structure has been slow, Latinos have contributed to the economic base of the community by owning and managing 38 businesses, including 8 markets, 1 large food warehouse, 1 bakery, 2 coffee shops, 5 restaurants, 6 clothing stores, 1 travel agency, 1 hairdressing establishment, 7 churches, 1 shoe store, and 1 barber shop (Rosa, 1985, p. 10).

Immigrants and School Policies: 1890-1920 and 1970-1990

Schooling from 1890 to 1920:
Standardization Meets Diversity

By 1890, the public school system in the community had taken roughly the form that it retains to the present, though the terminology and participation rates differed from today's. Children entered the school system in the first grade of a neighborhood primary school (there was no public kindergarten yet, though a charity kindergarten had been established); they remained in the primary school for at least three years. Ideally, the student completed one grade each year—an arrangement that we take for granted today, but which was just 20 years old in 1890. Students who had completed the work of the primary schools entered fourth grade in one of the grammar schools. The fourth grade class of 1890 was coeducational, but many of these students' older siblings had attended the gender-segregated grammar schools that existed from 1845 to 1888. In entering the grammar grades, students entered the school of the "great masses." The majority would end their formal educational careers sometime in the next six years, many *before* completing the ninth grade. Perhaps one in five of the fourth graders of 1890 would have entertained hopes of entering the high school, fewer still would have anticipated a high school diploma. The high school was established in 1846, long before most communities in the state or the nation had one, but like most high schools in this period, it enrolled only a small proportion of each age cohort until after World War I. Finally, 316 students in the primary and grammar grades attended the community's Irish Catholic parochial school in 1890 (compared to 3,518 in public primary and grammar schools). That single small school was established by the Irish immigrants of earlier decades, and proved a model alternative to the public system for other Catholics who arrived during the period.

Immigrants arriving in the period 1890 to 1920 found a school system similar in structure to the one we know today, but one which was newer in that form, and one that did not expect to retain all students even through the end of ninth grade. In addition to its structure, the system had a standard curriculum. State requirements and local demands added continually to the course of study. State legislation also required that students remain in school until their 14th year. Finally, as prelude to the developments between 1890 and 1920, we note that the state had already enacted a law requiring that public *and* private school instruction be carried out in the English language. The 1885 act allowed private schools only if "the teaching therein is in the English language, and . . . such teaching equals in thoroughness and efficiency the teaching in the public schools in the same locality" (School Committee, 1893, appendix).

Into this school system—recently standardized on dimensions of organization, administration, curriculum, and attendance—poured immigrant children, and the children of immigrants, who, as we saw above, accounted for 66 percent of the total population by 1900 and for 84 percent by 1915. (By way of comparison, Higham's figures [1975, p. 15] for the nation show that first- and second-generation immigrants, taken together, accounted for 34 percent of the population in 1900, and for 35 percent in 1910.) This proportional increase occurred simultaneously with an absolute increase in population from roughly 28,000 (in 1890) to 43,000 (in 1920), an increase of over 50 percent. Table 3 shows the growth in the population of school-age children and school enrollments between 1890 and 1920. The population of school-age children, according to the annual school census, grew from 4,445 to 11,810, an increase of 7,365, or *166 percent*. Parochial school enrollments, though much smaller, grew from 316 to 1,977 in the same period, an increase of *525 percent*. The growth in enrollments and in diversity created great challenges for the community's schools and for the children of the immigrant communities.

Whereas the schools were increasingly characterized by standardization, the student body between 1890 and 1920 was

TABLE 3

School-Aged Children and Enrollment by Level,
1890 to 1920

Year	Children of Compulsory School Age	Average Number Enrolled in Public Schools				Parochial
		Primary	Grammar	High School	All Public	
1890	4,445	1,720	1,798	295	3,813	316
1895	5,305	1,868	1,947	351	4,166	858
1900	6,023	2,368	2,444	378	5,189	622
19C5	7,232	2,476	3,286	385	6,147	673
1910	6,143	2,019	2,463	438	4,920	817
1916	9,579	—	—	—	8,202	1251
1920	11,810	—	—	—	9,988	1977

Source: School Committee, 1890, 1895, 1900, 1905, 1910, 1916 & 1920.

characterized by rapidly increasing *diversity*. The schools recognized this diversity largely as an issue of language, and found it to be a new experience. Though immigrants had made up 20 to 25 percent of the city's population during the standardization of the school system in the decades prior to 1890, most of them were immigrants from Ireland or from British North America, most of whom very likely spoke English. The immigrants of 1890 to 1920, in contrast, came with a variety of linguistic accomplishments; many of them were already multilingual upon arrival but were not fluent in English. Thus, the language of instruction presented a far greater challenge, in terms of the sheer number of students and in the diversity of languages, than ever before. The diversity of students' linguistic and educational backgrounds clashed with the standardized, age-to-grade-coordinated, prescribed curriculum found in the schools.

The strategies used by families and students in resolving these tensions constitute the legacy of expectations inherited by today's bilingual education program. The three alternatives available to immigrant children under 14 years old were: (1) to opt out of formal education and enter the labor market, an option that was perhaps less desirable in 1890 than it had been in 1850, but which remained more acceptable in 1890 than it is in 1990; (2) to seek education in the parochial schools, an option developed by Irish Catholic immigrants and utilized by other, later Catholic arrivals; or (3) to stay in the public schools and adjust to the standard curriculum, perhaps with the benefit of special intensive programs in English. We consider each of these alternatives below; since our main interest is in the role played by the public schools, however, we describe that alternative last and in greatest detail.

The educational alternative to the public schools were the parochial schools. By 1920, three parochial schools were established. The first such school had been founded by Irish parishioners in the 1880s, and continued to be an "Irish" school into the 20th century. For Catholic students, this school offered a religiously more compatible alternative. By 1910, the Polish Catholic church had also established a parochial school. The establishment of an alternative under the aegis of the ethnic church suggests that this was a response to the educational experience in the public schools. By 1916, a third parochial school had started serving the Franco-American community in the city.

The work place was, for many students, the only alternative. As noted above, half of the community's work force was employed in manufacturing, another quarter in clerical, domestic, and transportation services (Kopf, 1974). Entry-level employment was readily available around the turn of the century. Mary Antin's autobiographical novel provides an example of the choices made by immigrant families. Students were required by state law to attend school until age 14 unless their employment was needed by the family. Thus, some amount of schooling was inevitable for those children who were too young, by that era's standards, to work. The Antin sisters are a case in point as to the importance of age and family economic condition in determining the educational destiny of newly arrived immigrants in the last decade of the 19th century. Mary describes her own first day of school in the United States as the fulfillment of years of longing, but notes that her sister Frieda's fate was quite different:

> It was understood, even before we reached Boston, that she would go to work and I to school. . . . There was no choosing possible; Frieda was the oldest, the strongest, the best prepared, and the only one who was of legal age to be put to work. . . . My father . . . divided the world between his children in accordance with the laws of the country and the compulsion of his circumstances. (Antin, 1912, pp. 199-201)

The Antin family's experience in balancing educational opportunity against economic necessity was typical of many immigrant families.

Those who opted for the public schools entered a system where the momentum toward standardization of the educational program and of the student career path had not diminished. The schools initially placed newcomers on the basis of their linguistic abilities. Those who could not do the work of the grade to which their age corresponded were sent to the primary schools, and taught the rudiments of English until their linguistic abilities allowed them to be "main-streamed." This arrangement, however, was an unhappy one for all parties, and as the numbers of newcomers grew, the schools tried another arrangement, creating special programs for the "non-English speaking." The superintendent noted in 1891 that an "ungraded school"

> . . . was established to relieve the primary schools of children who seem out of place on account of age and size. . . . Very often children of foreign immigrants, such as the German, and the Russian Jew, find a home in [the city]. They cannot speak the English tongue and must begin with primary methods. . . . Here they receive that individual attention which only a special school of this kind can afford. [T]his school has been a useful auxiliary to the graded schools, and has proved successful beyond expectation. I have observed, with increasing wonder, the rapidity with which children of foreign birth learn to speak and read the English language, having no knowledge of either when they entered school. (School Committee, 1891, p. 18)

In 1891, 75 students were enrolled in the special school. Kopf's (1974) figures in Table 1 show that the changes in immigrant community composition were only beginning in 1890. Immigrants accounted for 29 percent of the city's population in 1890, and most of these, 25 percent of the total population, came from British realms. School committee figures likewise show only modest increases in numbers of children and enrollments for the first years of the decade. The schools responded, it would appear, to a relatively modest change in the student body.

There is irony in the results of compulsory attendance laws, for the compulsion works both ways; if the students were required to attend school until age 14, the schools were required to teach them. This compulsion was not exactly welcomed by a superintendent overwhelmed by the sheer number of students that crowded the classrooms. Six years later, the schools were bulging under the impact of sharp enrollment increases, the special classes described above had been discontinued, and the former practice of starting "over-age" students in the primary classrooms had been restored.

Superintendent Small's comments in 1897 describe the situation and the needs:

> To add to their labors, large, non-English speaking pupils are placed in these [primary school] rooms until they have acquired sufficient English to enable them to comprehend the work of the grades to which they properly belong. [T]hese pupils, large enough to be gathered together from all parts of the city, should be centralized in one place, under one teacher, and be given that individual attention which will produce the greatest progress. Such ungraded rooms are maintained in other cities, for relief to the regular grades and for the good of the pupils, *whose school life at best will be short* and who should be given every opportunity for acquiring sufficient education to fit them for future intelligent citizenship. Lack of room seems to forbid this at present. (School Committee, 1897, p. 15, italics added)

The comment on the likely "short school life" of these students, repeated in 1899 and 1900, reflects the expectation that many such students would not continue to study beyond their 14th year, the end of compulsory attendance. Employment was apparently an acceptable alternative to schooling from the school's perspective.

By 1899, growth had so strained the facilities of the system that the superintendent's comments took on a tone of still greater urgency.

> [T]he conditions which confront us . . . are rapidly becoming serious. The problem of education in this city is strikingly different from what it was even six years ago. Then the pupils came almost without exception from English speaking homes, while today there is a large number coming from non-English speaking homes. The influence is especially felt in two ways, in building demands and in manner of instruction. . . . Those [primary] rooms which are most heavily crowded are the rooms which have the largest percent of non-English speaking pupils. [W]e have coming to us at all times of the year, non-English speaking pupils, from 7 to 14, who must be admitted. They can only be placed in the primary rooms. The mixture is bad for them and bad for the smaller pupils. There is need today of two

> ungraded rooms, in charge of very skillful teachers of
> some conversational power in French and German, with
> whom the pupils can be placed in smaller numbers, not
> more than 20 per room; that they may be taught indi-
> vidually and be prepared for the Grammar Grades in
> the quickest possible time. . . . Under our present cir-
> cumstances that individual attention and instruction is
> not possible, except out of school hours and at the per-
> sonal sacrifice of the teachers. (School Committee,
> 1899, pp. 11, 16, 18)

In 1900, when the special rooms were re-established, their purpose and function was explained as follows:

> Each year there has been a steady influx of non-
> English speaking people, with children from 10 to 14
> years of age, many of whom have been to school, can
> read a foreign language, write, and do some arithmetic.
> In April, a special room was prepared for them . . .
> with 25 pupils. The aim . . . is to develop spoken and
> written English and ability to read, plus penmanship
> and arithmetic. *The stress however is on English.* The
> pupils come and go, but there has been stability enough
> to show the value of such a room. *Several have ac-
> quired English enough to enable them to obtain working
> certificates,* and several others have already gone di-
> rectly into the 4th grade where they are doing good
> work. (School Committee, 1900, p. 16, italics added.)

Once again, we see satisfaction with the *academic success* of *some* students expressed together with acceptance of *dropping out for employment* for others. In 1900, state law forbade the employment of children under the age of 13, and allowed employment of 13 and 14 year olds only if they had either attended school 30 weeks in the previous year (Martin, 1901) or been certified for work by the school com-mittee (certification being granted if a student could read and write at the fourth grade level).

Such special rooms, later called the Non-English Speak-ing Department came and went with fluctuations in immi-gration and enrollment. During the "100 percent American-ism" of World War I, the department disappeared, only to grow rapidly after the war. For one grammar school, the 1920-1921 school year began with 15 students seeking admission, and ended with 206 students and 6 teachers; the next year 330 students (out of 2,622 in that school) and 11 teachers were involved. As this program was available only to those newly arrived immigrants who could not "understand the teacher" in a regular class, it disappeared as soon as the immigration restriction laws of 1921 and 1924 sharply reduced new arrivals.

Those students who opted for the public schools received the standard school treatment, with a brief period of intensive instruction in English when that luxury could be afforded. As a result of this school experience, some students probably did indeed learn quite a bit of English quickly, though it was not necessarily the "decontextualized" or "cognitive-academic" linguistic ability needed in the schools (Cummins, 1986; Hakuta, 1986). The pace of language learning sounds impressive, yet one must consider the levels attained. To be certified for employment, 13- and 14-year-old students needed only be able to read and write at the fourth grade level. Students of high school age were most likely to enter employment, for relatively few students—native English speakers included—aspired to do so as the enrollment figures indicate.

In summary, we have seen: (1) recognition of the need for some accommodation to the linguistically diverse student population, and provision of such programs that placed students on the basis of ability level rather than age; (2) the strain on school facilities and personnel caused by growth in enrollments that led to discontinuation of those programs; (3) the intensive English classes served only small numbers of new arrivals, and were, in today's understanding, examples of a very intensive ESL program; (4) recognition of the work place as an alternative to the classroom for many students.

The records also suggest that, had there been less strain due to rapid enrollment increases, *the schools would have done more rather than less to make the transition to schooling smoother.* It would be untrue to the record to insist, as some do, that the "sink or swim" submersion approach was regarded as the only or the best possible arrangement. Though some accommodation was considered appropriate for the non-English speaking students in the public schools, the needs of the students were understood only in terms of learning English for the purpose of adapting to the norms of the system. While individual teachers might have been more culturally sensitive, the institutional policies were not.

Finally, we note that different ethnic groups tended toward different alternatives. Committee reports and interviews indicate that Jewish immigrant children tended to remain in the public schools; Polish, Franco-American, and other smaller groups of Catholic immigrants created and supported parochial schools. Many children from all groups were, like Frieda Antin, forced by the "compulsion of circumstances" to opt for the workplace. In a sense, little has changed; these three alternatives—to stay in the public schools, perhaps with some initial "special" assistance, to attend a private school with ethnic group affiliation, or to enter the job market—still exist today. But as we will argue more fully below, the significance of each alternative and the relationships between and among them are very different today.

The Bilingual Program: 1971 to 1990

In the five decades following 1920, immigration was greatly reduced through restrictive legislation. Schools in the community continued to be linked strongly to their neighborhoods. Present day teachers and administrators who grew up in the city in those years fondly recall the diversity of their own classmates, yet they regard the influxes of Spanish-speaking immigrants, beginning in the 1960s, and refugees from Southeast Asia, beginning in the late 1970s, as constituting significant changes in the life of the community and the schools.

From the perspective of the schools, state law played a much larger role in the response to the new immigrants, yet even before the passage of the state's transitional bilingual education (TBE) law in 1971, which took effect in April of 1972, the city had started offering Spanish language classes to their teachers and had developed classes in Spanish as a Second Language for some students. In-service courses in conversational Spanish for teachers were offered on a volunteer basis. In addition, as early as 1970, Spanish-speaking aides were hired to assist Spanish-speaking teachers and to speed up the students' transitions into regular classes. The School Committee called for a survey of Spanish-speaking students to "be certain that all students who should be attending school have been identified" (School Committee Minutes, March 1971). Prior to the passage of the TBE law, there were virtually no bilingual education programs anywhere in the state. That law stipulated that bilingual programs prepare students for "regular" English-only classes within three years, though at the parent's request or teacher's recommendation, a student may remain in the program longer than three years.

The Spanish bilingual program was developed in 1971 in response to the growing number of school-aged children in the Latino community; Cambodian bilingual and Vietnamese bilingual components were added in 1983 and 1986, respectively. The program's first classes were held in the basement of one of the schools. Gradually, bilingual classes spread through the grade levels, the subject areas, and into the three schools with the highest concentrations of non-English speaking students (NEP/LEP).

Currently, the TBE program serves 933 K-12 students in four of the city's six schools. Latinos, as the largest group, make up between 65 and 70 percent of the bilingual enrollment; Cambodians and Vietnamese combined account for 25 to 30 percent, with the remaining 10 percent representing diverse linguistic backgrounds. In 1988, Latino students numbered 1,486, 50 percent of the total system enrollment, of whom 523 were classified as unable to function in English in classroom work in 1989. Cambodian students numbered 260, Vietnamese 109, Chinese 31, Cape Verdeans 16, Portuguese 15 (Massachusetts Education of Linguistic Minority Students Bureau, surveys 1975 to 1988.) Table 4 shows the growth in enrollment and in proportion of linguistically diverse students.

Examination of school committee minutes from 1970 to 1988 gave clues as to the place of the bilingual program

TABLE 4

Linguistic Diversity and Enrollment,
1975 to 1988

Year	First Language Not English	(%)	Limited English Proficiency	(%)	Total System Enrollment
1975	534	13	324	8	4,146
1980	703	23	392	13	3,041
1985	1586	46	689	20	3,447
1988	1940	56	829	24	3,468

Source: Massachusetts Department of Education, October School Reports, 1975 to 1988.

within the school department's overall efforts. References to the bilingual program were categorized as relating to facilities, finances, personnel decisions, contract negotiations (with all teachers), and educational line issues. Educational issues were the least common references, and generally involved questions of textbook selection procedures, discipline policies, and traffic safety around the schools. The majority of the committee's involvement with the bilingual program, as with all programs, involved finances. As we have noted, our city is among the poorest in the state, and its school department holds the distinction of receiving monies from *every* available state and federal aid to education program. Every effort is made to keep expenses down (including refusal to raise the hourly wage of bilingual aides from $2.50 to $3.00 in 1974). Because funding for teachers in the bilingual program came from state and federal monies, they were less likely to be cut from the staff in the retrenchments of the 1970s and 1980s when budget matters dominated the committee's agenda.

The school committee minutes provide evidence of the committee's importance in city politics. The School De partment is one of many that shares the city budget, the mayor usually serves *ex officio* on the committee, and attention to the city's political machinations is consistent. The committee tended over the years to keep close watch on the administrators, and to hold the reins on power in the system. Though the committee consistently seeks outside expertise and outside funding, its control on the school system, until the late 1980s, extended to the smallest detail. Despite the presence of a growing bilingual program, *recognition* is given it by the school committee for staying under budget, for advancing students into colleges, community colleges, and vocational education programs. Legitimation of culture is relegated to cultural days and celebrations, but is not central to the core of schooling practices. The growing political power of the Latino community has attracted greater attention to *community* desires in the programs.

Analytical Framework: Critical Pedagogy and Bilingual Education

Understanding how immigrants were integrated into schooling in the past within this community affords us the opportunity to assess changes that have occurred at the policy and prescriptive levels. The immigrant experiences of the past are often used to criticize the effectiveness of bilingual education. Americanization programs, pushing students through grades in English-speaking classrooms are used as measures of success for earlier immigrants. Unstated are the explanations for those who did not make it, and the variations that were found within immigrant populations (Perlmann, 1988, 1990). In the historical memory of our community, schools at the turn of the century are characterized as the "great equalizers" of social cultural differences, the providers of equal educational opportunities. The culture of the home was to be maintained by families and neighborhoods, but schools afforded a common ground for culturally diverse students. Here, they could learn to communicate in one language and function within rules and responsibilities shared by all. But as policies, annual reports, school committee minutes, and interviews with teachers, administrators, and parents reflect, the integration of immigrant students, then as today, was not a smooth linear process. Other interests were in competition with basic education: economic interests in the labor market, political demands for national unity and "Americanization"—all of these influenced the configurations of schooling. In order to understand what these policies, then and today, imply and reflect about the education of immigrants, we turn to the analysis provided by critical pedagogy.

The critical pedagogy of Paulo Freire best frames the issues that we have uncovered in our research in this community and serves to articulate the operant power relationships held and used to explain the meaning of bilingual education for today's immigrants. Freire's (1970) basic tenets are: (1) that education can never be neutral, that it is essentially political in nature by the interests it represents; (2) that education for *liberation* is possible over education for *domestication,* (or as he calls it, a "banking education" in which students are depositories of learning, where they passively receive, memorize, and consume facts); and (3) that education must be dialogical, political consciousness is created out of the denunciation of oppressive learning. Rather than separating economic, political, and cultural explanations of schooling in society, he brings them together by problematizing the position of the school as reflecting the society. To learn, says Freire, is a dialogical process and a critical investigation of reality that must involve both teacher and students. "It is not education which shapes society, but society that shapes education according to those who have power," he noted in a 1985 appearance. Knowledge itself is seen as political. Thus, in his development of ideas, Freire attends to the learner in the act of learning. It is fundamental that the formulation of such learning be *context bound, historical,* and *experiential.* We apply this framework to the analyses of policies, historical documentation, and more recent data collected from interviews, school committee reports and minutes, focusing on the following:

Historicity: History provides an embedded sphere which allows for insertion of ideas.

> There is a need to appropriate the context and insert
> ourselves in it, not under time, but already in time. . . .
> We need to be subjects of history, even if we cannot to-
> tally stop being objects of history. And to be subjects,
> we need unquestionably to claim history critically. As
> active participants and real subjects, we can make his-
> tory only when we are continually critical of our lives.
> (Freire, 1986, p. 40, 199).

Historicity is imperative, and not in the sense of knowing the "facts" of how things turned out, or merely knowing the "final score" in terms of institutional structure, but rather in the sense of knowing the dynamic social facts, the alternative views, the concrete consequences of past social relations as they form the foundation for present day relations. History is regarded as the creation, not the creator, of human beings.

Anthropological concept of culture: Human beings are creators, makers of culture through their relationships to nature and others through their labor, actions, and work. "Culture is all human creation, thus it exists in a state of becoming" (Moll, 1986, p. 72). The sum of such creation constitutes the substance of social reality. Social reality can be transformed; it is created and re-created continuously and is not deterministically fated. Freire (1970) states: "If men produce social reality, then transforming that reality is a historical task, a task for men" (p. 36).

Conscientization: Consciousness is linked to people's social lives, thus as they transform reality, they too become historically and culturally conditioned and there are levels that are attained in the context of such cultural and historical reality (Freire 1970, p. 32). Conscientization requires critical awareness and reflection, with the capacity to create dialogue. There are three stages of consciousness/understanding/knowledge: the *intransitive*, naive stage which is unreflective; the *semitransitive*, and the *transitive*, critical, reflective stage. The transitive stage is the basis for dialogue and thoughtfulness. The democratic person arises in this stage with political participation.

Freire's conceptualization provides a lens for viewing schooling that sees people not as powerless, but as powerful;

it emphasizes issues of power relationships, and of shifts in the power bases as people are politicized; it also emphasizes the fluidity of culture, that people transform their situation and are not merely inputs transformed by the schools.

Discussion: Misconceptions in Bilingual Education Debate

Opponents of bilingual education place great importance on their version of the past. Appeals to history are ubiquitous; they are found in the writings of educational sociologists (e.g., Glazer, 1983), in letters to the editor (Hakuta, 1986), in discussions at schools of education, in school board debates, urban teacher's lounge discussions, and not least in the rhetoric of "English only" activists (e.g., Imhoff, 1990). Especially vocal in calling on the example of the past are those who lived through the immigrant schooling of the early 1900s. Hakuta (1986) reports that in a small survey of New Haven residents, most respondents were moderately favorable to bilingual education; those most opposed were individuals who had survived the "sink or swim" treatment dealt to earlier immigrants.

We have organized our discussion around misconceptions, or misconceptualizations, of bilingual education. We emphasize at the outset that we contest the use of history made by bilingual education's detractors—past social arrangements have no prescriptive claim on the present or the future. However, given the current state of the debate on bilingual education as we enter it, we first follow the lines of argument most commonly encountered before proposing a more appropriate and useful consideration of history. These are by no means the only misconceptions, but a representation of the *historical* ones; others have framed discussions and defenses of bilingual education in terms of "misconceptions" (Chen, n.d.; Dolson, 1988; Hakuta, 1986).

Misconception 1: The educational experience of immigrants was a uniform one; what "worked" for one group worked for all. No one expected special treatment.

On the face of it, the general uniformity of school provision for immigrants and native-born noted by Higham (1975) and Thompson (1920) confirms this idea, but only in describing the experience of those students *in a given time period, in a given community,* who *were in school.* These qualifications alone do away with any absolute claim of identical treatment, for as we have seen, important changes in the school system and in the importance of education have taken place continuously through history, and continue today. Within any given time period, while those who attended school received more or less the same schooling (more in terms of textbooks, less in terms of teachers' qualifications, quality of facilities, and teacher-to-student ratios—things that probably varied even *more* in the past than they do today), those who did *not* attend school had substantially different experiences. While the school treated people similarly, the school did not touch many people, especially immigrants. Not only has the quality of schooling changed through the decades, but the quantity available in the community has changed drastically over the years.

As to the variety of linguistic arrangements available in U.S. public schools, the historical precedent for the use of other languages, especially German, in public schools is discussed in Perlmann (1990), Tyack (1974), and Thompson (1920). In some rural areas of the Midwest, German was used as the sole language of instruction; in certain cities, German was used for half a day, or in German language instruction only. These practices decreased, though they were still common, especially in parochial schools, until World War I; they were banned in many states as nativism increased with the growth of war-time nationalism (Thompson, 1920, pp. 145-163, 282-302). Where and when one entered the public schools made a great deal of linguistic difference. In our community, however, bilingual education was not implemented in the public schools in the period 1890 to 1920. The earlier predominance of Irish immigrants whose homeland had for years been colonized politically and linguistically by England, and the later influx of people from British North America minimized the linguistic demands on the public schools prior to 1890. By the time Catholic groups other than the Irish established parochial schools—the Polish and the Franco-American— state law prohibited the teaching of required subjects in any but the English language. Instruction in other languages, as well as other historical and cultural traditions, would have been conducted in addition to the required curriculum. But though early immigrant experiences left no history of multilingual education, and though the nativist temper of the times led to legislation requiring monolingual education, the linguistic realities of schooling were not simple in the period of the "new immigration." Even in the Americanization-driven decades around World War I, people recognized that some academic accommodation was necessary, and established the special classes described above.

One side of the misconception of history is that the schools did not change their established practices for earlier immigrant groups. The assumption underlying such appeals to the precedent of institutional arrangements is that they are somehow immutable, machines not meant to be tinkered with by their current users. A critical perspective emphasizes the arbitrary nature of social institutions and knowledge. Thus, we view institutions *as social,* as constructions of their human participants. This linkage between the community and institutions is crucial. For our community, a substantial folklore has developed around the distinctive "educational enterprise" of Jewish students. Much of the thinking about historical group differences in educational success in the community turns on the contrast between Irish and Jewish students. Very different outcomes resulted from the same treatment.

Given these historical realities, a wide range of *expectations* for the present are conceivable. If anything, education is *more* critical for today's young immigrants than it was for those at the beginning of the century. The extent of educational needs has grown. Today's job-skill demands are different from those at the turn of the century. Skills needed today are those of the information technology sector; basic skills are not enough. Education needed for employment includes technical literacy, ability to continue learning, and to work in cooperative group efforts. Attendance requirements contained in the laws are also greater, but the real difference in pressure to succeed in school is more economic. It is crucial to recognize, however, that the linguistic skills needed to function in today's economy are more complex than they were at the turn of the century. It is no longer enough, as it was believed to be then, to be able only to read and write simple sentences in English. Significant content must be mastered, and higher levels of schooling completed. To suggest that the minimal educational efforts to promote immigrant adjustment in the earlier period should be a model for today's schools ignores significant differences in the nature of the schooling involved, as well as important precedents for bilingual education.

Misconception 2:   There was unanimity, *a consensus as to the role that schools, and the English language, should play in immigrant assimilation.*

The misconception of easy consensus is, historically, unfounded from both the perspective of the schools and of the immigrants. First, though immigrant students did participate in the schools, their presence there was not always welcomed, and special arrangements were made out of necessity and frustration. Second, from the students' perspective, tensions arose between family or immigrant community expectations and the expectations of the schools, especially in the area of religion. Lack of consensus in regard to religion added to the educational options in the community. For example, in 1859, Irish students refused to recite the morning lesson—the Ten Commandments and the Lord's Prayer—because the prayer was the Protestant version. One boy, the school's brightest student, persisted and was sent home by the two school committee members who came to set matters right. The next day, according to the local *Telegraph and Pioneer* (March 26, 1859), six more refused and were sent home. School regulations moved slowly towards accommodation of religious differences; by 1889, only the teacher was required to recite the prayers audibly—the students could remain silent (School Committee, 1889). The committee of 1891 would insist that "[s]ectarianism is unknown in our schools," yet assure the readers that, "virtues which are the outgrowth of our common Christianity, which are fundamental to our free institutions are faithfully inculcated. . . . We deem it but just to insist that we are not maintaining godless schools." (School Committee, 1891, p. 15). Yet sectarianism *did* remain an issue for Catholic citizens, and separate schools were established in response. As early as 1883 the school committee was aware of 259 students attending parochial schools. These schools became an integral part of the educational system.

As the immigrant groups changed, however, the issue of prayers in the school still caused controversy. Mary Antin relates an 1894 argument she had with a fellow Jewish student over whether they should participate in the optional recitation of the Lord's Prayer, or remain silent. The students were, ironically, reprimanded for bringing religion into the classroom, and admonished to leave their religion home—all were equal in the schools (Antin, 1912). The response of the Jewish immigrant community to this daily practice and to the reprimands that their children received for being absent during the High Holidays was to continue participation in the schools. Eventually, the community's schools *did* begin to celebrate Jewish holidays, and they continue to do so even though the number of Jewish families in the city has decreased. The Poles who arrived at around the same time, however, repeated the example of their Irish predecessors and established St. Stanislaus School. In this instance, the connection of Catholicity influenced the response to the terms of incorporation offered. These two groups responded differently, neither with acquiescence to the educational system as they found it.

Finally, it bears repeating that the tensions between immigrant expectations and the schools did not demand resolution because the workplace was an alternative route for those who were dissatisfied with schooling but could not construct alternative institutional arrangements. All school age children (those 14 and under) were required to be schooled in English, but those for whom the linguistic transition was not easy either attained sufficient ability to be certified to work, or stayed in the system until they reached age 14. Only those who could handle the work of the standard fourth grade were allowed to continue. Unfortunately, we don't know the percentages that took each route, but the fact that all those who stayed in school succeeded to a high degree should not be mistaken for meaning that all immigrant students did so.

Today's situation has more in common with the historical reality than with the idealized version of it. Schooling involves conflict for immigrants on several levels, and reaching consensus will require cooperation. First, many immigrants to this community today are undocumented, and are hesitant to enroll in school for fear of being found out by the Immigration and Naturalization Service (INS). Others await papers, but are in an administrative limbo until they are received. The political realities of adjustment are complex. Second, today's immigrants' experiences in coming to America differ from each others' as well as from those of earlier groups. Many are fleeing war-torn countries, and maintain strong contacts with their countries of origin. Because of disruption of schooling in their home countries, especially for those from war-torn Central American countries, many have not been in school for several years. Many are also illiterate in their native language, and are placed above their ability level on the basis of age. Students are then retained in grade, and therefore are likely to fail. Puerto Rican families, as U.S. citizens, move between the island and the mainland for family and economic reasons, interrupting the continuity and progress of their schooling and socialization. Third, and significantly for the community's schools, today's immigrants are younger than any before, and many young people are here as parts of sibling-headed households. The median age in the Latino community is estimated at 17.2 years. The support, encouragement, and advice from older family members is simply not available, and added family obligations, including the need to work, interferes with the older siblings' support of the school participation of the younger siblings.

Schools need to be more flexible in responding to the lived experiences and social relationships of these students, rather than relying on an unfounded version of a "consensus model," which assumes that all students learn the same way, in the same programs, with the same curriculum, with the same assessment measures, under the same scheduling. Teachers who advocate for their students are those who act from an of awareness of the students' actual situations, and not according to set procedures (Montero-Sieburth & Pérez, 1987). Community-based research is central to understanding the complexities of these students' lives, validating those experiences as well as the students' languages and cultures, and providing access to control and ownership of their own lives in the community.

Misconception 3: Bilingual education advocates are promoting their own "special interest."

There is an irony to this claim made by opponents of bilingual education. One part of the rationale for promoting "English only" legislation is that maintenance of separate linguistic traditions leads to political fragmentation. During the decades around World War I, the arguments were more direct; bilingual schools were accused of promoting divided loyalty, in contrast to the "100 percent Americanism" promoted in the monolingual schools (Thompson, 1920). On the surface, the arguments claim to envision a quicker political incorporation through the English language.

The experiences of earlier immigrant groups in gaining access to the political structure in the city, including the school committee and administrative posts in the schools, was a long process. The experience of the Latino community within the city in recent decades suggests that legitimation of linguistic and cultural identity by the presence of the bilingual program in the schools has encouraged entry into the political structure. Rather than slowing down political participation, it seems to have speeded it up. We suspect that political fragmentation is less feared by bilingual education's opponents than is the successful politicization of peoples which in fact occurs. The real issue is that the participation occurs through empowerment rather than through incorporation.

Finally, the related claim that proponents of bilingual education seek to protect jobs and benefits that are too expensive to justify otherwise is unsupported by the data. In our community, the per pupil expenditure for bilingual education programs in 1987-88 was $2,436, nearly $1,000 *less* than the $3,431 per pupil expenditures on the regular day program. For the local taxpayers, even this discrepancy understates the differences in cost. Two thirds of the cost of the day programs was provided by state assistance; *all* of the cost of the bilingual program was covered by state aid (figures provided by the State Department of Education). The bilingual program does *not* hire "extra" teachers or other personnel, but is cost-effective.

In summary, each appeal to history is a variation on the theme of a "golden past" when there was consensus and linearity about schooling and a uniform experience of immigrant adjustment and assimilation. Historical misconceptions claim that the experiences of earlier immigrants in the schools can be characterized as: (1) *uniform*, no one expected special treatment, and all immigrant groups in the past had to struggle with the language and go through the regular curriculum; (2) *unilinear*, assimilation was a one-way process to a better life in a better economic condition with a better culture, that it was all gain and no loss; and (3) *unanimous*, nobody argued about it, all parties were agreed as to method and outcome. The uniformity, unilinearity, and unanimity are products of the desire to find the "one best solution" to the challenges of diversity in the schools rather than conclusions based on the historical realities.

This manufactured version of history is not delivered as "merely history," however; historical assertions are coupled with contemporary allegations or accusations. Not only was the past golden, but the present is, in comparison, a great disappointment. Where they would like to see a re-creation of their own golden image of the past, critics see the present as deficient in: (1) *expectations*, educators are holding students back, keeping them from learning English by "ghettoizing" them on the basis of low expectations; parents and students who prefer bilingual education are likewise setting their aim too low, perhaps for lack of motivation or effort, or for the expectation of "entitlements" (Imhoff, 1990) or special treatment; (2) *efficiency*, not only is the use of two languages in the schools unnecessary, it is also inefficient;

bilingual education is an expensive luxury that takes resources away from other educational priorities; and finally, (3) *expedience*, politically, bilingual education, in promoting linguistic factionalism and segregation of ethnic groups defeats the American ideals of national unity and consensus; those who support bilingual education are accused of preserving their own political and administrative enclaves outside the mainstream of U.S. education and society. Claims about the past and complaints about the present are combined in misconceptualizations of bilingual education's nature and promise.

Our analysis revealed the following points:

1. Immigrants were incorporated into the established school practices at the turn of the century with the view that they would be educated by those already in power.

2. As newcomers, immigrants at the turn of the century were not viewed as making their own history. They had to "melt," or become like those whose presence in the community predated theirs. In the political turmoil around World War I, the emphasis on "making Americans" through the schools gained such momentum that the action of bilingual people as *subjects* in the historical moment was possible only outside the public schools.

3. In recent times, the mobilization of Latino parents and others to enact the state transitional bilingual education law made bilingual education possible in the community. The "push" of state law and the "pull" of state and federal monies provided the legal leverage for the development of the local bilingual program.

4. Conscientization of the power politics is evident in the rise to power of various groups within the city. Until the early 1900s, school administrators and city politicians were U.S.

natives. Following the first fire (1908), Irish
officials and administrators came to office.
Officeholders in the city and the schools today
have immigrant roots in the community
around the turn of the century. The lag between arrival in the schools and at the controls seems to be around 60 years during
which time each group learns the language
and politics of the community. They also in-
ternalize the oppressive conditions of their
own "welcome" and reproduce those social
relationships with newcomers.

5. Bilingual classrooms of today are embedded in
a historical context. While the debate about
bilingual education may be centered on
linguistic issues, the more important issues
involve having access to the socioeconomic
structures. The most crucial issues, today as in
the earlier period, are not access to schooling
alone, but access through schooling to
employment and political power.

Conclusion

In considering the record of one community, we have
shown that the situation of the earlier waves of immigration was not so simple or pleasant as some would have us
believe. School policies implied an education that was neither liberating nor dialogical for immigrants in the period
1890 to 1920; in spite of this, the responses of individuals
and groups show that they were far from "intransitive" in
Freire's terms. From the beginning, their responses included contestation, confrontation, and contradiction; alternative institutions were created in the form of parochial
schools. The schools, for their part, recognized that the
standard approach would not work, and established its own
fleeting alternatives. Yet the empowerment of previous
generations of immigrant groups to participate in the local
political structure was a slow process, not directly encour-

aged by the educational establishment. Productivity in employment or cultural conformity were the options presented by the system.

The situation of today's immigrants in the community is at once like and unlike that of previous groups. The local response to today's immigrants was much the same as to the arrival of immigrants around the turn of the century—some accommodation was made, but on terms decided by those who got there first. As the Latino community enters its fourth decade, changes are apparent, like those experienced by earlier groups when they entered business and politics in the community. But there are differences as well; though the bilingual program has never had a maintenance orientation, the legitimacy provided by the laws of the state and the presence of the bilingual program in the school has helped to preserve the cultural identity of the immigrant communities. Immigrant community members entering politics today enter as advocates of their communities, unlike their predecessors who were more likely to acquiesce to the melting pot ideology of their day. The state TBE law, which both required and subsidized the bilingual program in the community, created space for the reflection and conscientization that was denied in the context of educational institutions to previous immigrant generations. The connections between people's social realities in their communities and state policies need to be examined more closely in future research. Politically, the implication is that *both* community organizing and legislative action are imperative.

Facile comparisons to earlier days that fail to take into consideration the changing meaning of schooling in U.S. society at large, and/or the variations in different immigrant groups' experiences with the schools at any given period in history, are not valid arguments in today's policy debates. Because of greater resources in the society as a whole, we can do more today than we did in earlier days; because we are more conscious of the great price which was paid in the cultural losses in the earlier rush to Americanize immigrants, we are morally obliged to do better. While most immigrants in earlier periods came by their own decision seeking better opportunities, many of today's immigrants come fleeing U.S.-sponsored oppression and destabilization in Central America and elsewhere, or in the long-term aftermath of U.S. involvement in Southeast Asia. The international political and military roles played by the United States brings many people into its borders on terms it did not anticipate. The interdependency of nations and between foreign policy and domestic educational patterns must be considered.

In our community, Latinos sought election to the city government in 1977, 1982, and 1985. In 1989, the first Latina was elected to public office in the community—as a school committee member. Through encouraging parental involvement in parents' organizations connected to the bilingual program, the schools played a part in this access to political representation. In considering more adequate and relevant definitions of success for bilingual education programs, teachers and administrators need to include the long view, and consider the program's impact on the whole community. The development of community in the classrooms and of better relations between the school and the community are the real tests of success.

Notes

[1] The research reported in this study was supported by a grant from the Spencer Foundation, entitled "Analyzing the Use of Bilingual Teachers' Knowledge and Educational Processes in an Urban School Community to Improve Teacher Education," awarded to Dr. Martha Montero-Sieburth. The views expressed herein are solely the authors'; they do not reflect the policies or opinions of the Spencer Foundation nor the Harvard Graduate School of Education. The writers wish to acknowledge the staff of the community's public library, especially the Director, Mr. Nicholas Minadakis, who created a community historical archive where none existed before, and Mr. Robert Collins, the archivist, who brought relevant materials to our attention. The willing assistance of the whole library staff made this research possible.

[2] HyperCard is a trademark of Apple Computer.

[3] The term *Latino* is preferred by the authors over the term *Hispanic*, which was given common usage by government reporting requirements. The latter term is more properly used for solely linguistic purposes.

[4] In all references, [Northeast City] is inserted in place of the city's name.

References[4]

Antin, M. (1899). *From Plotzk to Boston*. Boston: W. B. Clarke and Company.

_____. (1912). *The promised land*. New York: Houghton Mifflin Company.

Beltran, X., Rodríguez, M., Straussman, J., & Zweig, E. (1976). *A view from under the bridge: A plan for Hispanics in [Northeast City]*. [Northeast City], MA: Care About Now.

Botsford, K. (1989, November/December). Assignment: [Northeast City's] schools; the whos, hows and whys behind [the] university's experimental management of that city's school system. *Bostonia*, pp. 33-41.

Chen, E. (n.d.). Why English-only is a civil liberties issue. Unpublished manuscript, American Civil Liberties Union Foundation of Northern California.

Commonwealth of Massachusetts, Department of Education. (1979). Briefing paper on Chapter 71A, the State Transitional Bilingual Education Act. Boston, MA: Author.

Cummins, J. (1986). Empowering minority students: A framework for intervention. *Harvard Educational Review, 56*(1), 18-36.

Dolson, D. (1988). *Common misconceptions regarding bilingual education*. Sacramento: California State Department of Education.

Freire, P. (1970). *Pedagogy of the oppressed*. New York: Seabury.

_____. (1986). *The politics of education*. South Hadley, MA: Bergin and Garvey.

Glazer, N. (1983). *Ethnic dilemmas: 1964-1982*. Cambridge: Harvard University Press.

Hakuta, K., (1986). *Mirror of language: The debate on bilingualism*. New York: Basic Books.

_____, & Gould, L. (1987). Synthesis of research on bilingual education. *Educational Leadership, 44*(6), 38-45.

Handlin, O. (1941, revised edition 1979). *Boston's immigrants 1790 to 1880: A study in acculturation*. Cambridge, MA: Belknap Press.

Higham, J. (1988). *Strangers in the land: Patterns of American nativism, 1860-1925*. (2nd ed.). New Brunswick, NJ: Rutgers University Press.

_____. (1975). *Send these to me*. New York: Atheneum.

Imhoff, G. (1990). The position of U.S. English on bilingual education. *The Annals of the American Academy of Political and Social Science, 508*, 48-61.

Kopf, E. (1974). *The intimate city: A study of urban social order, 1906-1915*. Unpublished doctoral dissertation, Brandeis University, Waltham, MA.

Martin, G. (1901). *The evolution of the Massachusetts public school system: A historical sketch.* New York: D. Appleton and Company.

Massachusetts Department of Education, Education of Linguistic Minority Students Bureau. Surveys, 1975-1988.

Moll, B. U. (1986). *Adult literacy training in rural Mexico: Practice, meaning, and theory.* Unpublished doctoral dissertation, Harvard University Graduate School of Education, Cambridge, MA.

Montero-Sieburth, M., & Pérez, M. (1987). *Echar Pa'lante*, Moving onward: The dilemmas and strategies of a bilingual teacher. *Anthropology and Education Quarterly, 18*(3), 180-189.

National Coalition of Advocates for Students. (1988). *New voices: Immigrant students in U.S. public schools.* Boston: Author.

Ogbu, J. (1987). Variability in minority school performance: A problem in search of an explanation. *Anthropology and Education Quarterly, 18*(4), 312-334.

Perlmann, J. (1988). *Ethnic differences: Schooling and social structure among the Irish, Italians, Jews, and Blacks in an American city, 1880-1935.* Cambridge: Cambridge University Press.

____. (1990). Historical legacies: 1840-1920. *The Annals of the American Academy of Political and Social Science, 508,* 27-37.

Pratt, W. M. (1930). *Seven generations: A story of Prattville and Northeast City.* Northeast City, MA: Author.

Rosa, M. (1985). Let's use our resources. Usemos Nuestros Recursos. A Bilingual Guide to Services in [Northeast City]. Guia Bilingue a Los Servicios en [Northeast City]. [Northeast City], MA: Mayor's Office of Community Development.

School Committee of [Northeast City]. *Annual report of the school committee* for years 1889, 1891, 1893, 1897, 1899, 1900, 1921.

____. Minutes, March 1971.

Snow, C., & Hakuta, K. (1987). The costs of monolingualism. Paper presented at the Institute on Bilingual Education, Harvard Graduate School of Education in collaboration with the Center for Language Education and Research, UCLA.

Spener, D. (1988). Transitional bilingual education and the socialization of immigrants. *Harvard Educational Review, 58*(2), 133-153.

Thompson, F. (1920). *Schooling of the immigrant.* New York: Harper and Brothers.

Tyack, D. (1974). *The one best system: A history of American urban education.* Cambridge, MA: Harvard University Press.

ETHNOTERRITORIAL POLITICS AND THE INSTITUTIONALIZATION OF BILINGUAL EDUCATION AT THE GRASS-ROOTS LEVEL

Armando L. Trujillo
University of Texas, San Antonio

ABSTRACT

The formation of federal bilingual education policy is posited as the outcome of the interaction of two factors: (a) policy decision making in governmental institutions and (b) grass-roots ethnoterritorial political movements. In order to explain the role of ethnoterritorial politics and policy responses on the part of the federal government, the Mexican American community is treated as an ethnoterritory in the Southwest. A case study of Aztlán City, in the Winter Garden region of South Texas, is used to illustrate the relationship between policy formation, ethnoterritorial politics, and the institutionalization of a bilingual, bicultural education program at the grass-roots level.

The emergence of a national bilingual education policy in 1968 in the form of the Bilingual Education Act (Title VII) has been hailed as "the triumphant passage" of an "historic bill" (Andersson, 1971, p. 429) and marks, some scholars argue, a definite turn toward supporting bilingualism in this country. In ethnic communities, bilingual education always has been seen as a more effective means of improving school-community relations, and as having the potential of including the language and culture of the community as part of the school's curriculum. The Bilingual Education Act allowed, for the first time, instruction in American public schools in languages other than English as well as allowing the preparation of bilingual teaching and learning materials. These areas of language policy and language planning are marked changes from United States language and education policy prior to 1968. Why did 1968 mark such a pivotal shift in policy if the national political agenda from

1880 to 1968 had been one of assimilating the culturally and linguistically different into the melting pot (Stein, 1986)? Was it because the national government suddenly turned into a benevolent promoter of ethnolinguistic rights and programs designed to meet the educational needs of the ethnolinguistic community, or did the ethnolinguistic community achieve new levels of political organization to influence a shift in national language and education policy?

Andersson (1971) argues that this change in policy was "the result of a lucky confluence of social, economic and political forces and of extensive research" (p. 30). He notes that the post-Sputnik age increased national interest in teaching science, math, and foreign languages. In addition, the public consciousness became more attuned to the educational problems encountered by low-income and ethnic-minority children given the accumulation of research.

A number of research studies conducted during the late 1950s and throughout the 1970s not only raised interest in bilingual education, but in the case of Mexican Americans, brought to the forefront the particular educational and social problems that Chicanos were experiencing (e.g., Carter, 1970; Gaarder, 1965; Gebler, Moore, & Guzmán, 1970; Fishman, 1965; Manuel, 1965; Texas Education Agency, 1957). Numerous educational conferences and congressional hearings also were held throughout the Southwest and in Washington, DC that addressed the educational problems of Mexican Americans and brought together representatives from various educational organizations as well as from local, state, and national governments (Andersson, 1971; Sánchez, 1973).

While the subsequent conference reports and congressional hearings elaborated on the major issues with respect to bilingual education as an alternative philosophy and pedagogy designed to address the educational needs of the Spanish-speaking child, little elaboration has been provided regarding the nature of the political forces influencing the development of national education policy. During the 1960s, Mexican Americans as a group became quite disenchanted with the lack of response the federal government was giving to the myriad social, economic, and educational problems confronting the Mexican American community

(García, 1989; San Miguel, 1987). This degree of disen-
chantment prompted the Chicano movement, a new kind
of political involvement at the grass-roots level based on
ethnic identity, militant rhetoric, and territorial affiliation
(Ericksen, 1970; Bongartz, 1969; Torgenson, 1970).

This new type of microlevel ethnoterritorial political
movement was intended to get policy responses from the
federal government, especially in the area of increased educational resources for the ethnolinguistic community. Very
little research has been done in the area of politics and bilingual education policy formation from a "bottom-up" perspective, i.e., investigating how ethnolinguistic community
struggles for equal educational opportunity influenced
bilingual education policy formulation and implementation. The few studies that have looked at the intervening
variables of politics and policy decision-making in governmental institutions usually view the formation of policy
from a top-down direction (cf. Edwards, 1976). In this chapter I argue that the emergence of federal bilingual education
policy involves a complex process embracing both the perception and interaction of macrolevel conditions and microlevel political behavior.

Historical Overview

In the 1960s, Chicanos as a people initiated a new type of
activism for civil rights, unionization, political enfran-
chisement, economic mobility, and equal educational opportunity. Initially this movement had strong regional and
nationalistic components—the United Farm Workers' push
for unionization in California, the land grant struggles in
New Mexico, the push for political mobilization and Chicano self-determination by both the Crusade for Justice in
Colorado and the Mexican American Youth Organization in
Texas. While each of these movements was spurred by its
own grass-roots regional ties, by the fall of 1967 representatives of these different movements came together to organize a series of Raza Unity Conferences. García (1989) notes
that the first unity conference was organized in El Paso,

Texas as a counter alternative to President Johnson's cabinet hearings on Mexican American affairs by those Mexican American leaders who had not been invited to the hearings. The unity conferences served to inform Chicanos about the different regional movements, while at the same time bringing together different segments of the Chicano community, middle-class and militant members alike, to exchange ideas and strategies for addressing the problems facing Mexican Americans.

For the newer Chicano organizations espousing a more militant ideology calling for ethnic separation and self-determination, these meetings were especially important in helping the groups to become better organized and more vocal in their language of confrontation and action. The political mobilization taking place in the barrios and rural areas also was fueled by cultural revitalization which reinforced the group's ethnic identity. Chicano cultural expression took form in song, dance, drama, poetry, art, and literature, much of it based on historical and cultural links that the ethnic community has to its indigenous roots and its territorial affiliation. The Chicano intellectual elite used this cultural revitalization to help a dispersed Mexican American population understand its history and cultural heritage by elaborating on the concept of Aztlán. Aztlán symbolized the unifying cohesion through which Chicanos could define the foundations of their ethnic identity; it also represented the reappropriated mythical homeland for the Chicano population in the United States (Anaya and Lomelí, 1989). By the end of the decade, the different movements had coalesced into an apparently united Chicano movement throughout the Southwest and had given birth to an alternative political party, *Partido Raza Unida*. The movement as a whole placed strong emphasis on cultural and ethnic pride and political mobilization intended to empower Chicanos in their struggle to control their community and the larger social institutions.

The militant stand and cultural nationalist position were influenced from the even more militant Black civil rights movement (García, 1989). Chicanos were among the first, followed later by other groups, to organize along ethnic lines and adopt the rhetoric, ideology, and tactics of Black militants. Organized as pressure groups, the militants sought to gain representation at all levels of public life and called for governmental action on behalf of their group in such areas as education, health, housing, and employment (Van den Berghe, 1981). Policy makers in Washington, under the Johnson administration, responded to the pressure exerted by these different wings of the Civil Rights Movement with a number of programs ushered in under the banner of the Great Society and the War on Poverty.

It was in the context of the Civil Rights Movement and the growing grass-roots political mobilization by Chicanos and other Latino and Native American groups that prompted the federal government to act in the area of educational equity. In terms of demographic strength, Spanish-speaking Latinos were by far the largest "other" language minority in the United States and foremost in exerting the political pressure resulting in the passage of Title VII (Ornstein-Galicia, 1979). The Bilingual Education Act, sponsored by Senator Ralph Yarborough and signed into law by a president from Texas, Lyndon B. Johnson, was an attempt to address not only the educational problems of Mexican Americans and other ethnolinguistic groups, but served to prevent the potentially violent public demonstrations that had occurred in the Black community (see e.g., García, 1989, pp. 29-33; Castro, 1974, pp. 139-141).

The passage of this landmark federal legislation prompted more than a dozen states to pass their own policies aimed at meeting the needs of language minority students. This proliferation of bilingual education policy gave impetus to what some scholars have labeled the bilingual education movement; since its inception, the movement has grown and now includes several hundred language and ethnic groups (Mackey & Ornstein, 1977). Nonetheless, research on the relationship between the bilingual education movement and its historical relationship to ethnic struggles for educational equity has seldom been conducted.

To illustrate the role that politics and policy play in ethnoterritorial conflicts, I will focus on south Texas as an example of an ethnoterritorial conflict between Chicanos and

Anglos for political control of community governing institutions. In south Texas, the Winter Garden region and Aztlán City (pseudonym) provide an exemplary case. The major issue that arose in this conflict was equal educational opportunity through bilingual education. Before proceeding to the analysis of the empirical data of the Winter Garden region and Aztlán City, it is important to discuss the theoretical framework that will help to conceptualize how different segments of society interact in the formation of policy.

Theoretical Framework

Federal and state bilingual education policy originated as the result of the interaction between policy decision-making in governmental institutions and grass-roots ethnoterritorial political movements for civil rights and educational equity. In other words, the formulation of bilingual education policy is the outcome of the role that politics and policy play in ethnoterritorial conflicts. The term ethnoterritorial, as used by Thompson and Rudolph (1989), is an overarching concept for various political movements and conflicts that are derived from a group of people who have some identifiable geographic base within the boundaries of an existing political system. They use the concept primarily to explain the role of ethnoterritorial politics and policy responses in Western Europe and Canada. In this section I apply Thompson and Rudolph's model to the United States context to explain the role of politics and policy in Chicano ethnoterritorial conflicts.

Within Thompson and Rudolph's model, politics and policy are recognized as intervening variables linking macrolevel conditions and microlevel political behavior. Figure 1 illustrates the intervening role political institutions play in ethnoterritorial movements. Thompson and Rudolph (1989) argue that at the macrolevel various concepts have been used to explain the "causes" of the emergence of ethnoterritorial conflicts. The causal conditions that have been postulated to give rise to dissatisfaction with, and resentment of, the pattern of existing politics and policy

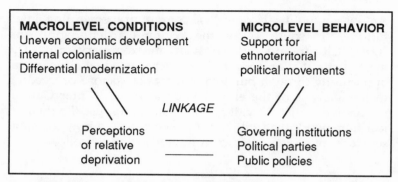

Figure 1
Linkage Role of Politics and Policy

include uneven economic development, perceptions of relative deprivation, internal colonialism, differential modernization, failure to assimilate ethnic elites, and postindustrialism (Thompson & Rudolph, 1989). They stress that "most of the 'causal' conditions concern the economic standing of the ethnoterritorial groups and regions in comparison to the dominant population groups and their central regions" (p.4). Because many of the regions have experienced differential rates and patterns of economic growth and integration, the region's ethnic population has (a) a lower standard of living and social status, (b) few if any high status political and economic positions, and (c) suffered denigration of their cultural distinctiveness. The value of the various concepts at the macrolevel is that they hypothesize that the historic economic and social conditions have created a context that generates the political prominence of the ethnoterritorial identity (Thompson & Rudolph, 1989).

The Mexican American community has comprised an ethnoterritory in the Southwest since the signing of the Treaty of Guadalupe Hidalgo in 1848, when Mexico ceded its northern territory to the United States following the war between the two countries. Numerous works have analyzed the historic economic and social context contributing to Chicano identity and to their subsequent political mobilization (Acuña, 1972; Barrera, 1979; Foley, Mota, Post, & Lozano, 1988; Montejano, 1987; Simmons, 1974; Webb, 1965; Shockley, 1974). García (1989) provides the most recent chronicle of Chicano political mobilization by analyzing the formation of an alternative political party—La Raza Unida. His study interprets how and why Chicanos organized an alternative political party locally and regionally at the onset and later at the national level.

Conceptually, however, the problem remains: How to connect the microlevel ethnoterritorial political movement to the macrolevel conditions such as internal colonialism. Thompson and Rudolph (1989) posit that governmental and political institutions are major actors and provide the linkage between the macrolevel conditions and the microlevel political behavior. But what actually leads to change or attempts to change the governmental and socioeconomic conditions to which ethnoterritorial movements object is political activity. Politics is multidimensional involving conflict, representation, and dialogue; the process through which different groups articulate their demands and compete for public resources (Thompson & Rudolph, 1989). Thompson and Rudolph add that through the action of politics, ethnoterritorial movements manifest their perceptions of past problems and future possibilities. However, the process of manifestation and the policy responses it generates from central decision-making institutions inherently transform the situation for the next set of ethnoterritorial actors and central decision makers.

This dialectic involves a complex process at various levels of society, be it the national, state, or local level. At the national level, one can get a glimpse of this process by tracing the changes in bilingual education policy since the enactment of the Bilingual Education Act in 1968. As noted earlier, by the latter part of the 1960s, the Chicano movement had coalesced into a multifaceted political struggle aimed at addressing the myriad problems facing the Mexican American community. The newer Chicano organizations

and their leadership had begun to espouse a militant nationalist rhetoric aimed at "liberation and nation-building"
(Gutiérrez, 1976). Nonetheless, the major aims that the
movement had, despite the nationalistic rhetoric on the part
of the more militant groups, were the operational goals of
getting appropriate governmental responses in such areas as
education, health, housing, and employment. In this respect, some of the demands made by ethnoterritorial
movements were more easily accommodated and were
more likely to incline leaders at the center to be accommodating toward them (Rudolph & Thompson, 1985). Thus,
the Chicano movement, as an ethnoterritorial movement
situated in the Southwest, was less concerned with achieving regional self-rule than with expanding their respective
region's share of government outputs.

In education, Chicanos demanded governmental responses aimed at addressing the poor educational treatment,
facilities, and outcomes by Chicano students. Since the demands were easily accommodated, the type of policy response forthcoming from the government is what Rudolph
and Thompson (1985) call economic and cultural output
concessions. The Bilingual Education Act as passed in 1968
provided both increased economic aid for education and
some cultural guarantees concerning the linguistic rights of
the ethnic group. However, if one follows the subsequent
changes made to the original bilingual education bill as introduced by Senator Yarborough and cosponsors in 1967, the
dialectical political process through which legislation takes
form becomes most apparent. Given the multicultural
makeup of the United States and the lobbying by different
interest groups, the final version of the bill signed into law
was very different from the original. At the federal level,
the focus of the bill was changed from legislation aimed
solely for Spanish-speaking Chicanos in the Southwest to
include all other ethnolinguistic groups (Sánchez, 1973;
Schneider, 1976). Thus, the techniques of accommodation
are such that the policy response in the form of output concessions (e.g., bilingual education policy), can both be seen as
an accomplished recognition of the legitimacy of ethnoterritorial demands and as an amplified response to include

other ethnolinguistic groups not involved in ethnoterritorial demands. In the end, the Chicano community obtained a policy response that provided increased economic aid for education and certain cultural guarantees of linguistic rights, but the policy was broadened to include other ethnolinguistic groups as well.

The federal policy has been the focus of continued political battles between ethnolinguistic groups, special interest groups, and systemwide leaders in the government. The basis for this continued conflict and controversy in bilingual education rests on the different views that special interest groups have toward the role that language and culture should play in the education of language minority groups (San Miguel, 1984). Conflicts among these different groups hinge on their particular philosophical perspectives. San Miguel (1984) has identified two clashing perspectives: (1) the pluralist perspective, shared largely by minority organizations and their political allies, which views the native language and culture of the minority child as integral to the instructional process, and (2) the assimilationist perspective, shared primarily by associations of school administrators and their political allies, which views the minority language and culture as incidental to the educational process.

According to San Miguel (1984), the conflict over bilingual education has persisted because of the push for major curricular reforms based on ". . . the role that non-English languages associated with low status minority groups should play in education" (p. 516). Because the pluralists and the assimilationists have clashing perspectives on how best to teach ethnolinguistic minorities and on the role that the student's native language should play in education, the conflict has persisted. The multidimensional nature of politics reflects this conflict over bilingual education policy in its 20-year history.

The key aim of the original Bilingual Education Act was to provide equal educational opportunity through experimental and innovative open-ended programs that could encompass any conceivable combination of time allocation to the two languages of instruction and include the history and culture of the ethnic group. However, the 1974 and 1978 amendments to the act emphasized educational equity through the mastery of English and limited both the number and type of students who could be served and the length of time they could receive native language instruction (Padilla, 1984). This change in policy fundamentally shifted the focus away from issues of equity through innovative programs to issues of equity for the individual student by emphasizing English competence. From a macrosocial structural perspective, the focus shifted from systemic institutional change to individual change. Further, there was a push for pedagogical efficiency concerning language of instruction and individual academic achievement in subject matter knowledge (Paulston, 1978). This pattern of change is again reinforced and its scope expanded with the 1984 and 1988 amendments whereby native language instruction loses more ground and English-only instruction programs gain prominence (August & García, 1988; San Miguel, 1987).

At the grass-roots community level, bilingual program policy implementation has followed a similar pattern despite heightened political involvement. The following section focuses on the microlevel political behavior of Chicanos in the Winter Garden region of south Texas by discussing the case of Aztlán City. I will attempt to show how the grass-roots political mobilization of Chicanos in Aztlán City helped them gain political control of their schools and city government. Once they controlled these key policy decision-making bodies, they initiated a number of reforms in the structure of schooling, community development, and community political organization. As part of the strategy for instituting schooling reforms, Chicanos used the 1968 federal bilingual education legislation to implement a comprehensive K-12 maintenance bilingual/bicultural education program as an integral part of their plan for community empowerment and Chicano self-determination.

The Winter Garden Region and Aztlán City

The Winter Garden region of Texas, spread over several counties, comprises an area of rich agricultural land with access to ample water for irrigation. It is climatically well suited for growing fresh vegetables in winter and early spring. Using Hansen's (1981) classification of subregions of the Southwest borderlands, it falls within the eight-county, middle Rio Grande border area and can be thought of as forming a particular ecological/agricultural zone within the plains portion of the region. As an economic unit, Winter Garden historically has been applied to concentrated winter-vegetable production in Maverick, Uvalde, Zavala, Dimmit, La Salle, and Frío counties (Tiller, 1971).

It is particularly important to note that the historical economic development of the Winter Garden as a vegetable-producing area has been due in large part to the abundance of cheap Mexican and Mexican American labor (Tiller, 1971; Foley, et al., 1988). The fact that Mexicans and Mexican Americans have provided the labor force on which the economic prosperity of the Winter Garden has developed demonstrates the structural relations between the Mexican American and Anglo ethnic groups (cf. Montejano, 1987). These relations established the Anglo group not only as the land-owning elite and businessmen but as the political force in control of community government and institutions. The Mexicanos became a wage laboring class who, if they complied with the existing social order, could with the passage of time gain access to privileged opportunities such as education.

These broader structural relations feed the causal conditions that have been postulated as giving rise to dissatisfaction within, and resentment of, the patterns of politics and policy, and have led to political demands to change the situation. Mexican American scholars have analyzed these structural relations from an internal colonial model arguing that the economic standing of Chicanos in comparison to the dominant population group is inferior because of the formation of a colonial labor system that led to differential rates and patterns of economic integration (Acuña, 1972; Almaguer, 1971; Barrera, Muñoz, & Ornelas, 1972). Closely tied with differential patterns of economic growth and integration are issues of race, which justify the lack of integration and social-economic mobility (De León, 1983; Monte-

jano, 1987; Foley, 1988). As a result of these structural relations, Chicanos in south Texas and the Southwest have a
lower standard of living and social status. They have few, if
any, high-status political and economic positions and their
cultural distinctiveness has been denigrated. In short, historically Chicanos have been second-class citizens.

In the 1960s, Chicanos sought to change their second-class
citizenship through political mobilization, community empowerment, and cultural revitalization. In Texas, the Mexican American Youth Organization (MAYO) played a major
role in this movement. MAYO was organized in 1967 by
five Chicanos, most of them university students in San Antonio, who met periodically to discuss the politics of organization. This group of astute, university-educated Chicano
activists felt that the established political parties, Republican
and Democratic, were not being attentive to the needs of the
Mexican American community in Texas and sought alternative ways of organizing. This group provided the linkage
between macrolevel conditions and microlevel political behavior. Well-read in political theory and involved in
community organizing, this new breed of leadership sought
to confront the internal colonialism that was keeping the
Mexican American people in a subordinate position. Their
goal was to mobilize the Chicano community to increase
their consciousness and draw responses from the governing
authorities. As a result, MAYO adopted a militant, con-
frontational style of politics to draw attention and possible
action to the problems and needs confronting the Mexican
American community. This new organization became involved in issues of discrimination, police brutality, labor organizing, and education, and attempted to foster a new pride
in being Chicano (García, 1989). From the start, educational
reform became one of MAYO's highest priorities.

Among the tactics that MAYO used to confront the educational problems of Chicanos in San Antonio and the rest
of Texas were demonstrations and school walkouts. Among
the more prominent demands for educational change was a
call for bilingual/bicultural education (García, 1989). Very
little research has been done on the demonstrations and
school walkouts supported by MAYO in Texas, however, the

evidence thus far indicates that the demonstrations and walkouts occurred at the same time that the Bilingual Education Bill was being discussed in Congress, or shortly after the bill became law (Navarro, 1974; García, 1989). What is most apparent in MAYO's short history is the success it had in forging a new world view of the Chicano barrio and its relationship to Anglo society.

In 1969, MAYO's political plans were to initiate a movement to redirect the social, political, and economic resources in a 10-county area of south Texas. At their semiannual state meeting held in San Antonio, the MAYO delegates decided that the counties of Zavala, Dimmit, and La Salle in the Winter Garden area would be the target in which to launch their plan (García, 1989). The organization sponsored the Winter Garden Project and named José Angel Gutiérrez, the first president of MAYO, as its director.

The Winter Garden area was chosen because the economic and political conditions experienced there by Mexicans were typical of South Texas. The project had four goals: (a) gain control of the educational system in Chicano communities, (b) bring democracy to the target counties through majority rule, (c) initiate a direct confrontation between Chicano and Anglo issues, and (d) initiate a program of rural economic development by ending Anglo economic domination and creating Chicano-controlled businesses and cooperatives (Gutiérrez, 1973). Aztlán City, the county seat of Zavala County, became the community base for the Winter Garden Project.

The Winter Garden Project unfolded on November 9, 1969, at a school board meeting where over 450 Mexican parents and students attended to support a Chicano student petition for relevant and equal quality education (Gutiérrez, 1973). The petition, which had been signed by Chicano students and parents, listed 14 demands, among them a call for bilingual/bicultural education, the creation of a Mexican American history course for credit, and the recognition of September 16 as a Mexican American holiday (*Zavala County Sentinel*, Nov. 6, 1969). However, the school board took no action on the different demands raised by the petition deciding to address these at their next regular meeting.

On December 8, 1969, the school board held a short business meeting but again did not discuss the points in the petition. The parents and students felt ignored, and as a result, they organized a boycott of classes (Gutiérrez, 1973). The boycott lasted three weeks and involved most of the Chicano students in the high school, junior high school, and some in the elementary schools. The school board finally agreed to meet with a committee of parents and students only after the Office of Civil Rights and the Justice Department intervened by sending a federal mediator to Aztlán City (Hardgrave & Hinojosa, 1975).

The struggle for relevant equal quality education highlighted by the walkout was effective and the students and parents won some initial concessions from the Anglo administration (Smith & Foley, 1975). However, the victory was more morale than substantive; it did not change the structure of ethnic power relations in the schooling domain. Nonetheless, the sense of victory for the ethnic group after the boycott ended is attributed to "viewing the walkout as a statement of contemporary ethnic identity [that] underscores the confrontation's historical significance" (Smith & Foley, 1975, p. 164). The victory signaled the end of the era of local Anglo control and ultimately led to Chicano control over schooling. Moreover, this sense of victory set in motion a series of events that changed the structure of ethnic relations in Aztlán City and much of the Winter Garden region (Shockley, 1974; Foley, et al., 1988).

Paralleling the organization and confrontation of the school authorities by the students, the parents organized into a civil rights/political organization (Lizcano, Melendrez, & Solís, n.d.) under the name of *Ciudadanos Unidos* (United Citizens). This group formed the nucleus through which José Angel Gutiérrez launched one of MAYO's Winter Garden Project aims, the formation of an alternative political party, La Raza Unida, which became the vehicle for political mobilization and political education. Through the Raza Unida party the Chicano community struggled to liberate itself from the political and socioeconomic domination that the Anglo minority had ruled since the turn of the century. In the local elections of 1970 the Chicano community gained political control of both the school board and city council.

After gaining local political control in Aztlán City, the *Partido Raza Unida*, initiated a variety of reform programs designed to empower a Chicano community that historically had been denied access to power positions. Among the reform programs initiated were a variety of housing, mental health, health care, economic, and education programs. Schools were particularly recognized for their importance in the processes of cultural maintenance and change and became the primary target for reform. Through the control of the school system, Gutiérrez hoped to ". . . force the educational system to extend to the Mexican student" (Gutiérrez, 1973, p. 2). Thus, by the fall of 1970 the changes initiated in curriculum and in policy were closely linked to the demands made by the student petitions and guided by the goals and philosophy of MAYO. Bilingual/bicultural education, Mexican American history courses, and the official school recognition of Mexican holidays such as the Diez y Seis de Septiembre and Cinco de Mayo were implemented as part of the schooling program (Hardgrave & Hinojosa, 1975).

With the initial political victories in the elections of 1970 and the subsequent initiation of reform programs, Aztlán City and La Raza Unida party became a major symbol for the Chicano Civil Rights Movement in Texas and throughout the Southwest (O'Brennan & Smith, 1981). The changes in the structure of schooling initiated in the early 1970s mark the era of Chicano control over schooling. To understand the intricacies of the role politics played in this change requires detailed analysis of the various school district, city, and county elections. That type of analysis, however, is beyond the scope of this chapter. A shorter route is to acknowledge that politics is the motor behind the change and continue the analysis focused only on bilingual program change. Therefore, the following section traces the changes brought about in the bilingual program by discussing the major shifts in the structure of the program without delving into the intricacies of the political battles.

The Implementation and Evolution
of Bilingual Education in Aztlán City

As explained above, the push for bilingual bicultural education came from the students and parents who struggled
for equal quality education in the spring of 1969. As the petitions developed, from the first one presented in April 1969
to the second in November 1969, and to the revised one in
December 1969, the wording and clarity of the demands became more apparent. MAYO as an organization founded in
1967 played a role by helping students to expand their demands from specific instances of discrimination in high
school culture (e.g., selection of cheerleaders and twirlers,
and the establishment of a student free-speech area, etc.) to
include more encompassing demands applicable to the Chicano school population as a whole (e.g., call for bilin-
gual/bicultural education, Mexican American history
courses, smaller class sizes, Mexican American counselors,
etc.). The amplification of the demands show a strong correlation between the goals of MAYO's Winter Garden Project
and the resultant school reforms introduced after the Chicano community gained control of the school system.

A bilingual education program began in the first and second grades with local funds during the fall of 1970. During
the 1971-72 school year, the district expanded the bilingual
program to include all kindergarten and third grades as part
of its newly funded five-year Title VII bilingual program
(*Cristal*, 1971; Lizcano, Meléndrez, & Solís, n.d.). During the
first year of the Title VII bilingual program, the administration held meetings throughout the district at different barrio
meeting places in order to get community input before
establishing the scope and direction of the bilingual program. Following these community meetings, the school
board established the scope and direction of the bilingual
program on February 1, 1973, and adopted a district policy
consisting of 22 recommendations, which served as a base
for the implementation of an acceptable maintenance bilingual program from grades pre-K through 12. The adoption
of these recommendations became district policies, which
served as a guide in designing the bilingual/bicultural pro-

gram for 1973-74 and subsequent years (Aztlán City Independent School District 22 Bilingual Recommendation[s], n.d.). To operationalize this new policy of restructuring the schools, the *partido* had put together a highly skilled and organized cadre of grant writers that was able to tap federal funding sources to get monies for various programs in the community (Foley, 1988). In the school district the *partido* obtained funding for various staff development programs that provided opportunities for local Chicano/as to (a) work as teacher aides and assist them in obtaining their B.A. degree and elementary teaching certificate, (b) assist Chicano/as with professional degrees to upgrade their credentials by helping them to obtain their Masters degree, and (c) assist Chicano/as with professional administrative experience by providing opportunities for them to obtain their superintendent's credentials and a master of arts degree (Lizcano, Meléndrez, & Solís, n.d.). In addition, new and remodeled schooling facilities were built and many new teaching materials were purchased or developed by incorporating the linguistic and cultural resources of the community and region.

The 22 bilingual recommendations adopted by the school board as educational policy reflects the empowered status of the Chicano community in 1973. The number of programs initiated in the district set in motion the goal of extending education to the Chicano. But perhaps the key symbol representing the new educational philosophy of the district rested on the bilingual/bicultural education program. The prekindergarten through twelfth grade bilingual/bicultural education program became the educational and philosophical plan through which the district sought to address the educational needs of the Chicano community. By 1973, the Anglo students, who had comprised the minority school population, were no longer attending the public schools (Shockley, 1974). Thus, the actions and programs approved by the board were aimed at the predominant Chicano school population.

The bilingual/bicultural education program, therefore, represents the cultural nationalist educational philosophy of

the *movimiento* as it developed through the 1970s. The
program remained virtually intact philosophically, as captured by the 22 board recommendations, through its federal
funding stage, which spanned from 1971 through 1979.
However, the political cohesion of the community underwent marked changes. In local elections, the Chicano community under the Raza Unida Party (RUP) had continued to
elect representatives to positions on the school board and
city council and by 1975 had won major political victories at
the county level of government. The *partido* had been very
successful in achieving the goals it established with the
Winter Garden Project. But unforeseen political events
took place in 1975 leading to major factionalization within
the *partido*, and this, in turn, led to division and polariza-
tion within the Chicano community.

Nonetheless, the RUP continued as the main overall political organization of the different factions competing for
control of the community institutions. Control of the
school board became one of the major battlegrounds where
the opposing factions engaged in political infighting. The effects of this political infighting eventually had its toll on the
bilingual/bicultural education program, the symbol of the
restructured schooling reform the *partido* had officially instituted in 1973. Locally these factions became known as
Raza Unida I, led by the founder of the *partido*, and Raza
Unida II, led by a number of local school professionals. This
schism is particularly evident when the superintendent of
schools, who had come in as an assistant superintendent in
the fall of 1970, left his post in August 1975 due to conflict
with several members of the school board who sided with
the the Raza Unida II faction. Thus, the 1975-1976 school
year was pivotal with respect to changes in the composition
of the school board and school administration.

As many of the members of the Raza Unida II faction
were school professionals, their strong hold was with the
schools. However, the composition of the school board
turned out to be a pivotal political arena for controlling the
direction of the educational programs, especially with respect to hiring and firing of school personnel. School board
elections were held yearly with either two or three positions

generally up for election. Starting with the school board elections in April 1975 and subsequently up until 1980, election campaigning for school board positions generated widespread community interest as both factions mobilized and canvassed for votes. Depending on which of the factions got control of the school board, the school administration composition with respect to superintendent, directors, supervisors, and some teachers often changed accordingly. Between 1975 and 1980, a total of five different superintendents were in charge of the public schools.

Despite all the changes at the district administrative level, the structure of the bilingual/bicultural education program did not change substantially because the 22 board recommendations were observed as district policy regardless of which faction was in control. The split in the *partido* was not so much over substantial ideological issues regarding the local movement as it was over competition for the few high-status, better-paying jobs within the district. Native Chicanos within the community who had obtained their administrative certification through the programs brought in by the *partido* and the district wanted access to administrative positions held by outsiders. Ideologically, native Chicanos espoused as strong a cultural nationalist perspective as the outsiders who had come in to staff the administrative positions. As a result, the local political battles often were over issues of who was more "Chicano" and supportive of programs intended to benefit the *raza* (cf. Barrios, 1981). Thus, when the RU II faction gained control of the schools in 1975, the philosophical base of the bilingual program did not change.

Furthermore, the program had a certain structural consistency due to the continued federal funding throughout the 1970s. This is not to say, however, that there were no controversies regarding the program. One of the more salient controversies took form in the latter part of the decade. An in-house debate took place among the administrators and teaching staff regarding changing the structure of the bilingual program. Some sought to maintain the policy as outlined in the 22 recommendations while others sought to include more English instruction as they felt that the students were not making the transition to English soon enough and were lagging behind in English reading. Concern over student's reading ability in English was heightened by low scores on achievement tests such as the California Test of Basic Skills (CTBS). Since the test was in English, students in the bilingual program, who were developing native language reading skills first, were at a disadvantage. With so much concern over the academic performance of students resting on standardized test scores, much of the push for change came from the teachers themselves (Interview with former Title VII and State Bilingual Program Director, October 2, 1989).

Concerns espoused by teachers and staff were over an observed discrepancy regarding progression and achievement of particular children enrolled in the bilingual program. The complaint was especially strong among those educators who had children enrolled in the school, and centered on the lack of progress their children were making in transitioning into the English reading track. They often stated that the children of the program directors and supervisors were not in the Spanish reading program because they were proficient English speakers. As such, they were placed in the English reading track, which was seen as facilitating faster academic progress than the children who were in the Spanish reading track and had not yet made the transition (Interview with former Title VII and State Bilingual Program Director, October 2, 1989). They add that these individuals did not practice what they preached with regards to the maintenance bilingual philosophy, and their actions were read as an attempt to keep their Spanish dominant children down academically without giving them access to the more prestigious English reading track.

Another concern among the teachers in the K-5 grade program was that the bilingual program was too spontaneous and lacked structure. Teachers often complained that the open classroom was too noisy and there were too many distractions, and were especially concerned that they did not have a good plan for implementing the program. District personnel, sensitive to this dissatisfaction, developed a bilingual management plan to help the teachers implement the program from prekindergarten through the fifth grade (Interview with Director of Curriculum and Instruction, June 20, 1988). This plan served to appease the teaching staff temporarily. In the end, however, a combination of all these factors had their effect in fueling the push to change the structure of the the bilingual program.

As pointed out above, the concern in the latter part of the 1970s among the teaching staff had been that students were not learning enough English to make the transition to English reading and this was having an adverse effect on their performance on standardized tests. The issue of test scores was particularly important because scores were compared with the test scores of the surrounding school districts. This issue became more salient given that anti-Raza segments, made up of Anglos and sympathetic Mexican Americans, were prone to criticize the troubled spots in Aztlán City in an attempt to discredit the RUP. In addition, teachers and supervisory personnel within the district often heard criticisms at professional meetings where they interacted with other professionals. The most often raised criticism against the Aztlán City ISD was its consistent low test scores when compared to those in surrounding districts and the presumed quality of teaching reflected in such scores. A similar type of criticism was directed at bilingual education programs at the national level (American Institute for Research, 1977; Baker & de Kanter, 1981).

Outside the school setting the political dynamics of the community also came to affect the direction of the bilingual program was to take in the 1980s. The years between 1975-1980 produced much discontent within the Chicano community as the two political factions skirmished for control of the local institutions. By 1979, the RUP lost its function as a political party. It was also the last year that RUP candidates ran in local elections. With the disbanding of the RUP much of the philosophy and ideology was also weakened. By late 1980, José Angel Gutiérrez had been ousted as county judge (Interview with County Commissioner, Pct. 3, Zavala County, Sept. 1, 1989). When José Angel Gutiérrez left town, members of RU I were left without their dynamic and charismatic leader. Their membership and unity continued

to dwindle without an organized political party espousing a
strong cultural nationalist line and focused on the needs of
the Mexicano community. As a result, many Chicanos
joined the Democratic Party or remained uncommitted.
With this sociopolitical change, the local Chicano movement modified and reorganized its course of action. In
short, with the decline of the RUP and the ouster of José
Angel Gutiérrez, the citizens of Aztlán City again had to
seek greater political and community stability.

With the demise of the RUP, the school district entered a
relatively long period of stability when a local Mexicano and
former leader of the RU II faction was hired as superintendent in July 1981. He pushed to get politics out of the
schools, and it was during his tenure as superintendent that
the bilingual program underwent substantial structural and
philosophical changes. With Title VII bilingual funding
ending in 1979, the start of the 1980s marked the start of an
essentially state-funded bilingual education program.

Restructuring the bilingual program began at the high
school level. The secondary bilingual/bicultural program
had ceased to be funded at the end of the 1970s and reduced
in scope to include the first two years of high school only.
By 1981, the program was operating only in the junior high
level where students were required to take Spanish I and II
as part of their coursework. However, by the 1984-85 school
year the Spanish Language Arts component in the junior
high was replaced by a required English reading course and
the bilingual program reduced to a prekindergarten through
fifth grade program. The factors that led to the institutionalization of a required English reading course for all students
were (a) the state of Texas legislation that called for an
English reading course for those students reading one year
or more below grade level as determined by standardized
tests such as the CTBS, and (b) a local school board policy directive that made the reading course a blanket policy for all
students in grades six through eight regardless of whether
they were reading below grade level or not (Interview with
former Title VII and State Bilingual Program Director,
June 14, 1988).

During the 1984-85 school term the bilingual program underwent further modifications. A 17-member committee consisting of teachers, elementary school principals, program directors and supervisors worked on a "Proposed Modifications in the Bilingual Program of Instruction Plan," which was submitted to the Board of Trustees for approval. The plan essentially restructured the bilingual program into a transitional prekindergarten through first grade program with emphasis on using the native language (Spanish) for instruction initially in facilitating the eventual transition to the English-only instructional track by the time the student started second grade. This document specifically stressed that if students had not reached the transitional level in Spanish by the time they started second grade they would, nonetheless, begin their reading and writing in the English language with the provision of further development of the oral language skills in English and the use of the Spanish language whenever the child did not understand a concept (School District Memo, Aug. 7, 1985).

Proponents of the transitional bilingual program approach in the community received credence from the state when the state bilingual program policy was changed to require parental consent in order to have a child enrolled in the bilingual program. Locally, this state policy change led the district to establish an English-only instructional track and a bilingual instructional program by the fall of 1985. The structure of the bilingual program in Aztlán City has remained the same since 1985 in spite of the fact that the state of Texas requires the provision of a bilingual program in grades kindergarten through fifth grade. During the spring of 1988, the Texas Department of Education made a monitoring visit to the district to observe the implementation of the bilingual education program. After the visit the agency found the district in noncompliance for failing to provide an adequate bilingual program for LEP students in second through fifth grade (Interview with the Principal of Zavala Elementary, July, 1989).

In a 20-year period the bilingual education program in Aztlán City has undergone substantial changes. In the mid-1970s, the kindergarten through twelfth grade maintenance bilingual/bicultural program was regarded as a model program throughout the Southwest and many educators made visits to the region to observe a model program in operation. However, in the late 1980s the bilingual program has been restructured into a prekindergarten to first grade transitional program where the ultimate goal is to get the children to function in English as soon as possible. The Texas Department of Education is now pushing the district to expand its bilingual program services in order to promote equal quality education. The pendulum of change has swung from one extreme to the other.

Conclusion

Bilingual education as national policy has undergone marked changes over a 20-year period. I have argued that the initial development and implementation of the original Bilingual Education Act of 1968 was the result of a complex process embracing both perception and interaction of macrolevel conditions and microlevel political behavior. In other words, the formulation of federal bilingual education policy is seen as the outcome of the role that politics and policy play in ethnoterritorial movements. Through political action and activity, ethnoterritorial movements manifest their perceptions of past problems and future possibilities. However, the process of manifestation and the policy responses it generates from central decision-making institutions inherently transform the situation for the next set of ethnoterritorial actors and central decision-makers.

Through the democratic avenue of partisan politics, Chicanos sought to decolonize their subordinate status within society by seeking control of community institutions. One of the most successful attempts at this strategy occurred in the Winter Garden region and Aztlán City. Aztlán City became an icon for the Chicano movement throughout the Southwest, the symbol of Chicano self-determination along with revitalized cultural and linguistic expression. The schools as an institution became one of the chief vehicles by which the community sought to achieve equal educational opportunity as well as recognize the validity and value of the cultural and linguistic resources of the Chicano. Through curricular reform, the community sought to reverse the process of cultural assimilation and language shift. It was, above all, an attempt to reverse the cultural denigration that the Mexican American community had suffered under internal colonialism. Ironically, although some success was achieved during the 1970s, by the decade of the 1980s, the plan for cultural and linguistic maintenance through the bilingual/bicultural education program in the schools had been weakened considerably. This decline, it is suggested, resulted from the confluence of national, state, and local bilingual education politics and policy.

At the community level, the political developments eventually had their toll on the citizenship. The citizens of Aztlán City were so saturated with the politics of the movement that the majority sought some semblance of normality, especially the teaching staff, where they could perform their duties as professionals and not have to be accountable to the broader political plan within the community. In a sense, they strove for the same type of recognition as mainstream Anglo teachers, and rejected being social change agents for the movement. Having obtained their credentials, the teachers needed to be recognized as successful professionals. In short, the majority of the professional class within the schools sought stability through the mainstream value of professionalism, devoid, so to speak, of political influence. In this manner they saw themselves as having achieved some sort of integration, and in this respect find that they now embrace the values that correspond to their class position within the mainstream culture.

To a large extent the professional class within Aztlán City now is the class segment that provides the leadership and direction within the school district, and city and county governments. Having achieved the goals of the movement, that is, gaining control of the educational system, achieving democratization through majority rule, and, to a lesser extent, ending Anglo economic domination, they no longer feel the need to push a strong cultural nationalist line. As one of the local leaders stated: "The Mexicanos are now in control. It is not so important now who wins in an election, because we know that it is going to be a Mexicano" (Interview with the Sheriff of Zavala County, Aug. 18, 1989). Before the Mexicanos gained community empowerment, it was important to initiate a direct confrontation of Chicano versus Anglo issues. Now that need is no longer viable. Essentially, the Mexicanos have decolonized the institutions within the community. The area where they have been less successful has been in achieving economic independence. It is in this area where credentials and levels of training are important that the language issue is so crucial.

National shifts in bilingual education policy have had a strong impact. At the state level, state policy in the early 1980s pushed for educational reform with the focus on making school reform meet the interests of the business community. Testing was stressed, especially with respect to English competence. The local professional class in Aztlán City responded by restructuring the bilingual program according to the direction provided by national and state educational policy directives. Not having achieved complete economic independence from the Anglo mainstream, the Chicano community continues to operate within the constraints of the political economy in the region, state, and nation.

The Chicano community of Aztlán City, made significant gains within the larger social, political, and economic structure, but their gains had limitations. They achieved new levels of empowerment and remain in control of the school system, and the municipal and county governments, yet their strong cultural nationalist stand has weakened. What appears now to be more important is a sense of integration and belonging to the national body politic. They still recognize their ethnicity and historical roots, but they argue that the school's role is not one of cultural and linguistic maintenance. Its proper role is for the transmission of English competence and mainstream values. They see the family as the proper institution for maintaining language and transmitting the ethnic culture. To what extent will the family succeed as the proper institution for language and cultural maintenance remains to be seen. When sociologist and language scholars such as Fishman (1989) argue that the process of language shift and cultural change is unavoidable without institutional support, among them schools, churches, and written media, one is left with a sense that the faith the local Chicano professional class is placing on the family is overly optimistic.

References*

Acuña, R. (1972). *Occupied America*. San Francisco: Canfield Press.

Almaguer, T. (1971). Toward the study of Chicano colonialism. *Aztlán, 2* (1), 7-20.

American Institute for Research. (1977). *Interim report, evaluation of the impact of ESEA Title VII, Spanish/English bilingual education programs*. Palo Alto, CA: Author.

Anaya, R. A. & Lomelí, F. A. (1989). *Aztlán: Essays on the Chicano homeland*. Albuquerque, NM: Academia/El Norte Publications.

Andersson, T. (1971). Bilingual education: The American experience. *Modern Language Journal, 55*(7), 427-440.

August, D., & García, E. E. (1988). *Language minority education in the United States*. Springfield, IL: Charles C. Thomas Publishers.

Aztlán City Independent School District. *Aztlán City Independent School District 22 Bilingual Recommendation*. (n.d.). Aztlán City: Author.

Baker, K. A., & de Kanter, A. A. (1981). *Effectiveness of bilingual education: A review of the literature. Final draft report*. Washington, DC: Department of Education, Office of Planning, Budget, and Evaluation.

Barrios, G. (Ed.). (1981). *La verdad: History of a Chicano newspaper*. Los Angeles: Posada Press.

Bongartz, R. (1969). The Chicano rebellion. *The Nation, 208*(9), 271-274.

Barrera, M. (1979). *Race and class in the southwest*. Notre Dame: University of Notre Dame Press.

____, Muñoz, C., & Ornelas, C. (1972). The barrio as an internal colony. In H. Hahn (Ed.), *People and politics in urban society: Urban affairs annual review, Vol. 6*, (pp. 465-498). Beverly Hills, CA: Sage Publications.

---

*In all references [Aztlán City] is inserted in place of city's name.

Carter, T. P. (1970). *Mexican Americans in school: A study of educational neglect.* New York: College Entrance Examination Board.

Castro, T. (1974). *Chicano power: The emergence of Mexican America.* New York: Saturday Review Press.

Cristal. (1971, September). Aztlán City, TX: La Raza Unida Party.

De León, A. (1983). *They called them greasers: Anglo attitudes toward Mexicans in Texas, 1821-1900.* Austin, TX: University of Texas Press.

Ericksen, C. A. (1970). Uprising in the barrios. In J. H. Burma (Ed.). *Mexican Americans in the United States: A reader* (pp. 289-294). Cambridge, MA: Schenkerman Publishing Co.

Edwards, J. R. (1976). Current issues in bilingual education. *Ethnicity, 3,* 70-81.

Fishman, J. A. (1965). The status and prospects of bilingualism in the United States. *The Modern Language Journal, 49*(4), 227-236.

_____. (1989). *Language and ethnicity in minority sociolinguistic perspective.* Philadelphia: Multilingual Matters Ltd.

Foley, D. E. (1988). The legacy of the Partido Raza Unida in south Texas: A class analysis. *Ethnic Affairs, 1* (2), 47-73.

_____, Mota, C., Post, D., & Lozano, A. (1988). *From peones to politicos: Ethnic relations in a south Texas town, 1900-1978* (rev. ed.). Austin: Center for Mexican American Studies, University of Texas Press.

Gaarder, A. B. (1965). Teaching the bilingual child: Research, development, and policy. *The Modern Language Journal, 49*(3), 165-175.

García, I. M. (1989). *United we win: The rise and fall of La Raza Unida Party.* Tucson: Mexican American Studies & Research Center, University of Arizona.

Gebler, L., Moore, J. W., and Guzman, R. C. (1970). *The Mexican-American people: The nation's second largest minority.* New York: The Free Press.

Gutiérrez, J. A. (1973). Aztlán: Chicano revolt in the Winter Garden. *La Raza Magazine,* pp. 36-49.

_____. (1976). *Toward a theory of community organization in a Mexican American community in south Texas.* Unpublished doctoral dissertation, University of Texas, Austin, TX.

Hansen, N. (1981). *The border economy: Regional development in the Southwest.* Austin, TX: University of Texas Press.

Hardgrave, R. L., & Hinojosa, S. (1975). *The politics of bilingual education: A study of four southwest Texas communities.* Manchaca, TX: Sterling Swift Publishing.

Lizcano, J., Melendrez, A., & Solis, E. (n.d.). *Cristal.* Aztlán City, TX: Aztlán City Independent School District.

Mackey, W., and Ornstein, J. (1977). *The bilingual education movement: Essays on its progress.* El Paso, TX: Texas Western Press.

Manuel, H. T. (1965). *Spanish-speaking children in the southwest: Their education and public welfare.* Austin, TX: University of Texas Press.

Montejano, D. (1987). *Anglos and Mexicans in the making of Texas, 1836-1986.* Austin, TX: University of Texas Press.

Navarro, A. (1974). *El partido de la Raza Unida in Aztlán City: A peaceful revolution.* Unpublished doctoral dissertation, University of California, Riverside, CA.

O'Brennan, J., & Smith, N. (1981). *The crystal icon.* Austin: Galaband Press.

Ornstein-Galicia, J. L. (1979). Comparative ethnic factors in bilingual education: The United States and abroad. In R. V. Padilla (Ed.), *Ethnoperspectives in bilingual education research: Bilingual education and public policy in the United States* (pp. 461-482). Ypsilanti, MI: Eastern Michigan University.

Padilla, R. (1984). Federal policy shifts and the implementation of bilingual education programs. In J. A. García, T. Córdova, & J. R. García (Eds.), *The Chicano struggle: Analyses of past and present efforts* (pp. 90-110). Binghamton, NY: Bilingual Press/Editorial Bilingüe.

Paulston, C. B. (1978). Rationales for bilingual educational reforms: A comparative assessment. *Comparative Education Review, 22*(3), 402-419.

Rudolph, J. R., Jr., & Thompson, R. J. (1985). Ethnoterritorial movements and the policy process: Accommodating nationalist demands in the developed world. *Comparative Politics, 17,* 291-311.

Sanchez, G. (1973). *An analysis of the bilingual education act, 1967-68,* Unpublished dissertation, University of Massachusetts, Amherst.

San Miguel, G., Jr. (1984). Conflict and controversy in the evolution of bilingual education in the United States - an interpretation. *Social Science Quarterly, 65*(2), 505-518.

____. (1987). *"Let all of them take heed" Mexican Americans and the campaign for educational equity in Texas, 1910-1981.* Austin, TX: University of Texas Press.

Schneider, S. G. (1976). *Revolution, reaction or reform: The 1974 bilingual education act.* New York: L.A. Publishing Co.

Shockley, J. S. (1974). *Chicano revolt in a Texas town.* South Bend, IN: University of Notre Dame Press.

Simmons, O. (1974). *Anglo-Americans and Mexican-Americans in south Texas.* New York: Arno Press.

Smith, W., & Foley, D. (1975). *The transition of multiethnic schooling in model town, Texas: 1930-1969* (Final Report NIE Project No. R020825 and No. 3-4003). Washington, DC: Office of Education, U.S. Department of Health, Education and Welfare.

Stein, C. B., Jr. (1986). *Sink or swim: The politics of bilingual education.* New York: Praeger Publishers.

Thompson, R. J., & Rudolph, J. R., Jr. (1989). The ebb and flow of ethnoterritorial politics in the Western world. In J. R. Rudolph & R. J. Thompson (Eds.), *Ethnoterritorial politics, policy and the western world* (pp. 1-14). Boulder, CO: Lynne Rienner Publishers.

Texas Education Agency, Division of Research. (1957). *Report of pupils in Texas public schools having Spanish surnames, 1955-1956.* Austin, TX: Author.

Tiller, J. W., Jr. (1971). *The Texas Winter Garden: Commercial cool-season vegetable production.* Austin, TX: Bureau of Business Research, Graduate School of Business, University of Texas at Austin.

Torgerson, D. (1970). "Brown power" unity seen behind school disorders. In J. H. Burma (Ed.). *Mexican Americans in the United States: A reader* (pp. 279-288). Cambridge, MA: Schenkerman Publishing Co.

Van der Berghe, P. L. (1981). *The ethnic phenomena.* New York: Elsevier North Holland, Inc.

Webb, W. P. (1965). *The Texas rangers: A century of frontier defense* (reprint). Austin, TX: University of Texas Press.

Zavala County Sentinel. (1969, November 6), p. 1.

Part Two

Improving Practice in Bilingual Education

TWO-WAY BILINGUAL/IMMERSION EDUCATION: THEORY, CONCEPTUAL ISSUES, AND PEDAGOGICAL IMPLICATIONS

Kathryn J. Lindholm
San Jose State University

ABSTRACT

Two-way bilingual/immersion education integrates bilingual education for language minority students with immersion education for language majority students with the goals of promoting academic achievement and language proficiency in two languages. The purpose of this paper is to review selected literature to discuss the theoretical and conceptual building blocks (i.e., social context of language, effective schools, language development, relationship between language and cognition) of two-way bilingual immersion education, and from this theoretical background, to discuss the pedagogical issues that are important in two-way bilingual/immersion education.

Two-way bilingual/immersion education is the marriage of bilingual education for linguistic minority children and immersion education for linguistic majority children. Because the two-way model promotes academic achievement and language proficiency in two languages for both language majority and language minority students in the same classroom, it has begun to receive attention at the national, state, and local levels. Still, there is little published information about two-way bilingual/immersion education, especially theoretical in nature, from which to develop the two-way program model.

Several pedagogical and conceptual issues, and theoretical building blocks can be implicated in the two-way bilingual/immersion model. The purpose of this chapter is to discuss the theory and conceptual issues relevant to two-way bilingual/immersion education, and from this background, discuss the important pedagogical issues in two-way bilingual/immersion education.

Defining Bilingual/Immersion Education

Two-way bilingual/immersion education programs are equally concerned with the language and academic development of both language minority and language majority children (Lindholm, 1990a). The students are integrated for all content instruction in a high-quality curriculum equivalent to the curriculum taught in mainstream classes. The major difference is that the language of instruction is the native language for the language minority students (e.g., Spanish) and a second language for language majority students (e.g., Spanish). (See Lindholm, 1990a, for a description of two-way bilingual/immersion programs.)

Variations in community and administrative needs mean that schools have varying goals for implementing two-way programs. However, three major goals of most programs include: (1) students will develop high levels of proficiency in two languages, (2) students will demonstrate normal to superior academic performance measured in both languages, and (3) students will show high levels of psychosocial competence and positive cross-cultural attitudes.

Theoretical and Conceptual Issues

Educational innovations must rely on sound educational theory in order for program models to be successful in meeting their goals. Bilingual/immersion has been constructed on four theoretical and conceptual building blocks to meet the language and academic needs of both native and nonnative speakers of English: (1) social context of language education, (2) effective schools, (3) language development, and (4) relation between language and thought. Each of these issues will be discussed separately.

Social Context of Language Education

The social context of language education programs, which refers to the attitudes and policies that are held regarding the language education program and its participants, can positively or negatively influence a program's outcomes

(Cortes, 1986; Troike, 1978).   If community, administration, and staff attitudes toward bilingualism and language minority students are favorable, then language education policies are more likely to result in high-quality programs and high levels of language and academic achievement among the program participants (Willig, 1985).

In contrast, when the community and administration attitudes toward bilingualism and language minority students are negative, then it is unlikely that language education programs will be implemented unless they are mandatory, and then they will tend to result in lower levels of academic achievement and language proficiency on the part of program participants.   As Linney and Seidman (1989) pointed out in their review of the literature on school and teacher effects on student outcomes, the quality of a child's school experience is important not only for academic and achievement outcomes, but for fostering self-esteem, self-confidence, and general psychological well-being.

School and teacher effects are reflected directly in program implementation and indirectly in policy statements regarding program implementation.   Thus, the social context in which a student is educated and learns language becomes critical.   Language education theorists and practitioners have discussed the social context of language learning in terms of the additive/subtractive bilingualism dichotomy.   Additive bilingualism is a form of enrichment in which "children can add one or more foreign languages to their accumulating skills and profit immensely from the experience—cognitively, socially, educationally, and even economically" (Lambert, 1984, p. 19).   Additive bilingualism is associated with high levels of proficiency in the two languages, adequate self-esteem, and positive cross-cultural attitudes (Lambert, 1984, 1987).

In stark contrast, subtractive bilingualism refers to the situation in which children are "forced to put aside or subtract out their ethnic languages for a more necessary, useful, and prestigious national language" (Lambert, 1984, p. 19). Subtractive bilingualism is associated with lower levels of second language attainment, scholastic underachievement, and psychosocial disorders (Lambert, 1984).   The reasoning

behind these negative consequences is tied to the relationship between language and thought. When children are
pressured to learn English as quickly as possible and to set
aside their home language, they lose the critical linguistic
foundation upon which their early conceptual development
is based.

Not only are linguistic minority children often subjected
to subtractive bilingualism contexts, but numerous studies
have shown that teachers interact differently with minority
students as opposed to majority students: the teachers tend
to have lower expectations for success, praise less often but
criticize more frequently, provide fewer opportunities for
minority students to respond in class, and give less time to
respond (see Brophy & Good, 1986, for a review of the literature). The gap between majority and linguistic minority
students is even greater because linguistic minority children
have additional barriers to overcome with accented English
speech, and greater difficulty in matching the grade level ex-
pectancies of their majority peers; language minority students are more likely than language majority students to be
placed in lower school tracks or assigned to special education
classes.

Research shows that expectations for white students are
higher than they are for ethnic minority students (except
Chinese, Korean, and Japanese), and expectations for
middle-class students are higher than those for lower-class
students. When studies include comparisons of white with
minority students of both social classes, different results
emerge. In research in which teachers are given verbal or
written *descriptions* of students, teachers do not base their
assessments on minority status, only socioeconomic status.
In contrast, when teachers are given *pictures* of students or
have the opportunity to listen to them, then teachers base
their assessments largely on minority group status. As a
consequence, social class and ethnic minority status have
different effects on teachers, where lower-class ethnic minority students have the lowest expectations and middle-
class white students the highest expectations (Dusek, 1985).
Language proficiency and immigration status are characteristics that produce the lowest expectations overall.

Differential treatment by teachers leads to differential academic outcomes on the part of students (Brophy, 1986; Brophy & Good, 1986). Students who are labelled as bright or high achievers are praised more frequently, and given more opportunities and more time to respond to the teacher in class. Given extra praise and attention, these students are able to maintain their perceived high achievement status. In contrast, students who are labelled as low achievers are given fewer opportunities to respond, less time to answer when they are called upon, and receive more criticism and less praise.

Although most teachers report that their expectations of students do not change over time, research shows that teacher attitudes and expectations toward students can be changed through professional development (Brophy & Good, 1986). When Kerman, Kimball, and Martin (1980) trained teachers to use positive interactions in an equitable manner with both perceived high and low achievers, all students showed significant achievement gains. Such intervention appears to be beneficial in its immediate effect on student achievement, and student attitudes and perceived competence (Brophy, 1986).

Student expectations toward each other are also important. Allowing only unplanned or incidental contact between majority and minority students may also reinforce negative expectations on the part of classmates. In his highly influential work on peer relations and school desegregation, Allport (1954) proposed four factors that are the core conditions for improving intergroup relations, and maximizing the achievement of minority and majority students. When minority and majority students have *equal status* in the classroom, *work interdependently* on tasks with common objectives, and have *opportunities to interact with each other as individuals*, student expectations and attitudes toward each other become more positive. Allport also pointed out that the effect of these contacts will be greatly enhanced if the contacts are *supported by teachers* and other authority figures.

Other researchers have provided evidence to support Allport's basic premises in demonstrating that instructional treatments that explicitly promote positive interdependence between minority and majority students result in positive outcomes in terms of an increased number of cross-racial friendships and greater self-esteem and academic achievement (Lambert, 1984, 1987). Particularly during the early school years, children are malleable in their cross-cultural attitudes. Children educated in immersion programs from early elementary school develop more positive cross-cultural attitudes than their non-immersion program peers (Lambert, 1987).

Cooperative learning methods, which were developed based on Allport's four factors, use heterogeneous grouping and shared group leadership with activities that require the students to work interdependently, with clear individual and group accountability for the achievement of all group members (Johnson, Johnson, & Holubec, 1986; Kagan, 1986; Slavin, 1983). Research demonstrates unequivocal support for cooperative learning in achievement, ethnic relations, and self-esteem (Slavin, 1983; see Kagan, 1986, for a review of this literature). When students work in ethnically mixed cooperative learning groups, they gain in cross-ethnic friendships. Most research also shows positive effects of cooperative learning on achievement. Strong achievement gains have been found with minority and typically low-achieving students, with little or no effect for white (non-Hispanic) and higher-achieving students. However, the gains of minority and low-achieving students are not made at the expense of majority or high-achieving students as these students also made gains at least as great, if not greater than, in traditional classrooms. Thus, cooperative learning methods close the achievement gap between minority and majority students, and have positive effects on the self-esteem and cross-cultural attitudes of both minority and majority children.

Bilingual/immersion education, then, is built on providing the language learner with the most positive social context in which to develop bilingual competence; in which both linguistic minority and majority students can benefit from an additive bilingualism environment; in which students develop in a social context in which both languages and cultures are equally valued and all students are treated equally; and in which students are integrated in a natural fashion to promote positive cross-cultural attitudes and psychosocial development, and higher levels of second language development and academic achievement.

Effective Schools

Over the past several years, a large literature has amassed on effective schools (Edmonds, 1983; Good & Weinstein, 1986). The conclusion of this research can be summarized as follows:

> A general finding across all the studies that distinguish effective from ineffective schools is the belief on the part of teachers in effective schools that all children can learn and that the school is responsible for that learning . . . schools make a difference. Variation in achievement among schools serving similar populations is often substantial and has significant implications for social policy (Good & Weinstein, 1986, pp. 1095-1096).

Several salient characteristics of effective schools have been identified:

1. a principal who is a good leader and shows leadership through concern for the quality of instruction
2. an instructional focus that is understood by all
3. an orderly and safe environment conducive to teaching and learning
4. teacher expectations and behaviors that demonstrate to the students that the students must obtain at least some minimal level of mastery
5. the use of student achievement as the basis for program evaluation (Edmonds, 1983; Linney & Seidman, 1989)

Bilingual and immersion education research also has demonstrated that effective bilingual programs are integrated with the total school program, strong support for the program is given from the school district administrators and local board of education, and the principal is very supportive of and knowledgeable about the program (Cortes, 1986; Troike, 1986).

Troike (1986), in a presentation to the U.S. House of Representatives Committee on Education and Labor, pinpointed a number of weaknesses in programs for linguistic minority students. One problem is the program's treatment by the school administration as peripheral to the central curriculum and organization of the school. The reason for this problem is due to a perceived "temporariness" about federally funded programs, which are expected to expire upon the cessation of government support. He also points out that school officials have applied for grants to supplement the regular school program, without any interest or commitment to the program for the linguistic minority students. Money, then, as opposed to concern for students, may motivate a school to institute such a program. In other cases, bilingual programs are viewed as a convenient way to help achieve school desegregation.

In contrast, according to Troike (1986), successful bilingual programs are more likely to be housed centrally, and closely integrated structurally and functionally within the total school system. In addition, they receive strong support from the central administration and from building principals. In schools with successful programs, the administration does not regard bilingual education as remedial or as merely a temporary program, but rather makes a commitment to providing an equal education for linguistic minority students even beyond any external funding and ensures that the program is an integral part of the basic program in the school system. The administration also devotes attention and resources to promoting acceptance of the program among the community and other school staff by informing them of its methods and results. In addition, it supports acceptance of the bilingual program staff as part of the regular staff by insisting on comparable standards of certification and competence and by facilitating interaction among them. Finally, there is a serious effort to obtain high-quality materials in the non-English language for the students. Resources are allocated for the purchase and development of appropriate materials for linguistic minority students.

In sum, successful bilingual/immersion programs, then, require effective and supportive administrative leadership, teachers with high expectations for achievement of all students, and actual integration within the total school program. In addition, they must be viewed as long-term enrichment programs, as opposed to temporary compensatory programs, and receive an equitable share of resources. High-quality educational materials in both languages and appropriate staff training are also essential for an enrichment program to develop high levels of student competence in *two* languages.

While many of these effective school issues are important in all educational programs, they are critical in bilingual/immersion programs (as well as bilingual programs) because of the usual compensatory label most bilingual programs possess as well as the increased attention many programs receive because of the added goal of promoting Spanish language and academic competence among the nonnative Spanish speakers. This added goal puts increased pressure on teachers and administrators to demonstrate as quickly as possible high levels of academic achievement for community assurance that the program is truly an enrichment program of benefit to both groups of participants, that is, language minority and language majority.

Language Development

Language development has been studied extensively for an understanding of how children acquire their first language, or two languages for bilingual children, and how children and adults develop a second or even third language.

Most language acquisition researchers agree that the capacity for native-like proficiency diminishes with age. Anecdotal evidence indicates that adults have considerable difficulty in learning a second language, and in fact, often never achieve native-like competence although they may be more effective language learners because of more efficiently developed language learning strategies (Genesee, 1987; Snow & Hoefnagle-Hohle 1982) and/or positive transfer from a fully developed first language system. Further, long-term research shows that individuals who begin second language learning early are more likely than those who begin later to achieve native-like levels of proficiency in their second language, particularly if given exposure to the language in extracurricular settings (Genesee, 1987). Research in the process of language development has demonstrated that this process is systematic and rule-governed, and involves the learner's active cognitive attempts to formulate linguistic rules that underlie competence in the language.

Considerable research has been conducted on language input in both first and second language acquisition to determine whether or how input influences language development (e.g., Gass & Madden, 1985). In first language learning, input has been studied by examining the type of speech mothers, and occasionally fathers or other caregivers, use with children—usually dubbed "motherese" in the literature. This literature has shown some distinct characteristics of speech addressed to young children, such as: slow rate of speech; simplified grammar, vocabulary, and concepts; repetitious; oriented to the here and now; and containing few corrections, with the corrections that occur being based on the truth value, or content, of the sentence rather than on the grammar (Lindholm, 1981). Second language researchers have also found similar input features in speech addressed to second language learners; this special language is often termed "foreigner talk" (e.g., Long, 1981). Research shows that regardless of the input a child receives, the process of language development follows systematic patterns.

A final note on language input for child bilinguals concerns language mixing versus language separation. Most research on child bilingualism supports the notion that keeping two languages as distinct as possible is the better strategy for promoting high levels of bilingualism in children (e.g., Hakuta, 1986; Padilla & Lindholm, 1984).

Strategies in which the languages are distinguished by individuals (e.g., mother speaks Spanish, father speaks English), environment (e.g., German in the home, English in the day care), or time (e.g., Japanese in the morning, English in the afternoon) help children to distinguish the two languages and provide consistent rules for which language is to be used in particular settings or with particular individuals (Padilla & Lindholm, 1984).

Bilingual/immersion, like immersion education, is grounded in language acquisition research in several respects. First, it is based on the premise that considerable language learning can occur naturally during nonlanguage arts classes, such as mathematics or social studies, which is similar to first language acquisition in which children communicate with each other about non-language-related issues (Genesee, 1984). Second, the learner can progress according to his or her own rate and style, again in much the same way that first language learners do (Genesee, 1987). Third, based on research regarding language learning and age, it has been argued that early immersion in a second language can facilitate a child's second language learning by taking advantage of his or her special neurolinguistic, psycholinguistic, and cognitive capacities to learn language (Genesee, 1984; Lambert, 1984). Fourth, language input to the students is adjusted to their conceptual and linguistic level, using many features of "motherese" to facilitate language comprehension and acquisition on the part of the students. Fifth, concentrated exposure to language is important to promote language development. Sixth, the two languages are kept distinct and never mixed during instruction.

Relationship Between Language and Thought

Many early studies examining the cognitive functioning of bilinguals concluded that exposure of young children to two languages often had deleterious effects on their intellectual development, as measured by standard tests of intelligence (for a review, see Hakuta, 1986). Careful examination of these early reports, however, led to questions concerning the validity of this conclusion. Almost without exception, the monolingual control groups in these studies who gave significantly higher performances on standardized intelligence tests were speakers of a sociolinguistically dominant language, dominant in the sense that it enjoyed greater prestige and greater communicative utility in the larger society from which the groups were selected. Moreover, in the majority of these studies, the bilinguals, regardless of their proficiency in the dominant language, suffered from socioeconomic and environmental factors specific to their lower status in the community. Because of these and other shortcomings having to do with the tests themselves, many of these studies have been dismissed for their lack of valid scientific inquiry.

In a classic study by Peal and Lambert (1962), perhaps the best controlled study comprising monolingual and bilingual children on a series of intellectual tasks, Peal and Lambert observed that exposure to two languages gave French-English bilinguals an advantage. Intellectually, their experiences with two languages seemed to result in mental flexibility, superiority in concept formation, and a more diversified set of mental abilities. In contrast, the monolinguals appeared to have more unitary cognitive structures, which restricted their verbal problem-solving ability.

A number of studies have been conducted with bilingual children that substantiate Peal and Lambert's results, although not all research is totally supportive of this position (for reviews, see Hakuta, 1986; Homel, Palij, & Aaronson, 1987). The important point is that there is evidence to suggest that bilingual development may facilitate cognitive functioning.

The extent to which cognitive development may be influenced by language proficiency has been discussed by Cummins (1979, 1987) and Toukomaa and Skutnabb-Kangas (1977). They speculate that there may be threshold levels of linguistic proficiency a child must attain to avoid cognitive disadvantages and to allow the potentially beneficial aspects of becoming bilingual to influence cognitive growth. This hypothesis assumes that a child must attain a certain minimum or threshold level of proficiency in both languages to enable bilingualism to exert a significant long-term effect and positively influence cognitive growth. However, if bilingual children sustain only a very low level of proficiency in L2 or L1, the range of potential interaction with the environment through that language is likely to be limited and there will not be any positive effect on cognitive development.

Cummins and Toukomaa and Skutnabb-Kangas in fact, argue that there are two thresholds. Attainment of the lower threshold level of bilingual proficiency would be sufficient to guard against negative consequences of bilingualism. However, for long-term cognitive benefits to be manifested requires achieving the second threshold of a higher level of bilingual proficiency.

Thus, the differential effects of bilingualism on cognitive development that have been reported in the literature have been explained by understanding the child's level of bilingual proficiency. In research showing negative effects on cognition, the threshold hypothesis would explain the negative effects by proposing that the bilingual children's proficiency in one or both languages was low enough to impede the interaction that occurred through that language in the school environment. Thus, these language minority children did not develop the school language to a sufficiently high level to benefit fully from their schooling. Conversely, children who attained the upper threshold of bilingual proficiency, or high levels of skills in both L1 and L2, have demonstrated rapid academic and cognitive development. The threshold hypothesis predicts neither positive nor negative consequences on cognition of children who attain full native proficiency in their first language, but develop only intermediate levels of proficiency in the weaker language.

The type of language proficiency is also important to examine because it influences our understanding of cognitive and academic functioning across languages. Cummins (1987), among others, has conceptualized language proficiency along two continua. The first continuum represents the range of contextual support available for expressing or receiving meaning. On one extreme of this continuum is context-embedded language and on the other end is context-reduced communication. These two ends of the continuum are distinguished by the amount of shared and real-world knowledge regarding the communication. In context-embedded communication, knowledge is shared among the speakers and the language is supported by a range of para-linguistic and situational cues. In context-reduced communication, knowledge may not be shared among the speakers, and thus there is a need for more precise and elaborated language and a dependence on the linguistic cues solely to interpret the communication. Examples of communicative behaviors going from left to right along the continuum might be talking with a friend, writing a letter to a close friend, reading (or writing) an article on theories of analogical reasoning. Context-embedded communication is more typical of everyday conversation whereas many of the linguistic demands of the classroom reflect communication that is closer to the context-reduced end of the continuum.

The second continuum addresses the developmental components of communicative proficiency with respect to the level of active cognitive involvement in the task or activity, where cognitive involvement is defined as the amount of information that must be processed simultaneously or in close succession by the individual in order to carry out the activity (Cummins, 1987). The level of skill mastery underlies this continuum, where new skills are cognitively demanding, but move up to cognitively undemanding as they are mastered and become processed automatically. For example, the acquisition of L1 phonology and syntax is cognitively demanding for a two-year old, but cognitively undemanding for a normal 12-year old. Thus, whenever new linguistic skills must be used to communicate, active cognitive involvement occurs. As mastery occurs, specific linguistic skills travel from the bottom to the top of the vertical continuum. Cognitive involvement can be just as intense in context-embedded as in context-reduced activities.

Two important points can be made about this model (California State Department of Education, 1982). First, all human beings acquire the language proficiency, in at least one language, necessary to complete context-embedded, cognitively undemanding tasks (e.g., everyday conversation). Second, among monolinguals, the ability to complete cognitively demanding tasks in context-reduced situations (e.g., reading or math proficiency) differs significantly among individuals. The ability to complete these tasks is probably highly related to an individual's intelligence and amount of formal schooling. The capability to access information in any of these areas depends on how it is stored in memory.

There are two major views of how bilinguals store and retrieve language. One view is that bilinguals develop the skills in each language independently and store them separately in the brain. According to this *separate underlying proficiency* model, efforts to develop proficiency in one language do not facilitate development in another language and may, in fact, impede second language development because of limited storage space in the brain. The opposing view, labelled *common underlying proficiency*, proposes that there is a common storage space and that the development of skills and knowledge in one language is not independent of the acquisition of information in a second language. Rather, developing knowledge and proficiency skills in one language facilitates learning in the second language (Cummins, 1987). Thus, acquiring the cognitively demanding tasks in context-reduced environments, typical of many school-related activities, in one language paves the way for the bilingual to perform similar tasks in the other language.

Considerable research supports the common underlying proficiency viewpoint. Studies of academic skills in a bilingual's two languages typically show high relationships, with correlations in the .60 to .80 range (Cummins, 1979; Lindholm, 1990b). Thus, a bilingual who performs well in math in one language is highly likely to perform well in math in a second language, even after only one or two years of schooling in the second language, once the student has the language proficiency skills for demonstrating that knowledge (Lindholm, 1990b).

Three critical educational implications emerge for two-way bilingual/immersion programs from these theoretical and conceptual points. First, bilingual development may facilitate cognitive functioning if the duo language development is sustained over a long period of time so that the child attains a high level of proficiency in the two languages.

Second, high levels of language proficiency require the development of both communicative and academic language skills in both languages.   Third, skills and knowledge learned in one language are accessible in another language as soon as the student possesses sufficient language proficiency to exhibit the knowledge.

Pedagogical Issues

In this section, three important pedagogical issues are presented and discussed based on the previous review. These issues include: (1) transfer of content across languages; (2) promoting high levels of academic achievement; and (3) discrepant language needs of linguistic minority and linguistic majority students.

Transfer of Content Across Languages

In the previous section, we discussed the theoretical notions related to transfer in the relationship between language and cognition. The pedagogical issue of transfer, that is, that content learned in one language is available or more easily acquired in the second language, is critical to any of the language education models—bilingual, immersion, or bilingual/immersion—as all three models assume that content need only be taught in one language.

In this section, I will discuss the evidence for transfer in bilingual/immersion programs, limitations of transfer, and pedagogical implications arising from the assumption of transfer.

In some of my own work in bilingual/immersion programs (Lindholm, 1990b; Lindholm & Fairchild, 1989, 1990), there is clear evidence of transfer of content demonstrated in the achievement performance of both native Spanish- and English-speaking children. Although these grade K-3 children received *all* of their math instruction in Spanish they were able to perform fairly well on math achievement tests in English (Bilingual = 50th percentile, English dominant = 44th percentile, Spanish dominant = 36th percentile), with some students even scoring above the 75th percentile on the CTBS test. Similarly, by the end of second grade, students had been instructed only in Spanish reading, yet many bilinguals and native English-speaking students were able to score above the 50th percentile in English reading achievement. A few bilinguals, but not dominant English speakers, even scored above the 75th percentile. These results show that some of the knowledge and skills learned through reading and math instruction in Spanish were available to students in English.

It is also clear that the transfer of content across languages has its limitations. The major limitation is that students can only demonstrate the transfer once they have acquired sufficient language skills to do so, and the level of language sufficiency will vary depending on the language requirements of the subject matter. For example, with bilingual/immersion students, there was a significant correlation between English reading achievement and Spanish reading achievement (in one study of third graders [Lindholm, 1989], $r = .35$, $p < .001$; in another study of sixth graders [Lindholm & Fairchild, 1989], $r = .56$, $p < .01$). The correlation was much higher between English math achievement and Spanish math achievement (in one study of third graders [Lindholm, 1989], $r = .65$, $p < .001$; in another study of sixth graders [Lindholm & Fairchild, 1989], $r = .83$, $p < .0001$). One reason for this difference in the relations across languages in math and reading skills is due to the level and type of language skills required to demonstrate competency in these areas.

In an examination of the predictors of reading and math achievement in English, the best predictor of *English math achievement* was *Spanish math achievement* ($R^2 = .47$), followed by *English language achievement* (R^2 change = .06). This result suggests that the math knowledge and skills learned in Spanish were transferred to English, but responses to math problems in English also required academic language proficiency in English, as one would expect.

On the other hand, the best predictor of *English reading achievement* was *English language achievement* ($R^2 = .65$), followed by *oral English proficiency* (R^2 change = .04). Thus, the best predictor was not Spanish reading achievement, but rather academic English language skills and oral English language skills. In fact, a significant amount of variance in English reading (R^2 = .69) was accounted for by these two distinct types of language skills. Spanish reading was correlated with English reading, but it was not the best predictor. Spanish reading was also highly correlated with English language achievement. While English language achievement was the best predictor of English reading, an important correlate of English language achievement was Spanish reading achievement. On the basis of these results, I would argue that students developed high levels of English language achievement because of the Spanish academic language they possessed. This point will be discussed further in the next section.

These results are important for three reasons. First, they provide clear evidence for transfer of content across languages. Second, such results demonstrate the distinction between the two types of language proficiency skills, academic and conversational, and they show the significance of both types of language skills in English reading. Third, conversational skills are significantly less important in achievement, both reading and math, than academic language skills, despite their overall saliency in the process of transitioning LEP students into mainstream English-only programs.

A significant pedagogical implication emerges from these results, which is that the two types of language skills, academic and conversational, need to be developed in both languages before one can expect to see high levels of achievement performance, especially in the nondominant language of the classroom. Developing both academic and conversational skills requires a considerable investment of time, which means that educators must be willing to wait patiently to see children performing at high levels of achievement in English. This is important because we often want to see instant success in both languages on the part of students in bilingual programs, and the results presented here show some compelling reasons why we do not see, nor could we expect to see, such academic success immediately.

Promoting High Levels of Language and Academic Achievement

In the previous discussion of transfer, we saw the importance of developing both academic and conversational skills to facilitate reading and math achievement. To understand the promotion of *high* levels of achievement requires elaboration of the role of language proficiency in achievement within the context of the threshold hypothesis (Cummins, 1987; Toukomaa & Skutnabb-Kangas, 1977).

The threshold hypothesis, as indicated previously, states that there are cognitive advantages for bilinguals who have reached a higher level of proficiency in the two languages, and neither advantages nor disadvantages for additive bilinguals who are proficient in one language but limited in proficiency in their second language.

In some of my own work in bilingual/immersion programs (Lindholm, 1990b), second- and third-grade students who have developed the conversational skills to be rated as orally proficient in both languages have scored higher, though not significantly higher, than students who were rated fluent in their first language but limited in their second language, in academic achievement tests in both English and Spanish. In examinations of the scores of the Spanish dominant, English dominant, and bilingual (who began school dominant or monolingual in Spanish) students from kindergarten through grade three (the latest grade for which there is appropriate data), the gap between students dominant in their native language and bilinguals, which is minimal or nonexistent in the early grades, increases across the grades.

One interpretation of this result is that as the students receive more instruction, those students who are proficient in the two languages, have developed better strategies for processing information, which has lead to their bilingual language proficiency. Of course, the alternative explanation is that more intelligent students acquire language faster and become bilingual, and these students, by virtue of their higher intelligence, also score higher in achievement tests. Regardless of the interpretation, there seems to be a link between level of bilingualism and academic achievement.

However, it is not enough for a bilingual to have high levels of conversational proficiency in the two languages to demonstrate advantages over a monolingual or a person dominant in one language. If conversational proficiency were sufficient for an academic advantage in language and reading achievement tests in English, then English speakers, because of several years of conversational English in their homes, should have an advantage over bilinguals who were originally native Spanish speakers and have only recently become classified as fluent in oral English. However, by third grade in the bilingual/immersion program, after only one academic year of reading instruction in English, bilingual students scored higher, though not significantly higher, than English dominant students in language achievement (16th vs 29th percentiles, respectively), but equivalent in reading (29th vs 30th percentiles, respectively). In addition, the bilinguals (B) outperformed the English (E) dominant and Spanish (S) dominant students in English math achievement (B = 50th percentile, E = 44th percentile, S = 36th percentile) and in Spanish reading achievement as well (B = 65th percentile, E = 19th percentile, S = 35th percentile).

To demonstrate the significance of academic language skills in academic achievement, we can look at the second graders who had received all of their instruction in reading and academic language in Spanish, and had received only oral English prior to the testing. At this second-grade level, bilinguals outperformed the English dominant students in Spanish reading achievement (English = 59th percentile, Bilinguals = 76th percentile), showing a richer knowledge base in Spanish academic language skills. Although the scores of the English dominant and bilingual students were comparable in English language achievement (English = 22nd percentile, Bilinguals = 22nd percentile), the bilinguals scored much lower in English reading achievement (English = 36th percentile, Bilingual = 21st percentile). Thus, prior to their introduction to English academic language and reading, while English speakers had English oral proficiency advantages over bilinguals, the bilinguals performed lower in English reading (B = 21st, E = 36th). However, after one year of formal instruction in English reading and academic language, while the bilinguals scored equivalent to the English dominant students in English reading (B = 36th, E = 36th, S = 36th), the bilinguals scored higher than the Spanish or English dominant students in Spanish reading (B = 76th, E = 59th, S = 65th). These results suggest that the bilinguals had a better developed framework through Spanish reading, and Spanish and English oral proficiency from which to integrate the new reading and language skills in English.

As these data and other bilingual theorists have indicated, then, the bilingual individual must develop full academic language proficiency in both languages in order for the cognitive and academic advantages to accrue. This means that a bilingual/immersion program needs a full maintenance model that completely develops both languages over an extended period of time to reap the cognitive and academic advantages.

Discrepant Language Needs of Language Majority and Language Minority Students

Another important assumption of bilingual/immersion programs is that they equitably meet the language and academic achievement needs of both language minority and language majority students. In a program such as bilingual/ immersion, there are very discrepant needs relating to the language proficiency levels of the two groups of students who enter the class. One group, consisting of English-only speakers, has minimal, if any, proficiency in Spanish, and the other group, comprising native Spanish speakers, speak Spanish proficiently. How can a teacher meet the demanding needs of the English speakers for a highly sheltered (i.e., motherese) form of Spanish instruction while still promoting the high levels of language proficiency needed for the Spanish speakers? The case is reversed for English language proficiency, with the range from proficient monolingual English speakers to non-English proficient speakers.

First, it is important to point out that despite the apparent discrepancy in students' language proficiency levels in Spanish, according to teacher ratings of the difficulty of meeting the communication needs of both groups of speakers, all teachers, who were experienced bilingual education teachers and aware of the language needs of both groups of students, indicated that this was not a problem at all (Lindholm, 1989).

There are several reasons for the teachers' confidence in this assertion. One explanation is that English speakers develop comprehension skills in Spanish quickly enough for teachers to move away from sheltered Spanish instruction after only a few months of instruction (Arambula, personal communication). Similarly, most LEP students become orally proficient in English by the time instruction in English content begins. In addition, instruction begins at grades K and 1, and instruction at those grade levels is often sheltered, or highly communication skill-based, with many contextual clues given to teach concepts and vocabulary. A related response to this question relates to the societal support that Spanish receives outside the classroom. Although Spanish is the dominant language of the class in the early grades, it is not the dominant language of society and thus it is not enriched as it would be in a Latin American country through media and greater community exposure. Thus, the Spanish of most Spanish-speaking students who have spent most of their lives in the United States would need strengthening because these children have not received the same enrichment they would have received if they lived in a Spanish-speaking country in which Spanish was the dominant language of the media and larger community, and was valued as the language of communication (Dolson, 1985).

Finally, interaction among the students—English speakers with Spanish speakers—provides additional settings in which to both learn one's second language and teach one's first language. Observations of bilingual/immersion classrooms clearly show that students often act as tutors or are tutored themselves in paired or small group activities. As language tutors, both Spanish and English speakers use academic language skills in their native language to help explain concepts, vocabulary, and structure to their classmates, thereby promoting their native language and metalinguistic skills. As recipients of tutorial assistance, students gain valuable one-on-one instruction and opportunities to practice the second language.

In sum, as long as the teachers are cognizant of the needs of both groups of students, there are several reasons why the bilingual/immersion model can meet the apparently discrepant language needs of both groups of students. Addressing these language needs adequately requires the implementation of small group activities, especially cooperative learning, the equitable distribution of tutorial responsibilities, and the creation of many opportunities for students to interact with each other.

In conclusion, I have reviewed the literature to show how bilingual/immersion education is theoretically and conceptually based in literatures on the social context of language, effective schools, language development, and the relationship between language and cognition. From some of these discussions, I have selected particular pedagogical issues that are significant to bilingual/immersion education. These issues reflect the salience of transfer, and the importance of developing both conversational and academic language skills in both languages to truly promote high levels of bilingualism and thereby provide cognitive and academic advantages to the program participants.

References

Allport, G. (1954). *The nature of prejudice.* Cambridge, MA: Addison-Wesley.

Brophy, J. (1986). Teacher influences on student achievement. *American Psychologist, 41,* 1069-1077.

___, & Good, T. (1986). Teacher behavior and student achievement. In M. Wittrock (Ed.), *Third handbook of research on teaching* (pp. 328-375). New York: MacMillan.

California State Department of Education. (1982). *Basic principles for the education of language minority students, an overview.* Sacramento: Office of Bilingual Bicultural Education.

Cortes, C. E. (1986). The education of language minority students: A contextual interaction model. In *Beyond language: Social and cultural factors in schooling language minority students* (pp. 3-33). Los Angeles, CA: Evaluation, Dissemination and Assessment Center, California State University, Los Angeles.

Cummins, J. (1979). Linguistic interdependence and the educational development of children. *Review of Educational Research, 49,* 222-251.

____. (1987). Bilingualism, language proficiency, and metalinguistic development. In P. Homel, M. Palij, & D. Aaronson (Eds.), *Childhood bilingualism: Aspects of linguistic, cognitive and social development* (pp. 57-73). Hillsdale, NJ: Lawrence Erlbaum Associates, Publishers.

Dolson, D. (1985). Bilingualism and scholastic performance: The literature revisited. *NABE Journal, 10,* 1-35.

Dusek, J. B. (1985). *Teacher expectations.* Hillsdale, NJ: Lawrence Erlbaum Associates, Publishers.

Edmonds, R. R. (1983). *Search for effective schools: The identification and analysis of city schools that are instructionally effective for poor children* (Final report). East Lansing: Michigan State University.

Gass, S. M., & Madden, C. G. (Eds.). (1985). *Input in second language acquisition.* Rowley, MA: Newbury House Publishers, Inc.

Genesee, F. (1984). Historical and theoretical foundations of immersion education. In *Studies on immersion education: A collection for U.S. educators* (pp. 32-57). Sacramento: California State Department of Education.

____. (1987). *Learning through two languages.* Cambridge, MA: Newbury House Publishers.

Good, T. L., & Weinstein, R. S. (1986). Schools make a difference: Evidence, criticisms, and new directions. *American Psychologist, 41,* 1090-1097.

Hakuta, K. (1986). *Mirror of language.* New York: Basic Books.

Homel, P., Palij, M., & Aaronson, D. (1987). *Childhood bilingualism: Aspects of linguistic, cognitive and social development.* Hillsdale, NJ: Lawrence Erlbaum Associates, Publishers.

Johnson, D. W., Johnson, R. T., & Holubec, E. J. (1986). *Circles of learning: Cooperation in the classroom.* Edina, MN: Interaction Book Company.

Kagan, S. (1986). Cooperative learning and sociocultural factors in schooling. *Beyond language: Social and cultural factors in schooling language minority students.* Los Angeles: California State University Evaluation, Dissemination, and Assessment Center.

Kerman, S., Kimball, & Martin (1980). *Teacher expectations and student achievement.* Downey, CA: Office of Los Angeles County Superintendent of Schools.

Lambert, W. E. (1984). An overview of issues in immersion education. In *Studies in immersion education: A collection for U.S. educators* (pp. 8-30). Sacramento: California State Department of Education.

____. (1987). The effects of bilingual and bicultural experiences on children's attitudes and social perspectives. In P. Homel, M. Palij & D. Aaronson (Eds.), *Childhood bilingualism: Aspects of linguistic, cognitive and social development* (pp. 197-221). Hillsdale, NJ: Lawrence Erlbaum Associates, Publishers.

Lindholm, K. J. (1981). *Communicative socialization: Parent-child and sibling interactions.* Unpublished doctoral dissertation, University of California, Los Angeles.

____. (1989). The Washington elementary school bilingual immersion program: Student progress after three years of implementation. Prepared for Washington Elementary School, San Jose Unified School District.

____. (1990a). Bilingual immersion education: Criteria for program development. In A. M. Padilla, H. H. Fairchild, & C. Valadez (Eds.), *Bilingual education: Issues and strategies* (pp. 91-105). Beverly Hills, CA: Sage Publications.

____. (1990b). Language proficiency and academic achievement in two languages: Theoretical assumptions and empirical evidence in two-way bilingual immersion education. Paper presented at the annual National Association for Bilingual Education conference, Tucson, Arizona.

____, & Fairchild, H. H. (1989). *Evaluation of an "exemplary" bilingual immersion program* (Technical Report No. 13). Los Angeles, CA: UCLA Center for Language Education and Research.

____, & Fairchild, H. H. (1990). First year evaluation of an elementary school bilingual immersion program. In A. M. Padilla, H. H. Fairchild, & C. Valadez (Eds.), *Bilingual education: Issues and strategies.* (pp. 126-136). Beverly Hills, CA: Sage Publications.

Linney, J. A., & Seidman, E. (1989). The future of schooling. *American Psychologist, 44,* 336-340.

Long, M. H. (1981). Input, interaction and second language acquisition. In H. Winitz (Ed.), *Native language and foreign language acquisition* (p. 379). New York: Annals of the New York Academy of Sciences.

Padilla, A. M., & Lindholm, K. J. (1984). Child bilingualism: The same old issues revisited. In J. L. Martinez, Jr., & R. H. Mendoza (Eds.), *Chicano psychology,* Second Edition (pp. 369-408). New York: Academic Press.

Peal, E., & Lambert, W. E. (1962). The relation of bilingualism to intelligence. *Psychological Monographs, 76,* 1-23.

Slavin, R. E. (1983). *Cooperative learning.* New York: Longman.

Snow, C. E., & Hoefnagel-Hohle, M. (1982). School-age second language learners' access to simplified linguistic input. *Language Learning, 32,* 411-430.

Troike, R. C. (1978). Research evidence for the effectiveness of bilingual education. *NABE Journal, 3,* 13-24.

____. (1986). *Improving conditions for success in bilingual education programs.* Prepared for Committee on Education and Labor, U. S. House of Representatives.

Toukomaa, P., & Skutnabb-Kangas, T. (1977). *The intensive teaching of the mother tongue to migrant children of pre-school age and children in the lower level of comprehensive school.* Helsinki: The Finnish National Commission for UNESCO.

Willig, A. (1985). A meta-analysis of selected studies on the effectiveness of bilingual education. *Review of Educational Research, 55,* 269-317.

A METACOGNITIVE APPROACH
TO TEACHING BILINGUAL STUDENTS[*]

María Cardelle-Elawar and José E. Náñez, Sr.
Arizona State University West

ABSTRACT

This article describes an approach, based on metacognitive theory, to teach students low on mathematical achievement. Also presented are the results of two experiments in which metacognitive techniques and Mayer's (1987) problem-solving model produced a significant increase in bilingual Hispanic elementary school childrens' mathematical achievement and attitude toward mathematics. We suggest, from the results of the two experiments, that the type of intervention used in the experiments could be tailored to classrooms where a majority of students have demonstrated low performance in mathematics. The article concludes with a call for researchers to aid policy makers by continuing to advance our knowledge and understanding of metacognitive processes and their relevance to the learner in the classroom.

Bilingual education programs have existed for some time (Title VII, 1968). However, bilingual Hispanic students have not been very successful in education (García, 1987, 1988). Merely presenting materials for students to learn and coaching them to learn specific materials has failed to help them become efficient thinkers. It is time to develop and test teaching approaches designed to foster self-evaluation and self-monitoring during the learning process.

Metacognitive theory may provide one practical approach for training teachers to guide students to develop well-organized thinking strategies. In addition to presenting a

[*]Support for this article was provided by a research support grant from the Hispanic Research Center, Arizona State University. We express our appreciation to Richard Durán and Raymond V. Padilla for their useful comments on earlier versions of the article.

brief overview of metacognitive theory, this chapter recommends ways for implementing metacognitive techniques designed to help the student become a competent, active participant in the learning process. The results of two empirical studies in which a metacognitive approach was utilized to significantly increase mathematical performance in low-achieving bilingual Hispanic children are also presented. The conclusion emphasizes the need for increased empirical research designed to find effective strategies for training teachers to use metacognitive skills in the classroom.

The Metacognitive Approach

A major problem with traditional teaching approaches is that they do not provide a clear indication of students' cognitive abilities or teacher effectiveness. Recent research findings indicate that a need exists to pressure schools to expand the breath and depth of curricular content (Costa, 1989; Resnick & Klopfer, 1989). These researchers assert that what is needed in today's classroom is an emphasis on the teaching of critical thinking processes and skills. Early cognitive theorists (Piaget, for example) stressed the need to include students as active participants in developing and expanding their cognitive abilities through active interaction with their learning environments. New theoretical conceptions regarding the psychological processes involved in learning and instruction emerged during the 1980s. These constructs represent a modern view of instructional theory, and have lead to a better understanding of individual differences in learning aptitude (Siegler, 1989). A major component of this modern educational view is the goal of helping students to ultimately become competent, flexible thinkers (Baron & Sternberg, 1987; Beyer, 1984; Costa, 1985; Norris, 1989; Snow, 1989).

Modern metacognitive theory indicates that the tools of inquiry by which one discovers and validates knowledge should be the transferable results of school. Consequently, emphasis should be given to developing these skills using course content as a means, not as an end, to learning. According to this approach, the primary goal of every teacher should be to help students accept mental challenge by creating a classroom environment where tackling the unfamiliar is exciting or at least nonthreatening. This can be accomplished by teaching students to think on their own, gage their productiveness through self-evaluation, test whether they are on track to the correct solution, and to implement self-corrective techniques when they are not. Experience with such skills is essential if education is going to fulfill the needs of our fast-growing, increasingly complex technological society. Unfortunately, this educational ideal has eluded many Hispanic students, particularly academic low-achievers from poor or educationally disadvantaged backgrounds. To include these students among the academically successful, teachers need to understand and learn how to teach metacognitive skills, such as abstract thinking, differential modes of inquiry, and higher order thought processes, and to incorporate them into their daily classroom practices (Brown & Palincsar, in press).

Although metacognition remains a broad, somewhat loosely defined concept, a reasonable degree of agreement exists among theorists concerning what the concept involves. Metacognition, as conceptualized in this chapter, refers to the complex cognitive processes involved in problem solving. These include the learner's ability to develop a systematic strategy during the act of problem solving and to reflect on and evaluate the productiveness of his or her own thinking processes. Metacognitive theorists (e.g., Haller, Child, & Walberg, 1989) summarize the essence of metacognitive instruction as including the following:

1. Creating students' awareness of the language, the meaning of words, and the information in the problem

2. Monitoring through self-questioning and paraphrasing to facilitate understanding

3. Regulating, by comparing and contrasting more possible solutions, of what students need to know when they fail to comprehend

4. Striving for greater student autonomy as well as increasing ability to master content and building the students' confidence

Current educational researchers are convinced that these metacognitive skills are essential for certain types of learning. For example, Brown and Palincsar (in press) stress the importance of self-regulation in learning effective reading skills. In their opinion, self-regulation strategies function in clarifying purpose, in activating a relevant knowledge base, in allocating attention to pertinent central content in the material being read, in drawing inferences, and the like. Self-regulating activities can be incorporated as an integral part of the classroom environment, to teach students how to monitor and evaluate their own activity, and to foster students' motivation to learn.

As an illustration, applying metacognitve strategies in teaching bilingual students to read would include teaching them to identify words that they do not know in the language being read, to look up their meaning in a dictionary, to formulate hypotheses regarding the use of the words in context, and to generate meaningful sentences using the words in both of their languages to evaluate and reinforce their understanding. For example, in reading a mathematical word problem, a student may run across the word *congruent*, as in "Which two angles are congruent?" Bilingual students often will fail to answer this type of question correctly on mathematics or geometry tests. It is not necessarily correct to assume that the student did not understand the concept of equal sides if we have not controlled for the possibility that he or she missed the question because of not understanding the meaning of the term *congruent*. The following is an actual case in which the bilingual instructor, in order to help students formulate their own definition of congruent, asked the students in Spanish to compare two desks in the classroom.

> The teacher asked the students to describe the two desks in as many ways as they could using both Spanish and English terms. Soon one student said *Son iguales!* The teacher then asked, "How would you say

that in English?" A student responded, "They are the same." Teacher: "What are other words that mean *igual* or the same?" A student said "They are equal." Teacher: "That's right, they are equal, the two angles are congruent."

Approaching a mental task through these techniques should help the students recognize the efficiency of using both of their languages in word recognition. It will also underscore the importance of building language competence in English in order to become academically successful, and fostering an appreciation for bringing previously acquired knowledge to bear on current text comprehension.

Research indicates that metacognitively based instructional techniques provide a promising approach to help teachers become more effective in the classroom and students to learn how to take control of their own learning processes. The metacognitive approach stimulates students to strengthen their thinking ability by providing insight into their ongoing mental processes (What am I doing?), redirecting the learner's activities when necessary during the act of problem solving through self-appraisal (How am I doing?), and transforming the classroom into an active, inquisitive learning environment by creating dynamic teacher-student interactions based on explicit discussion concerning how students process information.

Instructional plans utilizing metacognitive strategies must address a range of difficult issues and decisions. It is one thing to acknowledge the need to integrate deeper, richer, theory-based instructional practice. It is quite another to effectively train teachers to put metacognitive theory into practice in the classroom. It is also likely that since there are different subject areas to be taught, metacognitive instructional approaches should be adapted to the particular subject matter and to diverse student populations. For example, classroom teachers need to be sensitive to differences in the students' ability to comprehend and appreciate subject matter within and across content areas. Second, design of the curriculum should be sensitive to unique characteristics of individuals and to cultural, ethnic, racial, gender, and language diversity as well. The development of such programs has not yet received much attention in metacognitive re-search. Finally, metacognitive instruction should serve a diagnostic function in the identification and design of in-structional programs based on the needs of individual learners. That is, it should indicate logical alternatives or progressions for teaching a given learner. It should also help the researcher obtain explanations indicative of a learner's performance to date. This diagnosis serves to help the teacher make instructional interpretations and decisions about individual learners. The ultimate goal is to suggest fruitful directions for future research and to encourage the testing and implementation of metacognitive teaching techniques, especially with those Hispanic students who may exhibit difficulties in subject matter comprehension due to lack of English mastery.

Metacognitively based instructional techniques also allow the instructor to evaluate the student's learning strategies from the start and to initiate more effective step-by-step learning strategies as learning progresses. This approach allows rapid identification of markers indicating "break-downs" or difficulty in learning and teaching techniques. Each marker becomes a target for added coaching, practice, development of relevant strategies, and exercises. For example, if a cognitive analysis indicates that a bilingual student's poor performance can be traced to defective skills in executing a particular process, then the analysis serves a useful diagnostic function for suggesting remediation (Cardelle-Elawar, 1990). This approach minimizes working memory overload for the learner by minimizing the num-ber of novel cues or cognitive operations introduced at any one step, and allowing sufficient practice for automaticity in performance to be achieved at the current level before ad-vancing to the next higher level. The instructor attempts to promote flexibility in thought and learner-controlled search-ing for strategy improvement. The aim is also for a gradual transfer of control and responsibility for the learning process from the instructor to the learner.

Educators should become familiar with the variety of strategies that learners use to cope with particular tasks. They must also understand the circumstances under which students are likely to use each strategy, and the advantages that the use of varied strategies confers on the flexibility of the students' thought processes (i.e., there is often more than one approach to solving a given problem). Teachers might then be in a position to aid the learning process by modeling alternative strategies for students who may not have thought of them on their own. Teachers can accomplish this by comparing the advantages and disadvantages of alternative strategies, and by examining with the student why quite different approaches can be used to solve the same problem. This is far from the typical approach in mathematics classrooms, but it might well transfer to a deeper understanding of mathematical concepts. Students can learn to assess their own work in the same way that their teachers will judge it. This approach provides a basis for developing a metacognitive awareness of what are important characteristics of good problem solving, good writing, good experimentation, good historical analysis, and so on. Moreover, such an assessment can address not only the product one is trying to achieve, but also, in the process of achieving it, the learner may gain insight into the mental processes that contribute to successful problem solving. Teachers also must be knowledgeable about the learner's language of origin in order to know, for example, which words could interfere and which could aid learning in the new language (see Cocking & Mestre, 1989 for an excellent collection of papers addressing the teaching of mathematics to ethnic minorities and bilinguals).

We are particularly concerned with the failure of education to identify, develop, and implement research-based strategies for teaching cognitive skills to bilingual Hispanic students. The current educational literature primarily emphasizes the academic failure of Hispanic students on skills such as mathematics. García (1987, 1988) points out that while Hispanic students often receive supplementary teaching in English, they receive no instruction related to higher-order thinking processes that are essential to master basic skills. Thus, while it is well recognized that Hispanic students have traditionally fallen disproportionately into the academically low-achieving group, research aimed at understanding the "thinking about thinking processes" in this group of students is virtually nonexistent. Yet, this area of research is critical to developing models of cognition and, consequently, teaching procedures powerful enough to produce positive changes for Hispanic low-academic achievers. The metacognitive approach has the potential to yield diagnoses concerning problems or strengths in individual student learners that go beyond those possible with standardized achievement tests. Thus, metacognitive theory provides great promise as a practical approach for helping the largely underrepresented and traditionally underserved Hispanic student population.

A Metacognitive Approach to Teaching Mathematics

Perhaps the most direct lesson to be learned from metacognitive research on teaching concerns the development of research-based strategies for teaching bilingual students (Cardelle-Elawar, 1990). The experiments described here employed a metacognitive approach to significantly increase math achievement of low-math-ability Hispanic children. The results indicate that training in using metacognitive skills in Spanish and English increased performance of students in the experimental groups relative to comparison groups whose performance remained relatively unchanged.

The main purpose of the research was to assess whether using a metacognitive approach to teaching mathematics produced a positive effect on student's achievement and attitude toward mathematics. This was accomplished in two experiments in which Mayers' (1987) four types of knowledge served as a heuristic strategy for solving mathematics problems. In the first experiment, an "expert instructor" (the experimenter) employed the metacognitive approach described above to teach mathematics to low-achieving Hispanic elementary school children. The second experiment tested whether positive effects could also be achieved using this technique when the students' own teachers were trained to provide the metacognitive instruction. The major research questions addressed by the two experiments were: "What is the effect of metacognitive instruction on students' mathematics achievement?" and "What is the effect of this instruction on students' attitude toward mathematics?"

Experiment 1

Method

Subjects. The subjects were 90 sixth-grade bilingual Hispanic students selected from a suburban Arizona school with a majority Hispanic population. The subjects came from three separate classrooms with an average of 30 students each. The average age of the subjects was 11 years. All subjects came from lower SES families.

Procedure. The subjects were identified as low mathematics achievers based on their math scores on the Iowa Test of Basic Skills (ITBS). Their mean grade-equivalent ITBS mathematics scores were 4.40 with a standard deviation of 2.91. The subjects were further tested for mathematical knowledge prior to the beginning of the study by the administration of four mathematics pretests consisting of 20 questions each. One pretest was constructed for each of the four units to be covered in the student's regular classroom during the experimental period.

Two classrooms were randomly assigned to the experimental condition. The experimental classrooms were instructed by the experimenter using a metacognitive approach designed to

1. stimulate and develop students' thinking through insights into their own mental processes

2. redirect the students' activities during the act of problem solving by appraising their own thinking

3. transform the classroom into an active, inquisitive environment by displaying a

teacher-student interaction with explicit discussion of not only what is to be learned, but
also how to learn it, and why it is important to
learn it

The students were also taught problem-solving techniques in accordance with Mayers' (1987) teaching model.
Finally, the students were taught using a technique developed by Elawar and Corno (1985), which takes errors as a
source of information regarding students' problems with the
subject matter, and provides feedback tailored to individual
needs. The feedback includes both praise and constructive
criticism to guide the student's self-correction and
motivation. The remaining classroom served as a comparison group and was taught by the students' regular teacher,
who used a traditional teaching approach which consisted of
explaining the topic, lecturing, giving written assignments
to students, and correcting the assignments using a check
mark indicating the number of questions the students
answered correctly. For incorrect answers, the teacher provided the right answer for the whole class orally or in writing on the chalkboard.

To ensure that the comparison group teacher maintained
her traditional teaching approach, math lessons of the comparison group were audiotaped and observed by the experimenter on three different occasions. The audiotapes were
analyzed by two other teachers trained by the experimenter.
Observers were looking for how the teacher in the comparison group maintained her original teaching style. It was
found that the teacher kept her teaching style throughout
the duration of the experiment.

As stated above, in order to control for level of previous
mathematical knowledge, each class received a pretest on
the content to be covered in that unit to assess the initial
math ability of the learners. The pretest included 20 problems selected from the textbook used in the classroom.
These problems were followed by eight statements derived
from Mayers' teaching approach that required students to
analyze difficulties encountered in solving each problem.

Four of the statements were stated in the affirmative and four in the negative. The eight statements were:

1. "I don't understand the meaning of the following word(s) in this problem." (This is an example of Mayer's problem translation.)

2. "I don't have all the information to solve the problem. What type of information is needed?" (An example of problem integration and of lack of schematic knowledge.)

3. "I don't know how to organize the information to solve the problem, which steps to take, what to do first." (An example of lack of strategic knowledge.)

4. "I don't know how to execute the solution. Which operations do I have difficulty with?" (An example of problem execution.)

5. "I know all the words in this problem and I understand the main question." (Students were instructed to write down the question.)

6. "I have all the information needed to solve this problem." (Students were instructed to write the information needed.)

7. "I know which steps to follow in solving the problem; these steps are . . ."

8. "I know how to calculate the solution and work out the operation(s) needed."

These questions were probes designed to guide the student to focus both on the specific steps of mathematical problem solving and to increase his or her awareness of difficulties encountered during this process. Students' responses helped the teachers understand individual differences and similarities in the type of problems encountered by the students.

The experimenter established a lesson plan for the experimental classes with the teachers (trainees). The planning included an analysis of difficulties students experienced in solving the problems on the pretest. The experimenter reviewed and interpreted students' pretest performance with the following questions in mind: What are the key errors? Which type of difficulties, according to Mayers' model, are represented in each error? Was the error a result of a lack of linguistic knowledge or a problem in calculating the solution? What does the student say about his or her difficulties with the problem? How can I guide the student to correct the error on his or her own?

A three-stage lesson plan was followed. The first stage consisted of an introductory discussion. The experimenter reviewed the vocabulary of the problem, the specific question being asked, the schematic knowledge needed to integrate the information into a coherent representation, and the procedural knowledge needed to carry out the computations required in the plan. During this phase of instruction, one student was selected to explain on the chalkboard the problem from the book that she or he liked most. The rest of the class tried to solve it in their notebooks. They then compared their solutions with the solution of the student at the chalkboard and gave a rationale for any disagreements. The student at the chalkboard played the role of teacher, while the experimenter took the opportunity to provide relevant feedback as needed.

The second stage consisted of independent work. Students worked independently for 15 to 20 minutes solving problems similar to the ones provided in the pretest. During this time, the experimenter moved freely about the classroom providing individualized feedback. The feedback guided the students to focus on their errors and provided clues for self-correction. The experimenter assisted the individual student in monitoring his or her own thinking instead of simply providing the right answer when the student gave up.

During the final stage, a lesson summary was conducted by the students themselves as they answered questions asked by the experimenter. Two questions that were frequently asked by the experimenter were, "What did you learn today?" and "What did you learn about yourself in solving mathematics problems?" During this time, the experimenter also provided feedback to the students, re-

sponded to their questions, and provided positive reinforcement for their accomplishments. Because errors were
considered a source of learning, the experimenter considered every case in which a student improved his or her own
self-correction skills as an accomplishment.

Overall, the training emphasized self-directed inquiry to
foster positive transfer from the current problems to new
ones. The experimenter tailored the feedback to students,
while incorporating Mayer's model into a metacognitive
teaching perspective.

Instruments. The students were administered pre- and posttests designed to measure their attitude toward mathematics, their general mathematical abilities, and their
mathematical achievement.

Attitude toward mathematics was measured using
Aiken's (1974) Scales E and V. Scale E measures how much
the student enjoys mathematics; Scale V measures how
much the student values mathematics. General ability was
assessed using the Standard Progressive Matrices (Raven,
1958). Mathematical achievement was measured by spe-
cially designed, criterion-referenced tests consisting of 20
mathematics problems. The tests were designed by the experimenter in consultation with the students' teachers to
assess the mathematics content to be taught during the
seven-week experimental session. Three tests were designed to correspond with the three units covered during
the experiment. Students were administered the appropriate pretest before each corresponding unit.

Results

The main effects of teaching techniques were tested using
an analysis of covariance (ANCOVA) with repeated measures on both achievement and attitudes toward mathematics. The covariate consisted of the student scores on the
general ability pretest. The test for equivalence of the slopes
of the covariate against achievement and attitudes toward
mathematics was performed as described in Winer (1971,
p. 768). There were no differences between the slopes for
any of the groups. Table 1 shows the adjusted cell means

TABLE 1

Adjusted Cell Means and Standard Deviations for ITBS, General Ability, Mathematics Achievement, and Attitudes toward Mathematics

	Group	
Variable	*Experimental* *(N = 60)*	*Comparison* *(N = 30)*
*ITBS**		
Pretest		
Mean	4.20	4.60
S.D.	3.70	2.32
Posttest		
Mean	6.90	6.45
S.D.	2.10	2.50
General Ability		
Pretest		
Mean	33.28	33.84
S.D.	1.40	2.30
Posttest		
Mean	38.36	34.25
S.D.	2.70	3.00
Mathematics Achievement		
Pretest		
Mean	0.92	0.99
S.D.	0.88	0.66
Posttest		
Mean	15.30	6.15
S.D.	1.67	1.19

TABLE 1
(continued)

Variable	Group	
	Experimental (N = 60)	Comparison (N = 30)
Attitudes toward Mathematics		
Pretest		
Mean	32.00	31.00
S.D.	0.89	2.10
Posttest		
Mean	44.00	30.80
S.D.	1.15	2.10

*The ITBS was administered in April 1988 and April 1989 for the pre- and posttests, respectively.

and standard deviations for pre-post achievement measures, attitudes toward mathematics, ITBS, and general ability.

The experimental group exhibited significantly higher scores than the comparison group in all posttest measures except the ITBS. The similarity in the posttest ITBS scores for the experimental and comparison groups occurred because the posttest was administered after the comparison group had served as experimental group 2 in experiment 2 below. There were no statistically significant differences on pretest measures among the three classes.

The results of the repeated measures ANCOVA using general ability as the covariate show statistically significant differences between the experimental and control groups $F(1, 87) = 175.50$, s.d. $= 1.80$, $p < .001$. The pre-post mathematics differences in achievement were also statistically significant, $F(1, 88) = 312$, s.d. $= 3.34$, $p < .001$. Similar results were observed for the attitude toward mathematics measure $F(1, 87) = 154.10$, s.d. $= 2.3$, $p < .001$. For the pre-post differences, the results were $F(1, 88) = 213$, s.d. $= 4.56$, $p < .001$.

The significance of the results of experiment 1 will be discussed in conjunction with those of experiment 2.

Experiment 2

While the results of experiment 1 were very encouraging, there were two potential confounds in its design. First, it is possible that the results were attributable to an experimenter effect. That is, the experimenter instructed only the subjects in the experimental group while the control group was instructed by their regular teacher. Secondly, the mere presence of the experimenter in the classroom (e.g., a new teacher using new methods) may have produced a Hawthorne Effect. Study 2 was designed to control for the effects of these two possible confounds.

Method

Subjects. The subjects consisted of the students in the two experimental classrooms in experiment 1 (experimental group 1), the subjects from the classroom that served as the comparison group in experiment 1 (experimental group 2), and 32 students drawn from two classes from another school with the same population and curriculum characteristics as the first school (comparison group). The comparison group subjects were selected on the basis of their similar scores to the initial scores of experimental group 2 subjects who served as the comparison group in experiment 1.

Procedure. The rationale, teaching methods, and instruments administered to the students in experiment 2 were the same as in experiment 1. The experimental classrooms in experiment 2 were taught by the regular teachers who were trained by the experimenter during the first experiment.

The experimental and comparison groups were audiotaped and observed twice by the experimenter. The audio tapes were analyzed by the experimenter and the three teachers in the experimental group, who served as observers of each other's teaching. Each class observation was rated on a scale of 1 (low) to 5 (high) for teacher faithfulness to the metacognitive or traditional teaching techniques. The inter-judge reliability was .79.

Results

The design was a 3 (groups) X 2 (pre-posttests) repeated measures design. Table 2 shows the cell means and s.d. for the pre-post mathematics achievement differences, attitudes toward mathematics, and general ability tests.

The experimental groups exhibited higher scores than the control group in all posttest measures. Note that pretest means for experimental group 1 in experiment 2 consist of the group's posttest scores in experiment 1. Therefore, the differences in this group's pretest and posttest means for general ability, mathematics achievement, and attitudes toward mathematics shown in Table 2, are smaller than those for their corresponding categories in experimental group 2. The repeated measures ANCOVA with general ability pretest as a covariate revealed statistically significant differences for the groups main effect $F(2, 118) = 192.5$, s.d. $= 1.79$, $p < .001$. The pre-posttest differences in achievement also were significant, $F(2, 119) = 172$, s.d. $= 4.2$, $p < .001$.

Discussion

The findings of experiments 1 and 2 indicate that students who initially scored low on mathematics achievement progressed in efficiency of problem solving in a number of areas. They became better able at understanding how to approach a problem, at identifying the appropriate schemata for organizing the information, at recognizing that there may be more than one right way to solve a problem, and at verifying their solutions. Understanding how to approach a problem was improved by increasing their linguistic comprehension concerning the meaning of key words and sen-

TABLE 2

Cell Adjusted Means and Standard Deviations
for ITBS, General Ability, Mathematics Achievement,
and Attitudes toward Mathematics

Variable	Groups		
	Experimental 1	Experimental 2	Comparison
*ITBS**			
General Ability			
Pretest			
Mean	38.36	34.35	33.85
S.D.	2.70	3.00	3.60
Posttest			
Mean	44.20	39.40	35.75
S.D.	2.90	3.50	3.00
Mathematics Achievement			
Pretest			
Mean	15.30	6.15	6.90
S.D.	1.67	1.19	1.86
Posttest			
Mean	17.34	15.40	7.00
S.D.	1.67	1.34	1.19
Attitudes toward Mathematics			
Pretest			
Mean	44.00	30.80	33.00
S.D.	0.89	2.10	1.60
Posttest			
Mean	48.00	42.10	31.00
S.D.	1.10	2.36	1.70

*See Table 1 for ITBS pre- and posttest means.

tences. This improved comprehension, heightened their concentration on the problem, and reduced impulse-based responses. Recognition of multiple ways to solve a problem was evidenced by the students' new ability to describe their solution processes and to compare their processes to those used by other students. Students learned to verify their solutions by reflecting on their own thinking and examining the steps they took in working out solutions while checking the accuracy of calculations. Follow-up research is being conducted to assess the long-term effects of the metacognitive training in mathematics and possible transferable effects to reading ability.

The results of these experiments suggest several recommendations for teachers trying to help low mathematics achievers. First, the focus should not be on the students' labels (e.g., low achievers, minority, etc.), but on each student's individual behavior, abilities, and potential. Special consideration should be given to a student's uniqueness, strengths, and weaknesses. Second, low-performing students need a supportive atmosphere in which errors and mistakes lead to positive feedback and direction. Third, "low-achievers" seem to function better in a well-structured classroom situation. Having the task broken down into small segments of learning and mastery seemed to help. A major component of the necessary classroom structure is that the problem presentation be well organized and structured. The academic task presented to the student has a major influence on what the student learns because the key to a student's learning is his or her own thoughts and actions. To learn, the student must practice thinking and avoid simply applying procedures in rote fashion. Fourth, a great deal of interaction between teacher and student is required. Students learn best through involvement and through the teacher's mediation and use of constructive feedback. Such techniques can make mathematics a source of enjoyment rather than frustration. Finally, the two experiments presented in this paper show that the subjects profited from the self-reflective skills incorporated into the metacognitive teaching approach.

We would like to point out that the results of the two experiments also showed that low achievers do not lack the ability to use metacognitive learning skills. Rather, they lack explicit training on how to use such skills in problem-solving tasks. Preliminary results of a third experiment with third to seventh graders indicate that students in the experimental group showed evidence of higher mathematical achievement when compared with students in the comparison group, indicating that the positive effects of this metacognitive approach to teaching are robust.

It is very encouraging that legislators have begun to understand the importance of teaching students to become critical thinkers. This is evidenced by the fact that several states have already mandated the teaching of higher-order cognitive skills in their secondary school curricula (Nickerson, 1989). It is also encouraging that a number of other states are considering similar requirements. To help such policymakers, researchers need to continue to advance our knowledge and understanding of metacognitive processes and their relevance to learners in the classroom.

References

Aiken, L. R. (1974). Two scales of attitudes toward mathematics. *Journal for Research in Mathematics Education, 5,* 67-71.

Baron, J. B., & Sternberg, R. J. (1987). *Teaching thinking skills: Theory and practice.* New York: W. H. Freeman and Company.

Beyer, B. K. (1984). Improving thinking skills: Defining the problem. *Phi Delta Kappan, 65,* 486-90.

Brown, A. L., & Palincsar, A. S. (in press). Guided cooperative learning and individual knowledge acquisition. In H. Mandl, N. Stein, & T. Trabasso (Eds.), *Knowing and learning and comprehension of tests.* Hillsdale, NJ: Lawrence Erlbaum Associates, Publishers.

Cardelle-Elawar, M. (under review). Effects of teaching metacognitive skills on mathematics problem solving, *Contemporary Educational Psychology.*

____. (1990). Feedback tailored to bilingual students individual needs in mathematics word problems. *Elementary School Journal* (in press).

Cocking, R. R., & Mestre, J. P. (1988). *Linguistic and cultural influences on learning mathematics.* Hillsdale, NJ: Lawrence Erlbaum Associates, Publishers.

Costa, A. L. (1985). *Developing minds: A resource book of teaching thinking.* Reston, VA: Association for Supervision and Curriculum Development.

____. (1989). Forward. In L. B. Resnick & L. E. Klopfer (Eds.). *Toward the thinking curriculum: Current cognitive research.* Reston, VA: Association for Supervision and Curriculum Development.

Elawar, C. M., & Corno, L. (1985). A factorial experiment in teachers' written feedback on student homework: Changing teacher behavior a little rather than a lot. *Journal of Educational Psychology, 77,* 162-173.

García, E, (1987). Bilingual education in early childhood programs. *Teacher Education & Practice, 4,* 31-46.

____. (1988). Attributes of effective schools for language minority students. *Education and Urban Society, 2,* 387-398.

Haller, E. P., Child, D. A., & Walberg, H. J. (1989). Can comprehension be taught? *Educational Researcher, 17,* 5-8.

Mayer, R. (1987). Mathematics. In R. Mayer (Ed.), *Educational psychology.* Boston: Little, Brown and Co.

Nickerson, R. S. (1989). New directions in educational assessment. *Educational Researcher, 18,(9),* 3-7.

Norris, S. P. (1989). Can we test validity for critical thinking? *Educational Researcher, 18,(9),* 21-26.

Raven, J. C. (1958). *Standard progressive matrices.* New York: The Psychological Corporation.

Resnick, L. B., & Klopfer, L. (1989). *Toward the thinking curriculum: an overview.* Reston, VA: Association for Supervision and Curriculum Development.

Siegler, R. S. (1989). Strategy diversity and cognitive assessment. *Educational Researcher, 18,(9),* 15-20.

Snow, R. E. (1989). Toward assessment of cognitive and connative structures in learning. *Educational Researcher, 18,(9),* 8-14.

Winer, B. J. (1971). *Statistical principles of experimental design.* (2nd ed.). New York: McGraw Hill.

Sheryl L. Santos
Arizona State University

ABSTRACT

This chapter provides a critical analysis of the issues and
their potential solutions related to mathematics instruction
for limited- English-proficient (LEP) students in U.S.
schools. It touches upon sociopolitical, pedagogical, linguistic, and culturally related issues affecting motivation
and achievement. Programmatic initiatives through research and special projects also are described.

Mathematics Instruction in Bilingual Education: Issues and Initiatives

On a recent trip to Mexico City, where the dollars to pesos
exchange rate requires one to wear clothing with deep pock-
ets or carry a very large purse, I observed the proficiency
with which the street vendors' children carried out their
transactions. Negotiating with large amounts of currency,
even the youngest seemed adept at converting dollars to pesos, knowing the value of the items for sale, and giving customers' their change.

Again coming face-to-face with the underutilization of
potential of students from homes in which English is not
the native language upon my return to the States, I began to
hypothesize about the myriad of reasons why so many language minority students in the United States have not been
more successful in school mathematics.

The literature reports that adequate mathematics instruction has not found its way into enough classrooms (Bradley,
1984; Fernández, 1986; Tsang, 1984; Valverde, 1984). Given
that one of the most important academic subjects in a student's educational life in the United States is mathematics,
and that low achievement resulting in poor performance on

standardized examinations locks millions of students out of the college track ultimately limiting their career options and the potential for self-actualization, a critical analysis of the factors affecting mathematics achievement for limited English proficient (LEP) students has been long overdue.

This chapter will discuss the salient issues and innovative programmatic responses in mathematics education for students with limited English proficiency. While the focus is on linguistic diversity, the discussion cannot be divorced from culture, class, race, and gender. Ultimately, any initiative to improve educational opportunities for speakers of other languages in the United States will have to address the issues of racism, sexism, and classism.

Issues in Mathematics Education

A Decade of Educational Reform

The decade of the 1980s ushered in a national agenda for educational reform. In 1989, three major documents were published which addressed future directions for mathematics education in the United States (American Association for the Advancement of Science, 1989; National Council of Teachers of Mathematics, 1989; National Research Council, 1989). Without exception, the reports point to the need for improving access and equity for minority groups, including language minorities.

Three major issues affecting mathematics instruction and achievement for LEP students surfaced in the literature. They include sociopolitical, linguistic-cultural, and pedagogical issues.

Sociopolitical Issues

Sociopolitical issues broadly range from lack of adequate funding for programs and resources to political disenfranchisement of ethnolinguistic communities. The ultraconservative backlash of the Reagan era and the rise of neoracist groups such as U.S. English have poisoned public opinion against bilingual methodologies. This has had a negative effect on education and employment for language minority students (Spener, 1988).

Bilingual education research and programs have demonstrated the benefits of bilingualism, suggested effective pedagogical practices, and have contributed to American education (De Avila et al., 1987; Hakuta & Gould, 1987; Medrano, 1988; Pagni, 1989; Secada & Carey, 1989), and yet, the trend to thwart the use and maintenance of the native language continues. Bilingual education has been conceptualized by many administrators and nonbilingual educators as merely a bridge or a crutch to English. Programs nationwide have been underfunded and understaffed for the most part, and the teaching of English has been emphasized at the expense of academic subjects like mathematics, science, and social studies (Ochoa & Caballero-Allen, 1988).

Regardless of what research suggests about the benefits of native language instruction (e.g., Cummins, 1981; Cardenas, 1986; Willig, 1985), if those in decision-making positions have a mind-set not to provide adequate resources for public bilingual education programs, the issue of which language to use for instruction becomes moot. Despite the fact that for the past 22 years bilingual educators have led the way in providing a viable educational alternative for LEP students, and much progress has been made in understanding the value and importance of the native language in relation to cognition, intellectual development, and academic achievement, it appears that no amount of logic or appeals to reason are adequate enough to quell detractors from undermining these efforts. Such quests as making English the official language of the United States or attempting to repeal state bilingual education policies, as U. S. English tried to do in New York State through a deceptive media campaign (García, 1989), have become an ever present barrier to access and equity.

Furthermore, during the Reagan years, when "choice" became a buzz word for watering down bilingual content and funding, states began to permit the placement of LEP students into English as a Second Language (ESL) programs instead of providing them with much needed bilingual education programs (Spener, 1988). The results have not been positive. Many of these so-called ESL programs are pull-out programs offering only one half hour per day of instruction in English; the rest of the day the students attend regular classes languishing in the shadows of their English-proficient classmates with teachers who know little of their culture, language, or educational needs (González, 1980; Santos, 1986, 1990).

In short, support for quality programs depends upon many factors including the political mood of the country, the clear- headedness of national and state leaders, the availability of resources, a common knowledge base, the mass media, and the motivation and interest of the populations in question.

Linguistic and Cultural Issues

Issues pertaining to language and culture are numerous. Given the importance of problem solving, word problems, and other linguistic aspects of the mathematics curriculum, one must ask why students who don't even have basic English skills are expected to understand complex concepts in the English mathematics register. When a student fails an examination, does he/she fail because he/she doesn't know how to do math or because he/she cannot read nor understand either English nor the specialized language of mathematics?

In the "mathematics register" (Cuevas, 1984), words and concepts have meanings unique to mathematics. The use of symbols, formulas, and numerical representations have meaning only to the initiated. Consider the following excerpt from an international mathematics journal (Hulek, 1989, p.129): "*Fläche* vom *Geschlecht* 1. Eine kompakte Riemannsche Fläche vom Geschlecht 1 heißt auch *ellip tische Kurve.* " For speakers of English who do not know German, it is futile to make sense of it. It is in a foreign language.

Now consider the next excerpt from an article in English (Cohn, 1989, p. 209): "In the 'homogeneous' case, when $P = P_0 = \ldots$, the classical Markov chains theory provides a

detailed analysis of P^n: ..." Is this excerpt any more understandable than the one in German? If you are not a mathe-
matician, you probably understood as little as you did in
German!

An interesting model conceptualizing the variables affecting this relationship between language and mathematics
was developed by Cocking and Chipman (1988). The model
suggests that mathematics achievement is affected by both
linguistic and nonlinguistic factors. It encompasses the entry characteristics of learners (entry levels in both math and
language); opportunities to learn (provided by teachers and
parents); and motivation (attitudes, influential values of
friends, parents, and the cultural group, and expectations).

Let us apply the conceptual model of Cocking and Chipman (1988) to gain insight about the effects of culture and
values on mathematics achievement among Asian students
in the United States. A noteworthy survey of 7,000 students
in six San Francisco area high schools carried out by Stanford sociologist Sanford M. Dornbusch (Butterfield, 1990)
found that Asian Americans consistently received higher
grades than other groups. Among the most successful were
students from homes where English is not spoken and
whose families have been in the United States the least
amount of time. The concept of the melting pot as an advantage is being challenged by the reality that losing one's
native language and cultural identity is neither advantageous nor desirable.

Research suggests that differences in mathematics
achievement is not a function of IQ or innate talent, but
rather of family values, home study, and hard work. Comparisons of time spent on homework across ethnic groups
revealed that the group with the most time devoted to
homework, Asians, have the most visible achievements in
school. Dornbusch (in Butterfield, 1990) reports: "Asians
average 7.03 hours per week; whites, 6.12; Afro-Americans,
4.23; Hispanics, 3.98" (p. 5).

Asian student success is conjectured to be attributed to
hard work, which has its roots in Confucian philosophy, the
desire to bring honor to one's family, and closer physical and
cultural family ties.

For years educators have believed that mathematics was a language-neutral, culture-free, and value-free academic subject. Today, however, there is an increasing interest in examining mathematics as a "pan-human phenomenon" (Bishop, 1988). This means that "as each cultural group generates its own language, religious beliefs, etc., so it seems that each cultural group is capable of generating its own mathematics" (p. 180).

Gerdes (1988) demonstrates that mathematics is not culture-free by developing examples from Euclidean geometrical concepts using the traditional culture of Mozambique. He supports a methodology termed "cultural conscientialization" in teacher training. A reaffirmation of the grounding of mathematics in many cultures is expected to counteract racial and neocolonial prejudice.

Similarly, the thread of the relevance of culture to mathematics appears in the work of Bradley (1984), who writes about the relationship and importance of culture and language in mathematics education for Native American peoples. Bradley notes that the Navajo language does not have a word for *multiply, divide, if, cosine,* or *sine.* Without the conceptual language and framework, mathematics instruction can become threatening and irrelevant. But just as Gerdes (1988) used a culturally based curriculum to teach geometrical concepts, Bradley uses loom-woven beadwork as a basis for teaching geometry, number theory, and measurement.

A similar problem regarding language, meanings, and algorithms exists for students who have been educated in Spanish- speaking countries. In these cases, students' methods for subtraction, long division, the representation of decimals, and metric measures often causes cognitive confusion and frustration (Castellanos, 1980; Perez de Gerling, 1986) because they have been taught to conceptualize differently than U.S. students.

Pedagogical Issues

The spectrum of pedagogical issues encompasses: teacher training, staffing, textbooks, instructional materials,

computer-assisted instruction, quality and quantity of
classroom instruction, access to manipulatives, computers,
calculators, and other mathematical devices, classroom
environment, and the ability of the teacher to motivate
students.

It is interesting to note that there is a growing body of international literature concerning mathematics pedagogy
from nations with large numbers of ethnolinguistic minorities, such as former European colonies, Great Britain, Australia, South Africa, Mozambique, and many others (Berry,
1985; Bishop, 1988; Brodie, 1989; Dawe, 1983; Gerdes, 1988;
Presmeg, 1988). Many parallels in mathematics instruction
in bilingual education in nations that have been colonized
or have practiced colonization document the struggle for access and equity. This body of literature is very useful in that
the issues raised mirror those affecting ethnolinguistic populations in the United States.

Brodie (1989) questions the desirability of teaching mathematics in a nonnative language. She gives evidence that
learning mathematics in a foreign language can result in
"serious cognitive difficulties" (p. 40) thereby supporting the
pioneering research findings of Cummins, De Avila,
Krashen, and others. Brodie (1989) focuses on bilingual education as practiced in South Africa.

> South African society is made up of many different
> language groups . . . English and Afrikaans speakers
> are descendants of European colonists who arrived be-
> tween 1650 and 1900 . . . The majority of people, black
> South Africans, speak one or more of a number of
> African languages . . . and in South Africa they do not
> have the same status that is accorded to English and
> Afrikaans.

> Education for black students is usually in the vernacu-
> lar in the first years of primary school and in English
> in later primary and secondary schools . . . Thus the
> overall aim is for the student to make a transition from
> her first language to an official language. . . . (p.41)

Brodie also addresses the shortage of qualified bilingual
teachers and lack of adequate curriculum materials in the
vernacular, familiar pedagogical issues in the United States.

Testing is another important issue when we consider that examinations are used to exclude students from participation in higher education, professional careers, and other prestigious opportunities. Scores of many culturally and linguistically different students are unfavorably compared to those of native English speakers (Llabre & Cuevas, 1983). In the interest of equity, the issue of testing must not go unnoticed. How many students who do poorly on mathematics exams do so because they were unable to read the question or interpret words into mathematical statements or equations?

Considering the question of mathematics anxiety and avoidance as a persistent problem in the United States, let us look at a study by MacCorquodale (1988). Her findings indicate that the influence of social forces, English proficiency, sex-role stereotyping, the lack of role models, and role conflict have created a gap in mathematics achievement between Mexican American and Anglo female students. These issues should not be considered independently from one another. There is a tremendous need to understand the nexus between language minority students and how they best learn content instruction. As we seek to understand their interrelatedness, we will be moving toward developing a more coherent picture of the status quo along with a vision for a brighter future.

Programmatic Initiatives

At the core of many initiatives to improve mathematics instruction for LEP students is the push toward integrating second language and content area instruction in academic subjects such as mathematics, science, and social studies (Bilotta, 1985; Chamot, 1985, 1987; Crandall, 1987; Kessler, 1987; Levine, 1984; Supple, 1986; Willets, 1986).

One initiative to improve mathematics instruction developed by Cuevas (Dale & Cuevas, 1987) is the Second Language Approach to Mathematics Skills (SLAMS). This approach, which can be applied to any grade level, "is based on the assumption that in order for a student to master the mathematics concepts presented in class, the language of the concepts must be addressed and mastered" (p. 34). While there is no substitution for native language instruction, (Cardenas, 1986; Cummins, 1981; Hakuta & Gould, 1987; Willig, 1985), the present situation as previously discussed necessitates pragmatic and immediate responses. This does not imply that we remain paralyzed, but rather that we simultaneously seek to strengthen the bilingual education research agenda, dissemination efforts, grantsmanship skills, political advocacy, and community outreach to ethnolinguistic populations throughout the nation.

Several highly recommended nationwide projects available for classroom teachers are tackling the problems of mathematics anxiety, the historical lockout of women in math and the sciences, the alienation of minorities, and the need to go beyond traditional teacher training programs. Specialized workshops are available nationally through such programs as Equals, Family Math/Matemáticas para la familia, Math Their Way, Math for Early Childhood, Activities Integrating Math and Science (AIMS), Great Explorations in Math and Science (GEMS), and others. Most universities and local school districts have detailed information about these programs.

Research and Projects

The Center for Applied Linguistics (CAL) in Washington, DC has taken a leadership role in developing and implementing projects that integrate language and academic instruction for language minority students. Currently, CAL is funded by the Carnegie Corporation to improve articulation between language arts and mathematics and science instruction. This CAL project has five major components: (1) administration of a national survey to determine precollege program needs and subsequent conference to develop the content for project workshops, materials development, research, and dissemination; (2) development of an "Arithmetic Language Inventory" to provide teachers with a way of assessing students' language proficiency in mathematics; (3) production of a videotape illustrating promising practices; (4) implementation of training workshops; and (5) dissemination effort via conference presentations at national meetings of math, science, language, and minority student educators.

Two of the products of the CAL/Carnegie project to be widely disseminated are the Pre-Algebra Lexicon (PAL) and the Math/Science/Language Video. PAL is a useful tool for both math and language teachers in that it addresses the mathematics language needs of all students, LEP learners and others, in order to increase academic achievement. PAL contains specialized mathematical terms, instructional strategies, and diagnostic assessment techniques.

The Math/Science/Language Video is designed to assist math and science teachers who work with ethnic, linguistic, and racial minorities to increase communication and interaction in their classes. This project, funded by the Carnegie Corporation of New York and the Xerox Corporation in cooperation with CAL and the Media Group, presents sequences of students and teachers in which communication is emphasized; students are shown learning unfamiliar academic concepts in math and science, doing group work, word problems, peer tutoring, and playing competitive games in positive ways. (More information about these projects is available from the Center for Applied Linguistics, 1118 22nd Street, N.W., Washington, DC 20037.)

Development Associates, Inc. of Arlington, Virginia, with funding from the Office for Bilingual Education and Minority Languages Affairs (OBEMLA) of the U.S. Department of Education is currently engaged in the "Innovative Approaches Research Project." One of the four topic areas of the project, "Cheche Konnen: An Investigation-Based Approach to Teaching Scientific Inquiry," focuses on science/math instruction. The phrase "Cheche Konnen" means "search for knowledge" in Haitian. Some 70 students from various nationalities in urban Massachusetts are field testing an innovative instructional model to help LEP students become mathematically and scientifically literate through collaborative learning activities. A second project goal is the development of teacher resources to enable others to develop and implement an investigation-based approach in their classrooms. Researchers expect to make available a set of activities, a handbook, a training plan, and videotape materials. More information about Cheche Konnan can be obtained from BBN Systems & Technology Corporation, Cambridge, MA.

Another promising initiative, "A Naturalistic Study of Mathematics Teaching with Hispanic Bilingual Students," funded by the National Science Foundation, is being implemented at Washington State University, Department of Elementary and Secondary Education, Pullman, WA 99164-2122. The purpose of this project is to investigate linguistic factors (Spanish and English) that help or hinder mathematical understanding. Through the use of ethnographic research techniques, students with varying levels of language proficiency in English will be observed in four elementary classrooms. Contrasting data related to teacher-student interaction during mathematics instruction will be gathered.

The National Science Foundation has also funded Arizona State University's "Hispanic Math Project," which is designed to help sixth-grade migrant Hispanic students learn mathematics through a computerized system programmed to talk, show instructional videos, and provide individualized instruction.

This state-of-the-art tutoring system is based upon research in multicultural and mathematics education, cognitive psychology, and artificial intelligence. The Hispanic Math Project will provide a flexible, self-paced environment for learning mathematics. (For further information: The Hispanic Math Project, Arizona State University, Technology Based Learning and Research, Community Services Center at Papago, Tempe, AZ 85287-0908.)

The Santa Ana-Fullerton Elementary Mathematics Project (SAFEMAP), has been underway for two years in California. The purpose of this project is to upgrade teaching in mathematics to include new California requirements, and to encourage and motivate teachers to learn and like mathematics (Pagni, 1989).

A number of Title VII and other projects designed to meet the educational needs of LEP and minority students include goals and objectives that incorporate improvement in mathematics achievement. Many of the projects are multiyear programs offering recommendations for increasing math achievement at all grade levels.

Information concerning public school projects can be obtained from either the National Clearinghouse for Bilingual Education, 8737 Colesville Road, Suite 900, Silver Spring, MA 20910, or from ERIC Document Reproduction Service.

Conclusion

A sampling of several Title VII initiatives to improve mathematics instruction revealed an emphasis on the use of computers and computer-assisted instruction, a focus on learning mathematics in English as a Second Language, explorations in cooperative learning, and mathematics-related conceptual language development in English. Many of the Title VII projects do not focus exclusively on mathematics, but rather include it along with science and social studies.

The literature is very sparse concerning the use of the primary language for mathematics and science instruction. For the most part, compensatory transitional bilingual education continues to dominate the field, with some resources being channeled into two-way bilingual educator or maintenance programs. Considering the rapid rise in the national LEP population on a state-by-state basis and demographic predictions into the 21st century, efforts to initiate improvements in mathematics instruction are wholly inadequate. The issues are pernicious.

Solutions leading toward improvements in mathematics education for LEP students can only come about through concerted efforts by informed and caring citizens who mobilize their local education agencies, universities, community-based organizations, and policy-making bodies to collaboratively set an agenda of attainable short- and long-term goals.

References

American Association for the Advancement of Science. (1989). *Mathematics: A project 2061 panel report*. Washington, D.C.: Author.

Berry, J. W. (1985). Learning mathematics in a second language: Some cross-cultural issues. *For the Learning of Mathematics, 5*(2), 18-23.

Bilotta, C. (1985). (Ed.) *Proceedings of delivering academic excellence to culturally diverse populations* (Language Development through Math and Science Activities). Teaneck, NJ: Farleigh Dickinson University.

Bishop, A. J. (1988). Mathematics education in its cultural context. In A. J. Bishop (Ed.), *Mathematics education and culture* (pp. 179-191). The Netherlands: Kluwer Academic Press.

Bradley, C. (1984). Issues in mathematics education for Native Americans and directions for research. *Journal for Research in Mathematics Education, 15*(2), 96-106.

Brodie, K. (1989). Learning mathematics in a second language. *Educational Review, 41*(1), 39-53.

Butterfield, F. (1990, January 21). Why they excel. *Tempe Tribune* [*Parade,* suppl.], pp. 4-6.

Cárdenas, J. A. (1986, January). The role of the native language in bilingual education. *Kappan, 67*, 359-63.

Castellanos, G. G. (1980). Mathematics and the Spanish-speaking student. *Arithmetic Teacher, 28*(3), 16.

Chamot, A. U. (1985). English language development through a content-based approach. In *Issues in English language development* (pp. 49-55). Rosslyn, VA: National Clearinghouse for Bilingual Education (NCBE).

Cocking, R. R., & Chipman, S. (1988). Conceptual issues related to mathematics achievement of language minority children. In R. R. Cocking & J. P. Mestre (Eds.), *Linguistic and cultural influences on learning mathematics* (pp. 17-46). Hillsdale, NJ: Lawrence Erlbaum Associates.

Cohn, H. (1989). Products of stochastic matrices and applications. *International Journal of Mathematics and Mathematical Sciences, 12*(2), 209-233.

Crandall, J. (1987). Content-based ESL: An introduction. In J. Crandall (Ed.), *ESL through content-area instruction: Mathematics, science, social studies* (pp. 1-8). Englewood Cliffs, NJ: Prentice Hall Regents.

Cuevas, G. J. (1984). Mathematics learning in English as a second language. *Journal for Research in Mathematics Education, 15*(2), 134-144.

Cummins, J. (1981). The role of primary language development in promoting educational success for language minority students. In *Schooling and language minority students: A theoretical framework* (pp. 3-49). Evaluation, Dissemination, and Assessment Center, California State University at Los Angeles.

Dale Corasaniti, T., & Cuevas, G. J. (1987). Integrating language and mathematics learning. In J. Crandall (Ed.), *ESL through content-area instruction: Mathematics, science, social studies* (pp. 9-54). Englewood Cliffs, NJ: Prentice Hall Regents.

Dawe, L. (1983). Bilingualism and mathematical reasoning in English as a second language. *Educational Studies in Mathematics, 14*(4) 325-354.

De Avila, E. A., Duncan, S. E., & Navarrete, C. J., compiled by Valdez Pierce, L. (1987). Cooperative learning: Integrating language and content-area instruction. *Teacher resource guide series,* No. 2. Silver Spring, MD: NCBE.

Fernández, R. (1986). Bilingualism and Hispanic school achievement. *Social Science Research, 15,* 43-70.

García, R. (1989, August 18). Bilingual education means equal opportunity [Letter to the editor]. *The New York Times,* p. A30.

Gerdes, P. (1988). On culture, geometrical thinking and mathematics education. In A. J. Bishop (Ed.), *Mathematics education and culture* (pp. 137-162). The Netherlands: Kluwer Academic Publishers.

González, P. (1980). English as a second language in math education. *NABE Journal, 5*(1), 93-101.

Hakuta, K., & Gould, L. J. (March 1987). Synthesis of research on bilingual education. *Educational Leadership,* 39-45.

Hulek, B. K. (1989). Elliptische kurven, abelsche flachen und das ikosaeder. *Jahresbericht der Deutschen Mathematiker- Vereinigung, 91,* 126-147.

Kessler, C. (1987). Linking mathematics and second language teaching. (ERIC Document Reproduction Service No. ED 289 357).

Levine, L. N. (1984). Content area instruction for the elementary school ESL student. (ERIC Document Reproduction Service No. ED 274 182)

Llabre, M. M., & Cuevas, G. (1983). The effects of test language and mathematical skills assessed on the scores of bilingual Hispanic students. *Journal for Research in Mathematics Education, 14*(4), 318-324.

MacCorquodale, P. (1988). Mexican-American women and mathematics. In R. R. Cocking & J. P. Mestre (Eds.), *Linguistic and cultural influences on learning mathematics* (pp. 137-160). Hillsdale, NJ: Lawrence Erlbaum Associates.

Medrano, M. F. (1988). The effects of bilingual education on reading and mathematics achievement: A longitudinal case study. *Equity & Excellence, 23*(4), 17-19.

National Council of Teachers of Mathematics. (1989). *Curriculum and evaluation standards for school mathematics.* Reston, VA: Author.

National Research Council. (1989). *Everybody counts: A report to the nation on the future of mathematics education.* Washington, D.C.: National Academy Press.

Ochoa, A. M., & Caballero-Allen, Y. (1988). Beyond the rhetoric of federal reports. *Equity & Excellence, 23*(4), 20-24.

Pagni, D. L. (1989, Spring). Project SAFEMAP: An innovative approach to assist minorities in mathematics. *Educational Issues of Language Minority Students, 4,* 85-89.

Perez de Gerling, M. (1986, May). Una observación aritmética bicultural de la división. *Hispania,* 399.

Presmeg, N. C. (1988). School mathematics in culture conflict situations. In A. J. Bishop (Ed.), *Mathematics education and culture* (pp. 163-177). The Netherlands: Kluwer Academic Press.

Santos, S. L. (1986, Spring). High school LEPs: The forgotten minority. *NABE News, 9*(3), 5.

_____. (1990). [Teacher interviews]. Unpublished raw data.

Secada, W. G., & Carey, D. A., with activities by Schlicher, R. (1989, Summer). Innovative strategies for teaching mathematics to limited-English proficient students. *Program information guide series,* No. 10. Silver Spring, MD: NCBE.

Spener, D. (1988). Transitional bilingual education and the socialization of immigrants. *Harvard Educational Review, 58*(2), 133-153.

Supple, S. (1986). Teaching other subjects through the target language. (ERIC Document Reproduction Service No. ED 268 837)

Tsang, S. (1984). The mathematics education of Asian Americans. *Journal for Research in Mathematics Education, 15*(2), 114-122.

Valverde, L.A. (1984). Underachievement and underrepresentation of Hispanics in mathematics and mathematics-related careers. *Journal for Research in Mathematics Education, 15*(2), 123-133.

Willets, Karen F. (1986). Integrating Language and Content Instruction. (ERIC Document Reproduction Service No. ED 278 262)

Willig, A. C. (1985). A meta-analysis of selected studies on the effectiveness of bilingual education. *Review of Educational Research, 55*(3), 269-317.

LANGUAGE PROFICIENCY AND BILINGUALISM

Arnulfo G. Ramírez
Louisiana State University

ABSTRACT

The concept of bilingualism has been used to describe the behavior of speakers who habitually use two languages, the individual's own view of his/her two languages and/or identification with two linguistic communities, and the ever-hanging definition of language competence. Concepts of language proficiency have been depicted in terms of behavioral-structural models of language, a global language factor, a twofold approach consisting of basic interpersonal communication skills and context-reduced communication, and multidimensional concepts of communicative competence involving various systems of knowledge and skills such as grammatical, sociolinguistic, discourse, and strategic competence.

Recent developments in foreign language teaching have introduced the categories of language functions, content or topics, and levels of linguistic accuracy. This concept of language proficiency is currently being depicted in terms of particular performance levels and behaviors within the modalities of listening, speaking, reading, and writing. Moreover, these skills and behaviors appear to involve various systems of knowledge that go beyond the linguistic elements of language, including an understanding of cultural conventions, social factors, and a number of cognitive considerations. While it may not be possible to assess the true linguistic proficiency of bilingual children with current testing procedures, it is important to consider the special uses of language in the school setting and the nature of academic tasks.

Language proficiency and bilingualism can be seen as two linguistic constructs. The concept of bilingualism has been used to describe the behavior of individuals who habitually use two languages for different functions (Weinreich, 1967) while interacting in a bilingual society, or the alternate use of two or more languages by the same individual (Mackey,

1970). The concept has been also associated with the speaker's own view of his or her identification with two languages or two linguistic communities (Malmberg, 1977). Under this view, bilingualism can also be assigned to an individual based on the perception of other persons who come to regard a speaker as a native of two speech communities (e.g., a speaker can "act in both language groups without any disturbing deviance being noticed," Malmberg, 1977, p. 135). The definition of bilingualism according to linguistic competence has been redefined many times an continues to change with our views of languages: What does it mean to know a language?

This chapter describes the conceptions of language proficiency in relation to (1) the meanings associated with the term "communicative competence," (2) the components that constitute language proficiency, (3) functional language proficiency according to a trisectional formulation with respect to language functions, topics, and level of accuracy, (4) factors influencing language proficiency, and (5) language demands of school subjects. These aspects of language proficiency are associated with a linguistic approach to the concept of individual bilingualism rather than a social perspective involving the uses of two languages or an affective orientation considering the language attitudes of speakers and ethnolinguistic communities.

Dimensions of Communicative Competence

The notion of language "competence" was used to characterize a speaker's underlying knowledge of the system of a language, which includes the rules for generating grammatical sentences (Chomsky, 1965). Competence was viewed as the native speaker's internalized grammar consisting of a complex system of rules, operating at different levels—syntactic, lexical, phonological, semantic—to determine the organization of grammatical forms for various communicative purposes. This type of competence cannot be directly observed and is likened to an idealized speaker-hearer who does not display imperfect "performance" errors due to such factors as memory limitations, distractions, shifts of attention, and hesitation phenomena like repeats, false starts, pauses, omissions, and additions.

The term communicative competence has been used by a number of persons since the 1970s to depict a range of ability wider than that associated with a grammatical knowledge of language (Hymes, 1985). This broader linguistic competence involves such aspects as social and functional rules of language use and skills to negotiate meanings interpersonally within specific sociocultural situations (Hymes, 1972). Paulston (1974), for example, distinguished between "linguistic" and "communicative" competence to underscore the essential difference between the knowledge about language rules and structures and knowledge that enables a person to communicate effectively in face-to-face interactions.

Other terms associated with a broader view of grammatical competence have been proposed. Scholars concerned with verbal art conceive of "rhetorical" competence (Steinmann, 1982) and "narrative" competence (McLendon, 1977). Those concerned with interpersonal uses of language identify "conversational" competence (Kennan, 1974), "interactional" competence (Erickson & Schults, 1981), "social" competence (Cicourel, 1981), and "sociolinguistic" competence (Troike, 1970). These kinds of competence suggest a multitude of abilities or skills that constitute knowledge and command of a language.

Components of Communicative Competence

The depictions of linguistic abilities according to a behavioral-structural model of language tends to segment language into discrete, independently measurable components. Hernández-Chávez, Burt, and Dulay (1978) characterize language in terms of a three-dimensional matrix constructed with 64 possible separate proficiencies. One of the dimensions consists of the aspects of language—vocabulary, grammatical structures, pronunciation, and semantics. The second one includes the oral and written modalities of language, with comprehension and production abilities related to the oral channel and reading and writing abilities associated with the written mode. The third component incorporates sociolinguistic performance with respect to usage consideration (speech styles and communicative functions of language) and language varieties (standard and nonstandard dialects and sociolinguistic domains such as home, school, work, neighborhood, and church).

Oller (1978), on the other hand, argues that "there exists a global language proficiency factor which accounts for the bulk of the reliable variance in a wide variety of language proficiency measures" (p. 413). This single concept expression of proficiency, described as "expectancy grammar," is strongly related to cognitive variables and academic achievement measures and appears to exist across all four language skills—listening, speaking, reading, and writing (Oller, 1979). This global ability is attributed to the fact that "in the meaningful use of language, some sort of pragmatic expectancy grammar must function in all cases," and this perceptual ability is "a psychologically real system that sequentially orders linguistic elements in time and in relation to extralinguistic elements in meaningful ways" (Oller, 1979, p. 25). This position emphasizes the central role that expectation and prediction play across language tasks and that language itself cannot be meaningfully segmented into separate, discrete components.

A twofold approach for characterizing language proficiency has been proposed by Cummins (1980, 1983). Initially, he distinguished between basic interpersonal communicative skills (BICS) and cognitive/academic language proficiency (CALP). The BICS dimension of proficiency is the communicative capacity of language that all children acquire in order to be able to function in daily face-to-face exchange. CALP involves the ability to manipulate or reflect upon the features of language (reading a text, writing an essay), independent of extralinguistic supports (e.g., gestures, situational cues). The BICS-CALP distinction was later modified to include a developmental perspective for describing relationships between academic performance and language proficiency, creating a framework that conceptualized language proficiency along two continua. The horizontal continuum distinguishes between context-embedded and context-reduced communication.

In context-embedded communication (i.e., BICS), the participants can negotiate meaning through the use of gestures and feedback to indicate that the message has not been understood, and the language is supported by a wide range of situational cues. Context-reduced communication (i.e., CALP), in contrast, relies primarily on linguistic cues to establish meaning, and, in some cases, this may involve suspending knowledge of the "real" world so as to interpret or manipulate the logic of communication correctly. A good amount of classroom language is context-reduced, requiring linguistic messages to be elaborated precisely and explicitly so misunderstanding is minimized—as in writing a letter, answering an essay question, or reading an article. Context-embedded communication, on the other hand, is more typical of interactive situations outside the classroom. This form of communication derives part of its meaning from interpersonal involvement in a shared reality which makes it unnecessary to elaborate explicitly the linguistic message.

The vertical continuum addresses the developmental aspect of communicative proficiency in relation to the degree of active cognitive involvement in the task or activity. Cognitively demanding tasks such as persuading another person or writing a composition to explain a complicated process, require the individual to process a considerable amount of information simultaneously or in close succession in order to complete the activity.

Cognitively undemanding tasks, at the other end of the vertical continuum, consist of communicative activities that require little cognitive involvement because the linguistic requirements have become automatized as in greetings, asking for permission, filling out a form with personal information, or locating the title of a story/chapter.

A fourfold concept of communicative competence has been advanced by Canale (1983) based on a framework by Canale and Swain (1980) specifying three interacting factors. According to Canale (1984), linguistic communication can be characterized in terms of various systems of knowledge and skills noted in four areas:

1. Grammatical competence: mastery of the language code (verbal or nonverbal), concerned with such features as lexical items, and rules of sentence formation, pronunciation, and literal meaning.

2. Sociolinguistic competence: mastery of appropriate language use in different sociolinguistic contexts, with emphasis on appropriateness of meanings (e.g., attitudes, speech acts, and propositions) and appropriateness of forms (e.g., register nonverbal expression, and intonation).

3. Discourse competence: mastery of how to combine and interpret forms and meanings to achieve a unified spoken or written text in different genres by using (a) cohesion devices to relate utterance forms (e.g., pronouns, transition words, and parallel structures), and (b) coherence rules to organize meanings (e.g., repetition, progression, consistency, and relevance of ideas).

4. Strategic competence: mastery of verbal and nonverbal strategies (a) to compensate for breakdowns in communication due to insufficient competence or to performance limitations (e.g., strategies such as use of dictionaries, paraphrase, and gestures), and (b) to enhance the effectiveness of communication (e.g., deliberately slow and soft speech for rhetorical effect). (p. 112)

It is important to note that communicative competence here is used to refer to both "knowledge" and "skill" in using language. Actual communication involves the realization of various underlying systems on knowledge (e.g., linguistic and nonlinguistic knowledge of the world) and skills (e.g., using the sociolinguistic conventions of a given language) under limiting psychological and environmental conditions such as memory and perceptual constraints, fatigue, nervousness (Canale, 1983, p. 5). This framework of four subsystems does not describe how these factors interact with one another and how they develop among learners/users.

Attempts by Bachman and Palmer (1982) to validate Canale and Swain's (1980) hypothesized components of communicative competence resulted in the identification of three distinct traits—linguistic competence, pragmatic competence, and sociolinguistic competence. Grammatical competence includes morphology and syntax, both of which can vary in range and accuracy. Phonology and graphology are excluded since they are viewed as channels rather than components of communication. Pragmatic competence is associated with the ability to express and comprehend messages and includes as sub-traits vocabulary, cohesion, and organization (coherence). Sociolinguistic competence incorporates the ability to distinguish registers, nativeness, and control of nonliteral, figurative language and relevant cultural allusions. This framework appears to have the status of a model in that it establishes through confirmatory factor analysis the independence of the various components or traits. Yet, Cummins and Swain (1986) note that Bachman and Palmer were unable to distinguish grammatical competence from pragmatic competence among the ESL students from the university level. Similarly, among sixth-grade French immersion students, results of the factor analysis failed to show the validity of three postulated traits— grammatical, sociolinguistic, and discourse competence. Only grammar and discourse competence emerged as distinct traits among this group of language learners but only when they are considered in the wider context of immersion students along with native speakers of French.

Other frameworks for depicting communicative competence have been proposed more recently. Faerch, Haastrup, and Phillipson (1984) argue that communicative competence consists of phonology/orthography, grammar, vocabulary, pragmatics, discourse, communication strategies, and fluency. Bachman's (1987) model incorporates aspects from Canale and Swain in a different formulation. Language competence includes two major components—organizational competence consisting of grammatical competence and textual competence along with various subskills. Pragmatic competence involves the functional uses of language (illocutionary competence) along with sociolinguistic competence. Strategic competence is a set of general abilities that utilize all of the elements of language competence in addition to psychomotor skills in the process of negotiating meaning.

Conceptions of communicative competence have important implications for how language is tested and how language is taught within a communicative perspective. Determining the construct validity of the various components that make up the different models noted above may be a difficult task in terms of an absolute model of communicative competence. Cummins and Swain (1986) suggest the need to test how the various components or traits of communicative competence become differentiated from each other for particular groups of students in specific learning situations.

Functional Language Proficiency

The concept of proficiency, as reflected in the American Council on the Teaching of Foreign Languages (ACTFL) Guidelines (1986), organizes the characteristics of speakers at various levels according to function, context, and accuracy. Function refers to the communicative acts that the student must be able to accomplish such as enumerating events, asking questions, narrating past or future activities. Context refers to the topics or content—everyday survival situations, travel, professional interests—in which the functions are realized. Accuracy relates to how well the functions are performed or to what extent the message is found acceptable among native speakers. The trisectional description of proficiency is used to characterize hierarchical global performance in the areas of speaking, listening, reading, and writing. Ratings of an individual's proficiency are made by comparing performance with the integrated descriptions of linguistic abilities, taking all three factors into account.

Table 1 provides an example of the functional trisection of oral proficiency levels based on the 1982 ACTFL Provisional Proficiency Guidelines in collaboration with Educational Testing Service (ETS).

Students at the novice level are able to communicate minimally with memorized material. They are characterized by the ability to list and respond briefly to questions with words and phrases that have been memorized in first-year textbooks, such as colors, numbers, foods, days of the week, and names of family members. Speakers at this level function primarily at the vocabulary level. They will experience great difficulties in producing sentence-type utterances and will encounter numerous difficulties in being understood by native speakers. Students at the intermediate level are able to create language by combining or recombining learned elements. They are able to ask and answer questions, initiate and minimally sustain conversations about familiar topics such as home, school, friends, personal history, and family members. They can be understood by sympathetic interlocutors even though there are many problems in the area of grammatical accuracy and strong interference from the first tongue. Advanced level speakers have moved from sentence-level utterances to paragraph-length connected discourse. These speakers can narrate and describe present, past, and future activities. They talk about a variety of concrete topics—personal background, family, work, travel, interests, events they have experienced or read about. They are able to express facts, report incidents, and make comparisons, but are not able to support an opinion with examples or argue against an opposing viewpoint. Speakers at the Superior level are able to participate effectively in most formal and informal conversations on topics connected with practical, social, professional, and abstract concerns. They can support their opinions and hypothesize about abstract topics, offering detailed narration and description with native-like discourse strategies. These speakers

TABLE 1

Functional Trisection of Oral Proficiency Levels
ACTFL/ETS Scale

Oral Proficiency Level	Function (Tasks accomplished, attitudes expressed, tone conveyed)	Context (Topics, subject areas, activities addressed)	Accuracy (Acceptability, quality and accuracy of message)
Superior	Can converse in formal and informal situations, resolve problem situations, deal with unfamiliar topics, provide explanations, describe in detail, offer supported opinions, and hypothesize.	Practical, social, professional, and abstract topics; particular interests; and special fields of competence.	Errors never interfere with understanding and rarely disturb the native speaker. Only sporadic errors in basic structures.
Advanced	Able to fully participate in casual conversations; express facts; give instruction; describe, report, and provide narrative about current, past, and future activities.	Concrete topics such as own background, family, interests, work, travel, and current events.	Understandable to native speaker not used to dealing with foreigners; sometimes miscommunicates.
Intermediate	Can create with the language, ask and answer questions, participate in short conversations.	Everyday survival topics and courtesy requirements.	Intelligible to native speakers used to dealing with foreigners/learners.
Novice	Can list, enumerate, and recite.	Memorized (learned) material, such as time, date, basic objects, family members, etc.	Sometimes intelligible to native speakers used to dealing with foreigners/learners.

Source: Liskin-Gasparro, 1986, p. 93.

while not native-like in their linguistic abilities, are able to function effectively with most native speakers.

The ACTFL Proficiency Guidelines (1986) for speaking, listening, reading, and writing are presented in Appendix A. Generic descriptions for nine levels of proficiency for speaking and writing performance are offered along with 10 proficiency levels for listening and reading comprehension. Novice-level speaking performance is characterized in terms of three levels (Novice-Low, Novice-Mid, and Novice-High). The Intermediate speaker is also classified according to three levels (Intermediate-Low), Intermediate-Mid, and Intermediate-High). The Advanced learner can be categorized as either Advanced or Advanced-Plus, followed by the Superior level, learners who can interact successfully with native speakers on a variety of topics but still unable to tailor language to fit the audience or discuss in-depth a highly abstract subject. Writing performance levels are characterized in a similar manner. Listening and reading proficiency levels offers a tenth category of Distinguished, which is described as an ability to understand or read accurately most linguistic styles and forms within the cultural framework of the language.

Factors Influencing Functional Proficiency

Functional language proficiency is currently being depicted in reference to particular performance skills and behaviors within the language modalities of listening, speaking, reading, and writing. These skills and behaviors can involve various systems of knowledge that go beyond the linguistic elements of a language. Papalia (1983), points out that functional proficiency may depend on:

1. Interactional use of the language in the social context (roles of the participants, purpose for interacting, and appropriateness of utterances)

2. Linguistic competence (lexical, morphological, syntactic, and phonological features of the language)

3. Discourse and cultural inference (appropriate interpretation of connected sentences leading to a coherent, global and meaningful whole, and appropriate interpretation of cultural manifestations and values)

4. Strategic functions (manifestations for coping with a variety of factors dealing with misunderstanding, clarifying, pausing, taking time to collect one's thoughts, reactive listening, etc.) (p. 11)

Greetings in French involve considerations beyond when to use *tu* and *vous* forms. One needs to know when to shake hands or kiss, when to use first names, and what to say after the greetings. In Spanish, appropriate cultural scripts may be essential for going on a date, attending a wedding reception, or renting an apartment. What are the dating customs (cultural information)? What can one say on a date (topics and functions)? Where does one go (settings)? What is the sequence of events (meeting-invitation-date-departure)? How does one ask for the time in French when speaking to a friend, stranger, teenager, or adult? Is there a particular interactional sequence that should be followed?

A: Excuse me, (apology)
     Could you tell me the time? (request)
B: It's 2:30 p.m. (informative)
A: Thank you (thanking)

Along with an understanding of social conventions and the cultural context of language use, there are cognitive considerations. Current research efforts in the areas of the receptive skills suggest that reading and listening comprehension involve different types of cognitive tasks associated with kinds of texts (Canale, 1984; Dandonoli, 1987; Child, 1987). Lee and Musumeci (1988), for example, have established parallel hierarchies of text types with cognitive tasks with respect to reading skills (Table 2).

Students at the 0/0+ level (Novice) are expected to read signs, addresses, numbers and names, processes that involve the ability to recognize memorized elements. Students at the level 1 (Intermediate stage) will skim and scan orientational types of text such as travel forms and schedules, menus, and newspapers. At level 2 (Advanced), students need to engage in decoding and classifying tasks as they read factual reports, short narratives, labels, and invitations. At the Superior levels, students must employ numerous cognitive processes (infer, hypothesize, interpret, analyze, and verify) while reading editorials, literary texts, critiques, technical papers, and argumentative prose.

García (1980) argues that it may be impossible to assess the true linguistic proficiency of bilingual children with current language testing procedures usually administered by adults in a highly artificial student-teacher interview format. Bilingual children may use both languages in a complementary fashion, "as part of a single, fully integrated communication resource" (pp. 62-63) that represents his or her linguistic repertoire. A child, for example, might switch from Spanish to English at the word or sentence level while discussing hobbies, family life, or school experiences. Wald (1981) further notes that what a speaker can do orally with language is greatly influenced by the situation (e.g., formal, classroom context versus informal setting at home), the participants (e.g., teacher-student interaction, peer discussion), the topic (e.g., earning a living, travel plans, current politics), and the extent to which the speaker controls the topics under discussion.

Language Demands and Learning Tasks

The acquisition of basic skills involves, in part, the learning of several language varieties that will allow the student to send (speak or write) or receive (listen or read) messages with different purposes (interview for a job, write an essay

TABLE 2

Parallel Hierarchies of Text Types and Reading Skills Defining Levels of Foreign Language Reading Proficiency

Level	Text Type	Sample Texts	Reading Skills
0/0+	Enumerative	Numbers, names, street signs, money denominations, office/shop designations, addresses.	Recognize memorized elements
1	Orientational	Travel and registration forms, plane and train schedules, TV/radio program guides, menus, memos, newspaper headlines, tables of contents, messages.	Skim, scan
2	Instructive	Ads and labels, newspaper accounts, instructions and directions, short narratives and descriptions, factual reports, formulaic requests on forms, invitations, introductory and concluding paragraphs.	Decode, classify
3	Evaluative	Editorials, analyses, apologia, certain literary texts, biography with critical interpretation.	Infer, guess, hypothesize, interpret
4	Projective	Critiques of art or theater performances, literary texts, philosophical discourse, technical papers, argumentation.	Analyze, verify, extend hypotheses

Source: Lee and Musumeci, 1988, p. 174.

to persuade, read an editorial for point-of-view). To acquire this competence the individual may need to know and understand the specialized register (specific language structures and technical terminology) of the subject. Richards' (1978) study of language demands of subject learning reveals differences in the use of technical terminology and language variety (colloquial style of speaking, use of a scientific register).

He notes that English, history, geography, and languages share colloquial, personal, relatively less complex stylistic features and low scores for technical and special terms. Mathematics, physics, chemistry, and biology share formal, impersonal, relatively more complex stylistic features and high scores for technical and special terms (see Table 3). The occurrence of particular language structures is marked enough in the science subjects to suggest that the register of scientific English exerts a powerful influence on the language of science teachers in spite of their attempts to adapt their language to the needs of the pupils. Use of the register is particularly noticeable when material is being exposed, terms defined, and information recorded.

TABLE 3

Use of Technical and Nontechnical Terms

	Feature	
	---	---
Subject	Technical Term	Special Nontechnical Term
Mathematics	111	57
Physics	249	45
Chemistry	223	32
Geography	110	21
English	34	42
History	79	48
Languages	52	49
Biology	225	63

Source: Richards 1978, p. 90.

In addition to the use of specialized vocabulary, students are called to perform a number of pedagogical tasks that can involve a wide range of linguistics and nonlinguistic behaviors. The boundaries between linguistic competence and task performance are not easy to establish. Some tasks, for example, can involve one or more actions: "Open your book." "Write a letter to a friend." "Read chapter 10 and answer the first 5 questions."

Conclusion

Language proficiency and bilingualism can be seen as two linguistic constructs. The concept of bilingualism has been approached from the perspectives of language use, language attitudes, and language proficiency. Language proficiency, in turn, has been seen in terms of various dichotomies (linguistic/communicative competence, knowledge/use, context-embedded/context-reduced situations). Multicomponent perspectives such as frameworks from Canale and Swain (1980), Faerch, Haastrup, and Phillipson (1984), and Bachman (1987), illustrate the operation of various subsystems of language, types of knowledge, and skills. Functional language proficiency as reflected in the ACTFL Guidelines (1986) organizes the characteristics of speakers/users at various levels of performance according to integrated descriptions of linguistic abilities based on functions, context, and accuracy. Bilingualism approached from a functional perspective would result in a different view of the nature of language proficiency. At the same time, the assessment of functional proficiency across the four language skill areas would involve cognitive, cultural, and social factors.

Concepts of language proficiency and bilingualism, while inter-related, have not focused until recently on the nature of academic language and pedagogical tasks. Language proficiency independent of the special linguistic considerations on school success will not be particularly useful for student classification or placement. Bringing together the perspectives from ACTFL's functional proficiency along with other concepts of communicative competence and the nature of academic tasks, will enable us to formulate a more comprehensive view of language proficiency and individual bilingualism.

A linguistic view of bilingualism may be particularly useful in understanding the performance of bilingual individuals in different interactive situations (e.g., adult/child, child/child, brother/sister, teacher/student) and cultural settings, (e.g., home, school, church, workplace). Language proficiency appears to be an important factor that affects language choice among bilinguals. Individuals may use one language instead of another or employ both in a complementary manner given their relative degree of bilingualism and considerations such as the situation (e.g., location, participants, level of formality), discourse content (e.g., topics, lexical requirements), nature of the interaction (e.g., to create social distance, to include/exclude someone, to provide/obtain information). The type of bilingual proficiency can be seen as the behavioral manifestation of intergroup or intraethnic attitudes toward the languages themselves and their relative use in society.

References

ACTFL Provisional Proficiency Guidelines (1982, 1986). Hastings-on-Hudson, NY: ACTFL Materials Center.

Bachman, L. (1987). *Fundamental considerations in language testing.* Reading, MA: Addison-Wesley.

Bachman, L., & Palmer, A. (1982). The construct validation of some components of communicative proficiency. *TESOL Quarterly, 16,* 449-465.

Canale, M. (1983). From communicative competence to communicative language pedagogy. In J. Richards & R. Schmidt (Eds.), *Language and communication* (pp. 2-25). New York: Longman.

____. (1984). A communicative approach to language proficiency assessment in a minority setting. In C. Rivera (Ed.), *Communicative competence approaches to language proficiency assessment: Research and application* (pp. 107-122). Avon, England: Multilingual Matters.

____, & Swain, M. (1980). Theoretical bases of communicative approaches to second language teaching and testing. *Applied Linguistics, 1*(1), 1-47.

Child, J. R. (1987). Language proficiency levels and the typology of texts. In H. Byrnes & M. Canale (Eds.), *Defining and developing proficiency: Guidelines, implementation and concepts* (pp. 97-106). Lincolnwood, IL: National Textbook.

Chomsky, N. (1965). *Aspects of the theory of syntax.* Cambridge, MA: MIT Press.

Cicourel, A. (1981). Notes on the integration of micro and macrolevels of analysis. In K. Knorr-Cetina & A. V. Cicourel (Eds.), *Advances in social theory and methodology* (pp. 51-80). London: Routledge and Kegan Paul.

Cummins, J. (1980). The cross-lingual dimensions of language proficiency: Implications for bilingual education and the optimal age issue. *TESOL Quarterly, 14,* 175-187.

____. (1983). Language proficiency and academic achievement. In J. W. Oller, Jr. (Ed.), *Issues in language testing research* (pp. 108-126). Rowley, MA: Newbury House.

____, & Swain, M. (1987). *Bilingualism in education.* New York: Longman.

Dandonoli, P. (1986). ACTFL'S current research in proficiency testing. In H. Byrnes & M. Canale (Eds.), *Defining and developing proficiency: Guidelines, implementations and concepts.* (pp. 75-96). Lincolnwood, IL: National Textbook.

Erickson, F., & Schultz, J. (1981). When is a context? Some issues and methods in the analysis of social competence. In J. Green & C. Wallat (Eds.), *Ethnography and language in educational settings (Advances in discourse processes V)* (pp. 147-160). Norwood, NJ: Ablex.

Faerch, C., Haastrup, K., & Phillipson, R. (1984). *Learner language and language learning.* Copenhagen: Gyldendals Sprogbibliotek.

García, M. (1980). Linguistic proficiency: How bilingual discourse can show that a child has it. In R. V. Padilla (Ed.), *Ethnoperspectives in bilingual education research. Vol II: Theory in bilingual education* (pp. 62-74). Ypsilanti, MI: Eastern Michigan University, Foreign Languages and Bilingual Studies.

Hernández-Chávez, E., Burt, M. K., & Dulay, H. C. (1978). Language dominance and proficiency testing: Some general considerations. *NABE Journal, 3,* 41-54.

Hymes, D. (1972). On communicative competence. In J. B. Pride, & J. Holmes (Eds.), *Sociolinguistics* (pp. 269-293). London: Penguin.

____. (1985). Toward linguistic competence. *Revue de L'AILA, 2,* 9-23.

Lee, J. F., & Musumeci, D. (1988). On hierarchies of reading skills and text types, *Modern Language Journal, 72*(2), 173-187.

Liskin-Gasparro, J. (1986). Teaching and testing for oral proficiency: Some applications for the classroom. In A. Papalia (Ed.), *Teaching our students a second language in a proficiency based classroom* (pp. 91-99). Schenectady, NY: New York State Association of Foreign Language Teachers.

Mackey, W. F. (1970). The description of bilingualism. In J. A. Fishman (Ed.), *Readings in the sociology of language* (pp. 554-584). The Hague: Mouton & Co.

Malmberg, B. (1977). Finns halvsprakighet? *Sydsvenska Dagbladet,* 21(11), 133-136.

McLendon, S. (1977). Cultural presupposition and discourse analysis: Patterns of presupposition and assertion of information in Eastern Pomo and Russian narrative. In M. Saville-Troike (Ed.), *Linguistics and anthropology* (pp. 153-189). Washington, DC: Georgetown University, Round Table on Language and Linguistics.

Oller, J. W., Jr. (1978). The language factor in the evaluation of bilingual education. In J. E. Alatis (Ed.), *Georgetown University round table on languages and linguistics* (pp. 410-422), Washington, DC: Georgetown University Press.

____. (1979). *Language tests at school: A pragmatic approach.* New York: Longman.

Papalia, A. (1983). *Developing communicative proficiency and cultural understanding in secondary school language programs.* Schenectady, NY: New York State Association of Foreign Language Teachers.

Paulston, C. B. (1974). Linguistics and communicative competence. *TESOL Quarterly, 8,* 347-362.

Richards, J. (1978). *Classroom language: What sort?* London: George Allen and Unwin.

Steinmann, M. (1982). Speech act theory and writing. In M. Nystrand (Ed.), *What writers know. The language process and structure of written discourse* (pp. 291-324). New York: Academic Press.

Troike, R. C. (1970). Receptive competence, productive competence, and performance. In J. Alatis (Ed.), *Linguistics and the teaching of standard English to speakers of other languages and dialects* (pp. 63-74). Washington, DC: Georgetown University, Round Table on Languages and Linguistics.

Wald, B. (1981). The relation of topic/situation sensitivity to the study of language proficiency. In R. V. Padilla (Ed.), *Ethnoperspectives in bilingual education research, Vol III: Bilingual education technology* (pp. 281-306). Ypsilanti, MI: Eastern Michigan University, Foreign Languages and Bilingual Studies.

Weinrich, U. (1967). *Languages in contact. Findings and Problems* (5th printing). The Hague: Mouton and Co.

TOWARD A DEFINITION OF EXEMPLARY TEACHERS IN BILINGUAL MULTICULTURAL SCHOOL SETTINGS*

Christian J. Faltis
Arizona State University

Barbara J. Merino
University of California, Davis

ABSTRACT

The purpose of this paper is to offer a definition of exemplary teachers in bilingual multicultural classrooms that is derived from four traditions and to explore whether these traditions reveal exemplary teaching that is ethnic specific. Representative examples and critiques are presented for the teacher competency, the teacher effectiveness, the ethnographic, and the literary traditions. The paper ends with a call for an expanded definition of exemplary teaching, one that necessarily includes cultural knowledge and language proficiency.

Teacher preparation programs in bilingual multicultural education have as an implicit goal the development of exemplary teachers. At the national level this goal is being supported by efforts to connect teacher education to a national certification system designed to identify exemplary teachers in mainstream nonbilingual classrooms (Shulman, 1987). The purpose of this paper is to offer a definition of exemplary teachers in bilingual multicultural classrooms derived from several research and literary traditions, and in doing so simultaneously explore the question of whether the characteristics of exemplary teachers are ethnic specific.

Teachers who work in bilingual multicultural classrooms are distinct from mainstream teachers in at least three ways:

---

*The writing of this chapter was partially funded by a grant from the Far West Holmes Group.

1. They must be proficient in two languages and
   be knowledgeable of effective pedagogical
   strategies for manipulating instruction in
   those languages.

2. They must be skilled in the integration of
   students' work at mixed levels of linguistic
   and conceptual complexity.

3. They must know the rules of appropriate behavior of a least two ethnic groups and be able
   to incorporate this knowledge into the
   teaching process.

Teachers who are not proficient in two languages but
nonetheless work in classrooms that are ethnically and/or
linguistically diverse also must possess certain kinds of cultural knowledge beyond that espoused as effective for mainstream schooling. Therefore, our search for a definition of
what constitutes an exemplary bilingual multicultural
teacher perforce must involve all three factors and in the
case of nonbilingual multicultural teachers, the second and
third factors.

The fact that cultural knowledge necessarily figures into
the definition for bilingual and nonbilingual teachers is
especially interesting because it opens up the possibility that
some bilingual multicultural teachers may be more effective
with children from certain ethnic groups than they are with
others, depending on the cultural knowledge they possess
about the children in their classrooms. Accordingly, we
strive to offer a definition of exemplary bilingual multicultural teachers that is both cross-cultural and ethnic specific.

The definition we propose should not be considered as a
recipe for effectively teaching individual students who are
bilingual or from a particular ethnic background. Rather,
the definition, derived from multiple sources, may be especially useful for making general decisions about ways to improve the preparation of bilingual multicultural teachers.
We discuss this point in the final section of the paper.

Method

To achieve the goal of defining exemplary teaching in bilingual multicultural school settings, we examine four traditions, each contributing a distinct perspective on what makes a bilingual multicultural teacher exemplary. The four traditions are the *competency tradition*, the *teacher effectiveness tradition*, the *ethnographic study tradition*, and the *literary tradition*. For each tradition, we pose the following kinds of questions:

1. How is effective teaching portrayed?

2. In what ways can the portrayal be used in the preparation of bilingual multicultural teachers?

3. What are the strengths and limitations of the tradition in the way it portrays exemplary teachers?

4. Are certain skills and understandings emphasized as being essential for effective teaching with a particular language and/or ethnic group?

Answers to these questions enable us to focus on points of commonality across the four traditions and to explore points of difference associated with language and ethnic variation. Because the literature for each tradition is vast, and our space limited, we will highlight representative samples of each tradition and conclude by discussing the relationship among traditions in terms of the featured samples.

The Competency Tradition

In this tradition, linguists, educational psychologists, and expert educators generate lists of competencies considered necessary for teaching in bilingual multicultural settings. The first comprehensive list appeared in 1974, when a group of "leading bilingual educators from throughout the United

States" (Center for Applied Linguistics (CAL) in Alatis & Twaddell, 1976, p. 345) convened in Arlington, Virginia to draw up guidelines for the preparation and certification of teachers of bilingual/bicultural education. The CAL group developed eight areas of competency: language proficiency, linguistics, culture, instructional methods, curriculum utilization and adaptation, assessment, school-community relations, and supervised teaching. They then subdivided each area into more specific abilities that the teacher should be able to demonstrate. In the area of cultural competence, exemplary teachers need to demonstrate the ability to develop cross-cultural awareness in students and foster an appreciation for cultural diversity.

In an updated version of the CAL guidelines, Garza and Barnes (1989) list seven of the eight original areas of competency (supervised teaching is omitted) and add what they consider to be expert references to support the sub-abilities in each of major competency areas. Moreover, they added several new sub-abilities to the area of cultural competence, and stressed the importance of being sensitive to cognitive learning style preferences, suggesting that "individual differences [may] be correlated with membership in particular cultural groups" (p. 14). The expert reference for this sub-ability is Ramírez and Castañeda (1974), who argued that Mexican American children learn best with field-sensitive teachers and materials.

Cognitive learning style preference also has been listed as a potentially cultural- and ethnic-specific competency by Bennett (1990), and García (1990). However, these authors point out the danger of creating stereotypes that may be harmful to individual students who are members of the groups labeled as preferring one style over another.

The competency tradition also includes the work of a number of educators who are interested primarily in changing the existing school curriculum so that students acquire knowledge about a range of cultural groups and develop attitudes and abilities needed to function at some level of competency within various cultural environments (Banks, 1979; Baker, 1983).

As a whole, the competency tradition lacks empirical evidence to show whether the competencies generated by experts are associated with the competencies that exemplary teachers draw from to be effective in either cross-cultural or ethnic-specific settings. The one apparent exception to this rule is a study by Rodríquez (1980), who asked superior and average bilingual teachers to describe effective and ineffective ways of teaching in bilingual multicultural classrooms, and then thematically analyzed their responses into six major competency areas, all of which can be located in other competency lists. She found that the three most prominent characteristics mentioned by exemplary bilingual teachers were communicative skills, positive regard for children and their parents, and a nonauthoritative interaction style.

The Teacher Effectiveness Tradition

This tradition of identifying exemplary teaching has a rich research history which began with attempts to identify presage variables—teacher formative experiences, teacher-preparation experiences, and teacher personality factors—and relate these to student gains. The simple model evolved into a systematic research tradition that seeks to trace the influence of presage, contextual and process variables with student product variables such as student achievement, student attitudes to schooling, and the development of thinking strategies (Dunkin & Biddle, 1974; Rosenshine & Stevens, 1986). The bulk of this research has focused on mainstream classrooms in the United States. A few studies, however, have sought to identify effective instructional strategies in working-class populations, specifically Chapter 1 classrooms (Brophy, 1982; Crawford, 1989). This research tradition has been developing steadily in linguistically diverse settings, most notably in second language classrooms (Chaudron, 1988; van Lier, 1988), although to some extent also with bidialectal populations such as black English speakers (Politzer, 1980). In culturally diverse settings, this research tradition has focused on process research, particularly on identifying patterns of allocation of student turns differentiated by ethnicity and only rarely on relating classroom processes and student gains to teachers' and students' cultural backgrounds (Merino, in press; Wong Fillmore, Ammon, McLaughlin, & Ammon, 1985).

The research on teacher effectiveness is far too extensive to summarize here. Instead, we will highlight instructional strategies that have been shown to be effective in culturally or linguistically diverse settings in numerous research studies.

Student Participation. Giving students the opportunity to learn, providing them with academic learning time, stands out as one of the best documented instructional predictors of educational achievement in mainstream classrooms (Fisher, Berliner, Filby, Marliave, Cahen & Dishaw, 1980). This finding has been replicated in Chapter 1 classrooms (Crawford, 1989) and in bilingual classrooms (Tikunoff & Vásquez-Faría, 1982). While this finding may seem intuitively obvious, it is important to study because classrooms appear to vary considerably in the amount of time students are engaged in active learning. As reported by Crawford (1989), the highest achieving teachers in the Chapter 1 classroom that he studied allocated 90 percent of the available time to academic content. Tikunoff and Vásquez-Faría (1982) reported that exemplary teachers they studied were effective in making transitions from one lesson to the next and gave clear explanations. Moreover, students were aware of the goals of the lesson, and were actively engaged in learning. Clarity of presentation and clear articulation of classroom goals may be more important to some cultural groups than to others. Wong Fillmore (1985), for example, found that while Chinese students she studied could compensate for lack of clarity in instruction by becoming more attentive, Hispanic children were particularly vulnerable and did not perform as well with teachers who gave poor instructions and who did not clearly mark lesson boundaries.

Language Acquisition. A principal trend in current research on first and second language acquisition is that communicatively meaningful activities are essential for facilitating the language acquisition process (Linfors, 1987; Rigg & Allen, 1990). Depending on the child's stage of acquisition, different instructional strategies may be key to making language teaching meaningful. For second language learners, input that is comprehensible to the students appears to be critical at the beginning stages (Krashen, 1981). As the student progresses and begins a more active, productive phase, student output (Swain, 1985) and having the opportunity to negotiate language become more critical (Long, 1981). Engaging students with academic content that is intrinsically interesting and using reflective questions that require answers that go beyond memorized phrases are strategies that lead to greater amounts of output (Ramírez & Merino, 1990). While the direct link between negotiation and second language acquisition is still in the process of being established (Ellis, 1987), research on small group learning has consistently demonstrated that language minority students negotiate and use more talk in small group tasks than in whole class tasks (Au & Kawakami, 1984; Cohen, 1986).

Classroom Climate. Exemplary second language teachers are distinguishable by their enthusiasm for the learning of a second language (Moskowitz, 1976). Superior teachers keep interest alive by such strategies as varying the activities and using a quick pace to move through the lesson (Politzer, 1982; Ramírez & Stromquist, 1979), as well as by assigning intrinsically interesting tasks that encourage hands-on participation by students (Coughran, Merino, & Hoskins, 1986). Effective teachers in culturally and linguistically diverse classrooms have high expectations of their students (Payne, 1984) and provide a positive classroom environment where the culture of the student is actively used as a means for creating student interest and validation (García, 1988).

The Ethnographic Tradition

Under the influence of anthropologists such as Spindler (1974; 1982), Trueba and Wright (1980-81) and Heath (1983), classrooms, teachers, and students have become the focus of many ethnographic studies. In this section we present examples of effective teachers in culturally and linguistically diverse settings as well as examples that illustrate students' perspectives on exemplary teaching.

The Teacher Perspective. First, it is important to underscore that American classroom teachers, as transmitters of American culture, reflect a range of behaviors along which they vary, but which at the same time may be restricted by certain cultural orientations. Spindler and Spindler (1987) studied teachers and classrooms in a rural German community, Schönhausen, and in a comparable American, rural community, Roseville. They report interesting contrasts between the teachers' cultural knowledge. The beliefs that teachers hold about individual and group achievement is especially noteworthy. In Roseville, the assumption is that the function of the group is to make individual life and achievement possible, to establish a context in which individual students can pursue their goals. In Schönhausen, the teacher is regarded as responsible for whatever learning takes place. Motivating students is the teacher's job, as is bringing the students up to the group standard.

These distinguishing cultural features, if they are generalizable to other American contexts, have important implications for teaching in culturally diverse settings. To the extent that teachers' expectations differ from the expectations of students and their parents, "discontinuities" may ensue that seriously impair the students' learning opportunities. Moreover, to the extent that the dominant culture relegates minority students to a caste-like status, teachers as transmitters of mainstream culture may simply be institutionalizing lower expectations for achievement (Ogbu, 1982).

Delgado-Gaitán (1987) explored the continuities/discontinuities between the home and school in the context of Mexican families in an urban northern California community setting she calls Los Portales. One of the discontinuities she highlighted focuses on variations of authority in the home and school. At home, her informants were given a great variety of tasks to accomplish, from changing diapers, to conveying important messages and taking care of siblings. While some of the tasks were relatively simple, others required negotiation and the use of complex problem-solving strategies. Children also engaged in involved sequences of negotiation with their parents in establishing when and how the tasks will be completed. In sharp contrast to the home, at school, Delgado-Gaitán presented several classroom sequences in which teacher control stringently operates. In a third-grade classroom, for example, a handwriting lesson proceeded on cue, with the writing of first names and then last names, with the teacher controlling the talk and limiting any kind of consultation among students.

In Los Portales, teachers controlled not only the content of the tasks, but how the tasks were completed as well. Is the contrast in autonomy and control between the Roseville and Los Portales schools due to the content of lessons that focus on basic skills and mechanics? Are teachers less willing to give up control when teaching students from working-class backgrounds, as Wilcox (1982) found in her comparison of two working-class and middle-class classrooms? Whatever the ontogenesis for these behaviors, the teachers in Los Portales do not give the impression of being agents for the empowerment of their students.

Macías (1987) provided an alternative view of teachers consciously engaged in reducing the impact of home/school discontinuities in the Papago Reservation. Macías highlighted three different types of home/school discontinuities and Papago teachers' strategies to reduce the negative impact of these discontinuities. Here we will focus on Macías's discussion of autonomy and control.

Papago childrearing practices stress the autonomy of the child. Few limitations are placed on Papago children's freedom and parents are rarely punitive. Papago teachers faced with the demands of formal schooling and more rigid schedules use a "minimally directive interaction style." Classroom rules are presented as generalized warnings to the whole group: "We don't shout in the room." Misbehavior is not directly punished, instead good behavior is positively reinforced through pragmatic overt rewards such as allowing quiet children to be dismissed first. In those rare occasions when an individual continues to misbehave despite many generalized warnings, the child is called aside and without an audience, given instructions on how to behave more appropriately.

Many of the teachers in the Macías study were Papago as were most of the students in school. However, being a member of the same ethnic group as the children in the classroom is not necessarily a prerequisite to exemplary teaching. The challenge for classroom teachers working with students of different cultural backgrounds is to use instructional strategies that are in harmony with students' ways of talking and learning and at the same time that engender in students a respect for other ways of doing things (Faltis, 1989; Moll, 1988).

Allied to the anthropological research tradition is an emerging methodology that seeks to identify the cultural knowledge of exemplary or expert teachers. In an exciting study currently in progress, Foster (1989) has been interviewing exemplary black teachers who taught before desegregation. She has used a community nomination process as a way of identifying exemplary teachers. One common characteristic of these exemplary teachers is a stance of commitment to the learning of their students that goes far beyond what traditional American teachers tend to adopt. Foster notes that the teachers actively seek parents' help in getting the students to learn and that they are aggressive with their students in not letting them opt out of learning. These efforts may be critical with students who through continuous exposure to unemployment, job ceilings, and discrimination may have internalized a low effort syndrome (Ogbu, 1987).

The Student Perspective. The research on student perspectives concerning exemplary teachers is strikingly sparse. Spindler (1982) was perhaps the first ethnographer to give serious attention to the students' view of effective teaching in heterogeneous classroom. In 1952, Spindler studied Roger Harker's (a pseudonym) fifth-grade classroom in northern California. The class was comprised of children from upper-middle, middle-, and lower-class backgrounds who represented Mexican American, Anglo, and Japanese American ethnic groups. The school administration, his principal, and Harker himself were convinced that he was an exemplary teacher. Harker described himself as "fair and just to all my pupils," as making "fair decisions" and as "playing no favorites" (Spindler, 1982, p. 25). The children, however, viewed Harker quite differently. The minority children described him as "having special pets," as not always being fair to everyone, and as not someone who is easy to approach with personal or academic problems. Spindler concluded that Harker was tacitly informing the Anglo children that they counted, and informing the lower-class and non-Anglo children that they were less capable and hence, less worth his trouble. The children knew that Harker was discriminating, but the school system supported his classroom behavior without question.

Sizemore (1981) was interested in finding out whether black and white ninth- and twelfth-grade students look for the same characteristics in teachers. He hypothesized that teachers may have difficulty working with ninth-grade black and white students because these students perceive as important a set of behaviors and characteristics different from their twelfth-grade counterparts. The results indicated, however, that students' perceptions of good teaching differed more significantly according to grade level than to ethnicity. Within grade levels, however, the ninth-grade black students indicated a greater need than white students for warm, understanding and friendly behavior. At the twelfth-grade level, this need was still evident, but to a lesser degree. All students, regardless of ethnicity or grade level, said they wanted teachers who care, who explain materials thoroughly and in a meaningful way, and who help students master the material.

Two other studies examined student perspectives on effective teachers. Both of these studies were conducted in predominately black high schools in Chicago. Payne (1984), a black teacher, asked students open-ended questions about good teaching and how to tell if a teacher is concerned. The most significant response was that students wanted teachers to explain clearly and to provide students with some indication of progress. Students did not particularly like demanding teachers, but they generally viewed teachers who made them do work and who kept on them about attendance and homework as concerned about teaching.

Parkay (1983), a white teacher, found that underachieving students viewed teachers with a high degree of hostility and that all felt that only a few teachers were interested in helping them learn. Achievers, in contrast, viewed teachers positively and felt that teachers were doing their best given the kinds of students they must teach. These students expected teachers to be demanding and also felt that successful learning was a result of careful listening.

The Literary Tradition

This section is organized into two major foci: children's view of exemplary teaching in children's literature and exemplary teaching presented in popular literature and film.

Children's Literature. The perspective of ethnic minorities in children's literature has been slow to develop, but is fast becoming more influential. Initially, most childrens' stories with a minority perspective tended to be quasi-historical accounts, frequently written by white authors. O'Dell's *Island of the Blue Dolphins* (1960), a moving account of a Native American girl who must survive on an island by herself, is a well-known example of this genre. Partly as a result of the civil rights movement of the 1960s, stories whose central characters have a minority background have become more available. The *New York Times Parent's Guide to Best Books for Children* (Lipson, 1988) lists 56 titles with a minority theme, out of a total of 956. Many still are written by white authors (Greene, 1974; Fitzhugh, 1974), but often now there is an attempt to support the authenticity of the minority perspective by acknowledging interviews with minority members.

Another very important trend in minority children's literature is the perspective of minority authors who use their own bicultural heritage as an inspiration for their work. Frequently these stories draw heavily from the authors' family histories and their own experiences growing up. How do teachers figure in these stories? We have selected two examples to discuss the wide range of roles teachers play in this tradition of children's literature.

Yoshido Uchida in *Jar of Dreams* (1981) draws a powerful image of Rinko, an 11-year-old Japanese American girl growing up during the Depression in Berkeley, California. Her family struggles to start a home laundry and faces ruthless, racist competition from a white launderer. At the same time, Rinko struggles with racism at her school. From boys, prejudice takes the form of overt name calling and ethnic slurs "Jap" and "Ching Chong Chinaman." Girls employed a more subtle form of prejudice, "they talk over and around and right through me like I was a pane of glass" (Uchida, 1981, p. 6). Rinko wants to be a teacher even though her older brother Cal tells her that no public school in California would hire a Japanese teacher. It is Rinko's Aunt Waka, who comes to visit from Japan, who helps Rinko and her family deal with the racism they all encounter. Rinko, reflecting on her teacher, provides an example of what she considers to be white culture's lack of understanding of her culture. "My teacher at school is always asking me to repeat my answers. 'Rinko, you'll have to learn to speak up,' she says, as though having a soft voice was a fault I'd have to overcome." (p. 41).

Mildred Taylor, in *Roll of Thunder, Hear my Cry* (1976), gives a picture of a totally different teacher. Inspired by the stories her father told her as a child, Taylor creates a gripping story of a black family seeking to keep their land in segregated Mississippi during the Depression. Cassie Logan, the fourth grader narrator, vividly describes her growing awareness of the prejudice and discrimination all around her. Her mother teaches the seventh grade where her younger brother, Little Man, is crestfallen to receive a dilapidated reader as his first reading text. On its title page is a form list with the year, the condition of the book, and the race of the student. The book was first issued as new in 1922 to a white student. By 1933, the book's condition is very poor and the race of the student is marked as "nigra." Little Man, in disgust, throws it on the floor and stamps on it. His mother, upon hearing about the incident, covers the title page with a piece of brown paper and does the same to the books of all her students. Mrs. Logan knows that teaching does not mean simply transmitting academic subjects. She reacts to the prejudice the children face in the school and helps them find concrete actions to deal with it. She organizes a boycott to protest the murder of a black man. Her history lesson on slavery goes far beyond the watered-down version of the authorized school text.

Taylor's teacher reflects much of the stance that Foster (1989) reports from her interviews of exemplary black teachers before integration. These are teachers who know that they must help their students negotiate the double messages of a society that at times doles out justice capriciously.

Popular Literature and Film. Exemplary teachers have been depicted in several well-regarded novels and films. This genre of literature and film presents the story of a real teacher who successfully reaches children who other teachers and society as a whole feel are not worth the effort. E. R. Braithwaite's (1959) novel *To Sir, with Love* is one of the more popular examples of the genre. In this story, Braithwaite, a well-educated black electrical engineer born in Guyana takes a one-year teaching position in a predominately white high school in London's cockney East Side while he seeks a permanent position with an engineering firm. His first experiences with the students are fraught with confrontations and unsuccessful learning experiences. As a result of a disgusting classroom incidence, Braithwaite institutes a plan for promoting mutual respect among the students. He insists that the students learn certain manners, that he be called Sir, and that they use Mr. and Miss to refer to one another. Over time, the students grow to love and respect Braithwaite and in the process, become more responsible and caring in both their social and personal relations with others.

Jaime Escalante is the exemplary teacher portrayed in the film *Stand and Deliver* (Menéndez & Musca, 1988). In this story, Escalante, a bright computer scientist, leaves his profession in 1983 to teach computer science at Garfield High School, a predominately Mexican American school in East Los Angeles, California. However, since the computers did not arrive (for the second year in a row), Escalante is assigned to teach remedial mathematics or Math 1A to a group of unruly Chicano students. His first few weeks in the classroom demonstrate his extraordinary teaching acumen. He contextualizes teaching by showing students the meaning of mathematical concepts in ways that are immediately understood by the students. "Mathematics," he tells the students, "is in your blood," reminding them that their ancestors, the Mayas, were among the first to contemplate mathematical principles.

The school administration does not believe that the students are capable of learning beyond the basics. However, Escalante disagrees, asserting that students rise to the level of expectations. In class, Escalante repeatedly reminds students that they are tops, and that to stay on top they must have *ganas*, a will to survive. He meets with one of the parents of a good student when the student is forced by her parents to quit school to work in the family restaurant.

One day when Escalante takes his class to visit an engineering firm, he learns that a daughter of a computer scientist is taking calculus at her high school. He decides that his students should also have the same opportunities, and so he organizes a calculus class that in addition to meeting during school hours, meets before and after school, and on Saturdays as well.

After a semester's worth of hard work, the students in Escalante's class take the Advanced Placement Calculus exam. All of the students pass the exam, but are suspected of cheating by Educational Testing Service because they all have similar kinds of errors. Escalante and the students are devastated. "They were almost great," he laments, "but now the kids have learned that even if you try really hard, you still lose." After talking with the students, Escalante arranges for them to take the test over with only one day's notice. Again, all of the students pass the exam, most with a superior grade. That year, 1983, 15 Garfield High students passed the AP Calculus Exam, by 1987, the number had grown to 87.

Toward a Definition

The purpose of this paper is to offer a definition of exemplary bilingual multicultural teachers based upon four contributing traditions. For each tradition presented, we posed the following questions: How is effective teaching portrayed? In what ways can the portrayal be useful in the preparation of bilingual multicultural teachers? What are the strengths and limitations of the tradition? And lastly, are certain skills and understandings emphasized as being essential for effective teaching with a particular language and/or ethnic group?

First, exemplary bilingual multicultural teachers are skilled communicators. They articulate lesson goals clearly, give lucid directions for classroom tasks, and reach out to students in ways that are culturally as well as individually meaningful to students. Second, exemplary teachers who teach in culturally diverse settings are able to establish positive environments for learning by conveying a willingness to reach out to students and their families, at times in defiance of educational conventions. In a very real sense, their classrooms invariably approximate a family-like atmosphere of caring and responsibility to the group. Third, exemplary bilingual multicultural teachers have a definite agenda for teaching. They are convinced that the content and the classroom activities through which the content is learned are essential for socio-academic success. Finally, these exemplary teachers are sensitive to the cultural needs of their students, adapting teaching strategies, participant structures, and classroom materials to enhance meaningful student participation and benefit from schooling.

Each of the four traditions we examined comes with an identifiable set of strengths and weaknesses. The principal advantage of the competency tradition is that it is eclectic and thus can draw from theoretical, practical, and empirical sources to establish an agenda for teacher preparation. Its chief limitation is that it usually lacks an empirical foundation. As a result, the tradition may be affected by educational trends that are popular, but without empirical support.

The ethnographic tradition enjoys the advantage of presenting a valid representation of exemplary teaching based upon empirical observation over an extended period of time. An inherent feature of this tradition is that it is designed to pick out cultural variation within a particular setting, hence it can provide teachers with vital information about ethnic- and language-specific effective behaviors. In spite of the immense value of ethnography for learning about cultural differences, this tradition has not found its way into teacher education programs because learning to do ethnography of schooling requires advanced training and the amount of time needed for observation is practically prohibitive for most teachers.

A strength of the teacher effectiveness tradition is that it empirically defines teacher effectiveness across many classrooms rather than relying on expert and personal judgment or context-specific research. This tradition has also provided some insight about effective teaching that otherwise may not have been discovered; for example, teacher wait-time and allocating time on task. A principal disadvantage of the tradition is that it studies teaching out of context, focusing instead on isolated (usually low-inference) teaching behaviors and as a result, loses the whole picture. Another limitation is that the tradition depends on a high number of cases (classrooms) for statistical analysis. Consequently, it is difficult to sort out cultural differences because the finer details are lost in the analyses.

The popular tradition, including children's literature, has the advantage of presenting a skillfully crafted portrayal of exemplary teaching based on personal experiences with cultural differences. The tradition communicates directly to the teacher an author's perceptions of what it is like to be in a culturally diverse classroom. It offers the most powerful message to teachers about effective teaching. Yet, its major disadvantage is that the message in each story is not generalizable to other settings. Moreover, the stories told are difficult to translate into a usable framework for preparing teachers.

With respect to the question of whether certain teaching practices and understandings are essential for effectively teaching students of specific ethnic and/or linguistic backgrounds, the four traditions provide only hints. The ethnographic tradition addresses this question more directly than the other traditions, but at this stage, there is not one body of research that provides particular teaching practices for specific groups of learners. Macías' (1982) work with the Papago is one example of research that indicates that effective teaching may be culturally specific in single ethnic group classrooms. Wong Fillmore (1985) suggests that certain strategies may be more effective for Hispanic children than Chinese children. In classrooms where there are students from various ethnic and linguistic backgrounds, however, no identifiable patterns have emerged. Moreover, there is no research on the issue of portability of exemplary teaching from one cultural classroom setting to another.

Conclusion

Preparing teachers to work in bilingual multicultural school settings is a complex endeavor involving language, cultural, pedagogical, and content knowledge. In the past, teacher preparation programs have had to rely on competency lists, case studies, and individual judgments about how to best prepare teachers to work in culturally diverse classrooms. In this paper, we examined four major traditions that speak to effectiveness in teaching in an attempt to formulate a new definition of exemplary bilingual multicultural teachers, a definition that expands the universe of teacher knowledge to include cultural and language considerations. It became clear to us after looking across the four divergent traditions that exemplary bilingual multicultural teachers take and sustain a stance toward education beyond what mainstream literature (e.g., Carter & Richardson, 1989) defines as effective. Exemplary bilingual multicultural teachers take these abilities for granted and work additionally to connect with their students' community and family, and to develop a sense of professionalism that unrelentingly advocates for the culturally different child. These efforts merit consideration in the literature on excellence in teaching because it is this literature that informs teacher education programs and more importantly, the teacher evaluation movement currently underway nationally (Shulman, 1987).

A fundamental question remains for teacher educators. How can the knowledge and skills of exemplary teachers be transmitted to novice and prospective teachers? Traditionally, teacher education programs have relied on an apprenticeship under the tutelage of an experienced teacher. Alternatively, microteaching approaches have been used to teach novices the use of particular pedagogical skills, such as questioning and closure. These approaches can be successful in the acquisition of some skills, for example, the allocation of turns, but seem to be less workable in transmitting more complex behaviors. In the future, teacher educators must explore how to develop the skills and stances that are essential for working in culturally diverse settings. Researchers must establish which skills are portable across settings and learn more about how to effectively socialize beginning teachers to work for membership in the guild of exemplary teachers.

References

Alatis J., & Twaddell, K. (Eds.). (1976). *English as a second language in bilingual education*. Washington, DC: Teachers of English to Speakers of Other Languages.

Au, K. H., & Kawakami, A. J. (1984). Vygotskian perspectives on discussion processes in small-group reading lessons. In P. L. Peterson, L. C. Wilkinson, & M. Hallinan (Eds.), *The social context of instruction: Group organization and group processes* (pp. 209-225). New York: Academic Press.

Baker, G. C. (1983). *Planning and organizing for multicultural instruction*. Reading, MA: Addison-Wesley.

Banks, J. A. (1979). *Multiethnic/multicultural education: Conceptual, historical, and ideological issues*. Rosslyn, VA: National Clearinghouse for Bilingual Education.

Bennett, C. (1990). *Comprehensive multicultural education*. Boston: Allyn & Bacon.

Braithwaite, E. R. (1959). *To sir, with love*. Englewood Cliffs, NJ: Prentice-Hall.

Brophy, J. (1982). Successful teaching strategies for the inner-city child. *Phi Delta Kappa, 63*, 527-530.

Carter, K., & Richardson, V. (1989). A curriculum for an initial-year-of-teaching program. *The Elementary School Journal, 89*(4), 405-419.

Chaudron, C. (1988). *Second language classrooms: Research on teaching and learning*. New York: Cambridge University Press.

Cohen, E. (1986). *Designing groupwork: Strategies for the heterogeneous classroom*. New York: Teachers College Press.

Coughran, C., Merino, B., & Hoskins, J. (1986). *BICOMP: A science based, computer assisted curriculum for language minority students*. West Sacramento, CA: Washington Unified School District.

Crawford, J. (1989). Instructional activities related to achievement gains in Chapter 1 classes. In R. Slavin, N. Karweit, & N. Madden (Eds.), *Effective programs for students at risk* (pp. 264-290). Boston: Allyn & Bacon.

Delgado-Gaitán, C. (1987). Traditions and transitions in the learning process of Mexican children. In G. Spindler & L. Spindler (Eds.), *Interpretive ethnography of education: At home and abroad* (pp. 333-359), Hillsdale, NJ: Lawrence Erlbaum.

Duncan, M. J., & Biddle, B. J. (1974). *The study of teaching*. New York: Holt, Rinehart, & Winston.

Ellis, R. (Ed.). (1987). *Second language acquisition in context*. Englewood Cliffs, NJ: Prentice-Hall.

Faltis, C. (1989). Preparing bilingual teachers for socio-cultural diversity in the classroom. *New York Association of Bilingual Education Journal, 5*(2), 17-26.

Fisher, C., Berliner, D., Filby, N., Marliave, R., Cahen, L., & Dishaw, M. (1980). Teaching behaviors, academic learning time, and student achievement: An overview. In C. Denham & A. Lieberman (Eds.), *A time to learn*. Washington, DC: National Institute of Education.

Fitzhugh, L. (1974). *Nobody's family is going to change*. New York: Farrar Straus.

Foster, M. (1989). Exemplary Black teachers in the segregated South. Keynote Address at the Far West Regional Conference of the Holmes Group, University of Nevada, Reno.

García, E. (1988). Attributes of effective schools for language minority students. *Education and Urban Society, 20*(4), 387-398.

____. (1990). Instructional discourse in "effective" Hispanic classrooms. In R. Jacobson & C. Faltis (Eds.), *Language distribution issues in bilingual schooling* (pp. 104-117). Clevedon, England: Multilingual Matters, Ltd.

Garza, S. A., & Barnes, C. P. (1989). Competencies for bilingual multicultural teachers. *Journal of Educational Issues of Language Minority Students, 5*, 1-25.

Greene, (1974). *Philip Hall likes. I reckon, maybe.* New York: Dial.

Hadley, I. (Pseudonym for Hadley, L., & Irwin, A. (1987). *Kim/Kimi.* New York: Macmillan Publishing Company.

Heath, S. B. (1983). *Ways with words.* New York: Cambridge University Press.

Krashen, S. (1981). *Second language acquisition and second language learning.* Oxford: Pergamon Press.

Lipson, E. R. (1988). *The New York Times parents' guide to the best books for children.* New York: Random House.

Linfors, J. (1987). *Children's language and learning* (2nd. ed.). Englewood Cliffs, NJ: Prentice-Hall.

Long, M. (1981). Input, interaction and second language acquisition. In H. Wintz (Ed.), *Native language and foreign language acquisition.* No. 379 (pp. 259-278) New York: Annals of the New York Academy of Sciences.

Macías, J. (1987). The hidden curriculum of Papago teachers: American Indian strategies for mitigating cultural discontinuity in early schooling. In G. Spindler & L. Spindler (Eds.), *Interpretive ethnography of schooling: At home and abroad* (pp. 363-380). Hillsdale, NJ: Lawrence Erlbaum Associates, Publishers.

Menéndez, R., & Musca, T. (1988). *Stand and deliver.* Hollywood, CA: Warner Bros. Pictures.

Merino, B. (in press). Promoting school success for Chicanos: The view from inside the bilingual classroom. In R. Valencia (Ed.), *Chicano school failure and success: Research and policy agendas for the 1990's.* Stanford, CA: Stanford University Press.

Moll, L. (1988). Some key issues in teaching Latino students. *Language Arts, 65*(5), 465-742.

Moskowitz, G. (1976). The classroom interaction of outstanding foreign language teachers. *Foreign Language Annals, 9*, 135-143, 146-157.

O'Dell, S. (1960). *Island of the blue dolphins.* New York: Houghton Mifflin.

Ogbu, J. (1982). Cultural discontinuities and schooling. *Anthropology and Education Quarterly, 13*(4), 290-307.

____. (1987). *Minority education and caste: The American system in cross-cultural perspective.* Orlando, FL: Academic Press.

Parkay, F. W. (1983). *White teacher, Black school*. New York: Praeger.

Payne, C. M. (1984). *Getting what we ask for: The ambiguity of success and failure in urban education*. Westport, CT: Greenwood Press.

Politzer, R. A. (1980). Student reactions as indicators of teaching efficiency. In E. Blansitt & R. Teschner (Eds.), *Festschrift for Jacob Ornstein* (pp. 236-248). Rowley, MA: Newbury House.

_____. (1982). Effective language teaching: Insights from research. In J. Alatis, H. Altman, & P. Alatis (Eds.), *The second language classroom: Directions for the 1980's* (pp. 23-35). New York: Oxford University Press.

Ramírez, A., & Stomquist, N. (1978). *ESL methodology and student language learning in bilingual elementary schools*. Stanford University: Center for Educational Research at Stanford.

Ramírez, J. D., & Merino, B. (1990). Classroom talk in English immersion, early-exit and late-exit transitional bilingual education programs. In R. Jacobson & C. Faltis (Eds.), *Language distribution issues in bilingual schooling* (pp. 61-103). Clevedon, England: Multilingual Matters, Ltd.

Ramírez, M., & Castañeda, A. (1974). *Cultural democracy, bicognitive development and education*. New York: Academic Press.

Rigg, P., & Allen, V. G. (Eds.). (1990). *When they don't all speak English*. Urbana, IL: National Council of Teachers of English.

Rodríguez, A. (1980). Empirically defining competencies for effective bilingual teachers: A preliminary study. In R. V. Padilla (Ed.), *Theory in bilingual education: Ethnoperspectives in bilingual education research, Volume II* (pp. 372-387). Ypsilanti, MI: Eastern Michigan University.

Rosenshine, B., & Stevens, R. (1986). Teaching functions. In M. C. Wittrock (Ed.), *Handbook of research on teaching* (pp. 376-391). New York: Macmillan.

Sizemore, R. W. (1981). Do Black and White students look for the same characteristics in teachers? *Journal of Negro Education, 50*(1), 48-53.

Shulman, L. (1987). Foundations of the new reform. *Harvard Educational Review, 57*, 1-22.

Spindler, G. (Ed.). (1974). *Anthropology and education*. Stanford, CA: Stanford University Press.

_____. (1982). Roger Harker and Schönhausen: From familiar to strange and back again. In G. D. Spindler (Ed.), *Doing the ethnography of schooling* (pp. 20-46). New York: Holt, Rinehart and Winston.

____, & Spindler, L. (1987). Cultural dialogue and schooling in Schönhausen and Roseville: A comparative analysis. *Anthropology and Education Quarterly, 18,* 3-16.

Taylor, M. (1976). *Roll of thunder, hear my cry.* New York: Bantam.

Tikunoff, W., & Vásquez-Faría, J. (1982). Successful instruction for bilingual schooling. *Peabody Journal of Education, 59,* 234-271.

Trueba, H. T., & Wright, P. (1980-81). On ethnographic studies and multicultural education. *NABE Journal, 5*(2), 29-56.

Uchida, Y. (1981). *A jar of dreams.* New York: Atheneum.

van Lier, L. (1988). *The classroom and the language learner.* New York: Longman.

Wilcox, K. (1982). Differential socialization in the classroom: Implications for equal opportunity. In G. Spindler (Ed.), *Doing the ethnography of schooling* (pp. 456-488). New York: Holt, Rinehart and Winston.

Wong Fillmore, L. (1985). When does teacher talk work as input? In S. Gass & C. Madden (Eds.), *Input in second language acquisition* (pp. 15-50). Rowley, MA: Newbury House.

____, Ammon, P., McLaughlin, B., & Ammon, M. (1985). *Language learning through bilingual instruction: Final report.* Washington, DC: Department of Education.

Part Three

Bilingual Education and the Public Interest

BILINGUAL EDUCATION, PUBLIC POLICY, AND THE TRICKLE-DOWN REFORM AGENDA

John J. Halcón
University of Northern Colorado, Greeley

María de la Luz Reyes
University of Colorado, Boulder

ABSTRACT

The authors explore and analyze the impact of educational reform on bilingual education and the education of language minority children. They examine the "trickle-down" reform agenda, drawing parallels to present reform, and examining the influence of that reform on bilingual education policy.

The authors trace the brief history of bilingual education legislation at the federal level by documenting the political battles between pluralists and assimilationists in their two-decade-old struggle to control bilingual education policy. They point out that the shift from innovation as equity to equity through mastery of English (Padilla, 1984) has become the dominant paradigm in bilingual education. They draw parallels between bilingual education policy and the present reform agenda with a particular focus on former Secretary of Education William Bennett's pivotal role in present bilingual policy.

> "When states apparently place a higher reform priority on increasing student homework than on abolishing pervasive, segregated schooling of Hispanics, the excellence movement has both trivialized and eroded the foundation of our democratic republic." (Medina, 1988, p. 347)

Introduction

The current reform movement launched by the publication of *A Nation at Risk* in 1983, is the latest in a long, continuous cycle of organizational reform in the history of American education (Passow, 1984). The Excellence in Education movement, as it is popularly known, promises to improve the quality of elementary, secondary, and higher education by proposing tougher academic standards for high school graduation, and higher admissions standards for college. At the heart of the Excellence in Education movement is the assumption that, in the long run, everyone will benefit from improved quality in education. On the surface, it is difficult to disagree with this line of reasoning, but one needs to examine the implications of the reform agenda on the education of limited English speakers to realize that reform, as it is being touted, has very little to offer nonmainstream students. In fact, some reforms have actually reduced educational opportunities and limited access to education for Hispanics as well as other minorities.

In this chapter, we explore and analyze the impact of educational reform specific to bilingual education and the education of language minority children. In our discussion we will examine the impact of the "trickle-down" reform agenda, draw parallels to the present reform, and indicate the influence of that reform on bilingual education policy.

The Trickle-Down Reform Agenda

The cycle of reform in American education has been described as a pendulum continuously oscillating from left to right. Generally, these swings are governed by economic conditions in the environment. Oakes (1986) asserts that the level of resource allocation to schools is associated with the relative strength of the economy. For example, when economic conditions are strong, resources are available for expanding educational programs; when they are weak, resources are scarce and their distribution to school programs is dramatically reduced or eliminated.

The current pendulum swing presents two troubling concerns with regard to the education of Hispanics. First is the fact that in this era of conservatism, the fundamental inequalities inherent in a differentiated schooling system remain unchanged (Oakes, 1986). Regardless of economic conditions or available dollars, the educational system still promotes differentiated schooling: one for mainstream and the other for non-mainstream children. According to Oakes (1986), those differences mean that in current supply-side economic times, "Those who have, shall get" (p. 60). Second, the present reform movement refuses to recognize differences in the educational needs of students, especially limited English speakers (Halcón & Reyes, 1990). Evidence of this can be found in the contents of the major reform documents. A perusal of these, including *A Nation at Risk: The Imperative for Educational Reform* (National Commission on Excellence in Education, 1983), *A Nation Prepared: Teachers for the 21st Century* (Carnegie Corporation, 1986), *Tomorrow's Teachers* (Holmes Group, 1987), and *College: The Undergraduate Experience in America* (Boyer, 1987), shows that the reforms do not take into account minority needs. In fact, in each of these documents, America's youth is defined as "white, middle-class, suburban and non-minority" (Passow, 1984, p. 680).

These reform documents completely disregard the differences in educational problems of minorities. For example, the high dropout rate, one of the most pressing problems in Hispanic education today (Steinberg, Blinde, & Chan, 1984), was only briefly acknowledged in some reports, and the schooling of immigrants and language minority children in bilingual education programs (Spener, 1988) was not even mentioned. The fact is, according to Passow (1984), that "the implicit assumption in many of these [reform] reports is that disadvantaged youngsters are really no different from other students and to believe otherwise is both anti-intellectual and anti-democratic" (p. 680).

The homogenization of student educational needs in tough economic times allows reformers to minimize the present crisis in minority education, assuring that majority students are the intended, principal beneficiaries of the reform. Thus, minorities benefit only incidentally, if and when "excellence" is ultimately achieved. We refer to this approach as trickle-down reform. This trickle-down approach has been used as the primary means of addressing

Hispanic and minority educational concerns in the major reform reports.

The problem with trickle-down reform is that proposed initiatives designed for mainstream students are not necessarily the most appropriate for Hispanics and all other minorities. Quite the contrary, exposure to unequal schooling experiences have resulted in different educational needs for Hispanics, Blacks and Native Americans, a fact not seriously considered in the reform documents (Orum, 1986). Trickle-down reform, for example, ignores differences in academic achievement between mainstream students and minorities (García, 1979; Olmedo, 1979), differential treatment of students by their teachers (Carter, 1970; Carter & Segura, 1979) and deeply rooted discriminatory practices such as tracking, ability grouping, and segregation for language instruction (Carter, 1970; Carter & Segura, 1979). Trickle-down reform proposes to improve the quality of teaching without mentioning how teachers should change their low expectations of Hispanics which contributes, in large part, to low academic achievement in school. The reform fails to call for much-needed, specific preparation to teach the growing number of culturally and linguistically different children (Oakes, 1986). Instead, present reform initiatives propose to address minority educational concerns indirectly by "raising standards" and expecting "excellence" in every rung of the educational ladder. This trickle-down approach to minority education is both simplistic and naive, and destined to fail. We concur with Passow (1984) who says, "simply recommending that school personnel get tougher, stiffen academic demands and crash down on discipline problems without affecting necessary changes in pedagogy, curriculum and personnel is an inadequate solution" (p. 680).

As the reform movement gains momentum with publication of additional reports, and so long as Hispanic educational interests are not addressed specifically, we do not believe that bilingual children (the majority of whom are Hispanic) will benefit from the trickle-down reform agenda. On the contrary, it appears that this reform is already causing serious harm. Are there significantly more bilingual classroom teachers today than there were a decade ago, or have the numbers dwindled? Have bilingual classroom practices improved over the last decade, or is there an increase in "English-only" instruction in these classrooms? With more identified language minority children than a decade ago, are the majority of those children receiving appropriate and adequate primary language instruction (National Coalition of Advocates for Students, 1988)?

The significant educational gains made by Hispanics in the mid-1960s and 1970s, when financial aid, affirmative action, flexible admission to colleges and universities, and bilingual education were part of the Great Society's reform agenda, are thus threatened by trickle-down reform. Bilingual education, in particular, is in jeopardy because it is evident that the interests of limited-English-speaking students have not been a reform priority.

In the following section, we will trace the development of bilingual education policy from its inception in 1968 through the 1984 amendments to the Bilingual Education Act, when bilingual education policy and the reform movement become inextricably entwined.

Bilingual Education as Public Policy

The implementation of the Bilingual Education Act of 1968 dramatically changed educational policy in the United States. Over the last two decades, however, disputes between opposing forces in the social, political, and economic environment have led to the current bilingual policies, which reflect a departure from the original intent of the legislation. San Miguel (1984) refers to these opposing forces as the "pluralists" (its supporters) and the "assimilationists" (its detractors). While both camps view themselves as reformers, pluralists, composed primarily of minority organizations and their political allies, have pushed for primary language instruction but have failed to make the development of native language skills an integral part of learning for language minority children. The assimilationists include associations of school district administrators and their political allies. Never recognizing the value of bilingualism, they have lobbied to make English the official language of the country, thereby discrediting the importance of instruction in languages other than English (Sundberg, 1988).

Pluralists benefitted from the liberalism of the 1960s and early 1970s when they were able to mount successful campaigns to focus national attention on the educational plight of Hispanics and other non-English speakers. The political successes of pluralists are evident in the early bilingual education policies. The passage of the Bilingual Education Act was not only a political victory for pluralists (many of whom were Hispanic), but also constituted a fundamental educational policy change which was originated, developed, lobbied for, and implemented by them. It should not be surprising, then, that criticism of bilingual education policy today is often interpreted as an affront to the Hispanic community. Pluralists remind us that bilingual education legislation was written because of the failure of traditional English-only schools to meet the educational needs of limited-English-speaking students. To suggest, therefore, that current bilingual policy has failed and that the proper remedy is a return to English-only instruction is anathema to pluralists. Yet, this is precisely what assimilationists propose as appropriate educational policy for limited-English-speaking students.

Assimilationists began their political rise in the middle 1970s when the end of the Vietnam war, the oil crisis in the Middle East, and political unrest led to worsening economic conditions in the United States. These factors and others, signalled the beginning of a politically conservative era in American politics. Assimilationists began to attack bilingual education on grounds of disloyalty to country—dubbing it as anti-Americanism because it advocated instruction in a language other than English (Spanish, initially). Assimilationists saw the growth of bilingual education as a threat to fundamental American ideals. Schools became the battleground; English-only instruction became the central issue.

By 1980 the conservative movement reached the pinnacle of political influence with the election of Ronald Reagan to the presidency. Educational policy reflects this turn of events. In particular, educational policy toward limited-

English speakers shifted dramatically away from language and cultural maintenance to a focus on English-only language instruction. Assimilationists expanded their English-only philosophy to the broader society. Under the auspices of U.S. English, an ultraconservative right-wing political group, assimilationists today are advocating a constitutional amendment to make English the "official" language of the country. In 1987, U.S. English counted a membership of 275,000 and had introduced legislation to make English the official language in 30 states. They were successful in nine (González, Schott, & Vásquez, 1988).

The Bilingual Education Act of 1968

Federal participation in the education of limited-English-speaking students began in earnest with the implementation of Title VII (the Bilingual Education Act), an amendment to the Elementary and Secondary Education Act (ESEA) of 1965. There were three important aspects to the Bilingual Education Act. First, since these programs were demonstration projects, almost all programs addressing the needs of limited-English-speaking students were eligible for funding whether or not they indicated a specific methodology. Secondly, projects funded under this amendment were intended as compensatory programs to "make up" for the deficiencies limited English-speakers brought to school. Finally, the bilingual education bill retained the principle of local control, allowing school districts the option of participating or not participating in the program (San Miguel, 1984).

Despite the fact that this legislation was "decidedly ambiguous with respect to the goals of federally sponsored bilingual education" (Matute-Bianchi, 1979, p. 19), the Bilingual Education Act represents a major policy shift from "a monolinguistic public educational system to a permissive use of bilingual instruction" (Padilla, 1984, p. 91). As such it is probably the most important federal law affecting the education of linguistic minorities, a much-needed piece of legislation warranted by years of "educational neglect" toward language minority students (Coleman, et al., 1966; Carter, 1970; Carter & Segura, 1979). In essence, "the new policy recognized that the educational need of bilingual students could not be met effectively by monolingual schools" (Padilla, 1984, p. 92). The Bilingual Education Act represents a major victory for pluralists who believed that "the federal government should assume an important responsibility for the educational problems of linguistically and culturally different children . . ." (Matuti-Bianchi, 1979). Pluralists had won the first of many battles.

Resistance to the original Title VII legislation began almost immediately. At least three sources of opposition can be cited: (1) the Office of Education which felt that Title I or Title II of ESEA could be used to meet the needs of limited-English speakers, (2) those in the federal government who opposed demonstration programs because they feared proliferation and expansion of bilingual programs, and (3) assimilationists opposed to bilingual education because of their belief that it was an un-American activity (Matute-Bianchi, 1979).

From the onset, districts that chose to implement the new programs were confronted with four fundamental problems: (1) a lack of trained bilingual teachers and staff, (2) a lack of materials and technology, (3) a lack of public support, and most importantly, (4) a lack of established educational programs to prepare bilingual classroom teachers (Padilla, 1984). Despite these problems, pluralists were not deterred. They pressed forward with program implementation recognizing that as demonstration projects, snags were to be expected. Later, these problems became issues to be pursued in subsequent legislative amendments to the Bilingual Education Act of 1968. The important thing for pluralists was to get as many basic programs implemented as soon as possible. After the first year, 76 programs were in place (Gaarder, 1970). Only two years later, 131 programs were funded (Gilbert-Schneider, 1976). By 1980, that number had increased to 565 basic programs, 66 percent of which served only Spanish-English clients (Halcón, 1983).

The May 25th Memorandum (1970)

The successful implementation of Title VII became a symbol of pluralists' growing political power. Not content to sit back and wait, they went on the offensive. Within two years, they had already begun a move to "transform bilingual education from a minor curricular innovation aimed at teaching English-only into a major reform aimed at introducing the non-English languages of low-status groups into the public schools" (San Miguel, 1984, p. 506). To accomplish this goal, pluralists pressed the Office of Civil Rights to issue a policy statement clarifying to school districts their responsibility toward language minority children. On May 25th of that year, the Office of Civil Rights issued a statement which was sent to hundreds of school districts across the country.

The May 25th Memorandum, as it has come to be known, addressed several major topics of concern for the education of language minority children (Pottinger, 1970). The memorandum specifically prohibited local school districts from assigning non-English-speaking children to mentally retarded classes, or low-ability groups, solely on the basis of their language. It also specified the responsibility of school districts to notify minority parents of regular school activities in a language they understood. Also, the memorandum specifically addressed the question of rectifying the language deficiencies of non-English-speaking students.

> Where inability to speak and understand the English language excludes national origin-minority group children from effective participation in the educational program offered by a school district, the district must take affirmative steps to rectify the language deficiency in order to open its instructional rogram to these children. (Pottinger, 1970)

Although few school districts actually complied with the new policy statement, the May 25th Memorandum became a very important document in the development of bilingual education policy because, for the first time, the federal government actually specified to school districts how best to address the needs of non-English-speaking children (Matute-Bianchi, 1979). Federal intervention in classroom instruction and curriculum at the school district level became a rallying point for assimilationists who argued that the federal government had no place in local decision-making and that educational decisions were the exclusive domain of the local schools.

Lau v. Nichols (1974)

The importance of the May 25th Memorandum became apparent in the Lau decision (Matute-Bianchi, 1984) when the U.S. Supreme Court ruled that failure to provide students with instruction they could understand infringed on their basic right to equal educational opportunity.

The *Lau* case began barely two months after the issuance of the May 25th Memorandum. It was brought by the Chinese community against the San Francisco Unified School District. They argued that the school district was violating their civil rights by not providing them with adequate instruction to learn English. The school district denied this charge responding that they had no legal obligation to provide the Chinese students with special language services. After four years of litigation, the Supreme Court ruled in favor of the plaintiffs (San Miguel, 1984).

The court agreed that by failing to provide Chinese-speaking students with comprehensible instruction, the San Francisco Unified School District had indeed violated the plaintiffs' civil rights. With its decision, the Supreme Court essentially affirmed the May 25th Memorandum (Matute-Bianchi, 1979), and stated convincingly that "the imposition of a requirement that before a child can effectively participate in the educational program he must have already acquired those basic [English] skills is to make a mockery of public education" (*Lau v. Nichols*, 1974). The high court ordered appropriate remedies to be worked out.

Three important points can be made about the *Lau* decision. First, the Supreme Court did not specify a particular remedy, nor did it require bilingual education. Secondly, *Lau* relied on statutory (Title VI of the 1964 U.S. Civil Rights Act) rather than constitutional violations to press its case. Finally, the Court deemed it important to specify the number of students necessary to warrant special programs (Applewhite, 1979).

The *Lau v. Nichols* decision became an important tool for pluralists to push forward their aggressive agenda for the education of language minority children. Pluralists used *Lau* to demand more comprehensive language-based instruction for minority children and to shift the focus of bilingual education away from compensatory education (Orfield, 1978, cited in San Miguel, 1984). Today, pluralists consider the *Lau* decision the legal cornerstone of bilingual education in the United States. The string of legal and legislative victories which followed *Lau* clearly gave pluralists the upper hand up to this point, but the debate regarding the direction and intent of bilingual education became even more heated with the 1974 Bilingual Education Amendments.

The 1974 Bilingual Education Amendments

The 1974 Bilingual Education Amendments represented the first major revision of the Bilingual Education Act and constituted "a fundamental rethinking of federal support for bilingual education" (Padilla, 1984, p. 100). Two previous amendments had been relatively minor. The new bill differed significantly from the original legislation in that it: (1) changed the eligibility criteria from socioeconomic status to limited-English proficiency, (2) expanded the medium of instruction from English to instruction in the child's primary language to include knowledge of culture, and (3) established a national office aimed at overseeing bilingual education. Changes also included the development of bilingual teacher-training programs, development of technical assistance, research, and dissemination of bilingual education, and most importantly, the establishment of the Office of Bilingual Education and Minority Language Affairs with its own national director (San Miguel, 1984).

The 1974 amendments also brought the transition versus maintenance debate to the forefront (Matute-Bianchi, 1979) establishing the basis of the fundamental philosophical distinction between assimilationists and pluralists. Assimilationists argued that the proper goal of bilingual education was to promote English-language development and to transition children from bilingual instruction into the English-language classroom as quickly as possible. In contrast, pluralists argued for the maintenance of native language and culture in bilingual programs while students learned English. To the delight of pluralists, the 1974 amendments expanded the role of the federal government significantly, but not without major concessions to assimilationists whose influence was widely acknowledged (Padilla, 1984). In the end, the groups reached a compromise that resulted in a new definition of bilingual education. That definition affirmed the transitional goal of bilingual education, but did not specifically rule out maintenance programs (Matute-Bianchi, 1979). The result of this compromise was a fundamental shift in bilingual education that went virtually unnoticed. Padilla (1984) points out that the new amendments changed the focus of bilingual education as "equity through innovation to equity through mastery of English" (p. 100), a paradigm that continues to define the direction of educational programs for language minority children even after 15 years.

Not entirely satisfied with the compromise, pluralists moved to establish maintenance programs as the single acceptable source of bilingual instruction for limited-English speakers (San Miguel, 1984). To accomplish this, they developed two strategies. First, they returned to the Office of Civil Rights (OCR) and urged them to investigate and enforce *Lau* compliance at the local school district level. Secondly, pluralists participated in the formulation of the *Lau* remedies. With the support of a sympathetic national task force established to provide guidelines, pluralists outlined a document specifying an "appropriate educational approach for teaching non-English dominant students and for complying with the *Lau* decision" (San Miguel, 1984, p. 509). Among many, the most important aspect of the *Lau* remedies was the stipulation that English as a Second Language instruction by itself was not appropriate and instruction for limited-English speakers had to include both native language instruction and cultural enrichment (*Lau v. Nichols*, 1974).

Pluralists were still influential in the development of bilingual policies, and the implementation of the 1974

Bilingual Education Amendments proved to be a positive turning point in their favor. But, rather than an outright victory, pluralists had to settle for "a temporary truce between various constituencies within the federal bureaucracy" (Matute-Bianchi, 1979, p. 26).

The 1978 Bilingual Education Amendments

By the time of the 1978 Bilingual Amendments, assimilationists, supported by mounting criticism of bilingual education from virtually every sector of American life, had gained undeniable influence of public policy regarding bilingual education. Pluralists had to concede major changes that reflected that influence. The 1978 amendments, for example, defined bilingual education as one in which

> . . . there is instruction given in, and the study of, English and, to the extent necessary to allow a child to achieve competence in the English language, the native language of the children of limited English-proficiency, and such instruction is given with appreciation for the cultural heritage of such children, and of other children in American society, and, with respect to elementary and secondary school instruction, such instruction shall: to the extent necessary, be in all courses or subjects of study which will allow a child to progress effectively through the educational system. (cited in National Council of La Raza, 1985, p. 7)

The new definition of bilingual education in the 1978 amendments shows that assimilationists, with significant support in Congress, were successful in establishing the primacy of English language instruction and in deemphasizing the use of primary language instruction and cultural development. They were successful in limiting funds to those programs that stressed second language development. They were also able to include a proviso in the legislation eliminating federal funding to bilingual programs in districts that did not have long-term needs for continued assistance. Finally, they were able to insert a provision that would require school district applicants to demonstrate that they would institutionalize the program after withdrawal of federal monies (San Miguel, 1984).

In spite of the increasing limitations brought on by changes in the legislation, pluralists were successful in lobbying for expanding the scope of bilingual programs, increasing funding for bilingual programs, broadening the definition of program eligibility, and substantially increasing funding for teacher preparation, research, and graduate fellowships (San Miguel, 1984).

The 1984 Bilingual Education Amendments

By 1984, assimilationists were in their strongest position politically to challenge pluralists on bilingual education. Beginning with the 1974 amendments, their influence over Congress had increased steadily so that by 1980, with the election of Reagan to the White House, their English-only philosophy of instruction for language minority children was firmly entrenched in the psyche of the nation. Equally as important, organizations of school administrators (San Miguel, 1984), had successfully argued for flexibility in the development of programs for language minority children in their respective school districts. This flexibility is evident in P.L. 98-511, the 1984 amendments, which President Reagan signed into law on October 19 of that year. In signing them, he promised to further expand viable options in bilingual legislation (National Council of La Raza, 1985).

In light of increasing public criticism of cultural maintenance in the public schools (Epstein, 1977), pluralists began to retreat from their staunch position on language maintenance and cultural pluralism adopting a conservative posture that supported transitional bilingual programs. By 1984 their political influence had waned significantly, yet it was still viable enough to present a formidable opposition to the English-only thrust of assimilationists. The bipartisan compromises of the 1984 amendments clearly show this. These amendments created several new programs eligible for Title VII funding, changed definitions and eligibility requirements, and increased data collection and evaluation requirements in the law.

The 1984 amendments represented a very dramatic departure from the original legislation, however, and were clearly a compromise that completely satisfied neither pluralists nor assimilationists. For example, newly authorized instructional programs included programs of Academic Excellence intended to strengthen and replicate effective programs; programs of Developmental Bilingual Education intended to integrate native English speakers with language minority children, affording all children the opportunity to study in two languages; programs of Bilingual Education for Special Populations intended for preschool, handicapped, gifted and talented children; Family English Literacy programs intended for the families of limited-English proficient children; and Special Alternative Instruction Programs that did not utilize a child's native language for instruction (National Council of La Raza, 1985).

In particular, Special Alternative Instruction Programs (SAIPs), authorized by the 1984 amendments, present a dramatic departure from the original intent of bilingual legislation since 1968. These programs, which, in essence, are a return to English instruction for limited-English speakers, were created on the grounds that bilingual education might be impractical in some districts and bilingually trained teachers might not be available to provide adequate instruction (National Council of La Raza, 1985). While intended to provide school districts greater flexibility in designing programs for their specific populations, these programs in a strict sense, actually authorized schools to by-pass Lau remedies in educating limited-English-speaking students.

Reform and Bilingual Education:
Equity defined as English-Only

Parallels between present bilingual policy and the Excellence in Education movement can be easily made. The selection of William J. Bennett as Secretary of Education in the Reagan administration added controversy to the on-going bilingual debate. His major reform initiatives and controversial perspectives on such diverse topics as the legacy of American education (Bennett, n.d.), a standardized curriculum for all high schools (Bennett, December 1987), and a standardized "core" curriculum for all colleges and universities (Bennett, May 1987), all promoted the primacy of Western culture and civilization at the expense of minority perspectives (*Stanford Observer*, 1988). These views established him as a leading figure of the present reform movement (Western Interstate Commission for Higher Education, 1989). His statements regarding English-only instruction for limited-English speakers while Secretary of Education also positioned him as the leading individual antagonist toward bilingual education.

One of his first acts as Secretary of Education was to reappoint three former members to the National Advisory and Coordinating Council on Bilingual Education (NACCBE) who had openly opposed federal support for bilingual instruction during their previous tenure. These appointees quickly renewed their attack on bilingual education in public forums (National Council of La Raza, 1985). One appointee, for example, referred publicly to bilingual education as "the new Latin hustle," while another complained that bilingual education was a "job maintenance program for people who could not have gotten a job otherwise." Still a third called for "English immersion programs rather than waste money on unsuccessful bilingual approaches" (cited in Crawford, 1989).

Not to be outdone by his appointees, Secretary Bennett interpreted the Lau decision as endorsing a flexibility of teaching approaches, thus, he attacked the Office of Civil Rights for "misinterpreting the Legislation and [using] heavy handedness in enforcement of Lau" (National Council of La Raza, 1985). He also advocated alternatives to bilingual programs, and sought to allow school districts more flexibility (and resources) to expand their relatively small English-only programs. Most disturbing was Bennett's initiative to redefine equal educational opportunity for language minority children by permitting school districts to comply with Civil Rights guidelines by the "simple provision of instruction in English" (National Council of La Raza, 1987).

Secretary Bennett positioned himself as a "champion of innovative approaches who dared to challenge the powerful bilingual education lobby" (Crawford, 1989, p. 72) insinuating "that non-English speakers were less than loyal Americans" (Crawford, 1989, p. 73). Thus, with great fanfare, he officially launched his "new" bilingual initiatives, which were blatantly designed to neutralize previous bilingual legislation and to further the English-only cause of assimilationists. The new initiatives included three components: (1) support for Title VII grants that would favor programs emphasizing the transition to English as quickly as possible, (2) a mandate to the Office of Civil Rights to invite all 498 districts that had previously adopted bilingual education as their response to Lau to renegotiate their agreements, and (3) a mandate that the Office of Bilingual Education and Minority Language Affairs would remove all restrictions on Title VII funding for English-only approaches (Crawford, 1989, p. 74). These proposals were endorsed by President Reagan (National Council of La Raza, 1985).

When one examines major reform initiatives proposed by Secretary Bennett and others, such as The Task Force on Federal Elementary and Secondary Education Policy, it is not difficult to see Bennett's antibilingual/antipluralist influence. For example, their report entitled *Making the Grade* (1983), which was sponsored by the Twentieth Century Fund, denounced bilingual programs as "a grave error," and thus, recommended that bilingual programs be replaced with the equivalent of English-only instruction (cited in Oakes, 1986, p. 73).

After three years of bitter legislative infighting in both Houses of Congress, Secretary Bennett's scheme to sabotage bilingual education was complete. By early 1988, both pluralists and assimilationists reached a compromise that clearly favored English-only approaches to classroom instruction for non-English-speaking children. In the end, the Department of Education granted more flexibility in funding alternatives to bilingual education from Title VII funds and, except in special cases, set a three-year limit on student enrollment in bilingual programs before exiting to an English-only classroom. Pluralists, by comparison, won only minor concessions (Crawford, 1989).

Secretary Bennett's antibilingual position clearly set a negative tone at the national level that had far-reaching implications for state and local municipalities struggling to provide educational services to the growing number of non-English-speaking immigrants and to the rapidly growing limited-English-speaking minorities already in this country. His legacy is one of contributing little substance to much-needed bilingual programs at a time when they were most needed.

Conclusion

The heart of bilingual education—instruction in native languages while students also learned English—has been at the center of the 20-year controversy between pluralists and assimilationists. The changing political scene and economic swings have contributed to wins and losses on both sides of the debate. An examination of educational policies during these two decades leads us to conclude that bilingual education, initially intended to equalize educational opportunities for limited-English-speaking students, generally, has not been successful. This lack of success can be attributed in large part to a continuous cycle of compromises made by opposing political forces resulting in changing definitions of bilingual education. Ultimately, its original intent was lost. The 1968 Bilingual Education Act, for example, proposed bilingual education as a way to achieve equity for language minority students. By 1978, and since then, bilingual education, redefined as English-only instruction for limited-English speakers, has been perceived as the new way to achieve equity. On its surface, this policy shift appears to be a return to the original goal of the legislation; that is, to provide an opportunity for students to become proficient in English to succeed in school, but in reality it has been a major setback.

The trickle-down philosophy of the Excellence in Education movement fueled the debate that made this shift possible and has left Hispanics with limited access and even fewer opportunities to achieve equity. A reduction of primary language programs for linguistic minorities at a time when the demand is at an all time high due to increasing immigration and higher birth rates in the minority community can only be interpreted as a xenophobic response to the rapid growth among these groups. A continuation of educational policies along these lines can only result in an even larger percentage of minorities among the growing class of undereducated Americans, a consequence this country can ill afford.

References

Applewhite, S. (1979). The legal dialect of bilingual education. In R. V. Padilla (Ed.), *Ethnoperspectives in bilingual education research, volume 1: Bilingual education and public policy in the United States* (pp. 3-17). Ypsilanti, MI: Eastern Michigan University.

Bennett, W. (n.d.). To reclaim a legacy. *American Education, 21*(1), 1-14.

____. (1987, December). *James Madison high school: A curriculum for American students.* Washington, DC: U.S. Department of Education.

____. (1987, May 4). American education: Making it work. *The Chronicle of Higher Education*, p. A29.

Boyer, E. L. (1987). *College—The undergraduate experience in America.* New York: Harper and Rowe.

Carnegie Corporation (1986). *A nation prepared: Teachers for the 21st century.* New York: Author.

Carter, T. P. (1970). *Mexican Americans in school: A history of educational neglect.* New York: College Entrance Examination Board.

____, & Segura, R. D. (1979). *Mexican Americans in school: A decade of change.* New York: College Entrance Examination Board.

Coleman, J. C., et al. (1966). *The equality of educational opportunity.* Washington, DC: U.S. Department of Health, Education and Welfare.

Crawford, J. (1989). *Bilingual education: History, politics, theory and practice.* Trenton, NJ: Crane Publishing Co.

Epstein, N. (1977). *Language, ethnicity, and the schools.* Washington, DC: George Washington University, Institute for Educational Leadership.

Gaarder, B. (1970). The first seventy-six bilingual education projects. In J. Alatis (Ed.), *Bilingualism and language contact.* Washington, DC: Georgetown University Roundtable on Languages and Linguistics.

García, J. (1979). Intelligence testing: Quotients, quotas, and quackery. In J. L. Martinez, Jr. (Ed.), *Chicano psychology* (pp. 197-212). New York: Academic Press.

Gilbert-Schneider, S. (1976). *Revolution, reaction or reform: The 1974 bilingual education act.* New York: Las Americas.

González, R. D, Schott, A. A., & Vásquez, V. (1988, March). The English language amendment: Examining myths. *English Journal,* pp. 24-30.

Halcón, J. J. (1983, Spring). A structural profile of basic Title VII (Spanish-English) bilingual bicultural education programs. *The Journal of The Association for Bilingual Education, 7*(3), 55-73.

____, & Reyes, M. de la Luz (in press). Trickle-down reform: Hispanics, higher education and the excellence movement, *The Urban Review.*

Holmes Group Inc. (1986, April). *Tomorrow's teachers. A report of the Holmes group.* East Lansing, MI: Author.

Lau v. Nichols, 414 U.S. 563; 39 L. Ed2d 1, 94 S.Ct. 786 (1974).

Matute-Bianchi, M. E. (1979). The federal mandate for bilingual education. In R. V. Padilla (Ed.), *Ethnoperspectives in bilingual education research, volume 1: Bilingual education and public policy in the United States.* (pp. 18-38). Ypsilanti, MI: Eastern Michigan University.

Medina, M., Jr. (1988). Hispanic apartheid in American public education. *Educational Administration Quarterly, 24*(3), 336-349.

National Coalition of Advocates for Students. (1988). *Barriers to excellence: Our children at risk* (3rd ed.). Boston, MA: Author.

National Council of La Raza. (1985, October 31). *Secretary Bennett's education initiative: Historical perspectives and implications.* Washington, DC: Author. (ERIC Document Reproduction Service No. ED 263245).

____. (1987, July 2). *The proposed bilingual education act amendments of 1987.* (Issue Brief). Washington, DC: Office of Research Advocacy and Legislation. (ERIC Document Reproduction Service No. ED 285940).

National Commission on Excellence in Education. (1983). *A nation at risk: The imperative for educational reform.* Washington, DC: U.S. Department of Education.

Oakes, J. (1986). Tracking, inequality, and the rhetoric of reform: Why schools don't change. *Journal of Education, 68*(1), 60-80.

Olmedo, E. L. (1979). Psychological testing and the Chicano: A reassessment. In J. L. Martinez, Jr. (Ed.), *Chicano psychology* (pp. 175-195). New York: Academic Press.

Orfield, G. (1978). *Must we bus? Segregated schools and national policy.* Washington, DC: The Brookings Institute.

Orum, L. (1986). *The education of Hispanics: Status and implications.* National Council of La Raza, Los Angeles Conference.

Padilla, R. V. (1984). Federal policy shifts and the implementation of bilingual education programs. In *The Chicano struggle: Analyses of past and present efforts* (pp. 90-110). Binghamton, NY: National Association for Chicano Studies, Bilingual Press/Editorial Bilingüe.

Passow, A. H. (1984). Tackling the reform reports of the 1980s. *Phi Delta Kappan, 65*(10), 674-683.

Pottinger, S. (1970). *Memorandum of May 25, 1970 to school districts with more than five percent national origin-minority group children.* Washington, DC: Department of Health, Education and Welfare, Office for Civil Rights.

San Miguel, G. (1984, June). Conflict and controversy in the evolution of bilingual education in the United States—An interpretation. *Social Science Quarterly, 65*, 505-518.

Spener, D. (1988, May). Transitional bilingual education and the socialization of immigrants. *Harvard Educational Review, 58*(2), 133-153.

Steinberg, L., Blinde, P. L., & Chan, K. S. (1984, Spring). Dropping out among language minority youth. *Review of Educational Research, 54*(1), 113-132.

Sundberg, T. J. (1988, March). The case against bilingualism. *English Journal*, pp. 16-17.

Twentieth Century Fund. (1983). *Making the grade.* A Report of the Task Force on Federal Elementary and Secondary Education Policy. Washington, DC: Author.

Western culture: The decade's great debate continues . . . (1988, February). *Stanford Observer.*

Western Interstate Commission for Higher Education (WICHE). (1989). *Setting the agenda: Reform and renewal in undergraduate education.* Boulder, CO: Author.

SHIFTS IN BILINGUAL EDUCATION POLICY AND THE KNOWLEDGE BASE

Ursula Casanova
Arizona State University

ABSTRACT

Through the years, bilingual education has remained precariously balanced between two extremes. Until 1978 the balance favored a more benign outlook which led to increases in support. After 1978, and particularly after 1980, the balance shifted drastically toward the opposite side. Throughout the 1970s and 1980s the population of the nation's public schools experienced considerable increases in the number of language minority students, but only one-third of them are receiving appropriate educational services. Ironically, the declining curves of scholarly production and federal funding run counter to a quite different ascending curve: the research evidence supporting the cognitive advantages of bilingualism and the benefits of bilingual instruction for speakers of other languages. In the meantime, the academic failure of minorities, and specifically of Latinos, in the U.S. school system continues to motivate reform efforts. This paper examines the evolution of government policy and the increasing distance between it and the separately evolving knowledge base.

Bilingual education, born in 1968, was a true child of the 1960s: innovative, creative, valuing of cultural diversity, and demanding of civil rights. Its arrival was not uneventful. However, its appearance was not universally celebrated. While many hailed it as an appropriately generous national response to disenfranchised populations, many more saw it as a threat to political stability. Through the years, bilingual education has remained precariously balanced between these extremes. Until 1978, the balance favored a more benign outlook, which led to increases in support. After 1978, and particularly after 1980, the balance shifted drastically toward the opposite side. This change in political climate can be seen reflected in the rising, then declining number of scholarly articles about bilingual education compiled between 1974 and 1989 in the ERIC collection.

In 1974, when bilingual education was still in its infancy, the ERIC Cumulative Index included 44 articles on bilingual education, and 24 on bilingualism. The number of articles on each topic increased through the next few years and reached its maximum in 1983 when 92 articles were catalogued under bilingual education, and 43 under bilingualism. That is, the output on those two topics had doubled in less than 10 years. However, this productivity was already being eroded by a hostile administration in Washington, but due to the natural delay between research and publication, the effects were not yet noticeable. They are very noticeable now. The 1988 Index includes only 31 articles on bilingual education and 17 on bilingualism, below the output of 1974. The decline in scholarly production parallels the curve of federal funding, which went from $7 million in 1969, the first year of appropriations, to $170 million in 1980, and then down to $133 million by 1986. This curve of declining support runs counter to the demand for bilingual education.

Throughout the 1970s and 1980s, the population of the nation's public schools experienced considerable increases in the number of language minority students. In California, for example, about 40 percent of the school population is currently dominant in a language other than English, and this trend is expected to continue:

> . . . what is coming toward the educational system is
> a group of children who will be poorer, more ethnical-
> ly and linguistically diverse. . . . Most important, by
> the year 2000, America will be a nation in which one of
> every THREE of us will be non-white . . . making sim-
> plistic treatment of their needs even less useful.
> (Hodgkinson, p. 7)

Estimates on the number of linguistically different children, and their need for services, vary widely. According to the U.S. Department of Education the number ranges between 1.2 and 1.7 million. But a 1987 briefing report by the U.S. General Accounting Office (1987) questions the validity of the data and judges that figure to be an underestimation. Waggoner (1986) estimates a much higher figure of 3.5 to 5.3 million, of which only one-third are receiving appropriate educational services.

Ironically, the matching declining curves of scholarly production and federal funding run counter to a quite different ascending curve: the research evidence supporting the cognitive advantages of bilingualism and the benefits of bilingual instruction for speakers of other languages. Thus, while the knowledge base in bilingual education expands the supporting evidence for its effectiveness becomes more persuasive, and the population in need of bilingual education expands, the funds and the policy supports for bilingual education become more scarce. In the meantime, the academic failure of minorities, and specifically of Latinos, in the U.S. school system continues to motivate reform efforts. Rather than improving the performance of Latinos, at times these efforts seem almost perversely designed to ensure failure.

Latino students rank among the lowest in academic achievement. According to data of the High School and Beyond Study of 1980, 76 percent scored in the lower half on national achievement tests. While almost 75 percent of the nation's 18 and 19 year olds had completed high school in 1986, less than 55 percent of Latinos had achieved the same goal (Baker, 1989). Only 44 percent of those graduates, compared to 56 percent of whites, enrolled in college that same year (National Center of Education Statistics, 1988).

Reasons for this dismal record have been offered by many experts. Some speak of the cultural chasm between home and school; others allege lack of aspiration on the part of Latino families; still others blame the "language problem"; and a few would argue that in U.S. society Latinos are members of a caste group and, as a result, their skills and efforts have been shunted towards achievable goals within the constrictions of caste (Ogbu, 1987).

The solutions proposed by experts vary as widely. Some argue for tougher standards, and some think that raising academic standards will only worsen an already critical situation (McDill, Natriello, & Pallas, 1986). Some suggest ways to adapt the curriculum to the culture, while others argue against "diluting" the curriculum or fear contributing to "cultural separatism." Among the most heated exchanges in the exploration of possible solutions is the continuing argument over language.

It is the language issue that is the focus of this chapter, specifically the comparison of government policies with the knowledge base about bilingual education. I will first briefly track the path of federal government policies regarding bilingual education, and examine present research knowledge on the topic. In my conclusions I will assess the current situation and suggest directions for the future.

Federal Policy, Briefly Considered

Bilingual education has always been controversial in the United States. During the 19th century, bilingual education flourished among immigrant communities, but before long the fear of "foreignness" reasserted itself, partly as a reaction to the political situation that culminated in World War I. As has happened so often, language became the target of political differences (Ferguson & Heath, 1981).

In its more recent manifestation, bilingual education was a child of the civil rights struggle of the early 1960s, directly engendered through Title VI of the Civil Rights Act of 1964:

> "No person in the United States shall, on the ground of race, color, or national origin, be excluded from participation in, be denied the benefits of, or be subjected to discrimination under any program or activity receiving Federal financial assistance."

The Civil Rights Act was, in turn, the prime catalyst for the first federal law designed to aid elementary and secondary education: Title I of the Elementary and Secondary Education Act (ESEA) of 1965. The passage of ESEA marked an end to the impasse over federal intervention in the public schools. The limited assistance provided under this legislation legitimized the federal government's role as provider of the last resort. As such it was a legislative breakthrough

of the traditional congressional resistance to federal intervention in education. It was a short step from there to consideration of the needs of the limited English-speaking
(Schneider, 1976).

This occurred with passage of Title VII of ESEA, the
Bilingual Education Act (BEA) of 1968, which funneled
funds to programs designed to support the educational
needs of speakers of other languages (SOLs).[1] It heralded a
"new educational age" by authorizing funds specifically for
the education of linguistic minorities (Schneider, 1976).

Title VI of the Civil Rights Act was also the framework
upon which the Supreme Court based the landmark *Lau v.
Nichols* decision 10 years later. In this decision, the Court
ruled that the defendant's intention to discriminate was not
necessary to establish a violation of the law. It was enough
for the plaintiff to demonstrate that a given policy or action
had produced an adverse effect. Additionally, the Court
established that equal educational opportunity was also being denied when school officials took no steps whatever to
help speakers of other languages participate meaningfully in
the school program.

The *Lau* decision was followed by the Lau guidelines,
which did not have the force of law but were implemented
through the Department of Health, Education and Welfare's
(now the Department of Education) monitoring responsibilities. The Lau guidelines required a transitional bilin-
gual/bicultural education for SOLs. In 1980, the guidelines
were reviewed by the newly created Department of Education and its first Secretary, Shirley Hufstedler. Formal regulations, mandating bilingual instruction in any public
school enrolling 20 or more speakers of a given language
emerged from that review. But the proposed formal guidelines were never implemented. They were withdrawn soon
after President Reagan took office in 1980. His election also
led to the softening of the government's advocacy role in
civil rights and, therefore, the weakening of Title VI.

The BEA has been reauthorized a number of times, most
recently in 1988. Conflict over the relative emphasis on native-language instruction has surrounded each funding
cycle, since, in spite of its name, the Act did not originally re-

quire "bilingual" instruction. The requirement for native-language instruction was added by Congress in 1974. In addition, although the transitional goal of the bilingual programs would be retained, the possibility for maintenance programs, that is, programs where the native language and culture could be maintained throughout the elementary and secondary years, was not excluded.

The requirement for native language instruction, although gradually eroded, has been maintained through several reauthorizations. It survived a major attack in 1978 when the reauthorization hearings closely followed the publication of Noel Epstein's *Language, Ethnicity and the Schools* (1977), a vitriolic review of bilingual education. As a reporter for *The Washington Post*, Epstein's opinion was assured wide dissemination, even though his position was sharply criticized by some of the very people he had cited in his support. Fishman (1978), for example, called it "an ignorant critique . . . heaps bias upon bias, suspicion upon suspicion, misinterpretation upon misinterpretation . . ."(p. 16).

A second blow to the concept of bilingual education came through research conducted by the American Institute for Research (AIR) under the direction of Malcolm Danoff. The research was severely criticized on methodological grounds by O'Malley (1974) of the National Institute of Education, and others. Nonetheless, the results received wide publicity from the press and became a rallying point for the opposition during the 1978 hearings. In spite of these formidable adversaries, the program was retained in language close to the original legislation.

In 1984, in spite of vehement opposition on the part of the Reagan administration, Congress insisted on the preservation of native language instruction for at least 96 percent of the funded programs. The 1984 law prohibited a Department of Education known to be hostile to the concept from redefining the term.

The strife surrounding bilingual education was heightened between 1985 and 1988, during the tenure of Education Secretary William Bennett. It is, in fact, impossible to review recent U.S. government policies towards bilingual education without mentioning the contribution of former

Secretary Bennett to the shaping of those policies. Secretary
Bennett's opposition to bilingual education led him to make
a multitude of pronouncements across the country. His un-
questioning endorsement of "immersion" as the strategy of
choice for SOLs caused a reaction among those Canadian researchers who had originally successfully experimented
with immersion. They wrote in strong opposition to the
transfer of a strategy successful in a specific Canadian context
to the very different U.S. context (Tucker, 1980).

Previous to the 1988 reauthorization, the former Secretary of Education proposed to remove the specific reservation of funds for bilingual programs from the law. The supposed ambiguity in research and evaluation reports was
cited as the reason to oppose continuation of the requirement for native language instruction. In an effort to clarify
the issues, the House Committee on Education and Labor
requested the Government Accounting Office (GAO) conduct an independent review of the research evidence on
bilingual education. Their review culminated in the GAO 's
Bilingual Education: A New Look at the Research Evidence
(1987).

For this review the GAO staff collected specific department statements about bilingual education uttered between
1983 and 1986 and identified all instances in which research
and evaluation were cited in support of proposed changes in
the law; they then selected a representative collection of
those statements. For example, one of the statements selected by the department included: "the evidence that TBE
(transitional bilingual education) is an effective method for
improving . . . math performance . . . is neither strong nor
consistent." The GAO staff then searched for research
summaries or reviews and selected 10 that met their standards for coverage and quality. Finally, 10 nationally recognized experts in bilingual education and social science were
selected, five of them were nominated by Department of
Education officials, and five by the GAO staff. One of those
selected by the GAO had also been a consultant to the Department. Each expert was asked to compare the research
reviews with department statements to verify whether the

Department's statements were supported by the research. In their summary analysis the GAO concluded that:

> The experts' view on the official statements . . . indicate that the department interpreted the research differently in several major ways. First, only 2 of the 10 experts agree with the department that there is insufficient evidence to support the law's requirement of the use of native language to the extent necessary to reach the objective of learning English. Second, 7 of the 10 believe that the department is incorrect in characterizing the evidence as showing the promise of teaching methods [such as immersion] that do not use native languages. Few agree with the department's suggestions that long-term school problems experienced by Hispanic youths are associated with native-language instruction. Few agree with the department's general interpretation that evidence in this field is too ambiguous to permit conclusions (GAO, 1987, p. 3).

Thus, the GAO comparison of statements by Department of Education officials with the research evidence suggests that department officials either misinterpreted the evidence, or that, for their own reasons, they chose to misquote and misuse it. One could therefore choose to accuse the former Secretary of Education of deficient scholarship, or, less charitably, of duplicity. In spite of this questionable behavior Bennett, and other Reagan administration officials, managed to shift the apportionment of funds. In 1988, the portion set-aside for programs including native language instruction was reduced to 75 percent. Twenty-five percent of the program moneys were set-aside for "special instructional programs" even though Congress had received the GAO report and its members were therefore aware that there was no research evidence to support such programs (Crawford, 1989).

The threat to bilingual education became clear to its advocates, who had perhaps counted on the persuasive power of the research evidence, after the 1988 reauthorization hearings. While discussions pre-1980 addressed the relative value of maintaining the native language alongside English instruction versus using the native language purely as a transitional stage, the debate shifted after 1988 (See González, 1978; Trueba, 1976). Under the threat of possible total loss, the possibility of maintenance is no longer discussed, we now speak of immersion versus transitional. Is this shift justified?

The Knowledge Base

As noted earlier, these policy developments have taken place against an increasingly optimistic backdrop of research in bilingualism and bilingual education. In this section I will now briefly discuss selected findings from recent research on language and education that represent a sturdy knowledge base for bilingual education. The purpose here is not to consider the relative advantages of specific teaching strategies, but rather to consider whether there are any advantages or disadvantages to bilingualism. If so, to whom do they accrue? My assumption is that learning English is only one of the purposes of schooling for SOLs. They must also, if they are to compete successfully, gain appropriate academic skills. Regardless of the controversy on bilingual education, pedagogical strategies should be chosen on the basis of their contribution to the future well-being of students. School completion, advanced education, and better opportunities in the workplace, are among the criteria used to judge the long-term effectiveness of instruction. I will, therefore, review some of the ways in which proficiency in more than one language is related to those criteria.

Metalinguistic and Metacognitive Skills

Most of the research conducted before the early 1960s found bilingualism to be a language handicap. This research was sharply questioned in 1962 by Peal and Lambert. They reported that bilingual children performed better than monolinguals in a series of cognitive tests, when sex, age, and socioeconomic status were appropriately controlled. These researchers attributed the negative findings of earlier studies to the failure to differentiate degrees of bilingualism. They distinguished between "pseudobilinguals," and "true bilinguals." The latter having mastered both languages in childhood and being able to communicate effectively in both. Evidence of the sturdiness of the findings reported by Peal and Lambert is that they have been replicated many times since then.

Diaz (1985), in a well-substantiated review intended as a plea of support for bilingual education in the southwest United States, lists a number of studies that show the advantages of bilingualism: ". . . in measures of conceptual development (Liedtke & Nelson, 1968; Bain, 1974), creativity (Torrance et al., 1970), metalinguistic awareness (Cummins, 1978), semantic development (Ianco-Worrall, 1972), and analytical skills . . . (Ben-Zeev, 1977)" (p. 72). Diaz then adds his own research within groups of bilingual children. He found that children with higher levels of bilingual proficiency performed at a higher level than their peers on measures of analogical reasoning and tests of spatial relations.

In later research, Hakuta (in press) found that bilingual fourth and fifth grade children could complete Spanish to English and English to Spanish translations with a minimal number of errors, and demonstrated at grade five skills similar to those of advanced foreign language students.

Two other researchers have been carrying out a powerful series of experiments comparing the performance of bilingual and monolingual children in the solution of science problems. Kessler and Quinn (1987) compared sixth grade bilingual children in a southwestern barrio school to private school Anglo children in the same grade in the northeast and found that the bilingual children from the barrio exceeded the performance of the Anglo children in spite of the Anglo children's superior reading level (7.38 compared to 3.0). Barrio children from San Antonio achieved higher scores in all measures: in their ability to generate more (1,945 to 579) and higher quality (176 to 53) scientific hypotheses; to use more complex metaphors (26 to 19); and to produce more syntactically complex statements (182 to 130) while attempting to solve science problems.

Outcome Evidence

The notion that bilingualism impedes the educational achievement of Hispanic students is also belied by data from the National Center for Education Statistics' High School and Beyond (HSB) study. Fernández and Nielsen (1986) found that exposure to Spanish during upbringing was not a handicap but an asset: greater Spanish proficiency was associated with greater achievement in both verbal and nonverbal tests.

Data are also available regarding differences in aspirations. One might infer that students with higher aspirations are likely to also achieve at a higher level. In an analysis of language skills as they affected the school achievement of high school seniors, Nielsen and Lerner (1982) considered three measures of school achievement: educational aspirations, grade point average, and age. They found ability and socioeconomic status to be the strongest determinants for achievement, effects that are well-substantiated in the literature. However, they also found that *Hispanicity* (defined as self-reported Spanish proficiency and frequency of use of the language) *was the third strongest determinant of aspirations.* That is, among the group of bilinguals, *those who used Spanish more had higher aspirations.* Conversely, *English proficiency had no significant effect on these students' aspirations.* Regarding grades, the findings also support positive effects for Spanish language maintenance. Although ability was most highly correlated with grades, Spanish speakers attained a higher grade point average than students who did not use the language.

Along a similar vein, García (1981) found positive associations with bilingualism among Latinos. He found that when Spanish-dominant homes enhanced the Spanish fluency of children, the offspring developed higher levels of self-esteem, more ambitious economic plans, greater assuredness of achieving such plans, greater locus of control, and higher grades in college.

The research evidence is therefore quite conclusive in favor of Spanish language maintenance. Over and over we find that native language competence contributes, rather than detracts, from academic achievement.

Subtracting vs. Adding

The advantages that can accrue to children through the maintenance of their native language, while simultaneously learning English, are likely to be lost to most SOL students. Policies endorsing transitional bilingual education, or worse, those endorsing immersion, concentrate on the rapid acquisition of the second language through obliteration of the vernacular or native language. These policies are considered to be destructive in several ways. First, when a high-prestige, socially powerful language such as English is introduced as the exclusive language of instruction, children are being exposed to what has been called "subtractive" bilingualism. That is, they are forced to lose their native language in the process of learning the majority language (Cummins, 1979). This not only robs them of their ethnic heritage, but is also likely to impede effective learning of the second language. Second, and perhaps even more important, is the potentially devastating cognitive risk run by minority language children when they are forced to put aside the language upon which they have relied to think and express themselves since infancy, as though all knowledge accumulated up to the point of entrance into school were useless. In contrast, children who acquire "additive" bilingualism, that is, those who are allowed to retain and expand their native language as they add English to their linguistic repertoire, are heirs to the benefits described above.

Cummins (1986) has argued that the cognitive advantages to be derived from bilingualism are the result of additive bilingualism, that is, when children learn a second language without losing the first. He argues for the "empowerment of minority students" through the school's recognition of the home language and culture.

Cummins further posits that for children to gain the benefits of bilingualism, they may need to reach a threshold level of competence in their first language. For children with a high level of competence in their native language, particularly in what he calls "context-reduced" communication, such as that which is characteristic of classrooms, the language of instruction may be irrelevant. However, many language minority children may be proficient in "context-embedded" communication but lack experience in context-reduced communication. Context-embedded communication is characteristic of social interactions outside the classroom. Understanding in those situations is aided by contextual and paralinguistic cues. Thus a child may appear to be proficient in the second language and yet lack the competence in context-reduced communication that predisposes students for academic success.

The theories espoused by Cummins support early emphasis on the child's vernacular language and delay of second language instruction. This strategy has been successfully employed in a California preschool program where Spanish was the only language of instruction. Instructional emphasis was placed on language development, particularly problem-solving and higher-level thinking. After one year the readiness level of the children in this group exceeded that of another group of Spanish-speakers attending a bilingual preschool, and nearly equalled that of a group of English-speaking children (21.6, 14.6, and 23.2, respectively). After two years the Spanish-only group matched the readiness level of the English-speaking group. Most interesting was the fact that upon entry into kindergarten, the children from the all-Spanish group obtained high scores in *both* Spanish and English versions of the Bilingual Syntax Measure, even though they had received no instruction in English (Cummins, 1984).

According to Crawford (1989), research funded by the Office of Bilingual Education and Minority Language Affairs (OBEMLA) and conducted by Ramirez also showed the advantages of native language instruction when compared to structured English instruction. The data from this longitudinal comparison study strongly favored programs using the native language for a longer period, even when student progress was assessed through English language tests. Findings from this study have not yet been made public, although a draft report was issued more than two years ago.

The research evidence cited above leads us to two conclusions: (1) balanced bilingualism is an advantage rather than a detriment to intellectual development; (2) becoming a balanced bilingual requires parallel development of both the native and second languages. Instructional strategies in current use appear to reject this evidence since they place their emphasis on early obliteration of the native language. Is there any reason for rejecting the research evidence? Are there data to support the fears expressed by many regarding the detrimental consequences of bilingualism? It does not appear that way. Nonetheless, many government officials have charged that the continuing low academic performance of Hispanics is due to interference with the native language. For support they cite, for example, the high rate of drop-outs characteristic of this population. It appears that in their eagerness to blame "the language problem" these officials have overlooked a much more likely possibility.

Overagedness and Dropping Out

Overagedness, or grade delay, has been consistently found to be the strongest predictor of dropping out once all other variables are accounted for. That is, after controlling for gender, SES, achievement, race, and ethnicity, students who are older than their classmates will drop out of high school at a much higher rate (Hess, 1986). This is a particularly important consideration for Hispanics. Retention in grade has been a favored strategy for dealing with language differences.

In the research by Nielsen and Lerner (1982), cited earlier, Hispanicity was found to have a substantial effect on age, which had a corresponding negative effect on achievement. That is, students who used Spanish more often were more likely to have been retained in grade earlier in their school career. Students who were older also achieved at a lower level. Retention in grade was, therefore a confounding variable that might erroneously implicate Hispanicity as the cause for lower achievement. These researchers conclude that "the maintenance of Spanish is favorable to achievement" (Nielsen & Lerner, 1982, p. 33).

The relationship between overagedness and dropping out was also confirmed by Fernández, Paulsen, and Hirano-Nakanishi (1989). They found that age was the strongest predictor for dropping out for both male and female Hispanics. They also found, as had Nielsen and Lerner before them, that English proficiency had no significant effect on dropping out while Spanish proficiency did, but at a lower level. It appears that here also the greater likelihood of retention in grade for students who are Spanish speakers may have confounded the results.

Evidence contrary to the association of bilingualism, or the maintenance of the native language, with academic disadvantage can also be found in an analysis of the relative academic achievement of Hispanic subgroups. Cubans, among all Hispanics, attain the highest levels of schooling and academic achievement. As wage earners they also lead the aggregated Hispanic population in salary levels. And yet Cubans are also the most likely to retain the Spanish language, clearly, language is not a problem for them. In fact, current bilingual education policies owe much to the demands of Cuban immigrants in the early 1960s. We could be simplistic and argue that they are more successful *because* they retain the home language. However, differences in the socioeconomic conditions of Cuban immigrants, and the conditions of their immigration itself, are more likely explanations. Those same conditions, rather than the language difference, should be considered when the deficient school performance of less fortunate Hispanics is discussed (Steinberg, 1989).

The research evidence supporting native language competency is, therefore, quite persuasive. And yet, the persistence of the disadvantaged myth (now better known as the "at-risk" myth) is rather amazing. It is a curious situation. So many, including former Secretary Bennett, have endorsed foreign language competence as an advantage in the world of business and social interaction, but the same people consistently oppose native language instruction for SOLs. This suggests either that languages spoken by native speakers are not "foreign," or that children from language minority populations are not expected to fill positions where bilingual competence may be not only useful but required. The first explanation is illogical, the second smacks of racism. Whether due to faulty logic or to racism, these beliefs encourage policies that lead to subtractive bilingualism and contribute to the creation of our own disadvantaged populations.

The problem is, of course, political. "Bilingual education" should be enclosed in quotes because it has come to mean so many different things, most of them having little to do with pedagogy. This is so in part because the term offers a convenient handle and projects a set of images that serve a political purpose. That is, hearing the term triggers certain expectations in people.

The political purpose served by the use of bilingual education varies according to the audience. Among those who are native speakers of other languages, bilingual education has come to mean an education that takes into account the linguistic needs of their children and prepares them to be their parents' cultural heirs at the same time as they are prepared to assume competitive positions in the work world. Latinos have never been known to demand that their children be instructed only in Spanish, but they reason that bilingual instruction, by providing competence in two languages rather than one, will give their children a competitive advantage. Thus, for most Latinos, bilingual education elicits positive images which they relate to their children's education.

For U.S. citizens of the majority culture, bilingual education elicits a totally different set of images. While they tend to be favorably disposed towards the maintenance of heritage cultures and languages for all ethnic groups, their generosity stops at the schoolhouse door since they consider instruction in languages other than English inappropriate in the public school setting. However, this same group of parents considers bilingualism developed through schooling as a social, intellectual, and career advantage for their own children (Lambert & Taylor, 1986).

For many U.S. citizens bilingual education is a "threat to the American way of life." Images of separatism, of "another Quebec," and of mental incompetence associated with deficiencies in English, are often associated with the term when it is applied to SOLs. However, when applied to their own children, or to the general school population, bilingualism acquires an aura of scholarship and sophistication and is recognized as an asset.

These differences in perception are important because they make it possible for political manipulators to use the slippery label of "bilingual education" to promote fear and resentment among non-Latino whites. By presenting bilingualism as a threat to the "American way of life," they prey upon nationalistic tendencies; and by clothing their attacks on their supposed concern for increased academic performance among Latinos they attempt to dispel accusations of racism. At the same time the label bilingual education is attached to instructional programs that use the native language very sparingly, if at all, while immersing students in an English-language environment. In this way Latino citizens are lulled into thinking that the school is attending to their children's educational needs while they are actually being subjected to a drastic, pedagogically inappropriate transition into English.

As currently used, therefore, bilingual education is a socially constructed term without a clear pedagogical meaning. Although it may appear otherwise, it cannot be assumed to guarantee any particular instructional strategy. Borrowing from the jargon of mathematics, bilingual education is a pedagogically empty set. It has come to have no educational meaning.

For this reason I believe that it is time to discard bilingual education as a pedagogical term unless it is accompanied by a precise description of the activities it is meant to label. What we all want for our children is optimally effective instruction within the constraints of existing resources. We want them to succeed not only at school but also in the workplace. The uniqueness of SOL children, whether Chicano, Puerto Rican, Cuban, Vietnamese, Laotian, or any other, lies in their arriving at school as competent speakers of a language other that English. But when these children enter their classrooms they find that their home language does not count, or perhaps more accurately, it counts as a deficit often accompanied by the ominous label: "at-risk."

This means that school officials consider the child's home-grown competence in another language to be a life sentence to the academic junk pile: the future dropouts. The "remedy" applied then may be some version of bilingual education that really consists of English language immersion, and we are back to where we started back in 1968. Not surprisingly, the child, who is trying to learn simultaneously the English language and the academic content, falls further and further behind. The next step is retention in grade and thus begins the child's journey down the slippery slope that leads, in fact, to dropping out, and thereby to another fulfilled expectation.

Disadvantaged or Advantaged?

Ability to speak more than one language can be a source of pride as well as of material rewards such as salary increments, and promotions. The U.S. government itself has recognized the value of language proficiency. The Foreign Service, for example, offers substantial salary differentials for foreign language competence and often requires monolingual employees to learn a foreign language (GAO Report, 1980).

The lack of foreign language competence among our citizenry has been amply criticized and associated with the country's decreased competitiveness in international trade. Conscious of this national deficiency, former Secretary Bennett included two years of required foreign language instruction among the academic requirements for his proposed model school, Madison High.

Unfortunately, the value attached nationally to proficiency in other languages is limited to those who learned the second language in school. By contrast, those who learned another language at home, whether Spanish, Arabic, Urdu, Italian, or any others, are believed to be deficient. The only remedy for these disadvantaged youngsters is for them to learn English as quickly as possible (Bennett, 1985), and by inference, to forget they ever spoke another language, or at least until they reach high school when they will be required to learn a foreign language.

Although the advantages of bilingualism have been known for years, and the disastrous consequences of current policies, have been also documented, we have lost the initiative we had 20 years ago. At that time we seemed to be on the way to more enlightened policies. The argument was between "maintenance" and "transitional" programs. That is, between programs that provided children with competence in both languages, and those that used the native language purely as a transitional step towards a monolingual curriculum. The discussion has shifted. Afraid to lose it all, we are now willing to accept transitional bilingual education (TBE) as the enlightened position, because the alternative is immersion, which at best, provides some native language assistance to the children. At worst it allows the children to sit and listen for months to a language they do not understand. And yet, everything we have learned during the last two decades of research in bilingual education suggests that language transitioning is not enough. To inherit the advantages that are due them, children need to develop both their vernacular language and the English they learn in school. To accept less is to accept an intellectual loss our children can ill afford.

Conclusions and Recommendations

In the face of eroding support for bilingual education at a time of increased need, it appears that advocates of these programs may well need to resort once again to legal challenges if they are to prevent further damage. According to Heubert (1988), the federal law that most extensively protects the educational interests of speakers of other languages at present is the Equal Educational Opportunity Act (EEOA). The legal standard under the EEOA established by lower courts but recently reaffirmed by the Court of Appeals is based on a three-part test:

1. Is the theory acceptable?

2. Are the programs used reasonably calculated to implement the educational theory effectively?

3. Are language barriers actually being overcome?

Cases decided on the basis of the EEOA have thus far relied on the first and second part of the legal test. Based on these cases, it is unlikely that instructional approaches such as immersion will be invalidated by the courts on theoretical grounds. Violations of the EEOA have been based on inadequate implementation, such as employing nonbilingual teachers for bilingual instruction, and use of English language tests to evaluate the progress of children in bilingual programs. However, the EEOA offers two advantages. First, Congress can subject states to suit under the EEOA, and second, where violations of EEOA cause continuing problems, affected children may be able to obtain private remedial services at the expense of the offending educational agency. This avenue for redress is, therefore, worth pursuing, perhaps with a slight change in direction.

It is now time, under a new, more sympathetic administration, and with the increasing voting clout of the Hispanic community, to aggressively seek legal remedies as the most effective route to better schooling for SOLs. It may be more advantageous to seek legal action on behalf of the many children who are retained in grade because of perceived language difficulties. Retention in grade has been conclusively shown to be an inappropriate solution for academic difficulties (Holmes & Matthews, 1984). Surely it would be even less appropriate in cases where the child's slow progress is itself due to inappropriate instructional strategies. Thus, the first item of the three-part test would be satisfied: the theory is not acceptable. Furthermore, it is unlikely that examination beyond the labels would find the programs being used to aid SOLs and satisfy the *Lau* decision effective.

It is also time to demand clear language in a time of doublespeak. Regardless of what it is called, what our children need is <u>P</u>edagogically <u>A</u>ppropriate <u>L</u>anguage <u>I</u>nstruction *(PALI)*. Educators concerned with providing SOLs with

PALI will first recognize the unique advantage of SOL students, and then will seek to offer them the optimal balance of language instruction that will advance them towards academic and lifetime success. Variations will necessarily occur, depending on the context, but every effort will be made to preserve and expand the native language while developing the children's full bilingual competence.

Finally, I propose that we hold school districts accountable for the cognitive, social, and economic losses incurred by our children. The research I have cited here is not new. Within the recommendations of a 1982 report of the World Bank's Education Department, Dutcher (1982) cites "a growing body of research which indicates that children who have not learned their first language well will not learn well in their second . . . they will learn neither to read the second language well nor to acquire subject matter through the second language" (p. 23). They also encourage officials to accept that more instruction in the first language will promote better learning of and through the second.

We need to remember that the advantages of bilingualism are worth our efforts. The bilingual literature of the barrio is a forceful reminder of this fact. There, among the urban debris, creative bilingual minds, such as Tato Laviera and El Huitlacoche, construct poetry through linguistic acrobatics in two languages:

> assimilated? qué assimilated,
> brother, yo soy asimilao,
> así mi la o sí es verdad
> tengo un lado asimilao.
> you see, they went deep . . . . Ass
> oh . . . . they went deeper . . . SEE
> oh, oh, . . . they went deeper . . . ME
> but the sound LAO was too black
> for LATED, LAO could not be
> trans*lated*, assimilated,
> no, asimilao, melao,
> it became a black
> spanish word but
> we do have asimilados
> perfumados and by the
> last count even they
> were becoming asimilao

how can it be analyzed
as american? así que se
chavaron
trataron
pero no
pudieron
con el AO
de la palabra
principal, déles gracias a los prietos
que cambiaron asimilado al popular asimilao. (Laviera,
1981)[2]

Put in proper educational jargon, that is metalinguistics!

Notes

[1] The author considers the acronym LEP to be opposed to the best interests of the students it is supposed to identify on two counts: (1) because by starting out with "limited" it puts a negative cast on the linguistic skills of those students; and (2) because LEP itself calls to mind a historically excluded population. She has therefore adopted "speakers of other languages" as a more descriptively accurate way in which to identify these children. The phrase results in a much more positive acronym as well: SOLs.

[2] The poem cannot be translated without losing its deeper meaning. Roughly, it plays with the idea of assimilation and Puerto Rican resistance to it. Laviera suggests that assimilation into the U.S. is prevented by the black inheritance of Puerto Ricans.

References

Bain, B. (1974). Toward a general theory. In S. T. Carey (Ed.), *Bilingualism, biculturalism, and education: Proceedings from the conference at College Universitaire Saint Jean.* Edmonton: The University of Alberta, Canada.

Baker, C. O. (1989). *The condition of education, VI: Elementary and secondary education.* Washington, DC: U.S. Department of Education.

Bennett, W. J. (1985, February 25). Letter to the Speaker of the House of Representatives Thomas P. O'Neill, transmitting proposed changes in the Bilingual Education Act. As quoted in *Bilingual Education: A new look at the research evidence.* Washington, DC: U.S. General Accounting Office, March 1987.

Ben-Zeev, S. (1977). The influence of bilingualism on cognitive strategy and cognitive development. *Child Development, 48,* 1009-1018.

Crawford, J. (1989). *Bilingual education: History, politics, theory and practice.* Trenton, NJ: Crane Publishing Company.

Cummins, J. (1978). Metalinguistic development of children in bilingual education programs: Data from Irish and Canadian Ukrainian-English programs. In M. Paradis (Ed.), *The Fourth Locus Forum 1977.* Columbia, SC: Hornbeam Press.

_____. (1979). Linguistic interdependence and the educational development of bilingual children. *Review of Educational Research, 49,* 222-251.

_____. (1984). Wanted: A theoretical framework for relating language proficiency to academic achievement among bilingual students. In C. Rivera (Ed.), *Language proficiency and academic achievement.* Avon, England: Bilingual Matters, Ltd.

_____. (1986). Empowering minority students. *Harvard Educational Review, 56,* 18-36.

Diaz, R. M. (1985). The intellectual power of bilingualism. *The Quarterly Newsletter of the Laboratory of Comparative Human Cognition, 7,* 16-22.

Dutcher, N. (1982). *The use of first and second languages in primary education: Selected case studies.* Washington, DC: The World Bank.

Epstein, N. (1977). Language, ethnicity and the schools: Policy alternatives for bilingual-bicultural education. Washington, DC: Institute for Educational Leadership.

Ferguson, C. A., & Heath, S. B. (1981). Introduction. In C. A. Ferguson & S. B. Heath (Eds.), *Language in the USA.* Cambridge: Cambridge University Press.

Fernández, R. M., & Nielsen, F. (1986). Bilingualism and Hispanic scholastic achievement: Some baseline results. *Social Science Research, 15,* 43-70.

_____, Paulsen, R., & Hirano-Nakanishi, M. (1989). Dropping out among Hispanic youth. *Social Science Research, 18,* 21-52.

Fishman, J. (1978, March). A gathering of vultures, the "Legion of Decency" and bilingual education in the U.S.A. *NABE Journal, 2,* 2.

García, H. D. C. (1981). *Bilingualism, confidence and college achievement.* Baltimore, MD: Center for the Social Organization of Schools, Johns Hopkins University.

Gonzales, J. (1978, January). The status of bilingual education today: Un ristazo y un repaso. *NABE Journal, 2*(1), 13-20.

Hakuta, K. (in press). Language and cognition in bilingual children. In *Advances in bilingual education*. UCLA: Center for Language Education and Research.

Hess, G. A. (1986, Fall). Educational triage in an urban school setting. *Metropolitan Education, 2*, 39-52.

Heubert, J. (1988). Current legal issues in bilingual education. In A. N. Ambert (Ed.), *Bilingual education and English as a second language: A research handbook, 1986-1987* (pp. 118-157). New York: Garland.

Hodgkinson, H. J. (1983). *All one system*. Washington, DC: The Institute of Educational Leadership.

Holmes, C. T., & Matthews, K. M. (1984, Summer). The effects of nonpromotion on elementary and junior high school pupils: A metanalysis. *Review of Educational Research, 54*(2), 225-236.

Ianco-Worrall, A. D. (1972). Bilingualism and cognitive development. *Child Development, 43*, 1390-1400.

Kessler C., & Quinn, M. E. (1987). Language minority children's linguistic and cognitive creativity. *Journal of Multilingual and Multicultural Development, 8*(1)(2), 173-186.

Lambert, W. E., & Taylor, D. M. (1986, April). *Cultural and racial diversity in the lives of urban Americans: The Hamtrack/Pontiac study*. Preliminary Report. Toronto, ON: McGill University.

Lau v. Nichols, 414 U.S. 563 (1974).

Laviera, T. (1981). "asimilao" In *AmeRican* (p. 54). Houston: Arte Público Press.

Liedtke, W. W., & Nelson, L. D. (1968). Concept formation and bilingualism. *Alberta Journal of Education Research, 14*, 225-232.

McDill, E. L., Natriello, G., & Pallas, A. M. (1986, February). A population at risk: Potential consequences of tougher school standards for dropouts. *American Journal of Education, 94*, 135-181.

National Center of Education Statistics. (1988). *Digest of education statistics*. Washington, DC: U.S. Department of Education.

Nielsen F., & Lerner, S. J. (1982, October). Language skills and school achievement of bilingual hispanics. Unpublished manuscript. Chapel Hill, North Carolina.

Ogbu, J. U. (1987). Opportunity structures, cultural boundaries, and literacy. In J. Langer (Ed.), *Language, literacy, and culture: Issues of society and schooling* (pp. 149-177). Norwood, NJ: Ablex.

O'Malley, M. (1974). Testimony to the United States Congress. Reauthorization Hearings, Bilingual Education Act, Washington, DC.

Peal, E., & Lambert, W. E. (1962). The relation of bilingualism to intelligence. *Psychological Monographs, 76*(Whole No. 546), 1-23.

Schneider, S. G. (1976). *Revolution, reaction or reform: The Bilingual Education Act of 1974.* New York: L.A. Publishing Co.

Steinberg, S. (1989). *The ethnic myth.* Boston: Beacon Press.

Torrance, E. P., Wu, J. J., Gowan, J. C., & Aliotti, N. C. (1970). Creative functioning of monolingual and bilingual children in Singapore. *Journal of Educational Psychology, 61,* 72-75.

Trueba, E. T. (1976, December). Issues and problems in bilingual bicultural education today. *NABE Journal, 1*(2), 11-19.

Tucker, G. R. (1980, February). Implications for U.S. bilingual education: Evidence from Canadian research. *FOCUS, 2,* 1-4.

U.S. Congress. (1984). Bilingual Education Reauthorization Act.

U.S. Department of Education (1974, 1983, 1988). ERIC Cumulative Indexes. Washington, DC.

U.S. General Accounting Office. (1980, April 15). *More competence in foreign languages needed by Federal personnel working overseas.* Washington, DC.

_____. (1987, March). Bilingual education: A new look at the research evidence. Washington, DC.

_____. (1987, April). *Bilingual education: Information on limited English proficient students.* Briefing report to the Chairman, Committee on Labor and Human Resources. Washington, DC: United States Senate.

Waggoner, D. (1986). Estimates on the need for bilingual education and the proportion of children in need of being served. *NABE News, 9,* 6-9.

HISTORY AND STATUS OF BILINGUAL SPECIAL EDUCATION FOR HISPANIC HANDICAPPED STUDENTS[*]

Nadeen T. Ruiz
Richard A. Figueroa
University of California, Davis

Robert S. Rueda
University of Southern California

Carol Beaumont
University of California, Berkeley

ABSTRACT

This article focuses on three areas: (1) the empirical bases for questioning the role of special education in meeting the needs of Hispanic students who are either academically at-risk or who are handicapped, (2) the literature on bilingual special education and its underlying assumptions, and (3) the theoretical bases for proposing a new paradigm for meeting the needs of learning handicapped bilingual pupils, the Optimal Learning Environment (OLE).

The history of special education and the bilingual pupil is not a felicitous one. Other review articles have chronicled this history, primarily with a focus on the testing malpractices exercised upon bilingual students (e.g., Figueroa, 1990). Certainly, evidence continues to surface regarding the overidentification of bilingual children as mildly handicapped. A stark example is Ortiz and Yates' (1983) Texas study indicating a 300 percent overrepresentation of Hispanic students in the learning disabled category. So despite

*This research is funded by the California State Department of Education, Dr. Shirley Thornton, Deputy Superintendent for Special Programs; California Office of Migrant Education; and University of California Linguistic Minority Research Project. Special thanks to Carole Hinkle for the editorial work in the preparation of this manuscript.

attention to, first, the pitfalls of special education testing for Hispanic students (Cummins, 1984; Figueroa, 1989), and second, recommendations for improving this testing (Baca & Cervantes, 1989), Hispanic children continue to enter the special education process under suspect circumstances. Once there, Hispanic children seem to drop out of sight, at least in the literature. We essentially know very little about how they fare within the special education process (Carpenter, 1983a).

In this chapter we explore the history and status of Hispanic children in special education, but do not limit ourselves to testing issues in explaining the complex questions that exist. We believe that by considering both macro and micro levels of the structure of special education we can arrive at a fuller understanding of what gets Hispanic children into special education and what happens to them there. Furthermore, we believe that such an analysis provides directions for change in the status of Hispanic children in special education, directions that go beyond the illusory search for a "better" test or a "better" set of eligibility criteria, to a proposal for a dramatic restructuring of special education for at-risk children.

This chapter focuses on three areas: (1) the empirical bases for questioning the efficacy of special education in meeting the needs of Hispanic students who are either academically at-risk or who are handicapped, (2) the literature on bilingual special education, and (3) the theoretical and empirical rationale for proposing a new paradigm for meeting the needs of "mildly handicapped" bilingual pupils, the Optimal Learning Environment (OLE).

Reports on the Implementation of Public Law 94-142

In 1975, the 94th Congress passed the Education for All Handicapped Children Act, more commonly known as Public Law (P.L.) 94-142. This landmark piece of legislation for the first time guaranteed that all handicapped children in the United States had a right to a free and appropriate public education, an individualized education program (IEP), education in the least restrictive environment, nonbiased assessment procedures, and a series of due process protections.

P.L. 94-142 systematized the process through which a child becomes a special education student. The prescribed steps are a referral, a diagnosis (based on multiple assessments), an IEP team meeting, and a program placement. The power to determine which students can be designated as "handicapped" rests with the IEP team's decision, a decision that directly impacts on an individual's societal status and which must be made with the informed consent of the parents at every juncture in the decision-making process.

Since 1979, the U.S. Department of Education has published 11 reports to Congress on the implementation of P.L. 94-142 (U.S. Office of Education, 1979; U.S. Department of Education, 1980-1989). One of the most recent of these, the Eleventh Report, provides one of the most comprehensive profiles of how special education functions throughout the country. As is the case with the preceding reports, the Eleventh Report presents data on the preceding academic year, 1987-1988.

In the 1987-1988 academic year, there were 4,127,568 students (3 to 21 years of age) in the United States who received special education services (U.S. Department of Education, 1989). They were distributed among 10 categories of exceptionality: Learning Disabled (47%), Speech or Language Impaired (23.2%), Mentally Retarded (14.6%), Emotionally Disturbed (9.1%), Multihandicapped (1.9%), Hard of Hearing or Deaf (1.4%), Orthopedically Impaired (1.1%), Other Health Impaired (1.1%), Visually Handicapped (.6%), and Deaf-Blind (.0004%). These pupils made up 6.6 percent of the 3- to 21-year-old population in 1987-1988, a significant increase from the 4.8 percent reported in 1976-1977. In fact, the data in the Eleventh Report present many other perplexing anomalies.

These data show that across the 50 states and the District of Columbia, the percentages of children in special education (6 to 17 years old) vary tremendously, from a low of 6 percent to a high of 14 percent (U.S. Department of Education, 1989; Tables AA22a and AA23 on pages A36a and A37, respectively). The same data, broken down by exceptionality (Table AA23, p. A37), demonstrate in dramatic form that there are essentially two types of pupils in special education, those with biological symptoms (Hard of Hearing/Deaf, Multihandicapped, Orthopedically Handicapped, other Health Impaired, and Visually Handicapped) and with consistent incidence rates across states (at below 1 percent), and those with invisible symptoms with very inconsistent incidence rates throughout the country and whose primary symptom is an inability to profit from the regular education program (Learning Disabled, Speech Impaired, Mentally Retarded, and Emotionally Disturbed, with percentage ranges between 2 to 7, 1 to 3, 1 to 3, and 1 to 2, respectively).

Data on the 6- to 21-year-old population within each handicapping condition (U.S. Department of Education, 1989; Table AA15, p. A17) show that the learning disabled population doubles in numbers at the second grade (134,000), peaks between the fourth and seventh grades (+190,000), and then gradually diminishes (to 1,000). From an epidemiological perspective, learning disability appears to be a handicap that strikes in the second half of the elementary grades. The speech impaired category peaks at the first grade (204,000) and then either gets gradually "cured" by speech and language therapists or by growth and development (less than 1,000 at 21 years of age). The mentally retarded category increases steadily until the 10th grade (51,000) and then declines so quickly by the twelfth grade (34,000) that a dropout explanation seems compelling. The same appears to be the case for the emotionally disturbed category (from 34,000 to 11,000). All the other exceptionalities are very consistent across all the grades until the twelfth grade, again possibly implicating a dropout factor.

Finally, data indicate (U.S. Department of Education, 1989; Table AB1, p. 39) that the mandate in P.L. 94-142 to teach exceptional children in the Least Restrictive Environment (LRE) is disparately implemented throughout the United States. This applies to both the invisible categories. On this matter and with remarkable understatement, the Eleventh Report notes that "the extent of variability suggests that factors in addition to the characteristics of students determine educational placements, and that the decision-making power vested in the IEP process has not been sufficient to overcome these factors" (p. 29).

Minority Pupils in the Reports to Congress

There is one other area where the reports are bewildering. There are very little data on ethnic pupils. The Fifth Report is the only one that includes a small section directly affecting ethnic pupils. This section, "Efforts to Prevent Erroneous Classification," cites the 1980 Elementary and Secondary Schools Civil Rights Survey that, according to the Fifth Report, found overrepresentation in Educable Mentally Retarded and Trainable Mentally Retarded for Black and American Indian children but not for Asian or Hispanic children (a conclusion that does not coincide with what the National Academy of Sciences reported in 1982 using the same Civil Rights Survey [Heller, Holtzman, & Messick, 1982] and which will be discussed later).

The preponderance of this section on erroneous classification, however, dealt with the preliminary report of a study conducted by Applied Management Sciences, Inc. on procedures used "to prevent erroneous classification of handicapped children." Five hundred schools in 100 school districts were surveyed. The preliminary findings were: (1) overrepresentation of minority referrals occurred at the secondary but not the elementary grades; (2) the same number and types of tests were given to majority and minority children, thereby showing that there is no bias and that diagnosticians were being "conscientious"; (3) for minority and majority children, academic functioning was the most important factor in diagnosis and placement; (4) for minority students, teachers and diagnosticians rated five factors as being important: lack of support in the environment, socioeconomic disadvantage, "cultural deprivation," linguistic differences, and ethnic status; (5) diagnosticians judged twice as many minority pupils as "probably mentally retarded" (p. 24), though they did not place them in that proportion; and (6) in 1980, minority students were not being over-placed in special education. Finally, the Fifth Report notes that nondiscriminatory testing was an area in which some states required technical assistance. In essence, the conclusions from this study downplay problems with overrepresentation of minority students, with inappropriate testing practices, and with the misunderstanding and neglect of the impact of cultural factors on the special education process.

To repeat, except for a small section in the Fifth Report, the bilingual pupil is not a major concern in the 11 reports to Congress. The disconcerting part of all this is that appropriate placement and services to bilingual children has been a major problem to special education.

Literature from Special Education on Bilingual Pupils

The literature on bilingual pupils in special education holds that over the last 60 years, too many Hispanic children have been diagnosed as mentally handicapped and have been placed in special education programs. In 1933, Reynolds wrote a report, "The Education of Spanish-speaking Children in Five Southwestern States," for the U.S. Department of the Interior. Together with data on under-achievement, overageness, and dropout rates, she presented the following observation:

> A number of Mexican children are in development rooms which handle children who are for the most part below 65 IQ. In the words of a member of the research division staff [of the Los Angeles city schools], "The proportion of Mexican pupils in development rooms is probably somewhat higher than is their relative number in the general (pupil) population." (p. 51)

Almost 40 years later, little had changed. In 1969, the President's Committee on Mental Retardation recognized the phenomenon of "The Six-Hour Retarded Child" who was "diagnosed" as retarded only in the social context of school and nowhere else. In 1973, Mercer dramatically showed that the rate of disproportion of Hispanic students in EMR classes was some 300 percent above their representation in the Riverside School District. Ten years later, Ortíz and Yates (1983) documented a new trend in misdiagnosis of Hispanic children: a disproportionate swelling of the learning disabilities category.

Between 1970 and 1980, several major court cases had focused on this type of disparity (e.g., *Diana v. California State Board of Education*, 1970; *Ruiz v. State Board of Education*, 1971; *Covarrubias v. San Diego Unified School District*, 1972; *Guadalupe Organization Inc. v. Tempe Elementary School District*, 1978; *Dyrcias v. Board of Education*, 1979; *Jose P. v. Ambach*, 1979), and regrettably focused their remedies on either the assessment procedures (e.g., that testing be in the primary language) or on due process protections. The U.S. Commission on Civil Rights, in 1974, made the same points and the same mistake in attending only to testing practices. P.L. 94-142 and state laws and regulations followed suit and required use of the primary language for testing, parent permission and participation, and parent notification.

In 1982, the National Academy of Sciences investigated this problem of ethnic overrepresentation and published a report (Heller, Holtzman, & Messick, 1982) that articulated its general orientation with respect to minority overrepresentation. Regrettably, the academy failed to adequately consider the unique factors associated with bilingual overrepresentation (e.g., lack of primary language support in instructional programs, the role of interpreters in possibly biasing assessment, the lack of any viable or valid assessment instrument for bilingual children in the United States, the lack of instructional services in the primary language in special education, etc.). The report did make two important contributions, however. It suggested that the "handicapping condition" may be due to the quality of the instructional programs offered minority children. Of major importance to bilingual children, it concluded from an analysis of the 1980 Civil Rights Survey that:

> . . . the apparently similar EMR placement rates for Hispanic and non-minority students disguise enormous variation in practices among school districts. There are a number of districts in which Hispanic students are assigned to EMR programs in large proportions. They are distinguished from other districts by having

small enrollments that are often—but not always—
largely Hispanic; furthermore, they have small black
enrollments, small or nonexistent bilingual programs,
and high percentages of Hispanic students in SLD
[Specific Learning Disability] classes as well. Among
large districts with the greatest pool of resources, low
EMR disproportion and low SLD disproportion occur
where many Hispanic students participate in bilingual
programs (Finn, 1982, p. 374).

Bilingual Special Education Literature

The first major piece of literature on the needs of handicapped, bilingual learners appeared as a special issue of *Exceptional Children* (Bransford, Baca, & Lane, 1974). But, the
articles had little to do with special education. Instead, they
concentrated on sensitizing special educators to the cross-
cultural, linguistic, assessment, and overrepresentation
issues surrounding minority children placed in special education. The references cited in the articles dealt almost exclusively on minority children in general. None of the articles provided any empirical data on handicapped, minority
children, or on the social, policy, or delivery system
involved in supposedly meeting the needs of these pupils.
Part of this legacy remains. Bilingual special education has a
substantial amount of literature that is predominantly prescriptive on how to merge bilingual and special education,
but it has a very small empirical data base.

This literature can be divided into four categories: journal articles, unpublished reports, published books, and
school district and state manuals. Most of this literature appeared in the 1980s. In a recent, general discussion of this
literature, Rueda (1989) posited that most of it is grounded
in a system improvement or modification approach. According to Rueda, a system modification approach accepts
the system as currently structured, and attempts to improve
practices without making fundamental changes in the referral, assessment, placement system.

In order to analyze a representative sample (*n* = 64, see
Note 1) of the bilingual special education literature, a rating

scale was devised based on the theoretical considerations about special education noted by Rueda (1989), Poplin (1988a, 1988b), and Ruiz (1989b). Rueda (1989) outlines three possible approaches to the problems in special education: those that maintain the current system, those that try to modify it, and those that try to restructure it. The rating scale uses these three categories. Under each category, at least five mutually exclusive descriptors are identified and scored. The descriptors under System Maintenance are each given a score of 1, for System Modification a score of 2, and for System Restructuring a score of 3. Table 1 presents the matrix used to evaluate literature from the field of bilingual special education.

After each reviewed journal article, report, book, and manual was evaluated along the five dimensions covered, a score was given based on which descriptors best fit the text being rated. The average score for each text was then computed (based either on scores for each dimension or only for applicable dimensions). This mean score essentially locates each bilingual special education text along a continuum from System Maintenance to System Restructuring. A total score for each category of text (e.g., journal articles, unpublished reports, etc.) was also computed. Table 2 presents these results.

Based on the classification system outlined in Table 1 and the subsequent rating of bilingual special education texts (Note 1), it would appear that Rueda (1989) is correct. Bilingual special education does adhere to a System Modification approach (overall mean rating = 1.92). Bilingual special educators, by and large, see their profession as part of the existing special education delivery system. There appears to be little difficulty in supporting the assumptions and systems encompassed by special education. This includes the beliefs that mild handicaps actually exist within individuals, that these can be "diagnosed," and that these are best dealt with in separate, reductionist programs (from pull-out, mainstreamed placements to full-day special education classrooms).

However, the data in Table 2 do underscore some exceptions. Specifically, the empirical literature shows a trend

TABLE 1

Criteria Used to Evaluate Bilingual Special Education Literature

Dimension	Maintenance Score=1	Modification Score=2	Restructuring Score=3
Assessment	• For diagnosis	• For nondiscriminatory diagnosis (the "more" principle)*	• For enhancing instruction
Program	• Autonomous special education program • Funded: special education	• Coordinated (special education/bilingual education) • Funded: special education	• Like other "at risk" programs • Funded: multiple sources
Language Use	• English/ESL (L1 not acknowledged)	• Mostly L2 • L1 support bilingual aide • Use interpreters	• L1 and L2
Assumptions	• Medical model • Handicap in the person	• Modified medical model • Concern for false positives	• Social model (social context defines "exceptionality")
Paradigm	• Reductionism in L2	• Reductionism in L1 and L2	• Holism in L1 and L2

*If you do "more" pre-referral activities and "more testing," the assessment will be "more" valid.

TABLE 2
Ratings of the Bilingual Special Education Literature*

Type of Literature	N	$\overline{X}$	$\overline{SD}$
Journal Articles	31	1.89	.7
• Empirical	18	1.55	.59
• Nonempirical	13	2.35	.57
Reports	11	1.7	.51
• Empirical	6	1.5	.61
• Nonempirical	5	1.94	.19
Books	13	2.08	.50
Manuals	9	2.00	.00

Total N = 64 $\overline{X}$ = 1.92

*Based on whether the tests reflect a maintenance (Score 1), modification (Score 2), or restructuring (Score 3) approach to special education.

towards lower scores, indicating more of a System Maintenance orientation. The reason for this is that many of the empirical texts study the state and status of bilingual children in existing special education programs throughout the country. As an example, there are the data from the two federally-funded Handicapped Minority Research Institutes (García, 1985; Ortíz, 1986; Ortíz & Polyzoi, 1986; Ortíz & Yates, 1987; Rueda, Cardoza, Mercer, & Carpenter, 1984; Rueda, Figueroa, Mercado, & Cardoza, 1984; Willig & Swedo, 1987). The essential findings are that testing practices have not changed; that misplacement continues unabated, though in a different category of exceptionality (Learning Disabilities); that Spanish-language tests are as flawed as English tests; that factors associated with bilingualism are often confused with a learning disability; and that special education placement puts a bilingual child in greater academic risk.

Without federal statutory recognition, and without an empirical basis for recommending and documenting how bilingual and special education can (or should) merge, the needs of bilingual pupils in the current special education system will continue to be addressed by personnel whose belief systems may include the following:

> I believe that all assessment and placement of foreign-language youngsters, whether Latins or from groups which are more successful academically, should be aimed at the maximum integration of the children into English-speaking classrooms. . . . A more urgent concern [than issues around IQ] is the speedy training in English as a Second Language so that Latin youngsters can be mainstreamed into the regular classrooms, where they will be saturated in the majority language and culture (Page, 1980, pp. 479-480).

Conclusions from the Examination
of Macro Contexts of Special Education

The previous sections of this chapter essentially examine the macro context of education for Hispanic children in special education. They depend primarily on three sources: The reports to Congress on the implementation of P.L. 94-142, the literature from special education on bilingual pupils, and the literature from the field of bilingual special education. The first source reveals a systemwide, arbitrary nature to the incidence, determination, and placement of children with handicapping conditions. The arbitrariness factor is more dramatic for the "invisible" conditions, those of the mildly handicapped categories, but manifests itself even among the "visible" conditions, those with easily observed, biological indicators. Furthermore, these reports direct scant attention to bilingual pupils and, in a sense, minimize concerns about the possible inappropriate services dealt them.

The second source of information, the literature from special education on bilingual children, highlights the record of poor services provided to Hispanic children. The field of bilingual special education (the third source of information), as revealed in a review of some of its major "products" in the 1980s, has taken a peculiar position on these matters. The majority of its products accept the special education system as a given and propose only modifications; the prevailing assumptions, values, and structures remain intact.

The essential fallacy of the special education status quo is dramatically revealed in studies that have focused on narrower contexts of the education of special education children. The next section reviews research from the school district and classroom contexts, research that examines the impact of the special education system on actual services to children.

Narrowing the Lens: Special Education at the School District and Classroom Levels

Nearly 10 years ago Carpenter wrote a review of what we knew and what we did not know about bilingual special education (1983a). The most serious lack of knowledge within the discipline, according to Carpenter, was our ignorance of the process of education for bilingual students in special education, i.e., how students and teachers get down to the business of learning and teaching in day-to-day situations. Since that article, a few studies have focused on the special education process.

In a longitudinal ethnographic study of one school district in southern California, Mehan and his associates (Mehan, Hertweck, & Meihls, 1986) found that the entire decision-making process outlined in P.L. 94-142 was subverted by a system of trade-offs, in-house negotiations, and prearranged deals. Psychologists would test until the desired profile of scores met an eligibility requirement. Teachers would negotiate with each other before IEP meetings and would essentially write the IEP prior to the IEP meeting. Parents had little opportunity to exercise informed consent or to participate as equal partners in the decision-making process. Money and availability of services often predetermined what services a child would receive. These findings and others led Mehan and his colleagues to assert:

> . . . learning disabilities are more like touchdowns and property rights than like chicken pox and asthma. They are defined as real by a complex set of legal and educational practices and governed by school rules and policies. They are objects that are culturally constructed by the rules of the school, its laws and daily educational practices. Just as the rules of football constitute touchdowns, so too the rules of special education constitute learning disabilities and educational handicaps, (Mehan, Hertweck, & Meihls, 1986, p. 85).

More than any other study, this research vividly makes the case for the social construction of learning handicaps.

Other prominent researchers in special education bolster the findings from Mehan, et al. Ysseldyke and his colleagues for years have argued that the assessment procedures and tests used in special education are devoid of technical adequacy and that the categorical approach to serving the mildly handicapped is not supported by empirical findings (Ysseldyke, Algozzine, Shinn, & McGue, 1982; Ysseldyke & Algozzine, 1983). Coles (1987) and Kugelmass (1987) have reviewed the literature and studied the actual labeling process for Learning Disabilities and Severe Emotional Disturbance, respectively. They have made a compelling case for dispelling any biological or reliable basis for diagnosing most children who end up in these categories. For both authors, the Medical Model assumptions and procedures only serve to mask a sociopolitical failure in the educational system with children who are different and from different ethnic backgrounds.

Research like the Mehan, et al. (1986) study shows us how the arbitrary nature of special education, as revealed at the national level through incidence figures and the like, is enacted at the school district level. Adding to this picture are a few studies on a more micro context, i.e., the special education classroom where Hispanic children are placed.

We have found three studies on this topic: Ruiz (1988), Trueba (1987), and Willig and Swedo (1987). The results of these studies have been reviewed elsewhere (Ruiz, 1989b;

Figueroa, Ruiz, & Rueda, 1990). Though different in approach and subjects, all three studies point out the effects of contextual features of instruction on the academic performance of bilingual children in special education. An unfortunate common thread among these studies is a suggestion that a reductionist, mechanics-oriented and depersonalized approach predominates in the teaching of reading and writing to LEP students identified as learning disabled. In a more positive vein, two of the studies (Ruiz, 1988; Willig & Swedo, 1987) revealed certain conditions under which bilingual children in special education show greater academic success. The conclusions from these studies of the school district and classroom contexts provide further support for the position that educational handicaps are essentially social constructs.

A Proposal for System Restructuring: The Optimal Learning Environment

From a review of macro and micro contexts of special education for Hispanic students, two related themes emerge. The first deals with the social construction of learning handicaps (as opposed to a medical metaphor for their identification). The second concerns the effect of the social organization of instruction on children's academic performance.

These themes undergird our current research project which we call the Optimum Learning Environment (OLE) Project. In fact, the name derives from this theoretical underpinning. We suggest that only in an enriched, optimal learning environment can children's abilities be assessed and instructionally developed. We further suggest that students need not be categorized or labeled to receive this enriched instruction, and instead propose that the current eligibility system be changed to simply "request for assistance" (Gerber & Semmel, 1984).

Briefly, the OLE project is a longitudinal study aimed at implementing a new delivery system of special services to Hispanic students and examining the effects of this implementation. In the first year of operation, 1987-88, the project produced state-of-the-art papers for a special issue of *Exceptional Children* (Figueroa, Fradd, & Correa, 1989). In Year 2, 1988-89, the project began the Baseline phase of data collection at the selected school sites. In Year 3, 1989-90, the project has begun to phase in OLE classroom organizations and strategies. Five pull-out special education classes currently are involved: two in southern California in one of the largest school districts in the country and three in a northern California rural district. The northern California district has a large percentage of migrant pupils, a group that has been ignored by special education in spite of data that suggest considerable need (e.g., hearing impairments) and in spite of policy initiatives by Migrant Education (California State Department of Education, 1986).

The OLE project proposes a system change that begins with a dramatic paradigmatic shift. It proposes that a move away from reductionism towards holism/constructivism will produce better educational outcomes for underachieving bilingual children.

Those who adopt a holistic view of "mild mental handicaps" consider these special education categories and labels as social constructions (Mehan, Hertweck, & Miehls, 1986). For them, the assessment of learning disabilities is inseparable from the context in which they are observed and measured (Rueda, 1988; Rueda & Mehan, 1986; Ruiz, 1988). Effective instruction, from such a perspective, encourages students to construct meaning by integrating new knowledge with previous knowledge and by dealing with whole texts, in the company of trusted and experienced teacher/learners. It fosters interaction in high-interest activities that allow for authentic, functional end-products, a range of developmental abilities, personalization, risk-taking, and student influence on their learning activities (Diaz, Moll, & Mehan, 1986; Poplin, 1988b; Ruiz, 1989a; Tharp & Gallimore, 1988).

In contrast, the reductionist view considers learning handicaps to be a discrete phenomenon, essentially unaffected by contextual variables, and exclusively "owned" by the student. It considers the disability as remediable by segregating students into separate categories and by segmenting learning into parts. In reductionist instruction the diagnosis forms the intervention, typically consisting of a prepackaged curriculum controlled by the teacher. Student errors are viewed as behaviors to eliminate. Most classroom activities are funtionally artificial and their goal is simply to provide output for teacher evaluation (Poplin, 1988a; Rueda, 1989; Figueroa, Ruiz, & Rueda, 1990).

The OLE project used data from Year 2, the Baseline data phase, to conduct its own look at the status of services to Hispanic children in special education. We were interested in whether the classrooms, without experimental intervention by the OLE project, projected a reductionist or holistic view of learning abilities and disabilities.

Ruiz (1990) randomly selected a sample of videotaped instructional events (n = 22) from Year 2 of the OLE project. She analyzed them along a continuum of reductionism-holism adapted from Poplin (1988a, 1988b) and her own work. Figure 1 presents the rating scale used in this study. (See Ruiz, 1990 for a detailed theoretical and empirical rationale for the rating scale.)

The combined average for the OLE classrooms was a little more than two holistic characteristics per event out of a possible seven. Consequently, this study provides empirical data to support the frequently made claim for a reductionistic orientation in special education classrooms (Poplin, 1988a; Cummins & McNeely, 1987).

These data were in turn supported by two other studies emerging from the OLE project. Beaumont (1990) examined a randomly selected sample (n = 38) of student IEP's from the OLE project. She primarily relied on Ruiz's (1989a) OLE Curriculum Guide to develop a series of questions to pose for each IEP. Each question focused on a characteristic of holistic, effective instruction. Some of Beaumont's major findings regarding the IEP's were: (1) a reflection of a child-deficit orientation without regard for context of child performance, (2) failure to identify situations in which the children function at the upper range of their potential, (3) failure to include specific information on the children's curriculum context in regular education, (4) lack of attention to

CHARACTERISTICS OF HOLISTIC AND REDUCTIONIST LESSONS

Holism	*Reductionism*
a. Whole-part-whole	a. Learning segmented into parts
b. Student experience, background knowledge & interests influence content	b. Diagnosis forms intervention; prepackaged curriculum without link to student
c. Authentic; "real" purpose	c. Artificial; evaluation as goal
d. Meaning is emphasized first, followed by form	d. Primacy of form
e. Student activity; relatively balanced control of discourse (interactive nature)	e. Student passivity; teacher control (unidirectional, T. to S.)
f. Inclusion/recognition of personal interpretation and response	f. Emphasis on single, correct answer usually from source outside student, e.g., teachers or texts
g. Student-originated content	g. Teacher-selected content

Figure 1

Holistic Scale for Evaluating Lessons

children's range of language functions linked to academic success, (5) sparse information regarding the bilingual children's relative language proficiency in communicative context, (6) no discussion of students' cultural context and its impact on school performance, (7) no discussion of children's learning skills in evidence in out-of-school contexts, (8) no mention of children's literacy experiences, and (9) no mention of student interests and their connection to instructional strategies.

In a separate study, Rueda, Betts, and Hami (1990) looked at student work products from the OLE classrooms. Again, Rueda coded the work products for evidence of holistic characteristics, using a randomly selected subsample of students, evenly divided by language dominance (English and Spanish). Figures 2 and 3 dramatically illustrate the reductionist orientation of written work products for both Spanish-speaking and English-speaking children.

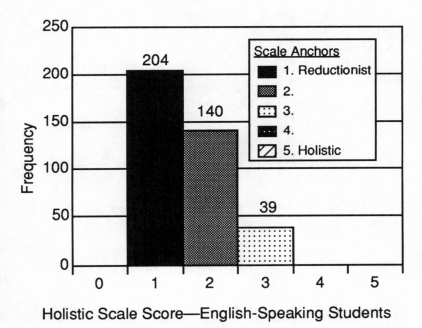

Figure 2
Frequency of Work Sample by Holistic Score—English-Speaking Students

The studies reported here constitute a first step in examining the instructional context of the students in the OLE project. They are limited in that they stop short of two important questions: Is a holistic lesson better in some way for Hispanic children in special education? How is it better? The OLE project is currently investigating these questions by

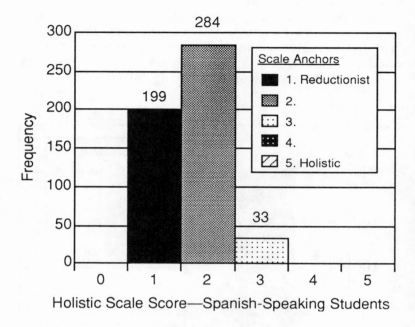

Figure 3
Frequency of Work Sample by Holistic Score—Spanish-Speaking Students

looking at changes in oral and written discourse patterns in holistic vs. reductionist lessons. It is also examining changes in the students' attitudes and metacognitive skills associated with literacy, as well as changes in more traditional measures, such as achievement scores, as the classrooms progressively represent more of an optimum learning environment.

Data from Year 3 of the OLE project suggest that changes are occurring in the OLE classrooms. Training in more holistic teaching strategies began in the academic year 1989-90. An initial look at the instructional events during the training phase of the OLE project has revealed a move towards holistic instruction. But the project has also noted that the move towards holism in the classroom context is constrained by the larger context in which special education functions and by the techniques that typify special education. For example, the high status accorded the special education teachers while regular education teachers try to get children placed in the Resource Specialist (RS) classroom (for mildly handicapped pupils) diminishes after placement. Regular education teachers do not send the students to the RS program if something "special" is going on, e.g., a movie is being shown. Furthermore, the RS teacher must often barter with the regular education teachers for times to pull out students for RS services. The result is sometimes an agreed-upon 45-minute session that in reality is substantially less than 45 minutes. Moreover, some of the OLE teachers, reflecting the behavioristic, reductionist training of their graduate programs, continue to use tangible reinforcers which are traded for special events or time off from instruction. Such "rewards" are given even when intrinsic motivation is clearly in evidence. For example, after a highly charged session of Writer's Workshop (an OLE strategy adapted from Graves [1983] and Atwell [1987]), OLE students repeatedly asked for more time to write.

These phenomena documented by the OLE project serve as a reminder that any serious attempts at reform of special education and bilingual special education has to take into account the multiple layers of context, from the micro context of student-teacher interaction to the larger, institutional contexts of the special education structure and its underlying techniques, beliefs, and value system.

Conclusion

This chapter has encompassed research from both special education and the newer field of bilingual special education. We have found a single paradigm to predominate throughout the past 70 years, known alternately as the Medical Model (Coles, 1987; Mercer, 1973; Rueda, 1989) or as reductionism (Poplin, 1988a, 1988b). Associated with this paradigm are anomalies that span macro and micro contexts of special education, such as substantially different incidence figures for handicapping conditions across states; overrepresentation of minorities in special classes; lack of differentiation between characteristics of low-achieving and learning disabled children; a simultaneous swelling of the LD category for Hispanic children and a shrinking of the EMR category; negotiation of labels for children based on available program options; and many others.

This historical look, along with recent data from our research project, lead us to conclude that the future for Hispanic children who come into contact with special education (and they will be many, given that the trigger for special education referral is simply low achievement) will not be much different than what we have described here; that is, unless the field begins to recognize these anomalies as arising from the inadequacies of the system and not the children.

Reversing these long-established trends will not be easy. What is needed is a sea change within special education, that is, a dramatic transformation. We believe that the holistic paradigm offers great potential as a new way of viewing learning and teaching. It accounts for and explains the anomalies in exposition here. More importantly, it relates recent work on learning and teaching from cognitive science, linguistics, and anthropology into a coherent approach, incorporating both theoretical and practical levels, that can help meet the needs of Hispanic children in special education.

Note

[1] Almada & Valdez, 1984; Anderson & Pearson, 1984; Baca & Amato, 1989; Baca & Bransford, 1982; Barnitz, 1986; Bergin 1980; Bernal, 1983; Carpenter, 1983b; Carrell, 1987; Cegelka, Lewis, & Rodriguez, 1987; Cegelka & Rodriguez, 1984; Chinn, 1984; Chinn & Hughes, 1987; Cummins, 1983; Cummins, 1984; Cummins, 1988; Cummins, 1989; Delgado, 1984; Diaz, 1989; Dien, Te, & We, 1986; Duran, 1989; Edelsky, 1986; Figueroa, 1980; Flores, Rueda, & Porter, 1986; Fradd & Correa, 1989; Fradd & Tikunoff, 1987; Fuchigami, 1980; Galang, Noble, & Halog, undated; Garcia & Yates, 1986; Goodman, 1969; Gumperz, 1982; Hopper, undated; Kamp & Chinn, 1982; Krashen, 1982; Landurand, Dew, Perlman, Schuhmann, & Napoliello, 1980; Langdon, 1989; Los Angeles Unified School District,

1988; Lynch & Stein, 1987; Martinez, 1981; Mendoza, 1983; Merced County Superintendent of Schools, 1986; Midwest National Origin Desegregation Assistance Center, 1982; New York City Board of Education, 1990; Omark & Erickson, 1983; Ortiz, 1987; Ortiz & Ramirez, 1988; Ortiz & Wilkinson, 1989; Ortiz & Yates, 1983; Ortiz, Yates, & Garcia, 1990; Perez, Brambila, Ingalls, Freeman, & Benevides, 1986; Plata, undated; Rueda, Rodriguez, & Prieto, 1981; Rueda, Ruiz, & Figueroa, 1989; Russell & Ortiz, 1988; Salend & Fradd, 1986; Simich-Dudgeon, 1986; Staff, undated; Swedo, 1987; Tinloy, Tan, & Leung, undated; U.S. Department of Education, Office for Civil Rights, San Francisco Region IX, undated; Weiss, 1981; Westby & Rouse, 1985; Wilkinson & Ortiz, 1986; Willig, 1986.

References

Almada, P., & Valdez, C. (1984). *Bilingual special education handbook.* Unpublished handbook developed for use in Montebello Unified School District, Montebello, California.

Anderson, R. C., & Pearson, P. D. (1984). A schema-theoretic view of basic processes in reading comprehension. In P. D. Pearson (Ed.), *Handbook of reading research* (pp. 255-291). New York: Longman.

Atwell, N. (1987). In the middle: Writing, reading and learning with adolescents. Portsmouth, NH: Heinemann.

Baca, L., & Amato, C. (1989). Bilingual special education: Training issues. *Exceptional Children, 56*(2), 168-173.

____, & Bransford, J. (1982). *An appropriate education for handicapped children of limited English proficiency* (Special education in America: Its legal and governmental foundations series). Reston, VA: Council for Exceptional Children.

____, & Cervantes, H. (1989). *The bilingual special education interface* (2nd ed.). Columbus, OH: Merrill.

Barnitz, J. G. (1986). Toward understanding the effects of cross-cultural schemata and discourse structure on second language reading comprehension. *Journal of Reading Behavior, 18,* 95-113.

Beaumont, C. (1990). *An analysis of IEP's in the OLE classrooms: Baseline phase.* Unpublished manuscript, University of California at Davis, Division of Education, Special Education Demonstration Project.

Bergin, V. (1980). *Special education needs in bilingual programs.* Rosslyn, VA: InterAmerica Research Associates, Inc. dba National Clearinghouse for Bilingual Education.

Bernal, E. M. (1983, Spring). New text on informal assessment [Review of *Informal assessment in education*]. *Bilingual Special Education News,*

2(1), 3. (Available from University of Texas at Austin, College of Education, Department of Special Education.)

Bransford, L., Baca, L., & Lane, K. (Eds.). (1974). Cultural diversity [Special issue]. *Exceptional Children, 40*(8).

California State Department of Education. (1986). *California policy workshop on special education needs of migrant handicapped students* (Proceedings Report). Sacramento, CA: Author.

Carpenter, L. (1983a). *Bilingual special education: An overview of issues* (NCBR Professional Papers). Los Alamitos, CA: National Center for Bilingual Research.

_____. (1983b). *Communication disorders in limited- and non-English proficient children* (Report). Los Alamitos, CA: National Center for Bilingual Research.

Carrell, P. A. (1987). Content and formal schemata in ESL reading. *TESOL Quarterly, 21,* 461-481.

Cegelka, P., Lewis, R., & Rodriguez, A. (1987). Status of educational services to handicapped students with limited English proficiency: Report of a statewide study in California. *Exceptional Children, 54*(3), 220-227.

_____, & Rodriguez, A. (1984). *Educational services to handicapped students with limited English proficiency: State of the art and future directions* (Technical Report). San Diego, CA: San Diego State University, Department of Special Education.

Chinn, P. C. (Ed.). (1984). *Education of culturally and linguistically different exceptional children.* Reston, VA: Council for Exceptional Children.

_____, & Hughes, S. (1987). Representation of minority students in special education classes. *Remedial and Special Education, 8*(4), 41-46.

Coles, G. (1987). *The learning mystique.* New York: Pantheon.

Covarrubias v. San Diego Unified School District. (1972). No. 70-394-T, San Diego, CA.

Cummins, J. (1983). Bilingualism and special education: Program and pedagogical issues. *Learning Disability Quarterly, 6,* 373-386.

_____. (1984). *Bilingualism and special education: Issues in assessment and pedagogy.* Clevedon, England: Multilingual Matters. Co-published in the United States by College-Hill Press, San Diego.

_____. (1988). *Theoretical matrix for the special education of bilingual pupils in California.* Unpublished manuscript, University of California at Davis, Department of Education, Special Education Demonstration Project.

____. (1989). A theoretical framework for bilingual special education. *Exceptional Children, 56*(2), 111-119.

____, & McNeely, S. N. (1987). Language development, academic learning and empowering minority students. In S. H. Fradd & W. J. Tikunoff (Eds.), *Bilingual education and bilingual special education: A guide for administration* (pp. 75-98). San Diego: College-Hill.

Delgado, G. L. (Ed.). (1984). *The Hispanic deaf: Issues and challenges for bilingual special education.* Washington, DC: Gallaudet College Press.

Diana v. California State Board of Education. (1970). No. C-70-37, United States District Court of Northern California.

Diaz, J. O. (1989). *The process and procedures for identifying exceptional language minority children.* University Park, PA: Pennsylvania State University, College of Education, Division of Curriculum and Instruction.

Diaz, S., Moll, L., & Mehan, H. (1986). Sociocultural resources in instruction: A context-specific approach. In Bilingual Education Office, California State Department of Education (Eds.), *Beyond language: Social & cultural factors in schooling language minority students* (pp. 187-230). Los Angeles: California State University, Evaluation, Dissemination, and Assessment Center.

Dien, T., Te, H. D., Wei, T. (1986). *Assessment of Vietnamese speaking limited English proficient students with special needs.* Unpublished training materials (plus reproductions of some published items) distributed at Vietnamese Assessment Seminar, Hayward, California. Developed for the Special Education Resource Network of the State Department of Education, Sacramento, California.

Duran, R. P. (1989). Assessment and instruction of at-risk Hispanic students. *Exceptional Children, 56*(2), 154-158.

Dyrcia S. v. Board of Education. (1979). C-2562, United States District Court, Eastern District of New York.

Edelsky, C. (1986). *Writing in a bilingual program: Habia una vez.* Norwood, NJ: Ablex.

Figueroa, R. A. (1980). Intersection of special education and bilingual education. In J. E. Alatis (Ed.), *Current issues in bilingual education* (147-161). Washington, DC: Georgetown University Press.

____. (1989). Psychological testing of linguistic-minority students: Knowledge gaps and regulations. *Exceptional Children, 56*(2), 145-152.

____. (1990). Assessment of linguistic minority group children. In C. R. Reynolds & R. W. Kamphaus (Eds.), *Handbook of psychological and educational assessment of children: Intelligence and achievement* (pp. 671-696). New York: Guilford Press.

___, Fradd, S. H., & Correa, V. I. (Eds.). (1989). Meeting the multicultural needs of the Hispanic students in special education [Special issue]. *Exceptional Children, 56*(2).

___, Ruiz, N. T., & Rueda, R. (1990). *Special education research project for learning handicapped Hispanic pupils: The OLE model* (federal proposal). Sacramento, CA: California State Department of Education.

Finn, J. D. (1982). Patterns in special education placement as revealed by the OCR surveys. In K. A. Heller, W. H. Holtzman, & S. Messick (Eds.), *Placing children in special education: A strategy for equity* (pp. 322-381). Washington, DC: National Academy Press.

Flores, B., Rueda, R., & Porter, B. (1986). Examining assumptions and instructional practices related to the acquisition of literacy with bilingual special education students. In A. Willig & H. Greenberg (Eds.), *Bilingualism and learning disabilities* (pp. 149-165). New York: American Library.

Fradd, S. H., & Correa, V. I. (1989). Hispanic students at risk: Do we abdicate or advocate? *Exceptional Children, 56*(2), 105-110.

___, & Tikunoff, W. J. (1987). *Bilingual education and bilingual special education: A guide for administrators.* Boston: College-Hill.

Fuchigami, R. Y. (1980). Teacher education for culturally diverse exceptional children. *Exceptional Children, 46*(8), 634-641.

Galang, R., Noble, V., & Halog, L. (n.d.). *Assessment of Pilipino speaking limited English proficient students with special needs.* Unpublished training materials. Developed for the Special Education Resource Network of the State Department of Education, Sacramento, California.

García, S. (1985, Fall). Characteristics of limited English proficient Hispanic students served in programs for the learning disabled: Implications for policy, practice and research (Part I). *Bilingual Special Education News, 4*, pp. 1, 3-6. (Available from University of Texas at Austin, College of Education, Department of Special Education.)

García, S. B., & Yates, J. R. (1986). Policy issues associated with serving bilingual exceptional children. *Reading, Writing, and Learning Disabilities, 2*, 123-137.

Gerber, M. M., & Semmel, M. I. (1984). Teacher as imperfect test: Reconceptualizing the referral process. *Educational Psychologist, 19*(3), 137-148.

Goodman, K. (1969). Analysis of oral reading miscues: Applied psycholinguistics. *Reading Research Quarterly*, 5, 9-30.

Graves, D. (1983). *Writing: Teachers and children at work*. Portsmouth, NH: Heinemann.

Guadalupe Organization v. Tempe Elementary School District. (1978). 587 F.2d 1022, U.S. Dist. Court of Arizona.

Gumperz, J. (1982). *Discourse strategies*. Cambridge: Cambridge University Press.

Heller, K. A., Holtzman, W. H., & Messick, S. (Eds.). (1982). *Placing children in special education: A strategy for equity*. Washington, DC: National Academy Press.

Hopper, M. (n.d.). *Understanding special education and bilingual education legislation, services and programs: Establishing a dialogue between bilingual and special educators*. Unpublished manuscript, California State Department of Education, Office of Special Education, Personnel Development Unit.

Jose P. v. Ambach. (1979). United States District Court, Eastern District of New York. C-270.

Kamp, S. H., & Chinn, P. C. (1982). *A multiethnic curriculum for special education students*. Reston, VA: Council for Exceptional Children.

Krashen, S. (1982). *Writing: Research, theory and applications*. Oxford, England: Pergamon Press.

Kugelmass, J. W. (1987). *Behavior bias and handicaps: Labeling the emotionally disturbed child*. New Brunswick, NJ: Transaction Books.

Landurand, P., Dew, N., Perlman, R., Schuhmann, A., & Napoliello, M. (1980). *Bridging the gap between bilingual and special education* (Report). Reston, VA: Council for Exceptional Children.

Langdon, H. W. (1989). Language disorder or difference? Assessing the language skills of Hispanic students. *Exceptional Children*, 56(2), 160-167.

Los Angeles Unified School District, Office of Bilingual-ESL Instruction. (1988). *Master plan for the education of limited-English-proficient students*. Los Angeles, CA: Author.

Lynch, E., & Stein, R. (1987). Parent participation by ethnicity: A comparison of Hispanic, Black, and Anglo families. *Exceptional Children*, 54(2), 105-111.

Martínez, H. (Ed.). (1981). Special education and the Hispanic child. *Proceedings from the second annual colloquium on Hispanic issues* (ERIC/CUE Urban Diversity Series, Number 74). New York, NY:

Columbia University, Teachers College, Institute for Urban and Minority Education.

Mehan, H., Hertweck, H., & Meihls, J. (1986). *Handicapping the handicapped.* Palo Alto, CA: Stanford University Press.

Mendoza, P. (1983, Summer). The role of language in psychological assessments of students. *Bilingual Special Education News*, 2(2), pp. 1, 4-5. (Available from University of Texas at Austin, College of Education, Department of Special Education.)

Merced County Superintendent of Schools. (1986). *Special education and the limited English proficient student: A guide to assessment, identification and educational planning for the LEP student.* Merced, CA: Author.

Mercer, J. (1973). *Labeling the mentally retarded.* Berkeley: University of California Press.

Midwest National Origin Desegregation Assistance Center. (1982). *Special education for exceptional bilingual students: A handbook for educators.* Milwaukee: University of Wisconsin.

New York City Board of Education. (1990). *The assessment of linguistically and culturally different students: A handbook for school based support teams.* Unpublished manuscript, Division of Special Education, Office of Bilingual Services, Project Recurso.

Omark, D. R., & Erickson, J. G. (Eds.). (1983). *The bilingual exceptional child.* San Diego: College-Hill.

Ortíz, A. A. (1986, Spring). Characteristics of limited English-proficient Hispanic students served in programs for the learning disabled: Implications for policy and practice (Part II). *Bilingual Special Education Newsletter*, pp. 1-5.

____. (1987, Spring). Communication disorders among limited English proficient Hispanic students. *Bilingual Special Education Newsletter, 5*, 1, 3-5, 7-8. (Available from University of Texas at Austin, College of Education, Department of Special Education.)

____, & Polyzoi, E. (Eds.). (1986). *Characteristics of limited English proficient Hispanic students in programs for the learning disabled: Implications for policy, practice and research* (Report Summary). Austin: University of Texas, College of Education, Department of Special Education, Handicapped Minority Research Institute on Language Proficiency.

____, & Ramirez, B. A. (Eds.). (1988). *Schools and the culturally diverse exceptional student: Promising practices and future directions.* Reston, VA: Council for Exceptional Children.

____, & Wilkinson, C. Y. (1989). Adapting IEPs for limited English proficient students. *Academic Therapy, 24*(5), 555-568.

____, & Yates, J. R. (1983). Incidence of exceptionality among Hispanics: Implications for manpower planning. *NABE Journal, 7*(3), 41-53.

____, & Yates, J. R. (1987). *Characteristics of learning disabled, mentally retarded, and speech-language handicapped Hispanic students at initial evaluation and re-evaluation.* Unpublished manuscript, University of Texas at Austin, College of Education, Department of Special Education.

____, Yates, J. R., & Garcia, S. B. (1990, Spring). Competencies associated with serving exceptional language minority students. *Bilingual Special Education Perspective* [formerly *Bilingual Special Education Newsletter*], *9*, 1, 3-5. (Available from University of Texas at Austin, College of Education, Department of Special Education.)

Page, E. B. (1980). Tests and decisions for the handicapped: A guide to evaluation under the new laws. *Journal of Special Education, 14*, 423-467.

Pérez, G., Brambila, A., Ingalls, P., Freeman, G., & Benevides, G. (1986, March). *Identification/assessment/strategies for L.E.P. kids in special education.* Unpublished training materials distributed at California Association of School Psychologists meeting, Oakland, California.

Plata, M. (n.d.). *Assessment, placement, and programming of bilingual exceptional pupils: A practical approach.* Reston, VA: Council for Exceptional Children.

Poplin, M. S. (1988a). The reductionistic fallacy in learning disabilities: Replicating the past by reducing the present. *Journal of Learning Disabilities, 21*, 389-400.

____. (1988b). Holistic/constructivist principles of the teaching/learning process: Implications for the field of learning disabilities. *Journal of Learning Disabilities, 21*, 401-416.

Reynolds, A. (1933). *The education of Spanish-speaking children in five southwestern states* (U.S. Department of the Interior Bulletin 1933, No. 11, Washington, DC). (Reprinted in *Education and the Mexican American*, [no editor or author listed; collection of five reprints]. New York: Arno Press, 1974)

Rueda, R. (1988). Eligibility criteria for special education for Spanish/English speaking pupils in California. Sacramento, CA: California State Department of Education, Special Education Demonstration Project I: Hispanic Pupils.

____. (1989). Defining mild disabilities with language-minority students. *Exceptional Children, 56*(2), 121-128.

____, Betts, B., & Hami, A. (1990). *A descriptive analysis of work products in OLE classroom sites: Baseline phase.* Unpublished manuscript, University of California at Davis, Division of Education, Special Education Demonstration Project.

____, Cardoza, D., Mercer, J., & Carpenter, L. (1984). *An examination of special education decisionmaking with Hispanic first-time referrals in large urban school districts* (Final Report—Longitudinal Study I Report). Los Alamitos, CA: Southwest Regional Laboratory, Handicapped-Minority Research Institute.

____, Figueroa, R., Mercado, P., & Cardoza, D. (1984). *Performance of Hispanic educable mentally retarded, learning disabled and nonclassified students on the WISC-RM, SOMPA and S-KABC* (Final Report—Short-Term Study One). Los Alamitos, CA: Southwest Regional Laboratory, Handicapped-Minority Research Institute.

____, & Mehan, H. (1986). Metacognition and passing: Strategic interactions in the lives of students with learning disabilities. *Anthropology and Education Quarterly, 17,* 145-165.

____, Rodriguez, R., & Prieto, A. (1981). Teachers perceptions of competencies for instructing bilingual/multicultural exceptional children. *Exceptional Children, 48*(3), 268-270.

____, Ruiz, N. T., & Figueroa, R. A. (1989, March). *Home language and learning practices among Mexican American children: Review of the literature.* Paper presented at the annual meeting of the American Education Research Association, San Francisco.

Ruiz, N. T. (1988). *Language for learning in a bilingual special education classroom.* Unpublished doctoral dissertation, Stanford University.

____. (1989a). *The Optimal Learning Environment (OLE) Curriculum Guide: A resource for teachers of Spanish-speaking children in learning handicapped programs.* Unpublished manuscript, University of California at Davis, Division of Education.

____. (1989b). An optimal learning environment for Rosemary. *Exceptional Children, 56*(2), 130-144.

____. (1990). *Instructional events in the OLE classrooms: Baseline phase.* Unpublished manuscript, University of California at Davis, Division of Education, Special Education Demonstration Project.

Ruiz v. State Board of Education. (1971). Superior Court of California, Sacramento County, Civil Action No. 218394.

Russell, N. L., & Ortíz, A. A. (1988, Fall). Assessment and instruction within a dialogue model of communication: Part I. *Bilingual Special Education Newsletter, 8,* 1, 3-4. (Available from University of Texas at Austin, College of Education, Department of Special Education.)

Salend, S. J., & Fradd, S. (1986). Nationwide availability of services for limited English-proficient handicapped students. *Journal of Special Education, 20*(1), 127-135.

Simich-Dudgeon, C. (1986). A multidisciplinary model to educate minority students with handicapping conditions. *Reading, Writing, and Learning Disabilities, 2,* 111-122.

Staff. (n.d. [1982]). Hispanics underrepresented in special education. *Bilingual Special Education News, 1*(1), 1-2. (Available from University of Texas at Austin, College of Education, Department of Special Education.)

Swedo, J. (1987, Fall). Effective teaching strategies for handicapped limited English proficient students. *Bilingual Special Education Newsletter, 6,* 1, 3-5. (Available from University of Texas at Austin, College of Education, Department of Special Education.)

Tharp, R. G., & Gallimore, R. (1988). *Rousing minds to life: Teaching, learning, and schooling in social contexts.* Cambridge: Cambridge University Press.

Tinloy, M., Tan, A., & Leung, B. (n.d.). *Assessment of Chinese speaking limited English proficient students with special needs.* Unpublished training materials developed for the Special Education Resource Network of the State Department of Education, Sacramento, California.

Trueba, H. T. (1987, April). Cultural differences or learning handicaps? Towards an understanding of adjustment processes. In *Schooling language minority youth: Volume III, Proceedings of the University of California Linguistic Minority Research Project Conference* (pp. 45-79). Los Angeles: University of California.

U.S. Commission on Civil Rights. (1974). *Toward quality education for Mexican Americans* (Report VI). Washington, DC: U.S. Government Printing Office.

U.S. Department of Education. (1980-1989). *Annual report toCongress on the implementation of The Education of the Handicapped Act* [second through eleventh reports]. Washington, DC: U.S. Government Printing Office.

_____, Office for Civil Rights, San Francisco Region IX. (n.d.). *A sample plan for the provision of special education services to limited English proficient students.* Unpublished manuscript. San Francisco, CA.

_____. (1979). *First annual report to Congress on the implementation of The Education of the Handicapped Act.* Washington, DC: U.S. Government Printing Office.

Weiss, R. S. (1981). INREAL intervention for language handicapped and bilingual children. *Journal of the Division for Early Childhood, 4,* 40-51.

Westby, C., & Rouse, G. R. (1985). Culture in education and the instruction of language learning-disabled students. *Topics in Language Disorders, 5*(4), 15-28.

Wilkinson, C. Y., & Ortíz, A. A. (1986, Fall). Reevaluation of learning disabled Hispanic students: Changes over three years. *Bilingual Special Education Newsletter, 5,* 1, 3-6. (Available from University of Texas at Austin, College of Education, Department of Special Education.)

Willig, A. C. (1986). Special education and the culturally and linguistically different child: An overview of issues and challenges. *Reading, Writing, and Learning Disabilities, 2,* 161-173.

____, & Swedo, J. (1987). *Improving teaching strategies for exceptional Hispanic limited English proficient students: An exploratory study of task engagement and teaching strategies.* Paper presented at the annual meeting of the American Educational Research Association, Washington, DC.

Ysseldyke, J. E., & Algozzine, B. (1983). LD or not LD: That's not the question! *Journal of Learning Disabilities, 16*(1), 29-31.

____, Algozzine, B., Shinn, M. R., & McGue, M. (1982). Similarities and differences between low achievers and students classified learning disabled. *Journal of Special Education, 16*(1), 73-85.

ASSESSMENT OF BILINGUAL PRESCHOOL CHILDREN

Maryann Santos de Barona
Andrés Barona
Arizona State University

ABSTRACT

Federal laws (P.L. 94-142; 1975; P.L. 99-457, 1986) coupled with a rapid increase of limited English proficient children residing in the United States have resulted in the potential for increased educational services for bilingual preschool children. Although the opportunities for increased services can have a positive impact on bilingual children and their families, a number of issues that can negatively impact bilingual preschool children such as identification, screening, assessment, and intervention, are identified and discussed. Recommendations designed to minimize potential negative impact and obstacles are also provided.

Assessment of Bilingual Preschool Children

During the past two decades, educational institutions have received great pressure to accurately assess the abilities and skills of bilingual children and to provide appropriate services based on the findings of that assessment. Such pressure has come from both judicial and legislative sectors and has involved issues related to parental informed consent for evaluation and placement, determining a child's primary language with subsequent evaluation in that language, the inappropriate use of standardized intelligence tests that underrepresent minority children in the norm sample, as well as the use of other tests that emphasize English language skills over general cognitive and achievement skills (*Diana v. Board of Education*, 1970; *Covarrubias v. San Diego Unified*, 1971; *Guadalupe v. Tempe Elementary School District*, 1971).

In 1975, Public Law (P.L.) 94-142, the Education for All Handicapped Children Act, was enacted. This pivotal law crafted a national policy from previous judicial and legislative actions to mandate that states provide special education and related services to all eligible children and youths between the ages of 6 and 17. As federal legislation, it had direct implications for assessing and providing services to ethnic minority children. Among its requirements were:

1. The use of valid, culturally appropriate and nondiscriminatory testing and evaluation materials and procedures by trained members of a multidisciplinary team

2. Procedural safeguards related to informed consent and due process

3. The use of multiple data sources such as observations, teacher recommendations, and adaptive behavior information in making classification and placement decisions

4. An individualized educational plan that specifies instructional goals of services to be provided in the "least restrictive environment"

5. The educational program be reviewed annually with a comprehensive review of the child's status to occur at least every three years (Bergan, 1985)

Although P.L. 94-142 was pivotal in that it required that services be provided to meet the unique developmental needs of children, it did not mandate services to children under the age of six. Rather, it merely allowed the provision of services to eligible preschoolers between three and six years if state law did not prohibit such services. Because only limited incentive funds were made available to states serving preschool populations, the number of states actually serving this population was quite low. This was particularly problematic in light of numerous studies showing the economic and educational benefits of early intervention for young handicapped children. In particular, research findings have shown that "the earlier intervention is started, the greater is the ultimate dollar savings and the higher the rate of educational attainment by handicapped children" (U.S. Department of Education, 1985, p. xvi).

P.L. 99-457, signed into law in 1986, remedied this situation by authorizing funds and providing guidelines to states "to help them plan, develop, and implement a statewide comprehensive, coordinated, multidisciplinary, interagency program of early intervention services for handicapped infants and toddlers and their families" (Garwood & Sheehan, 1989, p. 61). States failing to comply with the regulations risk loss of federal funds.

P.L. 99-457 takes a broad approach by dealing with early intervention rather than only with special education. As such, it permits emphasis on appropriate early intervention activities that may include family training, psychological services, limited medical and health services, screening and assessment services, and special instruction (SEC. 672.2.E). In addition, states may decide whether young children at risk for developmental delay will be served within its comprehensive intervention service system. Particularly significant components of this law are the recognition of the family and family members as integral members of both the evaluation and intervention processes and the flexibility to shape services according to unique family needs and circumstances.

The potential impact of these events for bilingual preschool children is great. The nation's Hispanic population presently totals over 20 million and, since 1980, has been growing at a rate five times as fast as the rate of the non-Hispanic population (U.S. Department of Commerce News, October 12, 1989). Estimates of the number of limited English proficient persons living in the United States are projected to near 40 million by the year 2000 (National Advisory Council on Bilingual Education, 1980-81) with the great majority having Spanish as their primary language. Demographic statistics indicate that the child at risk for school failure tends to be poor and an ethnic minority: 40 percent of Hispanic children currently live in families whose incomes fall below the poverty line (Halsell Miranda & Santos de Barona, 1990). In addition, the potential for school failure increases when the child is from a non-English speaking home, lives in a female-headed household, has parents who are young, unskilled, and themselves school dropouts, or has limited access to adequate health care (Committee for Economic Development, 1987; Halsell Miranda & Santos de Barona, 1990). Thus, it appears that young bilingual children are especially vulnerable to school failure and consequently may be able to greatly benefit from the opportunities presented by recent federal legislation.

While the opportunities for early intervention created by these recent federal mandates can positively impact the personal, educational, and vocational lives of bilingual children and their families by providing access to services before problems have become severe, several issues, related to identification, screening, assessment, and intervention, can negatively impact the at-risk bilingual preschool child in this process.

Identification

Providing early intervention services necessitates that children with problems first be appropriately identified. The process of identification involves a number of phases. First, parents must be aware that their child may be at-risk educationally and seek assistance. Screening must then be conducted to quickly and accurately separate those children with problems from those without. Those children identified in the screening phases as having problems must be thoroughly and appropriately assessed to obtain a clear picture of areas that require intervention. Based on the findings of this diagnostic phase, an intervention plan must be designed that will appropriately provide needed services in a manner that will be acceptable to the family. However, because of cultural, linguistic, and at times economic factors, the bilingual child may experience difficulty navigating each phase of this process and thus may be less likely than English-speaking children to receive needed services before learning and developmental problems become exacerbated. The following addresses potential problems likely to be experienced at each phase, along with suggestions for over-coming obstacles.

Parents must be aware that their child may be at-risk and seek assistance. Typically, young children, and particularly culturally diverse children from low socioeconomic house-holds, do not receive the attention of either the medical or educational professions unless significant and obvious health or development problems exist. Children with diag-nosed medical disorders for which there is a certainty for developmental delay, such as Down's Syndrome, epilepsy, or severe microcephaly, tend to be identified early in life and a variety of medical and educational services are provided to enhance their development. Problems of a more subtle or seemingly minor nature, however, such as low birth weight, slower development in walking or talking, problems in gross or fine motor coordination or frequent ear infections may not be recognized as symptoms of risk and parents therefore may not seek professional evaluation related to developmental concerns for their child. Still other factors exist that are primarily environmental in nature. These fac-tors, which include restricted access to health care and adequate nutrition, or low levels of physical and social stim-ulation may not be within the family's ability to modify yet adversely impact young children's development.

It is most important that parents, parent surrogates, and professionals in contact with bilingual preschool children be made aware of those factors that may be symptomatic of po-tential educational problems. Additionally, they must be made aware that services exist for their children as well as how to access available services. This will require that ex-tensive culturally sensitive outreach efforts be conducted whose aim is to publicize basic child developmental infor-mation and the availability of services, and to secure parental involvement.

Cultural differences must be addressed in outreach efforts because of their impact on both the family's value of ser-vices and its receptivity to outsiders' involvement in their child's care, treatment, and education. Some cultures con-sider a child's disability to be a source of shame and as a result some families may be reluctant to publicly acknowledge their handicapped child through referral lest they incur cultural stigma. In other cultures where there are few or no expectations for the disabled, intervention does not make sense and the family may see no reason to seek services for their child (Hanson & Lynch, 1989).

Screening

Information dissemination and screening efforts must be conducted in a culturally and linguistically sensitive manner. Individuals involved in these efforts, who themselves should be from diverse language and cultural backgrounds, must become familiar with all aspects of the culture, including perceptions related to disability and intervention. Interpreters or personnel who are primary language speakers need to be available to answer questions, and materials should be printed in the primary language. The values, beliefs, and traditions of the culture must be respected and, ideally, family involvement secured with culturally acceptable methods. As an example, if an elder's advice is regularly sought within the community, his or her assistance should be solicited (Hanson & Lynch, 1989).

Although numerous approaches to early childhood screening exist (Lichtenstein & Ireton, 1984, National Association of School Psychologists, 1989), many are not appropriate for culturally diverse children and communities. Most bilingual preschool children are not enrolled in either preschools or early childhood programs (Fradd, 1987) and so teacher or school-centered screening approaches are not feasible. Similarly, screening approaches that rely totally on parent-initiated referrals assume that the parents are both aware that their child's development may be atypical and know how to request and access needed services. This is often an unrealistic expectation for families who have limited English skills and a lack of familiarity with social, medical, and educational services. Rather, selective screening programs that provide direct screening for either demographic subgroups or geographic areas with a "substantial

number of underidentified children with special needs"
(Lichtenstein & Ireton, 1984, p. 12) may avoid this potential
problem.

*Screening must be conducted to quickly and accurately sepa-
rate those children with problems from those without.* The
screening process itself should be able to accurately identify
those children with problems so that they may receive further diagnostic evaluation. However, numerous factors
contribute to problems or ambiguity in screening for developmental problems. Problems associated with the screening
process include failing to identify a child with problems and
referring a child for further assessment who in fact does not
need this additional service.

The adequacy of screening procedures is particularly important since by definition these measures do not have high
levels of precision, may lack research support, and may not
be equally valid for children of varying economic and cultural backgrounds (Lidz, 1983). Many screening instruments
are available and may lack sufficient predictive ability, particularly regarding their validity and overall poor psychometric characteristics for culturally diverse children (Arffa,
Rider, & Cummings, 1984; Rubin, Balow, Dorle, & Rosen,
1978). In a study that screened kindergarten children for
school readiness (Gandara, Keogh, & Yoshioka-Maxwell,
1980), the predictive accuracy of kindergarten measures varied according to the ethnicity and language background of
the children. Although the measures used in the study
were not language or culture specific, they were significantly
predictive of Anglo English-speakers, less accurate for
Mexican American English speakers, and nonpredictive for
Mexican American Spanish speakers. Such differences are
critical and need to be widely known because of their significant and long-term consequences.

Differentiating abnormal from normal development in
very young children frequently is difficult since development occurs at a rapid and often unpredictable rate with
considerable variability in the range of individual children's
abilities (Lidz, 1983). A culturally diverse child of preschool
age typically receives most socializing influences from the

family since preschool programs reach less than 25 percent of minority three and four year olds (Fradd, 1987). To the extent that the family's values, experiences and behaviors differ from the mainstream Anglo culture, the bilingual child may share few common experiences with age peers. It therefore is extremely important that screening personnel be familiar with and understand the culture and language of the child.

Additionally, screening personnel may not be experienced or comfortable working with young children and may not know how to elicit optimal performance. If unfamiliar with the child's language and culture, it is entirely possible that such screening staff may misinterpret the child's behavior and responses during screening. The preschooler whose language and culture differ from mainstream American peers may also have different skills and styles of expression. Since young children's vocabulary is closely tied to their experiences, a culturally different child may react differently to assessment materials as well as the assessment situation in general. This is one reason why it is so important for screening personnel to be familiar with the unique characteristics of each culture. As an example, well-mannered Vietnamese children speak only when spoken to and refrain from spontaneous conversation lest they be considered rude or disrespectful. Similarly, it is considered impolite and even challenging for Hispanic children to maintain eye contact with an adult. American personnel unfamiliar with these culture-specific behaviors might erroneously conclude that the Vietnamese child was dull or unmotivated or that the Hispanic child was sneaky or devious rather than both behaving in a respectful manner as they had been taught in their culture.

Assessment

Once a child has been identified as requiring more indepth assessment, the need for acute sensitivity to cultural and linguistic differences increases. Federal law mandates that assessment be conducted using nondiscriminatory procedures and must "go beyond testing in the primary language. They must include consideration of the child's cultural history, economic status, and family value systems" (Danielson, Lynch, Moyano, Johnson, & Bettenburg, 1989, p. 10).

Nondiscriminatory procedures involve a number of important aspects related to development, language, and culture. Numerous problems are involved in the assessment of bilingual preschool children. These include issues related to preschool children, culturally and linguistically different children, as well as issues related to the measurement instruments. All must be considered carefully to ensure that the skills, abilities, and needs of bilingual preschoolers are accurately assessed.

Issues Related to Preschool Children. Evaluating preschool age children requires considerable skill, creativity, and fortitude. Young children typically are not constrained by social expectations. They frequently do not know nor are they concerned about appropriate behavior in specific situations. As a result, they tend to express their feelings easily and behave according to their immediate impulses. The length of time a young child can adequately invest in evaluation activities is quite short and often affected by the need for rest and food (Barona, 1990; Glenn, 1986; Ulrey, 1981). The examiner must be familiar and comfortable working with young children and should be ready to accommodate an individual child's needs by modifying the testing session. As one example, it may be necessary to have several short assessment sessions with the child if difficulties in maintaining attention and cooperation are experienced.

Young children's rate of development and learning is often variable and unpredictable, absent one day while clearly observable the next. This phenomenon has led to the recommendation that "particularly in the case of preschool children, assessment data should be viewed as a snapshot: a picture in time of the child's performance. That performance changes continually and it is not a good practice to use early assessment data to predict future performance, since the validity of these predictions is not very high (Rogers, 1986)" (NASP, 1989, p. 33).

Issues Related to Cultural and Linguistic Diversity. As mentioned earlier, unique cultural characteristics may result in behavioral differences that may be misinterpreted if not known. Some children may not speak until spoken to, may not volunteer information, or maintain eye contact because they are attempting to demonstrate courtesy and respect in the manner that they have learned (Barona, 1990). The evaluator may need to make special accommodations when assessing a culturally diverse child, modifying the style and tempo of the examination by becoming more direct, nurturing, affectionate, or reserved as the situation demands (Barona, 1990). In some instances, modifying the sequence of presentation of test items or conducting the test in a location more familiar to the child may result in significant and positive effects on test performance (Silverman, 1971; Zigler & Butterfield, 1968). The evaluator should be prepared to attempt a variety of strategies to reveal the child's current level of skill and knowledge and must be aware of those interactive styles that are judged proper and relevant to the child's cultural and linguistic experiences. Such awareness is critical for appropriate interpretation of test results although it does not ensure a valid assessment for every child. It is additionally essential that the evaluator be sensitive to the drawbacks of using many popular instruments.

Issues of Measurement. Traditional standardized methods of assessment have been criticized on the grounds that they limit the amount and nature of interaction between child and examiner. Only a narrow repertoire of responses are acceptable and many of these are unknown to a culturally or linguistically different child. Such a child may respond in a nonstandard manner that was not anticipated during test construction and therefore cannot be considered correct in scoring. Thus, the standardized nature of the assessment may not permit the child to adequately demonstrate his or her knowledge and abilities.

Many assessment instruments are hampered by an underrepresentation of culturally diverse individuals in the standardization sample. Many developmental scales used primarily white, middle-class populations as norms (Garber & Slater, 1983) and consequently are not useful when interpreting the test results of diverse populations. As noted earlier, the ability of many traditional methods and instruments to consistently predict outcomes is diminished with children from diverse backgrounds. These measures are most successful with white, middle-class children but "are generally unacceptable in their level of predictive ability for minority children" (Reynolds & Clark, 1983, p. 2). Two possibilities exist to explain this phenomenon. First, the content of test items may place a particular group at an advantage while placing others at a disadvantage through the use of information, concepts, or materials more familiar to some than to others (Wiersma & Jurs, 1985). The second possibility may be that these tests do not measure the same underlying constructs for all children. At least one study found the factor structure of a popular intelligence test to differ for white, black, and Hispanic school-age children (Santos de Barona, 1981) and it has been hypothesized that, for culturally diverse children, IQ tests may only measure the degree to which a child has become familiar with mainstream American society (Mercer, 1979) rather than an actual capacity to learn. Thus, interpretation, diagnosis, and long-range planning are hampered when children are not part of the American mainstream.

Finally, many assessment measures fail to provide sufficient specificity to enable useful decision making regarding educational programming. As a result, areas of deficit may not receive ample remediation. These limitations have caused much concern over the deleterious and lasting effects of premature labeling or possible misclassification and have resulted in many professionals postponing assessment for very young children.

As can be seen by this brief discussion, there are many factors that can interfere with the assessment process:

> The unique characteristics of the preschool period,
> which is often marked by uneven development and

growth spurts, combined with the effects of cultural variations in style of interaction, language issues, and problems associated with the assessment instruments, create significant difficulties in interpreting test results. This development-culture-instrument interaction makes it difficult to determine if test findings are attributable to cultural, linguistic, environmental, developmental, or measurement factors (Barona, 1990).

Ironically, however, such a determination is essential for the bilingual preschool child to avoid the negative effects of either denying needed services or providing unneeded services that carry the potential of lasting stigma

An extended process of assessment is suggested for use with the bilingual preschool child; this process allows for the systematic evaluation of the child's skills and knowledge and expands the frequency, length, and types of interaction with the bilingual preschool child so that more confident judgments regarding abilities and needs can be reached. This process is described in greater detail elsewhere (Barona, 1990) and is summarized here.

Preassessment Data. Prior to actual work with the child, comprehensive information about the child's language, motor, and social development should be obtained and concerns about the child discussed. Medical information, if pertinent, should also be obtained. Both parents and care providers should participate in this process to optimize information available about the child. In addition, information related to the family composition, status within the community, and level of acculturation can provide useful information about the child and help the evaluator decide how to structure the subsequent assessment.

Language Assessment. Language assessment is essential in the evaluation of bilingual children since it is necessary to separate problems related to limited English proficiency from either language disorders or slow development (Barona & Santos de Barona, 1987). For this reason, it is important that the evaluator be skilled in language assessment and fluent in the relevant language.

As part of the language assessment, it will be necessary to determine the child's home language and the degree, if any, to which the child has been exposed to English and then to assess the child's language structure and use of functional language (Barona & Santos de Barona, 1987). Both receptive and expressive aspects of language should be examined and should include vocabulary, comprehension, and syntax. This language assessment should result in a decision regarding the language or languages with which to conduct the remainder of the assessment and what, if any, modifications in the assessment procedure may need to be made to accommodate the child's language needs. Such modifications may include but are not limited to using commercial or local translations, determining the adequacy of such instruments, using interpreters when needed, and ensuring their skill.

The Traditional Assessment. This chapter has readily acknowledged the multiple problems associated with the use of standardized assessment instruments with culturally and linguistically different children. However, these instruments do serve a useful function in that they provide a systematic and relatively uniform way to collect data about the child in various domains. As such, they create a basis for comparison as well as a means with which to judge interactive styles. Results of standardized intelligence tests used with bilingual children should be viewed as a general estimate of the child's *current level of measurable functioning* rather than as an absolute index of cognitive functioning. As such, information regarding the child's demonstrated skills and knowledge can be compared relative to other children and can serve as a foundation for further assessment, if needed, or for making educational recommendations.

Test results should provide critical information regarding the relative level of functioning and whether test performance was affected by factors other than ability or achievement. Such factors might include the degree of the child's investment in evaluation tasks, how well the child appeared to understand the language of assessment, and whether language was a factor in test performance.

Test findings must be evaluated against all data gathered in earlier stages. As an example, a child who paid greater attention to test items presented in the native language probably is not experiencing an inability to attend but rather distractibility due to limited second language skills. Similarly, a Vietnamese child new to this country would not be expected to engage in elaborate or animated verbal interactions in any language and might warrant additional examination if observed to behave in this rather culturally atypical manner. This phase of assessment should be a way to integrate information about the child, generate and explore hypotheses, and develop strategies for either educational recommendation or for further assessment.

Even though the traditional standardized assessment was conducted with care, the evaluator may conclude that there is insufficient information with which to make decisions regarding the child. This conclusion may be a result of the influence on test results of language, developmental, or cultural factors such as difficulties in separating from the primary caregiver, concern over language involvement, or an inability to successfully work with a specific cultural interaction style. The evaluator may feel a need to obtain a more representative sampling of the child's skills and knowledge than that provided by the standardized instruments or may require more information concerning the way the child learns to get a clearer direction for instructional planning.

To ensure that developmental and cultural variables are accounted for while gathering useful information, the culturally different child should be sufficiently adjusted to the assessment setting. To this end, it is suggested that, prior to classification, the child undergo a diagnostic placement in an established preschool enrichment program where bilingual and bicultural personnel are available to assist the child with communication needs. This setting ideally should serve on a daily basis a high proportion of children of diverse ethnic and cultural backgrounds with apparently normal development to facilitate socialization and appropriate modeling behavior and to provide an informal means of comparison. Within a nurturing and supportive setting, the child's growth in motor, social, and cognitive areas can be facilitated with age-appropriate activities. Mediated learning experiences (Feuerstein, 1979) that encourage the children to explore a variety of problem-solving and information-seeking strategies in all developmental areas and that permit a close monitoring of the child's progress in accomplishing these tasks can be incorporated into the curriculum.

During the diagnostic placement, which would be expected to last for a period of three to six months, the child should be provided with continuous opportunities for appropriate social interactions and receive active encouragement for participation in activities. It is expected that children with separation difficulties will become accustomed to daily interaction with a number of adults and that this familiarity will result in increased responsiveness and attention to task when additional assessments are performed. Additionally, it is expected that the child will view new activities and information as a regular part of the daily routine, thus enabling the ongoing measurement of skills, learning styles, and progress in a relatively unobtrusive fashion.

A diagnostic placement can provide personnel with a way to observe the child in group situations, assess preferential language and learning styles, and determine effective teaching strategies over time. Since preschool teacher-pupil ratios are relatively low, it also is possible to monitor social adjustment in this setting and obtain a greater awareness of the child's overall personality and needs.

The effects of culture also can be determined more effectively since it is anticipated that children of both the same and different cultures will be in attendance as well as some personnel with similar language skills. Thus, throughout the placement interval, it will be possible to both measure and monitor the rate with which the child acquires new skills and concepts as well as to identify effective reinforcing conditions for a particular child. Finally, the diagnostic placement will result in a realistic estimate of the intensity of effort needed to work successfully with a particular child's needs.

Intervention

Typically, a review meeting is held with the parent and the professionals who were involved in assessing the child. It is at this meeting that a decision is made regarding whether the child is eligible for services and how to most appropriately meet the child's unique needs. The parent is an important part of the decision-making process and should have a major role in helping define the services to be provided. Too often parents who are not members of the mainstream American culture are not aware of this right or feel that they do not have the knowledge or skill to significantly contribute to the process; many parents view the school as an institution of authority and school personnel and evaluation specialists as experts. However, particularly where a young child is concerned, the parents and other family members are needed to participate in intervention activities; they have valuable and needed information that will be critical to a plan's success. Thus, ways must be found to solicit the family's input and participation during the design and implementation of the intervention. The degree of cooperation and investment of parents and other family members can be the key to the success or failure of enrichment and prescriptive services.

Here, too, it is critical that cultural and linguistic factors be carefully considered as they may significantly influence how a family responds to services. Some parents may have strong reservations related to labeling. As noted earlier, in some cultures a label such as mentally retarded may be perceived as shameful to the family and it is possible that a family might reject offered services since this action would publicly acknowledge a disability. Some may fear that, by agreeing that their child is handicapped, they and their child will be rejected by their community. Still others may be skeptical over the efficacy of services and hope that the identified problems are a transitory and normal part of development that will diminish over time.

It is important that the family understand why a particular intervention strategy is considered necessary for their child and how it will be implemented. If the family's involvement in intervention is considered to be important to the intervention, their ability to follow through must be determined. As an example, a family where the parents must work to make ends meet and who have limited transportation should not be assigned a primary role, particularly if such involvement requires regular participation in intervention activities where the child is being served. Rather, the family might be provided direction with some supplemental activities that can be implemented in the home. It is also important that the family's role in the intervention plan be clearly and concretely communicated and that the family perceive their involvement to be both appropriate and realistic. Again, it is important that, wherever possible, the design of the intervention reflect the unique cultural values of the family.

Summary

Federal law and the rapid increase of limited English proficient persons residing in the United States have resulted in the potential for increased educational services for bilingual children. However, these opportunities may be offset by problems related to accessing services. This chapter discussed several issues involving identification, screening, assessment, and intervention as they may negatively impact the bilingual child. Because the process of assessing bilingual preschool children is a complex one that requires great care, an expanded procedure for evaluation and diagnosis was suggested that includes obtaining culturally and linguistically relevant information at all stages of the assessment process.

Throughout the process, it is important that attention be paid to the various ways that culture and language impact evaluation results. Techniques must be found to obtain an accurate sampling of children's performance and this may require greater familiarity with the children's culture as well as extended and varied opportunities for observation and measurement. Test results may need to be interpreted with an eye to the bilingual child's culture. Finally, the needs and views of the parents and family must be considered and incorporated when intervention services are designed and implemented.

References

Arffa, S., Rider, L. H., & Cummings, J. A. (1984). A validity study of the Woodcock-Johnson Psychoeducational Battery and the Stanford-Binet with black preschool children. *Journal of Psychoeducational Assessment, 2,* 73-77.

Barona, A. (1990). Assessment of multicultural preschool children. In B. Bracken (Ed.), *Psychoeducational assessment of preschool children* (2nd ed.), (pp. 379-391). Boston: Allyn & Bacon.

_____, & Santos de Barona, M. (1987). A model for the assessment of limited English proficient students referred for special education services. In S. H. Fradd & W. J. Tikunoff (Eds.), *Bilingual education and bilingual special education: A guide for administrators* (pp. 183-210). Boston: College-Hill Press.

Bergan, J. R. (1985). *School psychology in contemporary society.* Columbus, OH: Charles C. Merrill.

Committee for Economic Development. (1987). *Children in need: Investment strategies for the educationally disadvantaged.* New York: Committee for Economic Development.

Covarrubias v. San Diego Unified School District, Civil Action No. 70-30d, (S.D. Cal., 1971).

Danielson, E. B., Lynch, E. C., Moyano, A., Johnson, B., & Bettenburg, A. (1989). *Assessing young children.* Washington, DC: National Association of School Psychologists.

Diana v. Board of Education, Civil Action No. C-70-37, (N.D., Cal., 1970).

Feuerstein, R. (1979). *The dynamic assessment of retarded performers: The learning potential assessment device, theory, instruments, and techniques.* Baltimore: University Park Press.

Fradd, S. H. (1987). The changing focus of bilingual education. In S. H. Fradd & W. J. Tikunoff (Eds.), *Bilingual education and bilingual special education: A guide for administrators* (pp. 1-44). Boston: College-Hill Press.

Gandara, P., Keogh, B. K., & Yoshioka-Maxwell, B. (1980). Predicting academic performance of anglo and Mexican-American children. *Psychology in the Schools, 17,* 174-177.

Garber, H. L., & Slater, M. (1983). Assessment of the culturally different preschooler. In K. D. Paget & B. Bracken (Eds.), *The psychoeducational assessment of preschool children* (pp. 443-472). New York: Grune & Stratton.

Garwood, S. G., & Sheehan, R. (1989). *Designing a comprehensive early intervention system: The challenge of Public Law 99-457.* Austin, TX: PRO-ED.

Glenn, G. L. (1986, October). Rich learning for all our children. *Phi Delta Kappan, 68,* 133-134.

Guadalupe v. Tempe Elementary School District, No. 3, Civ. No. 71-435 (D. Ariz., filed Aug. 9, 1971).

Halsell Miranda, A., & Santos de Barona, M. (1990). A model for interventions with low-achieving minority students. In A. Barona & E. Garcia (Eds.), *Children at risk.* Washington, DC: National Association for School Psychologists.

Hanson, M. J., & Lynch, E. W. (1989). *Early intervention: Implementing child and family services for infants and toddlers who are at-risk or disabled.* Austin, TX: PRO-ED.

Lichtenstein, R., & Ireton, H. (1984). *Preschool screening: Identifying young children with developmental and educational problems.* Orlando, FL: Grune & Stratton, Inc.

Lidz, C. C. (1983). Issues in assessing preschool children. In K. D. Paget & B. A. Bracken (Eds.), *The psychoeducational assessment of preschool children* (pp. 17-28). Orlando, FL: Grune & Stratton, Inc.

Mercer, J. (1979). *Technical manual: SOMPA: System of multicultural pluralistic assessment.* New York: Psychological Corporation.

National Association of School Psychologists. (1989). *The early childhood identification process: A manual for screening and assessment.* Washington, DC: NASP Publication Office.

National Advisory Council for Bilingual Education. (1980-81). *The prospects for bilingual education in the nation.* Washington, DC: Office of Bilingual Education and Minority Language Affairs, U.S. Department of Education (ERIC Document Reproduction Service No. ED 203 664).

Reynolds, C. R., & Clark, J. (1983). Assessment of cognitive abilities. In K. D. Paget & B. Bracken (Eds.), *The psychoeducational assessment of preschool children* (pp. 163-190). New York: Grune & Stratton.

Rogers, S. J. (1986). Assessment of infants and preschoolers with low income handicaps. In P. J. Lazarus & S. S. Strichart (Eds.), *Psychoeducational evaluation of children and adolescents with low-incidence handicaps.* New York: Grune & Stratton.

Rubin, R. A., Balow, B., Dorle, J., & Rosen, M. (1978). Preschool prediction of low achievement in basic school skills. *Journal of Learning Disabilities, 11*, 62-64.

Santos de Barona, M. (1981). A study of distractibility utilizing the WISC-R factors of intelligence and Bender error categories in a referred population. *Dissertation Abstracts International, 42*, 4775A.

Silverman, E. (1971). Situational variability of preschoolers' dysfluency: Preliminary study. *Perceptual and Motor Skills, 33*, 4021-4022.

Ulrey, G. (1981). The challenge of providing psychological services for young handicapped children. *Professional Psychology, 12*, 483-491.

U.S. Department of Commerce. (1989, October 12). [Census Bureau Press release]. Hispanic population surpasses 20 million mark; grows by 39 percent, Census bureau reports. (CB89-158).

U.S. Department of Education. (1985). *Seventh Annual Report to Congress on the Implementation of the Education of the Handicapped Act.* Washington, DC: Government Printing Office.

Wiersma, W., & Jurs, S. G. (1985). *Educational measurement and testing.* Boston: Allyn & Bacon.

Zigler, E., & Butterfield, E. (1968). Motivational aspects of changes in IQ test performance and culturally deprived nursery school children. *Child Development, 39*, 1-14.

MEXICAN AMERICAN STUDENT SEGREGATION AND DESEGREGATION IN CALIFORNIA

M. Beatriz Arias
Arizona State University

ABSTRACT

Mexican American participation in California school desegregation efforts is reviewed in this article, focusing on
the case of *Diaz v. San Jose Unified School District.*
Most desegregation remedies have ignored the language
component and have proceeded to create student assignment plans that achieve a maximum interethnic racial exposure. Clearly, the desegregation of San Jose Unified
has been accomplished. What is less clear is the extent to
which Mexican American parents and students had access
to the same range of choices available to majority students. Although it is still too early to determine differences in the educational experiences of Mexican American
students, the researcher did find that, on average, minority students (specifically, Mexican American) were performing 10 to 12 percentage points lower than majority
white students in all areas measured by achievement tests.
This and other data indicate that possibly the remedy for
relieving racial isolation must go beyond school assignment strategies to include the instructional components
required by programs for language minority students.

California recently gained the dubious distinction as a
state where the segregation of Hispanic students has increased significantly in the last 10 years. This segregation,
which today isolates most Mexican American and other
Hispanic students from Anglo and black students, is not a
recent development. School segregation both sanctioned
and unsanctioned has existed for decades. Now as a result of
the changing demographic character of California, where
majority students are rapidly becoming the minority in urban districts, segregation is merely more extensive.

California, like many other states, legally sanctioned
school segregative practices. Unlike other states, California's

segregationist policies were first articulated against two or three minority groups. For example, as early as 1901 "Mongolian" (primarily Japanese and Chinese students) rather than black children were denied access to equal school facilities. Later legislation focused on Native American (including Mexican American) students. With the repeal of the segregationist policies in 1947, California, like other southwestern states, had to integrate at least two minority groups with the majority Anglo student population: blacks and Mexican Americans.

This chapter briefly reviews Mexican American participation in California school desegregation efforts and focuses on one particular case: *Diaz v. San Jose Unified School District*. This chapter will describe the characteristics of the school desegregation plan in which Mexican American students were the excluded minority. A theme throughout this review is the proposition that in school desegregation cases with pluralistic constituencies the remedy for relieving racial isolation must go beyond school assignment strategies to include the instructional components required by programs for language minority students. Mexican American students, unlike black but similar to Asian and Native American students, have experienced linguistic as well as racial exclusion. Despite the importance of a linguistic remedy, most desegregation remedies have ignored the language component and have proceeded to create student assignment plans that achieve a maximum interethnic racial exposure. The thesis presented here is that increased educational opportunity for Mexican American students through school desegregation litigation must include access to English as well as exposure to majority students.

Historical Background

Segregated school facilities were legislatively sanctioned by public statute in California from 1874 to 1947. Early segregationist school policies were directed at Chinese and Japanese children, establishing schools for "Mongolian" children. Mexican American students while not specifically excluded by law from California schools were defined as "Indians" in order to apply segregationist practices. In the 1930s, California Attorney General U. S. Webb issued an opinion on the "Indianism" of Mexican students: "It is well known that the greater portion of the population of Mexico are Indians, and when such Indians migrate to the United States, they are subject to the laws applicable generally to other Indians" (Weinberg, 1977, p. 166).

The 1930s were a particularly difficult time for Mexican Americans in California. As a result of the economic depression there was less demand for unskilled labor, and the field laborers who had been imported years earlier were forcibly required to return to Mexico. In this climate, it is not surprising to witness organized opposition to the schooling of Mexican children as we shall see in the Lemon Grove case. In this vein, the amended California school code of 1935 protected the new found Indianism of Mexican American students:

> The governing board of the school district shall have power to establish separate schools for Indian children, excepting children of Indians who are wards of the United States government and children of all other Indians who are descendants of the original American Indians of the United States, and for children of Chinese, Japanese or Mongolian parentage. (School code of the State of California, 1937, pp. 147-148)

This provision of the education code allowed school authorities to separate Mexican students from their Anglo counterparts.

The official reasoning behind separate schools for Mexican American students has usually been a pedagogical one. School authorities proposed that in order to provide the students with help in English and to facilitate the "Americanization" of Mexican students, separate schools would be needed to best accomplish this goal. Yet these separate facilities were never an attempt to integrate the Mexican American students into the American society, rather they were an attempt to further isolate children from the mainstream. Typical of the school practices are those reported by Penrod (1948):

> In some instances school buses carrying Mexican children passed by one or more school houses designated for "Anglo" use only in order to deposit Mexican children from any section of town in a school set aside for the use of all Mexican residents of that community regardless of their proximity to other school facilities. Where Anglo and Mexican schools were situated on the same property, adjoining playgrounds were marked off so that one group would not trespass on the other's assigned area . . . (p. 47).

Commenting on the practice of establishing "Mexican Schools," the renowned scholar George I. Sánchez noted in 1943:

> . . . Judging from current practice, these pseudo-pedagogical reasons call for short terms, ramshackle school buildings, poorly paid and untrained teachers, and all varieties of prejudicial discrimination. The "language handicap" reason, so glibly advanced as the chief pedagogical excuse for the segregation of these school children, is extended to apply to all Spanish name youngsters, regardless of the fact that some of them know more English and more about other school subjects than the children from whom they are segregated. In addition, some of these Spanish named children know no Spanish whatsoever, coming from homes where only English has been spoken for two generations or more . . . (quoted in Carter, 1970, p. 4).

Segregation of Mexican children was a concern of the 1930s that endures today. The following section reviews Mexican American efforts against school segregation in California prior to the 1954 *Brown v. Board of Education* Supreme Court case.

Mexican American Participation in Desegregation before Brown

As was mentioned earlier, considerable evidence exists documenting the segregation of Mexican American students in California. Data from 1928 school records show that the enrollment of 64 schools in eight California counties was 90-

100 percent Mexican American. For this same time period, Weinberg (1977) noted segregated schools in San Bernardino, Orange, Los Angeles, Imperial, Kern, Ventura, Riverside, and Santa Barbara counties. Similarly, Taylor, in 1926, found that in the Imperial Valley, Mexican American children made up one-third of the population and were separated into Americanization and opportunity classes. "Segregation occurs in every town of the Imperial Valley" (Taylor, 1934, p. 83). Carter (1970), in reviewing the 1930 situation for Mexican American children, stated "Segregation, especially in the early grades was regularly recommended and commonly established" (p. 11). Separate schools and separate curricula were so prevalent throughout the Los Angeles area by this time that they had been the cause of official protest by the Mexican Consul.

An example of early Mexican American activism against segregation can be found in the Lemon Grove school case. In 1930, the Lemon Grove School District (a suburb of San Diego) found that its only school (K-8) was becoming overcrowded. To alleviate this condition the board proposed to build a makeshift two-room school house out of a barn in the Mexican neighborhood exclusively for Mexican American students. The Lemon Grove Mexican American parents challenged the school board's right to build and maintain a separate and segregated school for Mexican children. "We are not in agreement, which is very natural, nor do we consider just, the separation of our children without any reason, to send them to another establishment that distinguishes Mexican children from children of other nationalities" (*Alvarez v. Lemon Grove*, 1931).

The parents boycotted the new school and through a writ of mandate filed suit. *Alvarez v. Lemon Grove School District* represented the first California case where Mexican Americans protested segregative school practices. On March 13, 1931, San Diego Superior Court Judge Claude Chambers ruled in favor of the plaintiffs:

> I understand that you can separate a few children to improve their education, they need special instruction; but to separate all the Mexicans in one group can only be done by infringing the laws of the State of Califor-

> nia. And I do not blame the Mexican children because a few of them are behind (in school work) for this segregation. On the contrary, this is a fact in their favor. I believe that this separation denied the Mexican children the presence of the American children, which is so necessary to learn the English language. (*Alvarez v. Lemon Grove*, 1931)

According to Alvarez (1985), the court demanded an immediate reinstatement of the Mexican American children to the original schoolhouse and the reconverted barn was abandoned as a school site. Judge Chambers' analysis of the reason for the segregation of the Mexican students recognized in the 1930s what is all too evident in the 1990s: that in order to acquire the linguistic competence necessary for social integration, racial integration was necessary in the form of exposure to native English speaking models. Limited English speaking Mexican American students needed both linguistic and racial exposure.

Yet the Alvarez ruling was not sufficient to end the school segregation of Mexican American children in California. Sociologist Joan Moore (Grebler, Moore, & Guzman, 1970) has noted:

> No Southwestern state upheld legally the segregation of Mexican American children, yet the practice was widespread. Separate schools were built and maintained, in theory, simply because of residential segregation or to benefit the Mexican child. He had a "language handicap" and needed to be "Americanized" before mixing with Anglo children. His presence in an integrated school would hinder the progress of white American children. (p. 77)

In 1945, 15 years after the Alvarez case, Mexican American parents again used the courts to protest school segregation in California. *Méndez v. Westminster* represents the first federal case filed by Mexican Americans challenging school segregative practices. In a class action suit, five Mexican American fathers, representing 5,000 children in the Westminster, Garden Grove, Santa Ana and El Modeno Districts of Orange County, alleged a concerted policy and design of class discrimination against "persons of Mexican or

Latin descent or extraction" of elementary school age by school agencies in the conduct and operation of public schools, resulting in the denial of their equal protection. (64 F. Supp. 544)

In three of these school districts, official action had made language ability the basis for segregation. Non-English speaking children were required to attend schools designated by the board separate and apart from English-speaking pupils. Yet a language proficiency test had never been used to determining the extent of language ability in the students. While this language segregation did not affect all Mexican American students because some were monolingual English speakers, it did create schools exclusively for the non-English speaking Mexican American students. The class action suit argued that:

> The equal protection of the laws pertaining to the public school system in California is not provided by furnishing in separate schools the same technical facilities, text books, and courses of instruction to children of Mexican ancestry that are available to the other public school children regardless of their ancestry. A paramount requisite in the American system of public education is social equality. It must be open to all children by unified school association regardless of lineage. . . . The evidence clearly shows that Spanish speaking children are retarded in learning English by lack of exposure to its use because of segregation, and that commingling of the entire student body instills and develops a common cultural attitude among the school children which is imperative for the perpetuation of American institutions and ideals. (64 F. Supp. 544, p. 549)

The Alvarez and Méndez cases demonstrate two things: (1) that even before the 1954 *Brown v. Board of Education* case, Mexican American parents were challenging the imposition of segregated schooling in California, and (2) that language (non-English speaking) ability was often provided as the pedagogical rational for the further isolation of Mexican American students in California schools. Additionally, Méndez is significant not only because it represents the first action against school segregation in federal court by Mexican

American parents in California but also because it was upheld in 1947 by the Ninth Circuit Court of Appeals, thus making this the first time public school segregation was struck down in a federal court.

Influenced by the court of appeals position, the state legislature repealed the last remaining segregation statutes in the California Education Code in 1947. With this action, the education code no longer sanctioned segregation of minority groups in California public education. The legal battles, however, had just begun.

Demographic Changes

In the interim between Méndez in 1947 and the next major desegregation case involving Mexican American students, *Crawford v. Los Angeles Unified School District* in 1963, there were significant demographic changes in California's Mexican American population. Grebler, Moore, and Guzman (1970) noted that in the decade between 1950 and 1960 Mexican Americans urbanized more rapidly than Anglos or nonwhites, and this trend continued through the 1960s. Concurrently, California experienced the greatest increase in the numbers of Mexican Americans in the Southwest. The gain was more than twice the rate for Anglos. Grebler, et al. state, "California is the one state with a steadily increasing share of all persons of Mexican stock in the United States. Two fifths of the first, and second generation Mexican Americans in the U.S. lived in California in 1960" (p. 109). As the figures in Table 1 indicate, the increase in the number of Mexican Americans as variously estimated by the census (excluding undocumented workers) doubled in the 1950-1960 decade, increased by almost one million between 1960 and 1970 and increased by over two million in the 1970-1980 decade.

These are conservative figures given that the Census department was not consistent in the identification of Mexican Americans, defining them through the decades as Mexican, Spanish mother tongue, Spanish surname, and Spanish ori-

TABLE 1

California's Spanish Surname Population by Decade and Census Terminology

Census Period	U.S. Census Terminology	Spanish Surname Population	Total Population (%)
1980	Spanish origin	4,543,770	19.2
1970	Spanish origin	2,369,292	11.9
1969	Spanish origin	1,426,538	9.1
1950	Spanish surname	758,400	7.2
1940	Spanish mother tongue	416,140	6.0
1930	Mexican	368,013	6.4

Source: U.S. Bureau of the Census as reported in Camarillo (1984).

gin. Similarly the use of the term "Hispanic" creates a category which is overinclusive with respect to the counting of Mexican Americans. Consequently, although the counting of Mexican Americans has been unreliable, the fact that this is a group that has been on the rise is undeniable.

Table 2 shows that Mexican Americans were among the three major ethnic groups in California in 1970 and are expected to continue to be the most numerous through 2010.

In Table 3 we see how these demographic changes were reflected in the enrollment of the Los Angeles Unified School District (LAUSD) from 1966 through 1978. It is noteworthy that in 1966 black students were the larger minority in LAUSD, by 1973 Hispanic students began to outnumber blacks, and by 1977, outnumbered white students. Data compiled by the California State Department of Education show the statewide growth in minority student enrollment from 1967 to 1984.

TABLE 2

California's Major Ethnic Groups by Decade
(Projected to the year 2010)

Ethnic Group	1970	1980	1990	2000	2010
Whites	77.1	66.5	58.8	52.4	47.0
Hispanics	11.9	19.3	24.2	28.5	32.2
Blacks	7.0	7.5	7.5	7.4	7.2
Asians	4.0	5.6	8.3	10.6	12.5
Other	—	1.2	1.2	1.1	1.1

Source: "Population Change and California's Future" by L. Bouvier and P. Martin, 1985, *Population Reference Bureau*.

According to the California State Department of Education, in 1984 Hispanic students were the largest minority group comprising 27.9 percent of California's total student population of 4,151,110. As the numbers of Hispanic students have increased, so have their levels of segregation in California. There has been an increase in the number of schools 50 percent or more minority from 1967 through 1984. Approximately 2,694 schools in 355 California school districts were over 50 percent minority enrollment in 1984. Hispanic students in schools that were 50-100 percent Hispanic numbered 567,125. This means that, in 1984, 48.9 percent of all the Hispanic students in California attended schools that were significantly racially isolated. Compared with black and Asian students, Hispanic students were the most segregated in the state (California State Department of Education Intergroup Relations Office, 1984). As we shall see in Los Angeles, Mexican American students were more segregated there than elsewhere.

TABLE 3

Enrollment by Race/Ethnicity in the Los Angeles Unified School District and Annual Rates of Change, 1966 to 1978*

Year	Total	White	Black	Hispanic	Asian	Indian**
1966	627,219	352	134	117	24	1
1967	641,449	350	142	124	25	1
1968	648,577	348	147	130	23	1
1969	650,324	335	152	135	26	1
1970	638,277	318	154	139	26	1
1971	629,144	300	156	143	29	1
1972	615,673	283	155	147	29	1
1973	607,107	270	153	155	27	1
1974	598,314	251	148	166	31	3
1975	598,441	241	147	178	31	3
1976	592,931	219	143	190	35	5
1977	578,827	195	142	202	36	4
1978	555,755	165	137	214	36	3

*Data from 1966 through 1977 come from Annual Racial and Ethnic Surveys prepared by the Research and Evaluation Branch of the Los Angeles Unified School District. Data from 1978 come from an October 10 count of enrollment.

**Percentage changes in Indian enrollment based upon smaller numbers.

Desegregation and Bilingual Education

The pursuit of educational equity for Mexican American students in the 1970s was characterized by advocacy for bilingual education. With the advent of federal funds for ESEA Title VII bilingual programs in 1968, many educators sought to improve Mexican American student performance by addressing the language issues alone. Bilingual education was seen as a methodology that would facilitate access to English by using the student's native language to continue content area mastery as well as fostering an overall development of English fluency. Originally, federal bilingual program guidelines recommended that classroom composition approximate a one-third to two-thirds ratio of English speaking to non-English speaking students. The rationale was that exposure to native language models was critical for non-native speakers and that oral fluency would be aided by exposure and conversation with native speakers. Furthermore, many districts with high proportions of Hispanic limited English proficient (LEP) students were also segregated. Federal guidelines stated clearly that support would be withheld if evidence of student isolation was presented; hence the one-third to two-third ratio.

While it is not the purpose here to review the success of bilingual programs, it was clear from the inception of these programs that many fundamental components for success were lacking, partly because fund for bilingual education were limited, and partly because the methodology was innovative. An early evaluation of Title VII Spanish bilingual programs reported that only 50 percent of the teachers were fluent bilinguals (American Institute for Research, 1978). The availability of trained and certified instructional staff was and continues to be one of the main obstacles to successful program implementation.

Educators were pressed to maximize bilingual education services in spite of limited staff. The solution was to increase the concentration of LEP students in the classes despite the one-third to two-thirds recommendation. In districts where the need for bilingual services and integration was great, bilingual programs continued to prevail in segregated settings, exacerbating the conflict between bilingual education and integration. For example, in 1978 the Los Angeles Unified School District was under court order to desegregate over 500 schools. Mexican American community support for desegregation, however, was tempered by a concern for diminishing bilingual services. When Judge Paul Egly allowed the district to operate segregated bilingual programs in segregated schools, advocates of educational equity for Mexican American students feared that these students would never experience an integrated classroom. Similarly in Denver, Colorado, a federal desegregation case allowed Hispanic interveners to exclude a few bilingually impacted schools from full participation in the plan.

Perhaps the experiences in these districts prompted the popular misconception that bilingual services were competing with desegregation goals. Bilingual services required concentration, a "critical mass of students and faculty," (Arias, 1978), while desegregation required a reassignment of students along the lines of racial and ethnic characteristics.

This misconception has been addressed by González (1974) and more recently by Arias (1978). Arias maintains that both goals are attainable and not mutually exclusive, but that they require careful student identification and program planning that districts involved in desegregation litigation are reluctant to consider.

It is important to keep in mind that not all Mexican American students require bilingual services. The estimate is that approximately 25 percent of Mexican American students are LEP. Nevertheless, most Mexican American students are currently attending segregated schools. Desegregation of Mexican American students in California and the Southwest continues to be a serious and pressing educational and social issue. This issue can be explored further through an analysis of a desegregation plan that was implemented by a major school district where Mexican American students represent a significant percent of the population.

TABLE 4

Majority and Minority Student Enrollment
in the San Jose Unified School District
1971-1985

Year	Majority Total	Majority (%)	Minority Hispanic Total	Minority Hispanic (%)	Minority Other Total	Minority Other (%)	Minority Total	Minority Total (%)	Total Enrolled
1971-72	24,530	70	9,201	25	1,674	4.6	10,875	29.0	36,405
1979-80	22,507	65	9,176	26	2,745	8.0	11,921	34.6	34,429
1980-81	21,016	63	8,974	27	2,949	8.7	11,923	35.9	32,945
1981-82	19,943	62	8,975	27	3,242	10.0	12,217	37.0	32,184
1982-83	19,483	60	9,346	29	3,329	8.0	12,675	37.4	32,158
1983-84	18,245	58	9,499	30	3,398	10.9	12,897	41.3	31,174
1984-85	17,685	56	9,530	29	3,700	14.1	13,230	43.2	39,915

Source: "Summary of San Jose Unified School District Desegregation Action 1980-1984," October 29, 1984, *District Ethnic Recaps.*

The History of *Diaz v. San Jose Unified School District*

In 1971, parents of Mexican American children attending San Jose High School filed a class action suit against the San Jose Unified School District claiming a constitutional violation of access to equal educational opportunities. The parents claimed that the school board was responsible for inequitable distribution of resources. Evidence was introduced that showed that high schools in the suburban areas of San Jose offered a wider range of courses, including advanced placement, while San Jose High School lacked adequate libraries and laboratory facilities. From 1971 to 1985, the case made its way through the judicial system. Finally, in 1985, a federal court judge found the district guilty as charged and ordered the implementation of a desegregation plan. As is evident from the demographic figures presented in this chapter, much has changed in San Jose Unified School District over the 15-year period that it took for the case to be filed and the desegregation plan to be ordered (Arias, 1986).

Table 4 illustrates changes in majority/minority enrollment from 1971-1985. The table shows that San Jose has a significant decrease in white students coupled with a significant increase in Mexican American and other minority students. In 1985, San Jose Unified School District operated 37 schools. At that time San Jose had 24 elementary schools, 7 middle schools, and 6 high schools. Twenty schools were considered segregated according to the standard definition (plus or minus 20 percent of total white enrollment for that grade level). The most segregated schools were concentrated at the elementary school level ($n = 16$) with two junior high schools and two high schools exceeding the racial and ethnic percentage.

A characteristic of the San Jose Unified School District is its long, rectangular shape; the distance between the northern most and the southern most school is in excess of 26 miles. Using surface transportation routes, the minimum travel time from the northern most to the southern most school is 50 minutes. The district is further characterized by a concentration of predominantly minority residents of low income who live in the northern part of the district. The southern part of the school district is an area comprised of affluent, suburban-type homes, while the middle sector constitutes a "naturally" integrated residential area.

Characteristics of the San Jose Desegregation Plan

The San Jose Desegregation Plan can be characterized as a type of "controlled-choice" plan. In a controlled-choice plan, parents opt for schools within a designated attendance area with choices limited to the availability of space required to achieve racial balance. Controlled choice had been successfully implemented in Cambridge, Massachusetts, and Buffalo, New York school districts, also under court ordered desegregation.

As a student reassignment strategy for desegregation purposes, controlled-choice has the advantage of seeming to be voluntary and equitable; it is not as threatening to parents as mandatory student assignment plans. On the other hand, when given first choice, most parents choose neighborhood schools that reinforce existing residential patterns in school ethnic distributions. Controlled choice as operated in the San Jose district, generally favored those parents who were residentially stable, well-informed, anticipated reviewing their school programs, and participated in an entirely new enrollment procedure in the spring of the pre-implementation year. Parents were aware of time constraints (two weeks) needed for making their decisions. On the other hand, less informed parents, who were limited to access to school information networks, non-English speaking, unfamiliar with jargon such as "magnet," "alternative," and "enrichment," or who were away during those two crucial weeks, were seriously handicapped in participating in the choice process. The San Jose District promised to provide transportation to all students if their choice at the elementary level was more than one and a half miles from their home or separated by a major intersection; at the middle and high school level, transportation would be provided if the school of their choice was more than two and a half miles from their home. Unfortunately, the transportation program was not integrated with the school choice. Thus parents often made choices without knowing the distance involved or the type of transportation services available. Middle and high school students received either district transportation or free passes from the county transit system.

The controlled-choice system as implemented by San Jose Unified School District can be characterized as a two-phase system. Phase One occurs during a spring enrollment period, where students new to the district or who change grade levels (change from elementary to middle school for example) identify three schools of choice. Students who are aware that they can be in the school of their choice the following fall, make that decision early, with a high percentage of these selections being honored. After the spring enrollment period, a new student in the district must make his/her selection from those schools that have space remaining after Phase One. This, in effect, results in a type of mandatory assignment for most students who enroll during Phase Two. The limitation of choices for the second phase operates as a mandatory assignment practice in that the choices available are limited, both geographically and pragmatically. Language minority students in Phase Two generally choose schools outside their local attendance area that have limited experience with bilingual instructional methodology.

The 1985 Federal Court order in San Jose established the standards by which San Jose's schools would be desegregated; it outlined the controlled choice in general, set a timeline for achieving ethnic balance, and created an independent unit, the Compliance Monitor, to oversee the district's implementation of the desegregation order and who would report to the judge.

The timeline required that by December 1990, 100 percent of San Jose's schools must achieve racial and ethnic balance. In the first year of implementation, the district reduced its racially isolated schools from 20 to 10. In the second year of desegregation, the number of segregated schools decreased from 10 to 4. In 1988-89, 98 percent of the district's students attended racially balanced schools. By the fall of 1989, the district reported 100 percent of the students attending desegregated schools.

418   M. BEATRIZ ARIAS

These data suggest that controlled choice has been a successful strategy for reducing student racial isolation; the
schools are technically desegregated. Yet educators are concerned about the processes used by the schools to become desegregated. As Hawley et al. (1983) have noted:

> It is important to judge desegregation as one would
> judge any other school policy: whether and to what
> extent it achieves certain valued ends . . . seeing school
> desegregation as a process rather than as an outcome
> with its own justification has important implications
> for the way we proceed to determine the criteria
> which govern the assignment of students to schools.
> Thus, for example, "racial balance" would seldom be a
> sufficient factor on which to base a desegregation plan.
> (p. 45)

Policy Implications

After four years of court-ordered desegregation, all of the
schools in the San Jose Unified School District are within
the legally prescribed ethnic ratios. The school district maintains that controlled choice has been effective and that it has
allowed the district to achieve complete desegregation in
advance of the court's timeline. But it is appropriate to ask:
What have been the educational consequences of desegregated education for Mexican American students in San Jose?
Recall that the original plaintiffs in 1971 wanted equal access
to educational opportunity and maintained that the quality
of resources available to students in the northern sector of
the district severely limited student access.

As the district recently became desegregated in the fall of
1989, and San Jose High Academy, the original plaintiff's
school site and the last school to become integrated, it is still
too early to determine differences in the educational experiences of Mexican American students. The Court Monitor
has provided an achievement analysis based on the Comprehensive Test of Basic Skills (CTBS) administered to all
students K-12 since the inception of the court order. The
Monitor's report analyzed elementary student scores in
grades 2-5, to determine if there had been any noteworthy

changes in the performance of the most stable of the district's student population. Only scores for students present for testing in spring of 1987, 1988, and 1989 were analyzed. In general, majority students are performing at about the national norm in areas of language, reading, and math. On the average, minority students (specifically, Mexican American) were performing 10 to 12 percentage points lower than majority white students.

Reviewers of desegregation outcomes frequently note that if the desegregation strategy does not include instructional components, it is unrealistic to expect that mere social engineering, the reassignment of students, will have a positive impact on student performance. Rather, they suggest that informal indices of improvement be considered, such as reduction of drop-out rates, increased school attendance, increased parental participation in schools, increased curricular offerings for minority students, increased numbers of students taking advanced placement classes, and admission to college.

For language minority students, especially Mexican American students, informal indices that are relevant include access to instructional programs that provide either English as a Second Language (ESL) or bilingual curriculum. Increased parental participation is also an important educational objective for Mexican American students. In terms of these two areas, how has the desegregation plan in San Jose increased access?

The Court Monitor reviewed the availability and participation of Mexican American LEP students in bilingual or ESL programs one year after the inception of the court order. The monitor reported significant numbers of students in schools that had little or no ESL or bilingual resources, bilingual certified staff were in schools with no programs, and teachers who previously had little contact with LEP students were resentful of additional time requirements of reporting and identifying students.

In addition, the implementation of the controlled-choice system dismantled the role of the neighborhood school as the first point of contact for parents and the educational system. The new assignment strategy established an "assignment center" where students came for registration and school placement. This significantly altered the informational route utilized especially by minority parents for selecting school sites and programs. No longer were parents to go to the local school for information. School choice had to be made at the assignment centers, located at some distance from the neighborhood area.

A study by the Court Monitor of the information utilized by minority parents in selecting their school choices revealed important differences between minority (Mexican American) parents and majority (white) parents. Mexican American parents made their decision about school primarily on the information provided in the district catalog, and secondarily on information such as school reputation or school site visitation. On the other hand, majority parents made their decision on school site first based on familiarity with the school's program and reputation, secondly by visitation to a school site and thirdly, by the information provided in the catalog. This suggests that differential information networks are utilized by Mexican American parents and points to important structural considerations that need to be made if a choice system is to be truly equitable for majority and minority parents.

Clearly, the choice system has facilitated the desegregation of San Jose Unified. What is less clear, is the extent to which Mexican American parents and students had access to the same range of choices available to majority students. In the San Jose example, desegregation has increased the opportunity for majority students to interact with minority students. The educational consequences of participating in this desegregation effort for Mexican American students in the short term meant restriction of programmatic options. In the long run, as the choice becomes the routine for student assignment, the impact on Mexican American students may be less restrictive. Only time and future studies, access to greater educational resources was facilitated by student desegregation in San Jose.

References

Alvarez v. Lemon Grove School District, Superior Court of the State of California, County of San Diego, Petition for Writ of Mandate No. 66625, (February 13, 1931.)

Alvarez, R. (1985). *The Lemon Grove incident: The nation's first successful desegregation court case.* Unpublished manuscript, California State University, Sacramento, Center for Applied Sciences.

American Institutes for Research. (1977). *Evaluation of the impact of ESEA Title VII Spanish/English bilingual program: Vol. I. Study design and interim findings.* Washington D.C.: U.S. Office of Planning, Budgeting, and Evaluation.

Arias, M. B. (1978). *Report on the honorable judge Paul Egly in response to minute order no. C 822 854.* Los Angeles: University of California, Graduate School of Education.

____. (1986). The context of education for Hispanic students: An overview. *American Journal of Education, 95.*

Bouvier, L., & Martin, P. (1985). Population change and California's future. In *Population reference bureau.* Sacramento: State of California.

California State Department of Education Intergroup Relations Office. (1984). *Racial and ethnic survey of California public schools 1984.* Sacramento, CA: State Department of Education.

Camarillo, A. (1984). *Chicanos in a changing society.* Cambridge, MA: Harvard University Press.

Carter, T. (1970). *Mexican Americans in school: A history of educational neglect.* New York: College Entrance Examination Board.

____, & Segura, R. (1980). *Mexican American in school: A decade of change.* New York: College Entrance Examination Board.

Crawford v. Board of Education, 17 C.3d 280, Cal Rptr. 724, 511 P.2d 28.

Diaz v. San Jose Unified School District, 412 F. Supp. 310 (1976), 612 F.2d 411 (1979), 518 F. Supp. 622 (1981), 733 F.2d 660 (1984).

Farley, R. (1978). *Report to the Honorable Judge Egly in response to minute order no. C 822 854.* Ann Arbor: University of Michigan, Populations Study Center.

González, J. (1974). *Desegregation and bilingual education.* Arlington, VA: Bilingual Clearinghouse.

Grebler, L., Moore, J., & Guzman, R. (1970). *The Mexican American people: The nation's second largest minority.* New York: Free Press.

Haro, C. (1977). *Mexican/Chicano concerns and school desegregation in Los Angeles.* (Monograph No. 9). Los Angeles: University of California, Chicano Studies Center Publications.

Hawley, W. D., et al. (1983). *Strategies for effective desegregation.* Massachusetts: D. C. Health.

Méndez v. Westminster, 64 F. Supp. 544 (1946), aff'd 161 F.2d 744 (1947).

Mexicans in California: Report of Governor C. C. Young's Mexican fact finding committee. (1930). San Francisco: California State Printing Office.

Orfield, G. (1978). *Must we bus.* Washington, DC: Brookings Institute.

____. (1984, May). Lessons of the Los Angeles desegregation case. *Education and Urban Society, 16,* 338-353.

Payne, J. (1971). Race, reading and poverty in Los Angeles. *Integrated Education 9,* 20.

Penrod, V. (1948). *Civil rights problems of Mexican Americans in Southern California.* Unpublished master's thesis, University of Southern California.

Rangel, J., & Alcala, C. (1972). De jure segregation of Chicano in Texas schools. *Harvard Civil Rights Liberties Law Review, 7,* 9.

State of California. (1937). *State school code 1937.* Sacramento: State of California.

San Jose Unified School District. (1984). Summary of San Jose Unified School District desegregation action 1980-1984. In *District ethnic recaps.* San Jose, CA: San Jose Unified School District.

Taylor, P. (1934). *A Mexican-American frontier: Nueces County, Texas.* Chapel Hill: University of North Carolina Press.

U.S. Commission of Civil Rights. (1971-1974). Mexican American Education Study, 6 vols. *Ethnic Isolation of Mexican Americans in the Public Schools of the Southwest, 1.*

Weinberg, M. (1977). *A chance to learn: The history of race and education in the United States.* Cambridge, MA: Cambridge University Press.

CONTRIBUTORS

ADALBERTO AGUIRRE, JR. is an associate professor of sociology at the University of California, Riverside. His primary research interests are in the areas of sociolinguistics, bilingualism, and bilingual education. His articles have appeared in such journals as the *International Journal of the Sociology of Language, NABE Journal,* and *Social Science Quarterly.*

M. BEATRIZ ARIAS is an associate professor at Arizona State University, College of Education, and principal investigator and director of Arizona State University's Center for Bilingual Education and Research. She has published extensively and has written two books in the areas of Hispanic education and schooling in the Southwest.

ANDRES BARONA received his Ph.D. from the University of Texas at Austin in 1982. He is currently an associate professor and the coordinator of the School Psychology program in the Division of Psychology in Education at Arizona State University. His research interests include applied psychometrics as well as assessment with an emphasis on the evaluation of minority school children.

CAROL BEAUMONT is a doctoral student in special education at the University of California, Berkeley. Trained as a speech and language therapist, she specialized in meeting the needs of Hispanic bilingual children with communication handicaps. Her current research interests include the merging of holistic instructional principles with speech and language therapy. She is a research consultant to the OLE Project.

ALFREDO H. BENAVIDES received his Ph.D. from Michigan State University and served as a professor and director of Bilingual and Multicultural Teacher Education at the University of Iowa from 1976 until 1988. He is currently an associate professor of bilingual and multicultural education at Arizona State University. His main research interests include bilingual teacher education and ethnography of schools.

MARIA CARDELLE-ELAWAR received her Ph.D. from Stanford University and is currently Assistant Professor of Educational Psychology at Arizona State University West. Professor Cardelle-Elawar's research focuses on the area of infusion of the teaching of critical thinking on mathematics problems with at-risk students.

URSULA CASANOVA is an assistant professor in the Department of Educational Leadership and Policy Studies at the College of Education of Arizona State University. She was an elementary school principal for five years after several years of teaching experience. With Virginia Richardson, Peggy Placier, and Karen Guilfoyle, she coauthored *Schoolchildren at Risk* (1989). Her latest book is *Elementary School Secretaries: The Women in the Principal's Office* (1991).

LOURDES DIAZ SOTO is an assistant professor and the director of Pennsylvania State University's Comprehensive Bilingual Early Childhood Teacher Education Program. Her research focuses on the education of culturally and linguistically diverse young learners and their families. She currently serves as the Early Childhood Special Interest Group Chair of the National Association for Bilingual Education.

CHRISTIAN FALTIS is an associate professor of multicultural and bilingual education at Arizona State University. In 1990, he published *Language Distribution Issues in Bilingual Schooling* (with Rodolfo Jacobson) and *Language Minority Students and Computers* (with Robert A. DeVillar). His interests are second language teaching, bilingualism, and bilingual education.

RICHARD A. FIGUEROA is a professor of education at the University of California, Davis. Until recently, his primary area of research has been nonbiased assessment. In recent publications he has suggested that psychometrics may not be valid for bilingual populations. He is currently one of the directors of the OLE project.

JOHN J. HALCON is an assistant professor in the College of Education at the University of Northern Colorado, Greeley. His research centers on the organization of school districts and the development of public policy as it affects historically underrepresented and underachieving students. He is also interested in the training and socialization of teachers who work with minority populations.

MARK LACELLE-PETERSON is a doctoral student in the Harvard Graduate School of Education. His interest in bilingual education stems from experiences as an exchange student sponsored by the Rotary Youth Exchange Program. He earned a B.A. in Scandinavian Studies and an M.A. in International Development Education at the University of Minnesota where he also taught in the General College's Commanding English program.

KATHRYN J. LINDHOLM received her Ph.D. in developmental psychology from the University of California, Los Angeles in 1981. She is now an assistant professor of education at San Jose State University. Her main areas of interest are bilingual and second language development, and factors associated with school achievement in bilingual education programs.

BECKY LOPEZ MAEZ is a doctoral student in counseling psychology at Arizona State University. She has a B.S. from the University of Utah, and an M.A. from the University of California, Santa Barbara. Her APA internship was completed at the University of Arizona. She has taught graduate and undergraduate courses in counseling and career development.

BARBARA J. MERINO is an associate professor of education and linguistics at the University of California, Davis, where she also coordinates the bilingual and foreign language credentials programs. Her principal research interests are in language acquisition and language loss in bilingual children, classroom processes, language assessment, and curriculum development.

MARTHA MONTERO-SIEBURTH is an assistant professor of education and teaches courses in the analysis of curriculum, bilingual-multicultural education, and understanding the transfer of curriculum models. She is interested in the direct application of cultural anthropology and qualitative research to the development of culturally relevant instructional materials and curricula.

JOSE E. NAÑEZ, SR. received his Ph.D. in experimental child psychology from the Institute of Child Development, University of Minnesota-Twin Cities, and is currently an assistant professor of psychology at Arizona State University West. His main research emphases are visual perception and cognition in human infants and cognitive information processing in bilinguals.

AMADO M. PADILLA received his Ph.D. in experimental psychology from the University of New Mexico in 1969. He is currently a professor at the Stanford University School of Education. He has directed several national research center projects including the UCLA Center for Language Education and Research (CLEAR) and the National Center for Bilingual Research.

RAYMOND V. PADILLA is an associate professor in the Division of Educational Leadership and Policy Studies in the College of Education at Arizona State University and was the Director of the Hispanic Research Center from 1986 to 1991. He is the developer of HyperQual, a qualitative data analysis program for the Macintosh based on HyperCard. His research focuses on bilingualism and minority students in higher education.

ARNULFO G. RAMIREZ is currently Chair of Foreign Languages and Literatures and Professor of Linguistics and Spanish at Louisiana State University. He has taught at the University of California, Los Angeles, Stanford University, and The State University of New York at Albany. His major publications include *Bilingualism through Schooling, Teaching Languages for Communicative Proficiency and Cross-Cultural Understanding*, and *The English of Spanish-speaking Pupils in Bilingual and Monolingual School Settings*.

MARIA DE LA LUZ REYES is an assistant professor of education at the University of Colorado, Boulder. She is professionally involved with literacy for second-language learners, education of Hispanics, bilingual education, and teacher education. She has been a contributor to several scholarly books in these areas.

ROBERT S. RUEDA is a professor of special education at the University of Southern California. As a director of the Handicapped Minority Research Institute in southern California, he provided one of the clearest documentations of the assessment and decision-making process for His-

search Institute in southern California, he provided one of the clearest documentations of the assessment and decision-making process for Hispanic children in special education. He is one of the directors of the OLE Project.

NADEEN T. RUIZ is a research consultant in the Division of Education at the University of California at Davis. Her doctoral dissertation is one of the major ethnographic studies on bilingual special education for Hispanic communicatively handicapped students. Currently, her major research interests are the oral and written discourse patterns of Hispanic children in special education classrooms.

SHERYL L. SANTOS is a teacher educator at Arizona State University specializing in bilingual and multicultural education. Her experience in the field spans two decades and has included classroom teaching, international travel and research as a Fulbright Scholar, policy making, and consulting. Included in her current research interests are bilingual mathematics and science pedagogy for speakers of other languages.

MARYANN SANTOS DE BARONA received her Ph.D. from the University of Texas, Austin in 1981. Currently, she is an assistant professor in the Division of Psychology in Education at Arizona State University. Her research interests include assessment of preschool children, gender comparisons, and the education of minority school children.

ANTONIO SIMÕES is dean of the School of Education and Allied Professions at Fairfield University. Through the University of Lisbon, he is also serving as a consultant to the European Commission in Project Luxembourg. He was formerly at New York University as the director of bilingual education, and was chairperson of the Department of Curriculum and Instruction. Professor Simões has also served as director of the Bilingual Training Resource Center at Boston University and as an assistant deanat City University of New York.

HYEKYUNG SUNG is a Ph.D. student in the School of Education, Stanford University. She received her M.A. in Linguistics from Stanford University (1989) and in French from Seoul National University (1982). She taught French at the Hankuk University of Foreign Studies in Seoul, Korea. Her interests include second and foreign language education, bilinguals' memory, and language learning strategies.

ARMANDO L. TRUJILLO is an assistant professor of bilingual and bicultural studies at the University of Texas at San Antonio. He has extensive experience in education and has taught at the elementary, secondary, and college levels. He has also authored numerous articles and presented workshops throughout the United States. His areas of expertise and research include educational anthropology, and bilingual and migrant education.